Scott Foresman·Addison Wesley

enVisionMATH

California

Scott Foresman·Addison Wesley

enVisionMATH™ California

Authors

Randall I. Charles
Professor Emeritus
Department of Mathematics
San Jose State University
San Jose, California

Mary Cavanagh
Mathematics Consultant
San Diego County Office of Education
San Diego, California

Juanita V. Copley
Professor
College of Education
University of Houston
Houston, Texas

Warren D. Crown
Professor of Mathematics Education
Graduate School of Education
Rutgers University
New Brunswick, New Jersey

Francis (Skip) Fennell
Professor of Education
McDaniel College
Westminster, Maryland

Alma B. Ramirez
Sr. Research Associate
Math Pathways and Pitfalls WestEd
Oakland, California

Kay B. Sammons
Coordinator of Elementary Mathematics
Howard County Public Schools
Ellicott City, Maryland

Jane F. Schielack
Professor of Mathematics
Associate Dean for Assessment and
Pre K-12 Education, College of Science
Texas A&M University
College Station, Texas

William Tate
Edward Mallinckrodt Distinguished
University Professor in Arts & Sciences
Washington University
St. Louis, Missouri

John A. Van de Walle
Professor Emeritus, Mathematics Education
Virginia Commonwealth University
Richmond, Virginia

Consulting Mathematicians

Edward J. Barbeau
Professor of Mathematics
University of Toronto
Toronto, Canada

Sybilla Beckmann
Professor of Mathematics
Department of Mathematics
University of Georgia
Athens, Georgia

David Bressoud
DeWitt Wallace Professor of Mathematics
Macalester College
Saint Paul, Minnesota

Gary Lippman
Professor of Mathematics and Computer Science
California State University East Bay
Hayward, California

Editorial Offices: Glenview, Illinois • Parsippany, New Jersey • New York, New York
Sales Offices: Boston, Massachusetts • Duluth, Georgia • Glenview, Illinois
Coppell, Texas • Sacramento, California • Mesa, Arizona

Consulting Authors

Stuart J. Murphy
Visual Learning Specialist
Boston, Massachusetts

Jeanne Ramos
Secondary Mathematics Coordinator
Los Angeles Unified School District
Los Angeles, California

Verónica Galván Carlan
Private Consultant Mathematics
Harlingen, Texas

ELL Consultants/Reviewers

Alma B. Ramirez
Sr. Research Associate
Math Pathways and Pitfalls WestEd
Oakland, California

California Reviewers

Martha Borquez
Teacher
Los Angeles USD

Elsa M. Campos
Teacher
Corona-Norco USD

Lynn Cevallos
K-12 Mathematics Consultant
Los Angeles, CA

Jann Edwards
Teacher, GATE Coordinator
Los Angeles USD

Katherine J. Jones
Teacher, District Math Coach
Newark USD

Kevin M. Kazala
Math Specialist K-6
Corona-Norco USD

Karen Jae Ko
Teacher
Long Beach USD

Kristin Leidig-Sears
Teacher
Los Angeles USD

Ariana R. Levin
Teacher
Los Angeles USD

Patrick A. McCormack
Special Education Teacher
Los Angeles USD

Stefani Maida
Teacher
Berkeley USD

Misook Park-Kimura
Professional Development Mentor
Long Beach USD

Elgin Michael Scott
Educator
Los Angeles USD

Doris L. Sterling
Teacher/Math Facilitator
Sacramento City USD

Amy N. Tindell
Math Coach
Los Angeles USD

Rachel M. Williams
Math Curriculum Associate/Teacher
North Sacramento School District

Scott Foresman · Addison Wesley
enVisionMATH™
California

ISBN-13: 978-0-328-27290-7
ISBN-10: 0-328-27290-6

Scott Foresman·Addison Wesley

en**Vision**MATH™ Californi

Topic Titles

Table of Contents

MATH STRAND COLORS

Number Sense

Algebra and Functions

Measurement and Geometry

Statistics, Data Analysis, and Probability

Problem Solving

Mathematical Reasoning, which includes problem solving, is infused throughout all lessons.

Numeration

🕐 NS 1.0, 1.1 ▱, 1.2 ▱, 1.1, Gr.3, SDAP 1.0, MR 1.1

Topic 2 — Addition and Subtraction Number Sense

🕐 NS 1.0, 1.3 ▱, 2.1, 3.0, 3.1 ▱, MR 1.0, 1.1, 2.1, 2.3, 2.4, 2.5

Problem-Solving Handbook

Use this Problem-Solving Handbook throughout
the year to help you solve problems.

Don't
give up!

Everybody can
be a good
problem solver!

There's almost always
more than one way to
solve a problem!

Don't trust
key words.

Pictures help me
understand!

Explaining helps me
understand!

Problem-Solving Process

Read and Understand

? What am I trying to find?
- Tell what the question is asking.

? What do I know?
- Tell the problem in my own words.
- Identify key facts and details.

Plan and Solve

? What strategy or strategies should I try?

? Can I show the problem?
- Try drawing a picture.
- Try making a list, table, or graph.
- Try acting it out or using objects.

? How will I solve the problem?

? What is the answer?
- Tell the answer in a complete sentence.

Strategies
- Show What You Know
- Draw a Picture
- Make an Organized List
- Make a Table
- Make a Graph
- Act It Out/ Use Objects
- Look for a Pattern
- Try, Check, Revise
- Write an Equation
- Use Reasoning
- Work Backward
- Solve a Simpler Problem

Look Back and Check

? Did I check my work?
- Compare my work to the information in the problem.
- Be sure all calculations are correct.

? Is my answer reasonable?
- Estimate to see if my answer makes sense.
- Make sure the question was answered.

Using Bar Diagrams

Use a bar diagram to show how what you know and what you want to find are related. Then choose an operation to solve the problem.

Problem 1

Carrie helps at the family flower store in the summer. She keeps a record of how many flower bouquets she sells. How many bouquets did she sell on Monday and Wednesday?

Carrie's Sales

Days	Bouquets Sold
Monday	19
Tuesday	22
Wednesday	24
Thursday	33
Friday	41

Bar Diagram

TOTAL: Total number of bouquets she sold →

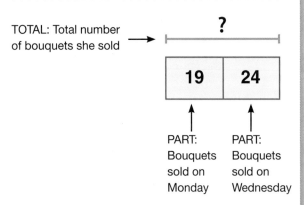

PART: Bouquets sold on Monday   PART: Bouquets sold on Wednesday

$$19 + 24 = ?$$

 Think I can add to find the total.

Problem 2

Kim is saving to buy a sweatshirt for the college her brother attends. She has $18. How much more money does she need to buy the sweatshirt?

$32

Bar Diagram

TOTAL: Cost of the sweatshirt →

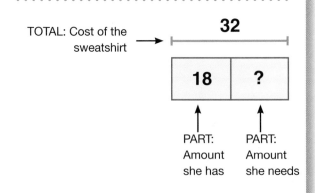

PART: Amount she has   PART: Amount she needs

$$32 - 18 = ?$$

 Think I can subtract to find the missing part.

Pictures help me understand!

Don't trust key words!

Problem 3

Tickets to a movie on Saturday cost only $5 each no matter what age you are. What is the cost of tickets for a family of four?

Bar Diagram

TOTAL: Total cost of the tickets →

?			
5	5	5	5

↑
PART:
Cost of
each ticket

4 × 5 = ?

 Think I can multiply because the parts are equal.

Problem 4

Thirty students traveled in 3 vans to the zoo. The same numbers of students were in each van. How many students were in each van?

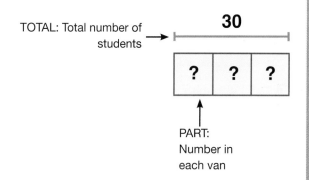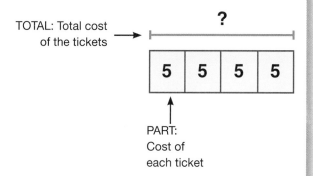

Bar Diagram

TOTAL: Total number of students →

30		
?	?	?

↑
PART:
Number in
each van

30 ÷ 3 = ?

 Think I can divide to find how many are in each part.

Problem-Solving Strategies

Strategy	Example	When I Use It
Draw a Picture	The race was 5 kilometers. Markers were at the starting line and the finish line. Markers showed each kilometer of the race. Find the number of markers used.	Try drawing a picture when it helps you visualize the problem or when the relationships such as joining or separating are involved.

Start Line — Finish Line

Start Line   1 km   2 km   3 km   4 km   Finish Line

Strategy	Example	When I Use It
Make a Table	Phil and Marcy spent all day Saturday at the fair. Phil rode 3 rides each half hour and Marcy rode 2 rides each half hour. How many rides had Marcy ridden when Phil rode 24 rides?	Try making a table when: • there are 2 or more quantities, • amounts change using a pattern.

Rides for Phil	3	6	9	12	15	18	21	24
Rides for Marcy	2	4	6	8	10	12	14	16

Strategy	Example	When I Use It
Look for a Pattern	The house numbers on Forest Road change in a planned way. Describe the pattern. Tell what the next two house numbers should be.	Look for a pattern when something repeats in a predictable way.

3   6   10   15   ?   ?

Everybody can
be a good
problem solver!

Strategy	Example	When I Use It
Make an Organized List	How many ways can you make change for a quarter using dimes and nickels?	Make an organized list when asked to find combinations of two or more items.

1 quarter =
1 dime + 1 dime + 1 nickel
1 dime + 1 nickel + 1 nickel + 1 nickel
1 nickel + 1 nickel + 1 nickel + 1 nickel + 1 nickel

| **Try, Check, Revise** | Suzanne spent $27, not including tax, on dog supplies. She bought two of one item and one of another item. What did she buy?

$8 + $8 + $15 = $31
$7 + $7 + $12 = $26
$6 + $6 + $15 = $27 | Use Try, Check, Revise when quantities are being combined to find a total, but you don't know which quantities. |

Dog Supplies Sale!
Leash $8
Collar $6
Bowls $7
Medium Beds $15
Toys $12

| **Write an Equation** | Maria's new CD player can hold 6 discs at a time. If she has 204 CDs, how many times can the player be filled without repeating a CD?

Find $204 \div 6 = n$. | Write an equation when the story describes a situation that uses an operation or operations. |

Even More Strategies

Strategy	Example	When I Use It
Act It Out	How many ways can 3 students snake each other's hand?	Think about acting out a problem when the numbers are small and there is action in the problem you can do.
Use Reasoning	Beth collected some shells, rocks, and beach glass. **Beth's Collection** 2 rocks ●● 3 times as many shells as rocks ●● ●● ●● 12 objects in all How many of each object are in the collection?	Use reasoning when you can use known information to reason out unknown information.
Work Backward	Tracy has band practice at 10:15 A.M. It takes her 20 minutes to get from home to practice and 5 minutes to warm up. What time should she leave home to get to practice on time? Time Tracy leaves home ? ← 20 minutes ← Time warm up starts ← 5 minutes ← Time practice starts **10:15**	Try working backward when: • you know the end result of a series of steps, • you want to know what happened at the beginning.

I can think about when to use each strategy.

Strategy	Example	When I Use It

Solve a Simpler Problem 	Each side of each triangle in the figure at the left is one centimeter. If there are 12 triangles in a row, what is the perimeter of the figure?
	
	 I can look at 1 triangle, then 2 triangles, then 3 triangles.
	
	  perimeter = 3 cm
	
	  perimeter = 4 cm
	
	  perimeter = 5 cm
		Try solving a simpler problem when you can create a simpler case that is easier to solve.

Make a Graph	Mary was in a jump rope contest. How did her number of jumps change over the five days of the contest? 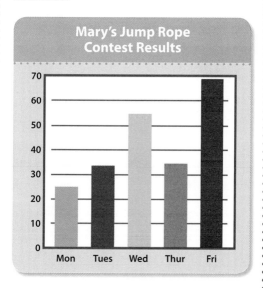	Make a graph when: • data for an event are given, • the question can be answered by reading the graph.

Writing to Explain

Here is a good math explanation.

Writing to Explain What happens to the area of the rectangle if the lengths of its sides are doubled?

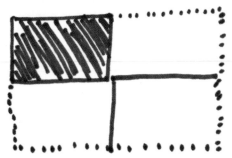

■ = $\frac{1}{4}$ of the whole rectangle

The area of the new rectangle is 4 times the area of the original rectangle.

Tips for Writing Good Math Explanations....

A good explanation should be:
- correct
- simple
- complete
- easy to understand

Math explanations can use:
- words
- pictures
- numbers
- symbols

This is another good math explanation.

Explaining helps me understand!

Writing to Explain Use blocks to show 13 × 24.
Draw a picture of what you did with the blocks.

First we made a row of 24 using
2 tens and 4 ones. Then we made
more rows until we had 13 rows.
Then we said 13 rows of 2 tens is
13 × 2 tens = 26 tens or 260.
Then we said 12 rows of 4 ones is
13 × 4 = 52. Then we added the parts.
260 + 52 = 312   So, 13 × 24 = 312.

Problem-Solving Recording Sheet

Name __Jane__

Teaching Tool
1

Problem-Solving Recording Sheet

Problem:
On June 14, 1777, the Continental Congress approved the design of a national flag. The 1777 flag had 13 stars, one for each colony. Today's flag has 50 stars, one for each state. How many stars were added to the flag since 1777?

Find?

Number of stars
added to the flag

Know?

Original flag
13 stars

Today's flag
50 stars

Strategies?

Show the Problem
☑ Draw a Picture
☐ Make an Organized List
☐ Make a Table
☐ Make a Graph
☐ Act It Out/Use Objects

☐ Look for a Pattern
☐ Try, Check, Revise
☑ Write an Equation
☐ Use Reasoning
☐ Work Backwards
☐ Solve a Simpler Problem

Show the Problem?

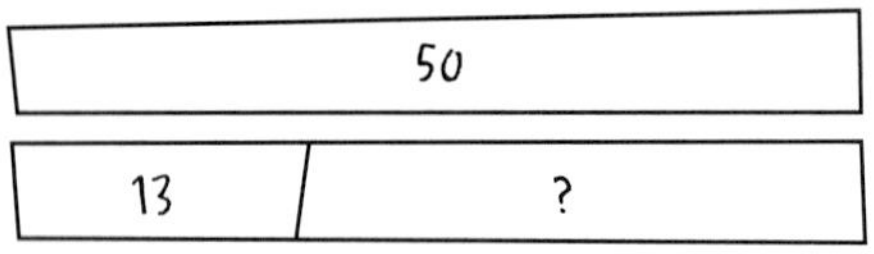

50

13	?

Solution?

I am comparing the two quantities.
I could add up from 13 to 50. I can also subtract 13 from 50. I'll subract.

$$\begin{array}{r} 50 \\ -\ 13 \\ \hline 37 \end{array}$$

Answer?

There were 37 stars added to the flag from 1777 to today.

Check? Reasonable?

37 + 13 = 50 so I subtracted correctly.

50 – 13 is about 50 – 10 = 40
40 is close to 37.   37 is reasonable.

Teaching Tools • 1

Name _Benton_

Teaching Tool
1

Problem-Solving Recording Sheet

Problem:

Suppose your teacher told you to open your math book to the facing pages whose pages numbers add to 85. To which two pages would you open your book?

Find?	**Know?**	**Strategies?**
Two facing page numbers	Two pages. Facing each other. Sum is 85.	Show the Problem ☑ Draw a Picture ☐ Make an Organized List ☐ Make a Table ☐ Make a Graph ☐ Act It Out/Use Objects ☐ Look for a Pattern ☑ Try, Check, Revise ☑ Write an Equation ☐ Use Reasoning ☐ Work Backwards ☐ Solve a Simpler Problem

Show the Problem?

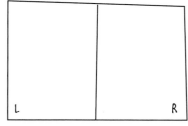

L + R = 85
L is 1 less than R

Solution?

I'll try some numbers in the middle.
40 + 41 = 81, too low
How about 46 and 47?
46 + 47 = 93, too high
Ok, now try 42 and 43.
42 + 43 = 85.

Answer?

The page numbers are 42 and 43.

Check? Reasonable?

I added correctly.
42 + 43 is about 40 + 40 = 80
80 is close to 85.
42 and 43 is reasonable.

Teaching Tools • 1

Topic 1

Numeration

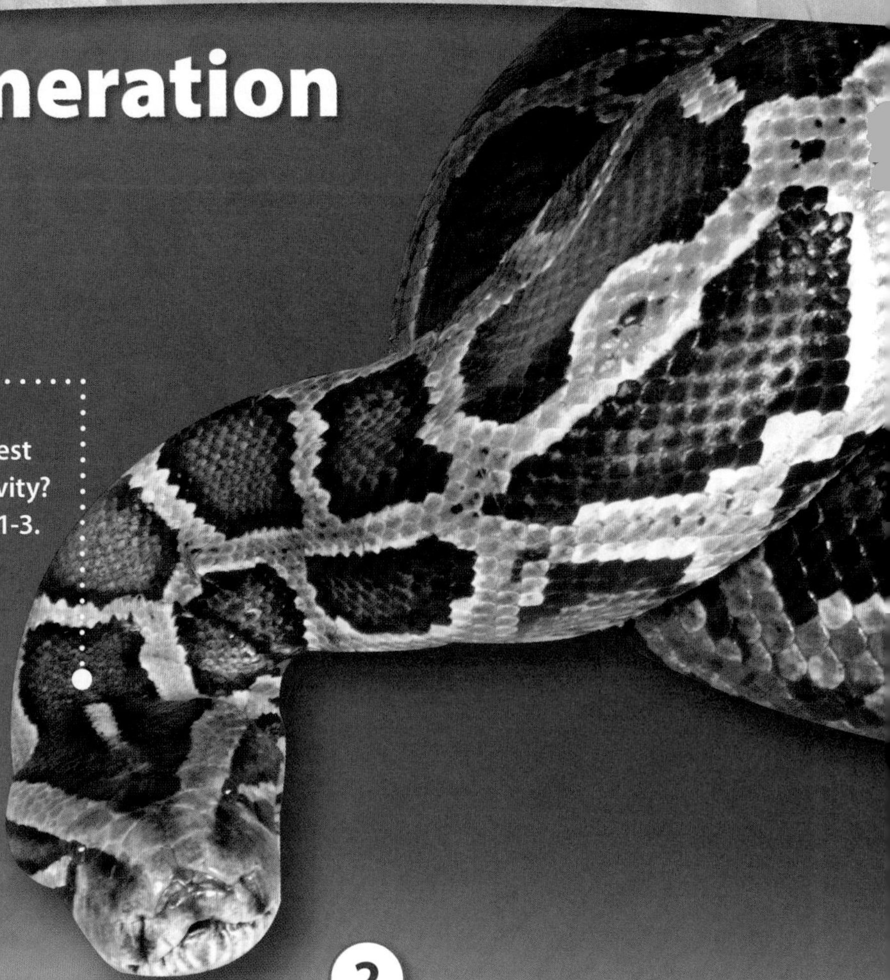

1 "Baby," the snake, weighs 403 pounds. Is it the heaviest snake that is living in captivity? You will find out in Lesson 1-3.

2 How many towns and cities were there in California in 2004? You will find out in Lesson 1–1.

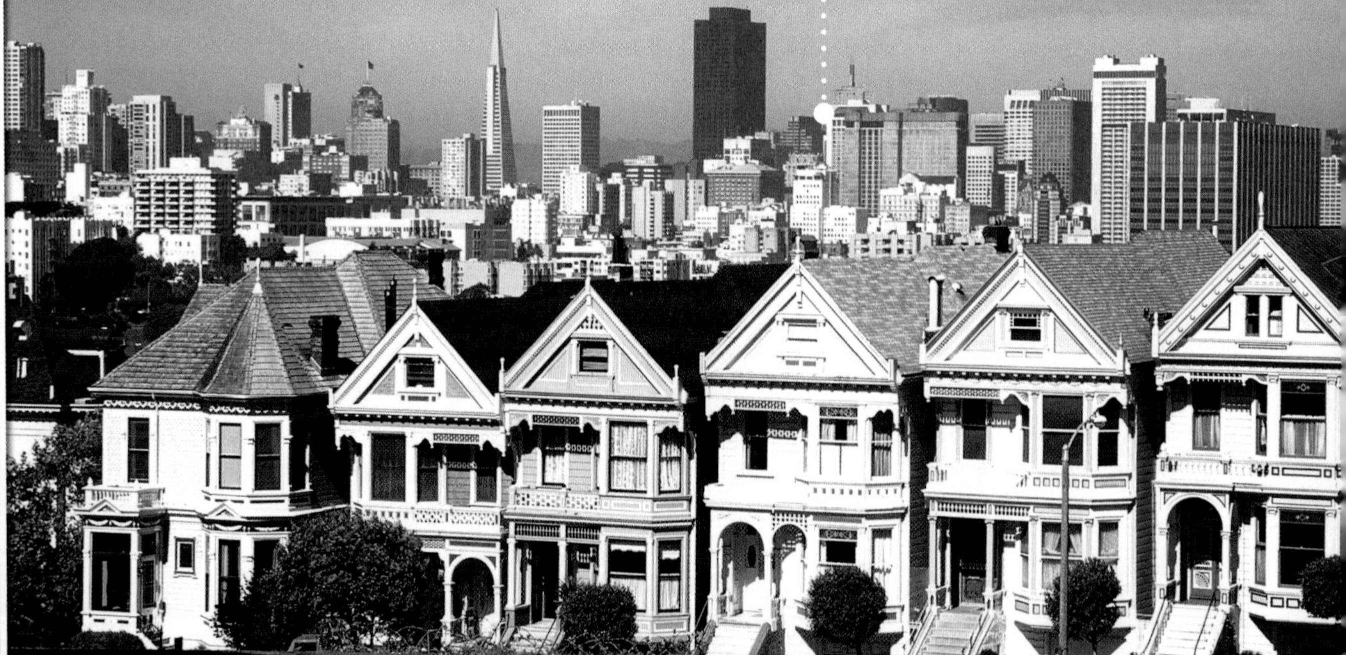

Vocabulary

Choose the best term from the box.

> • digits   • period
> • compare   • number line
> • even   • odd

1. A group of three digits in a number separated by a comma is a ? .

2. A ? is a line that shows numbers in order using a scale.

3. The number 8 is an ? number.

4. The number 5 is an ? number.

Comparing Numbers

Compare. Use >, <, or = for each ◯.

5. 13 ◯ 10   **6.** 7 ◯ 7   **7.** 28 ◯ 29

8. 14 ◯ 5   **9.** 43 ◯ 34   **10.** 0 ◯ 1

11. 52 ◯ 52   **12.** 13 ◯ 65   **13.** 22 ◯ 33

Place Value

Tell if the underlined digit is in the ones, tens, or hundreds place.

14. 34<u>6</u>   **15.** <u>1</u>7   **16.** 9<u>2</u>1

17. <u>1</u>06   **18.** 3<u>3</u>   **19.** <u>4</u>7

20. <u>2</u>17   **21.** 3<u>2</u>0   **22.** 81<u>0</u>

23. 1,00<u>6</u>   **24.** <u>9</u>99   **25.** 1,4<u>0</u>5

26. Writing to Explain How does using commas to separate periods help you read large numbers?

3

How much gold is stored in Fort Knox? You will find out in Lesson 1-2.

Lesson

1-1

NS 1.0, Grade 3
Understand the place
value of whole numbers.
Also **NS 1.0.**

Thousands

Hands-On
place-value blocks

What are some ways to represent numbers in the thousands?

An altimeter measures height above sea level. Jill's altimeter shows she is 3,241 feet above sea level. There are different ways to represent 3,241.

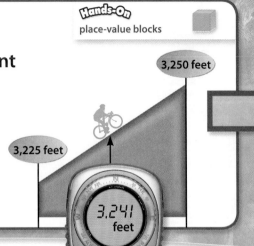

3,250 feet

3,225 feet

3.241 feet

Another Example How do you read and write numbers in the thousands?

Another bicycle racer's altimeter shows he is 5,260 feet above sea level. Write 5,260 in standard form, expanded form, and word form.

When writing a number in standard form, write only the digits: 5,260.

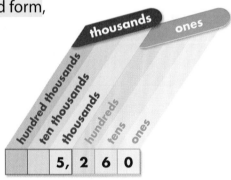

thousands   ones

hundred thousands
ten thousands
thousands
hundreds
tens
ones

5, 2   6   0

Each group of 3 digits starting from the right forms a period.

A number in expanded form is written as the sum of the value of the digits: 5,000 + 200 + 60 + 0.

Use periods in the place-value chart to write 5,260 in word form: five thousand, two hundred sixty.

Explain It

1. Explain why the value of 5 in 5,264 is 5,000.

2. Is the expanded form for 5,260 the same as for 5,206?

You can represent numbers using place-value blocks.

3,000 + **200** + **40** + **1**

You can represent numbers on a number line.

3,241

3,200   3,250   3,300

Guided Practice*

Do you know HOW?

In **1** through **4**, write the word form, and tell the value of the red digit in each number.

1. 15,324

2. 135,467

3. 921,382

4. 275,206

In **5** and **6**, write the expanded form.

5. 42,158

6. 63,308

Do you UNDERSTAND?

7. If Jill climbed 100 feet more, what would her altimeter read?

8. What is the value of the 2 in 3,261? the 3? the 1?

9. Write one hundred one thousand, eleven in standard form.

Independent Practice

Leveled Practice In **10** through **13**, write each number in standard form.

10.

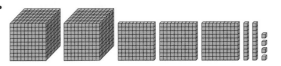

11.

12.

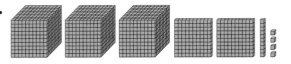

13.

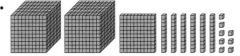

Animated Glossary, eTools
www.pearsonsuccessnet.com

In **14** and **15**, write each number in standard form.

14. Eighty-three thousand, nine hundred two

15. Three hundred twenty-one thousand, two hundred nine

In **16** and **17**, write each number in expanded form.

16. Four hundred ninety-seven thousand, three hundred thirty-two

17. Twenty-one thousand, eight hundred seven

In **18** and **19**, write each number in word form.

18. 300,000 + 8,000 + 20 + 9

19.

Problem Solving

20. Reasoning The pedometer below counts the number of steps you walk. It can show 5 digits. What is the greatest number it can show?

21. A town library has 124,763 books and 3,142 DVDs. This year, they bought 1,000 books and 2,000 DVDs. How many books does the library have now?

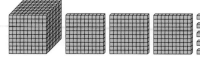

  A 5,142 books   **C** 125,763 books

  B 23,142 books   **D** 134,763 books

22. Number Sense Which digit is in the same place in all three numbers below? Name the place-value position.

574,632   24,376   574,632

23. Reasoning What is the greatest 4-digit number you can write? What is the least 4-digit number?

24. In 2004, California had 1,080 towns and cities. Use place-value blocks to represent 1,080. If this number increases by 300 in ten years, how many towns and cities will there be in ten years?

Mixed Problem Solving

1. How many more Kemp Ridley's Sea Turtles were there in 1947 than in 1968?

2. Did the population of Kemp Ridley's Sea Turtles increase or decrease between 1991 and 2000?

3. How many fewer Kemp Ridley's Sea Turtles were found nesting in 1991 than in 1968?

Data

Kemp Ridley's Sea Turtles	
Year	Female Kemp Ridley's Sea Turtles Found Nesting
1947	40,000
1968	5,000
1991	200
2000	6,000

4. Which is taller: the California jewel-flower or the Calistoga popcorn flower?

5. Which is shorter: the Calistoga popcorn flower or the Slender-horned spineflower?

6. Order the California jewel-flower, the Sacramento Orcutt grass, and the Slender-horned spineflower from tallest to shortest using their heights.

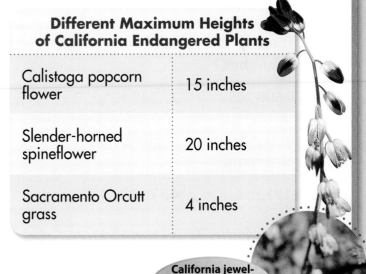

Different Maximum Heights of California Endangered Plants

Calistoga popcorn flower	15 inches
Slender-horned spineflower	20 inches
Sacramento Orcutt grass	4 inches

California jewel-flower: Grows up to about 40 inches tall

For **7** and **8**, use the information below.

California has a total area of 163,707 square miles. Of this total, 155, 959 square miles is land.

7. Which digit in the number 155,959 is in the thousands place? What does the 1 mean in this number?

8. **Strategy Focus** Solve the problem using the strategy Write and Equation.
   How many square miles of California's total area is covered by water?

Millions

What are some ways to represent numbers in the millions?

From 2001 through 2005, 356,039,763 fans attended professional baseball games. Write the expanded form and word form for 356,039,763. Use a place-value chart to help.

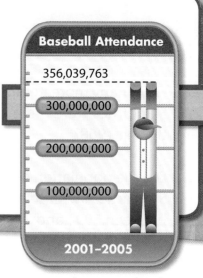

Baseball Attendance

356,039,763

300,000,000

200,000,000

100,000,000

2001–2005

Guided Practice*

Do you know HOW?

In **1** and **2**, write the number in word form. Then, tell the value of the red digit in each number.

1. 75,600,295

2. 249,104,330

In **3** through **6**, write the number in expanded form.

3. 6,173,253

4. 75,001,432

5. 16,107,320

6. 430,290,100

Do you UNDERSTAND?

7. What is the value of 5 in 356,039,763?

8. What is the value of 9 in 356,039,763?

9. Between 1996 and 2000 335,365,504 fans attended games. Which digit is in the millions place in 335,365,504?

Independent Practice

In **10** through **12**, write each number in standard form.

10. 300,000,000 + 40,000,000 + 7,000,000 + 300,000 + 10,000 + 6,000 + 20 + 9

11. 900,000,000 + 20,000,000 + 6,000,000 + 20,000 + 4,000 + 10

12. 80,000,000 + 1,000,000 + 600,000 + 20,000 + 900 + 40 + 8

In **13** through **16**, write the number in word form. Then, tell the value of the red digit in each number.

13. 7,915,878

14. 23,341,552

15. 214,278,216

16. 334,290,652

For another example, see Set B on page 20.

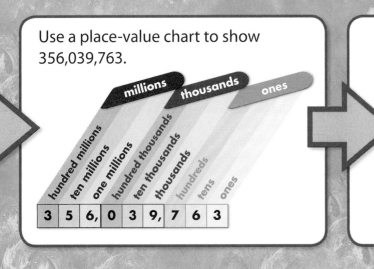

Use a place-value chart to show 356,039,763.

millions thousands ones

hundred millions / ten millions / one millions / hundred thousands / ten thousands / thousands / hundreds / tens / ones

| 3 | 5 | 6, | 0 | 3 | 9, | 7 | 6 | 3 |

There is a 3 is in the hundred millions place. Its value is 300,000,000.

Expanded Form: 300,000,000 + 50,000,000 + 6,000,000 + 30,000 + 9,000 + 700 + 60 + 3

Word Form: Three hundred fifty-six million, thirty-nine thousand, seven hundred sixty-three

In **17** through **20**, write the number in expanded form. Then, tell the value of the red digit in each number.

17. 7,330,968

18. 30,290,447

19. 133,958,840

20. 309,603,114

Problem Solving

21. Writing to Explain Which number will take less time to write in expanded form, 800,000,000 or 267,423?

22. Write the expanded form of 123,456,789 and 987,654,321. Which digit has the same value in both numbers?

23. In 2005, seventy-four million, nine hundred fifteen thousand, two hundred sixty-eight fans attended baseball games. Which choice shows this number in standard form?

   A 74,015,268   **C** 74,905,268

   B 74,900,268   **D** 74,915,268

24. Write the standard form of a 9-digit number with a 5 in the millions place and a 9 in the tens place.

   a Write a number that is ten million more than the number you chose.

   b Write a number that is one million less than the number you chose.

25. Number Sense Fort Knox holds 147,300,000 ounces of gold. Write the number that is one million more.

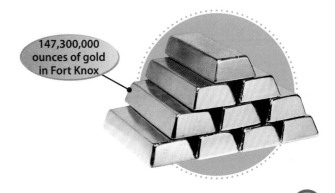

147,300,000 ounces of gold in Fort Knox

Comparing and Ordering Whole Numbers

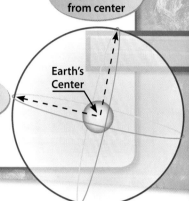

North Pole
6,356 km
from center

How do you compare numbers?

NS 1.2 Order and compare whole numbers and decimals to two decimal places.

Earth is not perfectly round. The North Pole is 6,356 kilometers from Earth's center. The equator is 6,378 kilometers from the center. Which is closer to the Earth's center: the North Pole or the equator?

Equator
6,378 km
from center

Earth's Center

Another Example How do you order numbers?

The areas of 3 continents on Earth are shown in the table at the right. Which shows the areas in order from **least** to **greatest**?

A 9,450,000; 4,010,000; 6,890,000

B 4,010,000; 9,450,000; 6,890,000

C 6,890,000; 9,450,000; 4,010,000

D 4,010,000; 6,890,000; 9,450,000

Data

Continent	Land Area (in square miles)
Europe	4,010,000
North America	9,450,000
South America	6,890,000

Step 1 Plot the numbers on a number line.

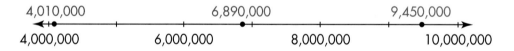

4,010,000   6,890,000   9,450,000

4,000,000   6,000,000   8,000,000   10,000,000

Step 2 Order the numbers. On a number line, numbers to the right are greater.

Reading from left to right, 4,010,000; 6,890,000; 9,450,000.

The correct choice is **D**.

Explain It

1. Describe how you would order the continents' areas using place value.

2. **Reasonableness** How can you rule out choices A and C as the correct answer?

Use place value to compare numbers.

Write the numbers, lining up places. Begin at the left and compare.

6,356
6,378

The thousands digit is the same in both numbers.

Look at the next digit.

6,356
6,378

The hundreds digit also is the same in both numbers.

The first place where the digits are different is the tens place. Compare.

6,356   5 tens $<$ 7 tens,
6,378   so 6,356 $<$ 6,378

The symbol $>$ means is greater than, and the symbol $<$ means is less than.

The North Pole is closer to Earth's center than the equator.

Guided Practice*

Do you know HOW?

In **1** through **4**, copy and complete by writing $>$ or $<$ for each ◯.

1. 2,643 ◯ 2,801   **2.** 6,519 ◯ 6,582

3. 2,643 ◯ 731   **4.** 6,703 ◯ 6,699

In **5** and **6**, order the numbers from least to greatest.

5. 7,502   6,793   6,723

6. 80,371   15,048   80,137

Do you UNDERSTAND?

7. Writing to Explain Why would you look at the hundreds place to order these numbers?

32,463   32,482   32,947

8. Compare the area of Europe and South America. Which is greater?

Independent Practice

In **9** through **16**, copy and complete by writing $>$ or $<$ for each ◯.

9. 221,495 ◯ 210,388

10. 52,744 ◯ 56,704

11. 138,752 ◯ 133,122

12. 4,937 ◯ 4,939

13. 22,873 ◯ 22,774

14. 1,912,706 ◯ 1,913,898

15. 412,632 ◯ 412,362

16. 999,999,999 ◯ 9,990,999

Leveled Practice In **17** through **20**, copy and complete the number lines. Then use the number lines to order the numbers from greatest to least.

17. 27,505   26,905   26,950

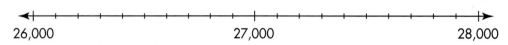

26,000   27,000   28,000

18. 3,422,100   3,422,700   3,422,000

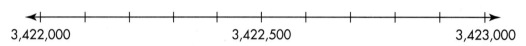

3,422,000   3,422,500   3,423,000

19. 7,502   7,622   7,523   7,852

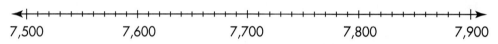

7,500   7,600   7,700   7,800   7,900

20. 3,030 3,033 3,003

3,000   3,050

In **21** through **28**, write the numbers in order from least to greatest.

21. 57,535 576,945 506,495

22. 18,764 18,761 13,490

23. 25,988 25,978 25,998

24. 87,837 37,838 878,393

25. 43,783 434,282 64,382

26. 723,433 72,324 72,432

27. 58,028 85,843 77,893

28. 274,849,551 283,940,039 23,485,903

Problem Solving

29. Estimation Aaron added 57 and 20 and said the answer is greater than 100. Is Aaron correct?

30. Number Sense Write three numbers that are greater than 780,000 but less than 781,000.

31. Reasoning Could you use only the millions period to order 462,409,524 463,409,524 and 463,562,391?

32. Describe how to compare 7,463 74,633 and 74,366 from least to greatest.

33. The heaviest snake living in captivity is a Burmese Python named "Baby." An average Anaconda snake weighs 330 pounds. Which snake weighs more?

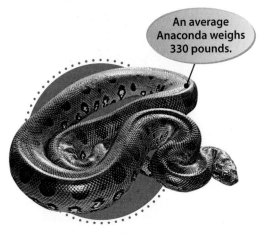

An average Anaconda weighs 330 pounds.

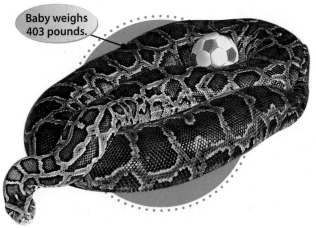

Baby weighs 403 pounds.

34. Which list of numbers is in order from least to greatest?

A	1,534	1,576	1,563
B	18,732	18,723	18,765
C	234,564	234,568	234,323
D	383,847	383,848	383,849

35. Asia and Africa are the two largest continents on Earth. Which continent is larger?

Continent	Land Area (square miles)
Africa	11,608,000
Asia	17,212,000

36. The chart below shows the number of game cards owned by the top collectors in one school. Which student had the most cards?

A Shani   **C** Ariel

B Lin   **D** Jorgé

Collector	Number of cards
Shani	3,424
Ariel	3,443
Lin	2,354
Jorgé	2,932

37. The Atlantic Ocean has an area of 33,420,000 square miles. This area is between which numbers?

A 33,400,000 and 33,440,000

B 33,000,000 and 33,040,000

C 33,100,000 and 33,419,000

D 33,430,000 and 33,500,000

Lesson

1-4

NS 1.2 ⌐⚬⚬⌐ Order and compare whole numbers and decimals to two decimal places.

Understanding Zeros in Place Value

How do you compare and order numbers with zeros?

Lena wrote three book reports. Which report used the most disk space on her computer? Use expanded form to compare and order numbers.

Book Report	File Size (bytes)
The Great Kapok Tree	9,050
Coyote School News	9,005
Grandfather's Journey	9,500

Guided Practice*

Do you know HOW?

In **1** and **2**, write each number in expanded form. Then write > or < for each ◯.

1. 6,400 ◯ 6,004   **2.** 1,002 ◯ 1,020

In **3** and **4**, order the numbers from greatest to least.

3. 7,002   7,200   7,020

4. 8,006   8,600   8,060

Do you UNDERSTAND?

5. Number Sense Write a 5-digit number with 0 in the hundreds place and 0 in the ones place. Then, write your number in expanded form.

6. Looking at the chart above, which book report used the least amount of disk space on Lena's computer? How much disk space did it use?

Independent Practice

Leveled Practice In **7** through **17**, compare. Write > or < for each ◯.

7. 1,040 = 1,000 + 40
1,004 = 1,000 + 4
1,040 ◯ 1,004

8. 18,020 = 10,000 + 8,000 + 20
18,200 = 10,000 + 8,000 + 200
18,020 ◯ 18,200

9. 2,070 ◯ 2,700   **10.** 13,200 ◯ 13,020   **11.** 5,406 ◯ 5,460

12. 4,130 ◯ 4,103   **13.** 31,002 ◯ 30,102   **14.** 26,008 ◯ 26,800

15. 10,250 ◯ 10,205   **16.** 60,802 ◯ 68,002   **17.** 42,910 ◯ 42,901

*For another example, see Set D on page 21.

Compare the first two numbers. Which is greater, 9,050 or 9,005?

$$9,050 = 9,000 + 50$$
$$9,005 = 9,000 + 5$$

$$50 > 5$$
So, $9,050 > 9,005$.

Write the numbers from greatest to least.

9,050   9,005   9,500

Write the numbers in expanded form.

$$9,050 = 9,000 + 50$$
$$9,005 = 9,000 + 5$$
$$9,500 = 9,000 + 500$$

$$500 > 50 > 5$$
So, $9,500 > 9,050 > 9,005$.

Grandfather's Journey took up the most disk space on Lena's computer.

In **18** through **21**, order the numbers from greatest to least.

18. 3,007 3,070 3,700

19. 9,800 9,008 9,080

20. 30,200 30,002 32,000 30,020

21. 40,060 40,006 40,600 46,000

Problem Solving

For **22** and **23**, pick four numbers between 143,000 and 144,000. Include exactly two zeros in each number.

22. Order the numbers you chose from least to greatest.

23. What do the numbers have in common?

For **24** and **25**, use the chart at the right.

24. Which month were the most carnival tickets sold?

25. Writing to Explain Explain why this statement is **NOT** correct: More tickets were sold in June than August because $40 > 20$.

Data	Month	Carnival
	June	12,040
	July	14,200
	August	14,020

26. The chart at the right shows the results of this year's reading contest. Which could **NOT** be the missing number?

   A 32,006   **C** 33,060

   B 33,006   **D** 34,006

Data	Class	Place	Pages Read
	Ms. Sharma	first	34,600
	Mr. Fox	second	
	Ms. Kim	third	32,060

MR 1.1 Analyze problems by identifying relationships, distinguishing relevant from irrelevant information, sequencing and prioritizing information, and observing patterns. Also **SDAP 1.0.**

Problem Solving

Make an Organized List

Arthur is tiling a bathroom wall. He has 520 wall tiles. He wants to arrange them in patterns of hundreds and tens.

Using only hundreds and tens blocks, how many ways can he make 520?

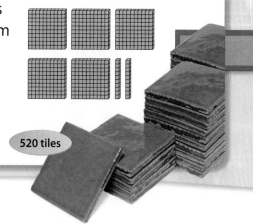

520 tiles

Guided Practice*

Do you know HOW?

Solve. Make an organized list to help you.

1. It costs Celia 50¢ admission to enter the aquarium. How many different ways can Celia pay the admission using only quarters, dimes, and nickels?

Do you UNDERSTAND?

2. What were the titles for the columns of your list in Problem 1?

3. **Write a Problem** Write a problem that you can solve using an organized list.

Independent Practice

Solve.

4. Using only hundreds blocks and tens blocks, list the ways to show 340.

5. Simon asked Margaret to guess a number. He gave these hints.
   - The number has 3 digits.
   - The digit in the 100s place is less than 2.
   - The digit in the 10s place is greater than 8.
   - The number is even.

   What are the possible numbers?

6. Make a list showing the ways you can make a dollar using only quarters, dimes, and nickels using no more than one nickel and no more than 9 dimes.

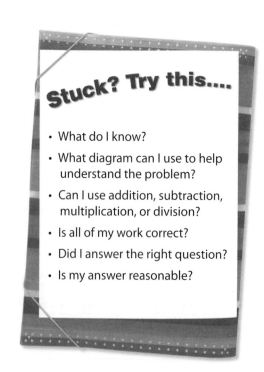

Stuck? Try this....

- What do I know?
- What diagram can I use to help understand the problem?
- Can I use addition, subtraction, multiplication, or division?
- Is all of my work correct?
- Did I answer the right question?
- Is my answer reasonable?

What do I know? I can use only hundreds blocks and tens blocks.

What am I asked to find? All of the combinations that show a total of 520

Record the combinations using an organized list.

Hundreds	5	4	3	2	1	0
Tens	2	12	22	32	42	52

There are 6 ways to make 520.

---

7. Lou's sandwiches are made with either wheat or white bread and have only one type of cheese— Swiss, Cheddar, American, or Mozzarella. How many different kinds of sandwiches can Lou make?

8. A magazine has a total of 24 articles and ads. There are 9 articles. How many ads are there?

24 articles and ads

9	?

9. Janie is making a bracelet. She has 1 red bead, 1 blue bead, and 1 white bead. How many possible ways can Janie arrange the beads?

10. Reasoning What two numbers have a sum of 12 and a difference of 4?

11. Alan has a cat, a goldfish, and a dog. He feeds them in a different order each day. How many different ways can he feed his pets?

12. Heather is writing a 3-digit number. She uses the digits 1, 5, and 9. What are the possible numbers she can write?

13. At the driving range, James wants to buy 200 golf balls. The golf balls are sold in buckets of 100, 50, and 10 golf balls. How many different ways can James buy 200 golf balls?

50 golf balls

100 golf balls

10 golf balls

1. Which of the following is another way to write the numeral 10,220? (1-1)

 A One thousand, two hundred twenty

 B Ten thousand, two hundred two

 C Ten thousand, two hundred twenty

 D Ten thousand, twenty-two

2. Which statement is true? (1-4)

 A 230,400 > 234,000

 B 230,400 < 230,040

 C 230,040 > 230,004

 D 234,000 < 230,040

3. Betsy is making a flag. She can choose three colors from red, white, blue, and yellow. How many choices does Betsy have? (1-5)

 A 3

 B 4

 C 6

 D 24

4. The diameter of Saturn at its equator is 120,536 kilometers. Which of the following is greater than 120,536? (1-4)

 A 126,600

 B 120,535

 C 102,660

 D 106,260

5. California has about forty million, two hundred thousand acres of forested land. Which of the following is this number in standard form? (1-2)

 A 40,200

 B 40,000,200

 C 40,020,000

 D 40,200,000

6. The table shows the areas of four states. Which of the four states has the least area? (1-3)

State	Total Area (square miles)
Montana	147,042
Oklahoma	69,898
Oregon	98,381
California	163,696

 A Montana

 B Oklahoma

 C Oregon

 D California

7. What number is best represented by Point *P* on the number line? (1-1)

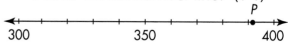

 A 378

 B 382

 C 388

 D 392

8. In 2000, the population of the city of Los Angeles, California was 3,694,820. Which number is less than 3,694,820? (1-3)

A 3,699,280

B 3,697,082

C 3,691,028

D 3,696,820

9. Carrie has 340 marbles to put in vases. The vases hold either 100 or 10 marbles each. Which is a way she can arrange the marbles? (1-5)

A 34 hundreds

B 3 hundreds 40 tens

C 1 hundred 24 tens

D 2 hundreds 24 tens

10. The table shows the areas of four countries in Europe. Which of the four countries has the greatest area? (1-3)

Country	Total Area (square miles)
Finland	130,558
Germany	137,846
Norway	125,020
Poland	120,728

Data

A Finland

B Germany

C Norway

D Poland

11. The place-value chart shows how many feet above sea level Mt. McKinley, the highest point in the United States, is. Which of the following is another way to write the number in the place-value chart? (1-1)

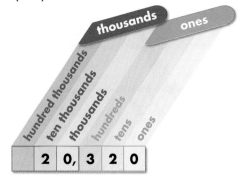

A 20,000 + 300 + 20

B 20,000 + 3,000 + 200

C 2,000 + 300 + 20

D 2,000 + 30 + 2

12. Which of these equals 8,205,006? (1-2)

A Eight million, two hundred five thousand, six

B Eight million, two hundred five thousand, sixty

C Eight million, two hundred fifty thousand, six

D Eighty million, two hundred five thousand, six

Set A, pages 4–6, 8–9

Use a place-value chart to write the expanded form and word form of 26,500.

Expanded form: 20,000 + 6,000 + 500

Word form: twenty-six thousand, five hundred

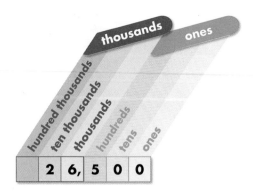

Remember that periods can help you read large numbers.

Use place-value charts to write each number in expanded form and word form.

1. 7,549   **2.** 27,961

3. 321,209   **4.** 3,454

5. 6,792,365   **6.** 15,164,612

7. 413,109,657   **8.** 83,251

9. 4,806   **10.** 6,138,405

Set B, pages 10–13

Write > or < for each ◯.

45,423 ◯ 44,897

Step 1 Use place value to compare.

Step 2 Start comparing from the left.

Step 3 Look for the first digit that is different.

45,423

44,897

5 > 4

So, 45,423 > 44,897.

Remember that a number line can be used to compare numbers.

Write > or < for each ◯.

1. 11,961 ◯ 12,961

2. 23,901 ◯ 23,899

3. 42,661,907 ◯ 42,659,824

4. 735,291,000 ◯ 735,291,001

5. 6,103,582 ◯ 6,130,449

6. 462,918 ◯ 461,349

7. 8,457 ◯ 8,451

8. 163,492,708 ◯ 163,492,807

9. 38,605 ◯ 38,650

10. 871,943 ◯ 871,934

Set C, pages 14–15

Use expanded form to compare and order numbers.

Which is greater, 3,500 or 3,005?

3,500 = 3,000 + 500
3,005 = 3,000 + 5
500 > 5

So, 3,500 > 3,005.

Write the numbers from greatest to least.

    3,050   3,005   3,500

Write the numbers in expanded form.

3,050 = 3,000 + 50
3,005 = 3,000 + 5
3,500 = 3,000 + 500
500 > 50 > 5

So, 3,500 > 3,050 > 3,005.

Remember to use a place-value chart to help compare and order numbers.

Write each number in expanded form. Then, copy and complete by writing > or < for each ◯.

1. 8,500 ◯ 8,005

2. 2,002 ◯ 2,020

3. 3,600 ◯ 3,006

4. 7,004 ◯ 7,040

Order the numbers from greatest to least.

5. 1,009   1,900   1,090

6. 6,008   6,800   6,080

Set D, pages 16–17

Using only hundreds and tens blocks, how many ways can you make 440?

What do I know?   I can use only hundreds blocks and tens blocks

What am I asked to find?   All of the combinations that show a total of 440

Record the combinations using an organized list.

Hundreds	4	3	2	1	0
Tens	4	14	24	34	44

Remember that the way you organize a list can help you find all the possibilities in a problem.

Solve. Make an organized list to help you.

1. A game has yellow, red, black, and green counters. How many 2-color combinations can you make?

2. Troy collects plastic banks. He has three different plastic banks: a pig, a cow, and a frog. How many ways can he arrange his banks on a shelf?

Addition and Subtraction Number Sense

1 About how many people visit the Los Angeles Zoo each year? You will find out in Lesson 2-2.

2 When was The Washington Monument completed? You will find out in Lesson 2-4.

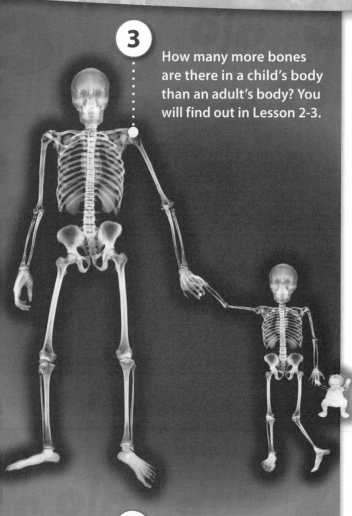

3 How many more bones are there in a child's body than an adult's body? You will find out in Lesson 2-3.

4 The lunar rover set the surface speed record on the moon. Find out the rover's estimated speed in Lesson 2-6.

Review What You Know!

Vocabulary

Choose the best term from the box.

- rounding
- mental math
- sum
- tens
- difference
- regroup

1. In order to subtract 141 from 530, you need to _?_.

2. _?_ tells about how many or about how much.

3. When you subtract two numbers, the answer is the _?_.

4. When you add numbers together, you find the _?_.

Addition Facts

Find the sum.

5. 4 + 6   **6.** 7 + 5   **7.** 9 + 8

8. 14 + 5   **9.** 3 + 7   **10.** 37 + 7

11. 9 + 6   **12.** 6 + 5   **13.** 15 + 7

14. 3 + 8   **15.** 14 + 6   **16.** 25 + 5

Subtraction Facts

Find the difference.

17. 27 − 3   **18.** 6 − 4   **19.** 15 − 8

20. 11 − 8   **21.** 6 − 2   **22.** 17 − 8

23. 16 − 4   **24.** 20 − 5   **25.** 11 − 6

26. 14 − 6   **27.** 15 − 10   **28.** 13 − 7

29. Writing to Explain Why does 843 round to 840 rather than to 850?

NS 1.3 ◦━━ Round whole numbers through the millions to the nearest ten, hundred, thousand, ten thousand, and hundred thousand.

Understanding Rounding

Why do you round numbers?

Rounding <u>replaces one number with another number that tells about how many or how much</u>.

The Golden Gate Bridge's towers reach a height of 746 feet. What is 746 rounded to the nearest ten? to the nearest hundred?

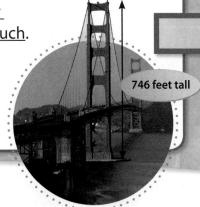

746 feet tall

Guided Practice*

Do you know HOW?

In **1** through **4**, use a number line to round each number to the place of the underlined digit.

1. 2,<u>2</u>86

2. 5,7<u>4</u>7

3. 1<u>5</u>3

4. 8,<u>6</u>39

Do you UNDERSTAND?

5. In the number lines above, why are the halfway point numbers different?

6. In New York, the Verrazano-Narrows Bridge's towers reach a height of 693 feet. What is 693 rounded to the nearest ten?

Independent Practice

Leveled Practice For **7** and **8**, use the number line to round each number to the place of the underlined digit.

7. 656

650   655   660

8. 9,128

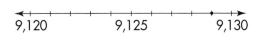

9,120   9,125   9,130

For **9** through **23**, use a number line to round each number to the place of the underlined digit.

9. 7,<u>2</u>41 **10.** 3,4<u>1</u>4 **11.** 2,<u>6</u>39 **12.** <u>5</u>61 **13.** 2<u>9</u>5

14. 2<u>0</u>6 **15.** 6,0<u>2</u>8 **16.** 8<u>7</u>3 **17.** 1<u>2</u>3 **18.** 1,9<u>9</u>9

19. 4,1<u>8</u>3 **20.** 6<u>4</u>7 **21.** 3,<u>8</u>09 **22.** 79<u>2</u> **23.** 8,<u>2</u>99

DIGITAL Animated Glossary
www.pearsonsuccessnet.com

For another example, see Set A on page 50.

Use a number line to round 746 to the nearest ten.

Compare 746 to the halfway point, which is 745.

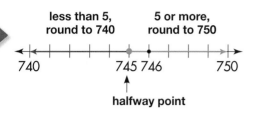

746 is to the right of the halfway point, so round to 750.

Use a number line to round 746 to the nearest hundred.

Compare 746 to the halfway point, which is 750.

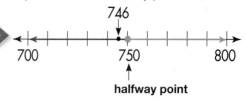

746 is to the left of the halfway point, so round to 700.

Problem Solving

For **24** and **25**, use the table at the right.

24. Write the number of cities in each state in expanded form. Then order the numbers from greatest to least.

25. Round each number in the table to the nearest 10 meters. Then order the rounded numbers from least to greatest.

State	Number of Cities
California	478
Georgia	528
Idaho	200

26. Number Sense Write four numbers that round to 500 when rounded to the nearest hundred.

27. The attendance at a football game at California Memorial Stadium was 54,387. What is this number rounded to the nearest hundred?

28. At a football game, a scoreboard showed the attendance at the game to be 35,396. Which choice is this number rounded to the nearest ten?

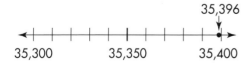

A 35,000   **C** 35,390

B 35,300   **D** 35,400

29. Writing to Explain Use the number line below. A car rental agency recorded the mileage of three cars in its fleet. What place can you round each number to and still be able to accurately order the numbers? Explain.

Mileage of 3 rental cars

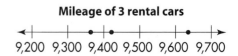

Lesson

2-2

NS 1.3 🔑 Round whole numbers through the millions to the nearest ten, hundred, thousand, ten thousand, and hundred thousand.

Rounding Whole Numbers

How can you round numbers?

Round 293,655,404 to the nearest thousand and to the nearest hundred thousand. You can use place value to round numbers.

293, 655, 404

281, 421, 906

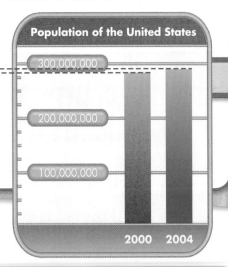

Population of the United States

300,000,000

200,000,000

100,000,000

2000   2004

Guided Practice

Do you know HOW?

In **1** through **6**, round each number to the place of the underlined digit.

1. 12<u>8</u>,955

2. 85,6<u>3</u>9

3. <u>9</u>,924

4. 1,1<u>9</u>4,542

5. <u>1</u>60,656

6. <u>1</u>49,590

Do you UNDERSTAND?

7. Writing to Explain Explain how to round a number when 7 is the digit to the right of the rounding place.

8. In 2000 the population of the United States was 281,421,906. Round 281,421,906 to the nearest hundred thousand.

Independent Practice

Leveled Practice In **9** through **28**, round each number to the place of the underlined digit. You may use a number line to help you.

9. 493,<u>2</u>95

⬜⬜⬜,000

10. 3<u>9</u>,230

⬜⬜,000

11. 77,2<u>9</u>2

⬜⬜,⬜0

12. <u>5</u>4,846

⬜0,000

13. 4,0<u>2</u>8

14. 6,6<u>6</u>8,365

15. 45<u>3</u>,280

16. 1<u>7</u>,909

17. 1,4<u>0</u>6

18. 55,<u>5</u>60

19. 21,6<u>7</u>9

20. 3,41<u>7</u>,547

21. 117,<u>8</u>21

22. <u>7</u>5,254

23. 9,<u>0</u>49

24. 1,666,<u>8</u>21

25 2,4<u>2</u>0

26. 9,0<u>0</u>0,985

27. <u>9</u>,511

28. 73,0<u>6</u>5

Round 293,655,404 to the nearest thousand.

thousands place

293,65<u>5</u>,404

If the digit to the right of the rounding place is 5 or more, add 1 to the rounding digit. If it is less than 5, leave the rounding digit alone.

293,65<u>5</u>,000

Since 4 < 5, leave the rounding digit as is. Change the digits to the right of the rounding place to zeros.

So, 293,655,404 rounds to 293,655,000.

Round 293,655,404 to the nearest hundred thousand.

hundred thousands place

293,<u>6</u>55,404

The digit to the right of the rounding place is 5.

293,<u>7</u>00,000

Since the digit is 5, round by adding 1 to the digit in the hundred thousands place.

So, 293,655,404 rounds to 293,700,000.

Problem Solving

For **29** and **30**, use the table at the right.

29. For each zoo in the chart, round the attendance to the nearest hundred thousand.

30. Reasoning Which zoo had the greatest number of visitors?

Zoo Attendance	
Los Angeles Zoo	1,396,538
Brookfield Zoo	1,872,544
Oregon Zoo	1,350,952

31. Number Sense Write four numbers that round to 700 when rounded to the nearest hundred.

32. Reasoning Write a number that when rounded to the nearest thousand and hundred will have a result that is the same.

33. Jonas read that about 1,760,000 people will graduate from high school in California in the next four years. Jonas thinks this number is rounded to the nearest ten thousand. What would the number be if it was rounded to the nearest hundred thousand?

34. Liz had attended class every day since she started school as a kindergartner. She said she had been in school for about 1,000 days. What could the actual number of school days be if she rounded to the nearest ten?

35. When rounded to the nearest ten thousand, which number would be rounded to 120,000?

    A 123,900   **C** 128,770

    B 126,480   **D** 130,000

36. A fruit market sold 3,849 apples, 3,498 oranges, and 3,894 pears in one day. Write these number in order from greatest to least.

Lesson

2-3

NS 2.1 Estimate and compute the sum or difference of whole numbers and positive decimals to two places.

Using Mental Math to Add and Subtract

How can you use mental math to add and subtract?

Properties can sometimes help you add using mental math. How many years have Ms. Walston and Mr. Randall been teaching? What is the total number of years all of the teachers in the chart have been teaching?

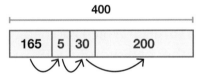

Teacher	Years Teaching
Ms. Walston	12
Mr. Roy	5
Mr. Randall	30

Other Examples

Add using mental math.

Find 135 + 48.

135	48

? (over whole)

Use **breaking apart** to find a ten.

Adding 5 to 135 is easy. Break apart 48.

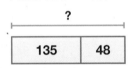

135	5	43

135 + 5 = 140
140 + 43 = 183
So, 135 + 48 = 183.

Use **compensation**.

135 + 48
135 + 50 = 185

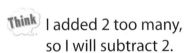 **Think** I added 2 too many, so I will subtract 2.

185 − 2 = 183
So, 135 + 48 = 183.

Subtract using mental math.

Find 400 − 165.

Use **counting on**.

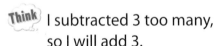

400

165	5	30	200

165 + 5 = 170
170 + 30 = 200
200 + 200 = 400

5 + 30 + 200 = 235
So, 400 − 165 = 235.

Use **compensation**.

Find 260 − 17.

It is easy to subtract 20.

260 − 20 = 240

Think I subtracted 3 too many, so I will add 3.

240 + 3 = 243
So, 260 − 17 = 243.

What do I know? The average weight of a chimpanzee brain is 420 grams. The average weight of a human brain is 1,350 grams.

What am I asked to find? The difference between the weights.

Draw a picture.

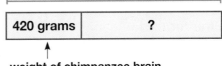

1,350 grams in all

| 420 grams | ? |

↑
weight of chimpanzee brain

Write an equation. Use subtraction to solve.

1,350 − 420 = ▢

The human brain weighs 930 grams more than the chimpanzee brain.

---

6. The American Kennel Club recognizes 17 breeds of herding dogs and 26 breeds of terriers. Draw a picture that could help find the total number of herding dogs and terriers.

7. Using the information in Exercise 6, write an equation to find how many more breeds of terriers than herding dogs there are.

For **8** through **10**, use the table to the right.

8. There are about 200 more animals in the Minnesota Zoo than in the Phoenix Zoo. About how many species of animals are in the Minnesota Zoo?

9. About how many more species are in the Indianapolis Zoo than the Phoenix Zoo?

10. How can you find the number of species of animals at the San Francisco Zoo?

Name of Zoo	Approximate Number of Animals
Phoenix	200
Minnesota	
San Francisco	
Indianapolis	360
Total Animals	1,210

Data

---

11. A parking lot had a total of 243 cars in one day. By 6:00 A.M., there were 67 cars in the lot. In the next hour, 13 more cars joined these. How many more cars would come to the lot by the end of the day?

243 cars in all

| 67 | 13 | ? |

12. A shoe store sold 162 pairs of shoes. The goal was to sell 345 pairs. How many pairs of shoes did they **NOT** sell?

345 pairs of shoes

| 162 | ? |

For **13** and **14**, use the table at the right.

13. What equation can you write to help find the cost of the shoes and socks together?

14. What equation can you write to help find the difference between the cost of the shirt and the shorts?

Cost of Gym Clothes	
Shirt	$12
Shorts	$19
Shoes	$42
Socks	$2
Hat	$15

15. Byron spent $7.75 on popcorn and a drink at the movie theater. The popcorn was $4.25. How much was the cost of the drink?

$7.75 in all

$4.25	?

16. Each school day, Mikaela sold the same number of tickets to the school play. On Monday she sold 4 tickets. How many tickets did she sell all together in 5 days?

? Tickets sold in all

4	4	4	4	4

tickets sold on one day

17. Writing to Explain Ken makes 2 nametags in the time it takes Mary to make 5 nametags. When Mary has made 15 nametags, how many has Ken made?

18. Mr. Lee had 62 pencils at the beginning of the school year. At the end of the school year he had 8 pencils left. How many pencils were given out during the year?

62 pencils in all

8	?

Think About the Process

19. Carlene bought a book for $13.58. She paid with a $10 bill and a $5 bill. Which expression would find the amount of change Carlene would receive?

A $15 − $13.58   **C** $10 + $5

B $15 − $1.42   **D** $13.58 + $1.42

20. Terrence rode 15 rides before lunch at the county fair. He rode 13 rides after lunch. Each ride requires 3 tickets. Which expression represents the number of rides he rode during the day?

A 15 − 13   **C** 15 − 3

B 15 + 13   **D** 13 − 3

Find each sum. Estimate to check
if the answer is reasonable.

1.   4,572
    + 2,391

2.   73,901
    + 5,799

3.   3,468
    + 947

4.   247
    + 312

5. 5,474 + 723   **6.** 47,090 + 2,910   **7.** 6,685 + 37

Find each difference. Estimate to check
if the answer is reasonable.

8.   4,087
    − 496

9.   8,354
    − 2,568

10.   9,115
    −   76

11.   6,000
    − 1,473

12.   6,249
    − 123

13. 5,302 − 88   **14.** 2,249 − 51   **15.** 8,001 − 4,832

Error Search Find each sum or difference that is not correct.
Write it correctly and explain the error.

16.   543
    + 29
    ─────
     562

17.   6,043
    + 972
    ─────
    7,025

18.   76,248
    + 19,046
    ──────
    95,294

19.   354
    − 74
    ────
    320

20.   14,953
    − 10,834
    ──────
     4,119

Number Sense

Estimating and Reasoning Write whether each
statement is true or false. Explain your answer.

21. The number 213,753 is ten thousand more than 223,753.

22. The sum of 6,823 and 1,339 is greater than 7,000
but less than 9,000.

23. The sum of 42,239 and 11,013 is less than 50,000.

24. The difference of 7,748 − 989 is greater than 7,000.

25. The sum of 596 + 325 is 4 less than 925.

26. The difference of 12,023 and 2,856 is closer
to 9,000 than 10,000.

1. Joe got 9,867 points playing a video game, and Shari got 7,375 points. How many more points did Joe get than Shari? (2-7)

A 2,592

B 2,512

C 2,492

D 1,492

2. The table shows tickets sold to the school play.

Tickets Sold	
Thursday	320
Friday	282
Saturday	375

Which is the best estimate of the total tickets sold? (2-4)

A 1,100

B 1,000

C 900

D 800

3. Dan bought a 3-ring binder for $4, a package of pencils for $1, and two packages of paper. What information is needed to find the total amount Dan spent before tax? (2-5)

A The cost of a package of paper

B The cost of a package of erasers

C The color of the binder

D How much money Dan gave the clerk

4. The U. S. Constitution contains 4,543 words, including the signatures. What is 4,543 rounded to the nearest hundred? (2-1)

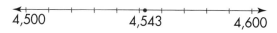

A 4,000

B 4,500

C 4,540

D 4,600

5. To find $239 + 149$, Garrett made a multiple of ten, as shown below. What is the missing number? (2-3)

$239 + 149 = 240 + \boxed{} = 388$

A 129

B 130

C 147

D 148

6. A musical group made 8,000 copies of a CD. By the end of the year, the group sold 6,280 copies. How many copies did they have left to sell? (2-8)

A 2,720

B 2,280

C 1,820

D 1,720

7. What is 500-126? (2-8)

A 626

B 484

C 426

D 374

8. In April, 5,326 books were checked out of the library. In May, 3,294 books were checked out. How many books were checked out in all? (2-6)

A 8,620

B 8,610

C 8,520

D 8,510

9. What number makes the number sentence true? (2-3)

28 + 79 = ▢ + 28

A 51

B 78

C 79

D 107

10. What is 22,456 + 694 + 1,121? (2-6)

A 24,271

B 24,171

C 23,271

D 23,161

11. The last total solar eclipse seen in Phoenix, Arizona, was in 1806. The next one will not be seen until 2205. Which number sentence shows the best way to estimate the number of years between the eclipses, using rounding? (2-4)

A 2000 − 1800 = 200

B 2200 − 1810 = 390

C 2210 − 1810 = 400

D 2210 − 1800 = 410

12. Daria's book has 323 pages. She has read 141 pages. Which picture models how to find the number of pages she has left to read? (2-9)

A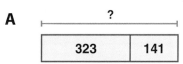

B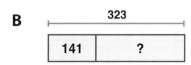

C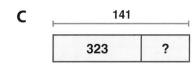

D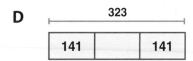

13. Last month, Mr. Chase's class read a total of 6,437 pages. This month they read 3,529 pages. How many more pages do the students need to read to reach the total from last month? (2-7)

A 2,908

B 2,912

C 3,108

D 3,112

14. What is 543,259,809 rounded to the nearest ten thousand? (2-2)

A 540,000,000

B 543,250,000

C 543,259,810

D 543,260,000

Set A, pages 24–25

Use a number line to round 837 to the nearest ten.

Compare 837 to the halfway point, which is 835.

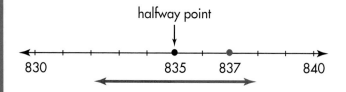

837 is to the right of the halfway point. So, 837 rounds to 840.

Remember to use the midpoint of the number line as a guide for rounding.

Use a number line to round each number to the place of the underlined digit.

1. 3,<u>7</u>67   **2.** 2,51<u>5</u>

3. 4<u>3</u>4   **4.** 6,<u>7</u>24

5. 1,6<u>2</u>3   **6.** 4,<u>2</u>93

7. 5,<u>1</u>93   **8.** <u>9</u>26

9. <u>4</u>67   **10.** 8,4<u>2</u>7

Set B, pages 26–27

Round 346,764,802 to the nearest hundred thousand.

hundred thousands place

346,<u>7</u>64,802   The digit to the right of the rounding place is <u>6</u>.

346,<u>8</u>00,000   Since 6 > 5, round by adding 1 to the digit in the hundred thousands place.

So, 346,764,802 rounds to 346,800,000.

Round 28,216 to the nearest thousand.

thousands place

2<u>8</u>,216   The digit to the right of the rounding place is <u>2</u>.

2<u>8</u>,000   Since 2 < 5, the digit in the rounding place stays the same.

So, 28,216 rounds to 28,000.

Remember to look at the number to the right of the rounding place. Then change the digits to the right of the rounding place to zeros.

Round each number to the place of the underlined digit.

1. 166,<u>7</u>42   **2.** 7<u>6</u>,532

3. <u>5</u>,861   **4.** 2,43<u>2</u>,741

5. <u>1</u>32,505   **6.** <u>2</u>57,931

7. 3<u>8</u>,427   **8.** 6,925

9. 2<u>4</u>3,819   **10.** <u>6</u>93,587

11. 15,<u>1</u>83,297   **12.** 4<u>9</u>3,620,761

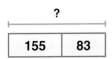

Set C, pages 28–30

Add 155 + 83. Use mental math.

?

155	83

Look for a ten and use the breaking apart method. Adding 5 to 155 is easy.

Break apart 83.

?

155	5	78

155 + 5 = 160

160 + 78 = 238

So, 155 + 83 = 238.

Remember that when you use compensation, you must adjust the sum or difference.

1. 53 + 88   **2.** 372 + 226

3. 734 − 223   **4.** 147 − 56

5. 5,342 + 1,826   **6.** 283 − 169

7. 6,000 + 0   **8.** 854 + 353

9. 1,854 + 362   **10.** 3,874 + 121

11. 363 + 784   **12.** 841 + 1,024

13. 676 − 521   **14.** 1,089 − 961

15. 899 − 275   **16.** 1,444 − 1,225

17. 2,401 − 1,025   **18.** 2,499 + 2,601

Set D, pages 32–33

Estimate   1,579
         − 1,248

Round each number to the nearest hundred.

1,579 rounds to 1,600.

1,248 rounds to 1,200.

Subtract   1,600
         − 1,200
            400

Estimate   534
         + 246

Round each number to the nearest ten.

534 rounds to 530.

246 rounds to 250.

Add   530
      − 250
         780

Remember that you can round numbers to the nearest hundred or thousand when estimating sums and differences.

1. 473 + 465   **2.** 8,352 − 3,421

3. 586 − 483   **4.** 4,094 + 246

5. 1,440 − 933   **6.** 748 − 392

7. 981 + 193   **8.** 725 + 635

9. 318 + 567   **10.** 4,806− 295

11. 743 − 188   **12.** 607 − 492

13. 3,593 + 1,208   **14.** 6,921 + 451

15. 7,264 − 2,835   **16.** 1,847 + 3,086

Set E, pages 34–35

Cathy had $8. She bought a sandwich, a fruit cup, and a milk at the snack bar. She spent a total of $6 on the sandwich and milk.

How much did Cathy have left?

What do I know?	Cathy had $8. Cathy bought a sandwich, a milk, and a fruit cup. Cathy spent $6 on the sandwich and the milk.
What am I asked to find?	The amount of money Cathy had left.

Is there missing information needed to solve the problem?

Yes, I need to know the cost of the fruit cup so I can find the total spent. Then I can find how much Cathy had left.

Is there extra information not needed to solve the problem?

No, there is no extra information.

Remember some problems have information you do not need.

Solve.

1. At the zoo, Doug saw 14 wallabies. He saw 5 Agile wallabies. The rest of the wallabies he saw were Rock wallabies. How many Rock wallabies did Doug see?

2. At the same zoo, Helen went to the Bat House exhibit to look at the Horseshoe bats. Min went to the same exhibit and saw 12 different bats. How many bats did Helen and Min see all together?

Set F, pages 36–38

Add 359 + 723.

Estimate: 400 + 700 = 1,100

Add the ones. Regroup if necessary.

```
  1
  359
+ 723
─────
    2
```

Add the tens. Regroup if necessary.

```
  1
  359
+ 723
─────
   82
```

Add the hundreds.

```
  1
  359
+ 723
─────
 1,082
```

The answer is reasonable.

Remember to regroup if necessary when adding whole numbers.

1. 215 + 8,823   2. 14,296 + 444

3. 2,417 + 3,573   4. 572 + 941

5.
```
  32,834
+ 17,384
```
6.
```
  14,382
+  9,243
```

7.
```
  10,294
+ 26,326
```
8.
```
  14,896
+  8,274
```

Set G, pages 40–41

Find 831 − 796.

Estimate: 830 − 800 = 30

Subtract the ones. Regroup if necessary.	Subtract the tens. Subtract the hundreds. Regroup if necessary.	Add to check your answer.
$\begin{array}{r} \text{2 11} \\ 8\,3\,\cancel{1} \\ -\ 7\,9\,6 \\ \hline 5 \end{array}$	$\begin{array}{r} \text{7 12 11} \\ \cancel{8}\,\cancel{3}\,\cancel{1} \\ -\ 7\,9\,6 \\ \hline 3\,5 \end{array}$	$\begin{array}{r} \text{1 1} \\ 8\,3\,1 \\ +\ 7\,9\,6 \\ \hline 8\,3\,1 \end{array}$

The answer is reasonable.

Remember you may need to regroup before you subtract.

1. 415 − 323   **2.** 673 − 294

3. 186 − 77   **4.** 4,978 − 2,766

5. $\begin{array}{r} 18,823 \\ -\ 4,634 \\ \hline \end{array}$ **6.** $\begin{array}{r} 728 \\ -\ 419 \\ \hline \end{array}$

7. $\begin{array}{r} 1,296 \\ -\ 377 \\ \hline \end{array}$ **8.** $\begin{array}{r} 866 \\ -\ 477 \\ \hline \end{array}$

Set H, pages 42–43

Find 400 − 378.

Estimate: 400 − 380 = 20

Regroup 4 hundreds to tens and ones.

$\begin{array}{r} \text{9} \\ \text{3 10 10} \\ \cancel{4}\,\cancel{0}\,\cancel{0} \\ -\ 3\,7\,8 \\ \hline 2\,2 \end{array}$ 4 hundreds =
3 hundreds + 9 tens + 10 ones

The answer is reasonable.

Remember to use the inverse operation to check your answer.

1. 700 − 255   **2.** 1,054 − 438

3. 320 − 111   **4.** 4,508 − 2,613

5. $\begin{array}{r} 18,005 \\ -\ 6,291 \\ \hline \end{array}$ **6.** $\begin{array}{r} 601 \\ -\ 482 \\ \hline \end{array}$

Set J, pages 44–46

The standard weight of a penny is 2.50 g, a standard nickel is 5.0 g, and a standard half dollar is 11.34 g. Estimate how much greater the weight of a half dollar is than a nickel.

What am I asked to find?   Estimate the difference between the weights.

Use subtraction to solve.

11.34 = 11

11.0 − 5.0 = 6.0

Remember you can draw a picture or diagram to model the problem.

1. A 7-kilometer run had markers at the starting line and at the finish line. Markers were placed at each kilometer. How many markers were used for the race?

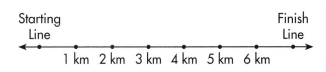

Multiplication and Division Meanings and Facts

1 How many years were in one full cycle of the Aztec calendar? You will find out in Lesson 3-4.

2 How many miles long is the Appalachian Trail? You will find out in Lesson 3-3.

3

Gouramis go to the surface of a fish tank to breathe air directly. How many gouramis can you keep in a 15-gallon tank? You will find out in Lesson 3-6.

4

How many years will it take the U.S. Mint to release all of the 50 state quarters? You will find out in Lesson 3-7.

CALIFORNIA
1850
JOHN MUIR
YOSEMITE VALLEY
2005
E PLURIBUS UNUM

CALIFORNIA
1850

Vocabulary

Choose the best term from the box.

- breaking apart
- factor
- product
- multiples

1. In the number sentence $8 \times 3 = 24$, 8 is a _?_.

2. In the number sentence $2 \times 6 = 12$, 12 is the _?_.

3. $26 + 4 = (20 + 6) + 4$ is an example of using the _?_ strategy.

4. To find _?_ of the number 3, multiply numbers by 3.

Patterns

Find the term that comes next in the pattern.

5. 2, 4, 6, 8, ▢   **6.** 20, 25, 30, 35, ▢

7. 6, 9, 12, 15, ▢   **8.** 8, 16, 24, 32, ▢

9. 7, 14, 21, 28, ▢   **10.** 11, 22, 33, 44, ▢

Arrays

Copy each array and circle equal groups of 3.

11. ▢▢▢▢▢
▢▢▢▢▢
▢▢▢▢▢

12. ▢▢▢
▢▢▢

13. Writing to Explain Henry is thinking of a whole number. He multiplies the number by 5, but the result is less than 5. What number is Henry thinking about? Explain.

NS 3.0 ⊶ Solve problems involving addition, subtraction, multiplication, and division of whole numbers and understand the relationships among the operations.

Meanings of Multiplication

How can multiplication be used when equal groups are combined?

How many ducks are there in 4 rows of 3? To find the total, multiply the number of equal groups by the number in each group. <u>Objects arranged in equal rows form an</u> array.

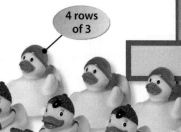

4 rows of 3

Another Example **How can multiplication be used when you only know the number in one group?**

You have learned addition facts. Now you will use them to help you learn to multiply.

Rudi and Eva collect plastic frogs. Rudi collected 5 frogs. Eva collected 3 times as many frogs. How many frogs did Eva collect?

A 3 frogs

B 5 frogs

C 10 frogs

D 15 frogs

Rudi's frogs

Eva's frogs

Eva collected 3 times as many frogs as Rudi.

Multiply by 3:

$3 \times 5 = 15$

Eva collected 15 frogs. The correct choice is **D**.

Explain It

1. Write an addition sentence that shows how many frogs Eva collected.

2. Draw an array of 16 frogs. Then, write a multiplication sentence describing the array.

There are 4 rows. Each row has 3 rubber ducks.

Repeated Addition: $\underbrace{3 + 3 + 3 + 3}_{\text{adding 4 rows of 3}} = 12$

Multiplication: $4 \times 3 = 12$

factors   product

The product is the answer to a multiplication problem. Factors are the numbers multiplied together to find the product.

The same rubber ducks can be arranged in another way.

Each group has 4 rubber ducks.

Repeated Addition: $4 + 4 + 4 = 12$

Multiplication: $3 \times 4 = 12$

There are 12 rubber ducks in all.

Guided Practice*

Do you know HOW?

In **1** and **2**, write an addition sentence and a multiplication sentence for each picture below.

1.

2.

Do you UNDERSTAND?

3. Beth saw 2 groups of 4 moths. Draw a picture to show 2 groups of 4. Then draw an array to show 2×4.

4. How could you use repeated addition to find the total number of objects in 3 groups of 2?

5. Martha has 5 rubber ducks. Jim has twice as many rubber ducks. How many rubber ducks does Jim have?

Independent Practice

Leveled Practice In **6** through **8**, write an addition sentence and a multiplication sentence for each picture.

6.

7.

8.

In **9** through **11**, write a multiplication sentence for each addition sentence.

9. $3 + 3 + 3 + 3 = 12$ **10.** $5 + 5 + 5 + 5 + 5 = 25$ **11.** $8 + 8 + 8 = 24$

DIGITAL   Animated Glossary   www.pearsonsuccessnet.com

12. Which number is three hundred three million, thiry-three thousand, three in standard form?

   A   300,333,003

   B   330,303,003

   C   300,303,033

   D   303,033,003

13. Reasoning Frank wrote 3 × 6 to describe the total number of paper clips shown. Alexa wrote 6 × 3. Who is correct? Explain.

14. Jacob, Hannah, and their grandmother visited the petting zoo. One scoop of animal food cost two dollars. How much did their grandmother pay to buy a scoop for each child?

15. Writing to Explain Without multiplying, how do you know that a 4 × 4 array will have more items than a 3 × 3 array?

16. Taylor helped his father with the grocery shopping. He bought three bags of cheese sticks. Each bag contained 8 cheese sticks. How many cheese sticks were there in all?

   A   3 cheese sticks

   B   16 cheese sticks

   C   24 cheese sticks

   D   30 cheese sticks

17. Sam is setting the table for a family dinner. He needs to put two forks at each place setting. Ten people will come for dinner. Write a multiplication sentence to show how many forks Sam needs.

18. **Think About the Process** Harry arranged the marbles in the pattern shown to the right. Which number sentence best represents Harry's arrangement of marbles?

   A   3 groups of 9 marbles   **C**   2 groups of 13 marbles

   B   4 groups of 5 marbles   **D**   4 groups of 7 marbles

19. Lisa has 2 rings. Tina has 4 times as many rings. How many rings does Tina have?

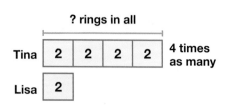

Mixed Problem Solving

California has several state animals in addition to the Grizzly Bear.

They are listed in the table below.

California State Animal	Facts
Animal: Grizzly Bear	5 claws on each paw
Marine Mammal: Gray Whale	Baby whales, called calves, drink 50-80 pounds of milk each day
Bird: California Valley Quail	Adopted in 1931, is characterized by a black bib with white stripe under the beak
Reptile: Desert Tortoise	Travels at a solid pace of 20 feet per minute
Insect: California Dogface Butterfly	Appeared on U.S. postage stamps in 1976
Marine Fish: Garibaldi	Adopted in 1995, takes 2-3 weeks for eggs to hatch

1. If a baby whale drinks 55 pounds of milk each day, how many pounds of milk can a calf drink in 4 days?

2. How many years after the California Valley Quail was adopted did California recognize the Garibaldi as the official state marine fish?

3. How many claws does a grizzly bear have in all?

? claws in all

5	5	5	5

4. The Golden Trout is the state fish of California. What is the difference in the number of eggs that a female may lay?

Californian Golden Trout	
Number of eggs	From 700 to 7,000
Life span	Up to 7 years
Identifying feature	10 dark oval musks called "parr marks"

5. If a female lays, on average, 4,000 eggs each year, how many eggs might she lay in her lifetime?

NS 2.2, Grade 3
Memorize to automaticity the multiplication table for numbers between 1 and 10.

Patterns for Facts

What are the patterns for multiples of 2, 5, and 9?

A multiple is the product of any two whole numbers.

○ multiples of 2

□ multiples of 5

△ multiples of 9

1	②	3	④	⑤	⑥	7	⑧	△9	⑩
11	⑫	13	⑭	15	⑯	17	⑱	19	⑳
21	㉒	23	㉔	25	㉖	27	㉘	29	㉚
31	㉜	33	㉞	35	㊱	37	㊳	39	㊵

Guided Practice*

Do you know HOW?

In **1** through **4**, skip count to find the number that comes next.

1. 2, 4, 6, 8, ▨

2. 20, 22, 24, ▨

3. 20, 25, 30, ▨

4. 36, 45, 54, ▨

In **5** through **8**, find the product.

5. 9×1

6. 2×8

7. 5×4

8. 9×2

Do you UNDERSTAND?

9. In the chart above, what pattern do you see for the numbers that have both red circles and green squares?

10. How do you know that 63 is not a multiple of 2? Explain using the pattern for multiples of 2.

11. Felix is sorting socks. He has 11 pairs of socks. How many socks does he have in all?

Independent Practice

In **12** through **15**, skip count to find the number that comes next.

12. 18, 27, 36, ▨

13. 12, 14, 16, ▨

14. 5, 10, 15, ▨

15. 88, 90, 92, ▨

In **16** through **30**, find each product.

16. 2×6

17. 5×3

18. 9×2

19. 5×8

20. 9×1

21. 2×7

22. 5×7

23. 9×3

24. 9×6

25. 2×8

26. 2×3

27. 5×9

28. 5×6

29. 4×7

30. 5×4

DIGITAL
Animated Glossary
www.pearsonsuccessnet.com

For another example, see Set B on page 86.

To find multiples of 2, skip count by 2s.

(2),(4),(6),(8),
(10),(12),(14),(16)...

All multiples of 2 are even numbers.

To find multiples of 5, skip count by 5s.

| 5 | 10 | 15 | 20 |
| 25 | 30 | 35 | 40 | ...

All multiples of 5 have a 0 or 5 in the ones place.

To find multiples of 9, skip count by 9s.

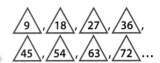

The digits of multiples of 9 add to 9 or a multiple of 9.

For 99, for example, 9 + 9 = 18, and 18 is a multiple of 9.

Problem Solving

31. How many arms do 9 starfish have

   a if each starfish has 6 arms?

   b if each starfish has 7 arms?

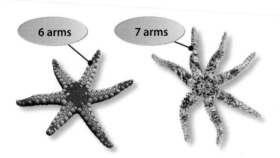

32. In wheelchair basketball, players use sports chairs that have 2 large wheels and 3 small wheels. If there are 5 players, how many

   a large wheels do the sports chairs have?

   b small wheels do the sports chairs have?

   c wheels do the sports chairs have in all?

33. Jody is working on her model train. She adds 9 pieces of track. Each piece of track is attached with 4 screws. How many screws does she need in all?

   A 18 screws   **C** 54 screws

   B 36 screws   **D** 72 screws

34. Geometry Each pentagon shown below has 5 sides. How many sides are there in all? Skip count by 5s to find the answer. Then, write the multiplication sentence.

35. Use the digits 3, 4, and 6 to make as many 3-digit numbers as you can. Put the numbers in order from least to greatest.

36. Which is equal to 7 dollars, 8 dimes, and 7 pennies?

   A $8.87   **C** $7.87

   B $8.78   **D** $7.78

Lesson

3-3

NS 2.6, Grade 3
Understand the special properties of 0 and 1 in multiplication and division.

Multiplication Properties

How can properties help you multiply?

Multiplication properties can help you remember basic facts.

3 groups of 2 (6 in all)

Commutative Property of Multiplication
Two numbers can be multiplied in any order and the product will be the same.

2 groups of 3 (6 in all)

$3 \times 2 = 2 \times 3$

Guided Practice*

Do you know HOW?

In **1** through **4**, find the product.

1. 0×5 **2.** 1×6

3. 1×0 **4.** 1×9

In **5** and **6**, copy and complete.

5. $4 \times 7 = 7 \times \boxed{}$

6. $6 \times 10 = \boxed{} \times 6$

Do you UNDERSTAND?

7. When you multiply any number by one, what is the product?

8. In a soccer tournament, Matt's team scored zero goals in each game. They played a total of 6 games. Write a multiplication sentence to show how many goals they scored in all.

Independent Practice

In **9** through **18**, find the product.

9. 1×5 **10.** 5×0 **11.** 3×9 **12.** 0×8 **13.** 0×3

14. 4×0 **15.** 9×4 **16.** 6×7 **17.** 5×6 **18.** 1×1

In **19** through **26**, find the missing number.

19. $4 \times 5 = \boxed{} \times 4$ **20.** $9 \times 12 = 12 \times \boxed{}$ **21.** $5 \times 0 = \boxed{} \times 5$ **22.** $9 \times 8 = \boxed{} \times 9$

23. $8 \times 11 = \boxed{} \times 8$ **24.** $1 \times 9 = \boxed{} \times 1$ **25.** $6 \times 4 = \boxed{} \times 6$ **26.** $7 \times 5 = \boxed{} \times 7$

*For another example, see Set C on page 86.

Zero Property of Multiplication
The product of any number and zero is zero.

2 groups of 0

$2 \times 0 = 0$

Identity Property of Multiplication
The product of any number and one is that number.

1 group of 7

$1 \times 7 = 7$

Problem Solving

For **27** and **28**, use the table at the right.

27. Annie has 6 packages of tennis balls. How many packages of yellow ping-pong balls would Annie need to have so that she has an equal number of ping-pong balls and tennis balls?

28. If Annie and her three friends each bought 1 package of baseballs, how many baseballs do they have in all?

Type of Ball	Number in each Package
Baseball	1
Tennis Balls	3
Ping-Pong Balls	6

29. Writing to Explain How do you know that $23 \times 15 = 15 \times 23$ without finding the products?

30. The Appalachian Trail is 2,174 miles long. If Andy hiked the entire trail one time, how many miles did he hike?

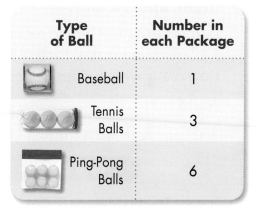

Katahdin, Maine

Appalachian Trail: 2,174 miles long

31. Mrs. Grayson has 27 students in her class. She wants to rearrange the desks in equal groups. If the desks are in 9 groups of 3 desks now, what is another way that she could arrange the desks?

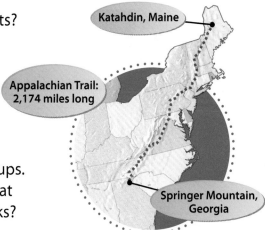

Springer Mountain, Georgia

Tip *Use a multiplication property.*

A 3 groups of 9 desks

B 2 groups of 13 desks

C 5 groups of 6 desks

D 4 groups of 7 desks

Lesson

3-4

MR 1.2 Determine
when and how to break
a problem into simpler
parts. Also NS 2.2

3, 4, 6, 7, and 8 as Factors

Each skateboard
has 4 wheels.

How can you break apart facts?

Darnel is replacing the wheels on
8 skateboards. Each skateboard has
4 wheels. How many wheels does he
need in all?

Use the Distributive Property to break
apart a problem into two simpler problems.

Another Example Are there different ways to
break apart a fact?

Darnel's boss asks him to replace the wheels on
7 inline racing skates. Each skate has 5 wheels.
How many wheels does he need?

Find 5×7.

You can break apart the first factor or the second factor.

One Way	**Another Way**

The first factor, 5, can be
broken into $3 + 2$.

The second factor, 7, can be
broken into $4 + 3$.

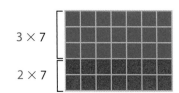

3×7

2×7

$5 \times 7 = (3 \times 7) + (2 \times 7)$

$21 + 14 = 35$

Darnel needs 35 wheels.

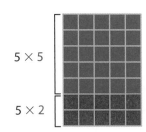

5×5

5×2

$5 \times 7 = (5 \times 5) + (5 \times 2)$

$25 + 10 = 35$

Explain It

1. In the example above, explain how the products
21 and 14 were found.

2. What is another way to break apart the fact 5×7?

Find 4 × 8.

Break apart 8 into 3 + 5.

$$4 \times 8 = (4 \times 3) + (4 \times 5)$$
$$12 + 20 = 32$$

So, 4 × 8 = 32

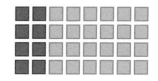
Find 4 × 8.

Break apart 8 into 2 + 6.

$$4 \times 8 = (4 \times 2) + (4 \times 6)$$
$$8 + 24 = 32$$

Darnel needs 32 wheels in all.

Guided Practice*

Do you know HOW?

In **1** through **3**, use breaking apart to find each product.

1. $6 \times 8 = (6 \times 4) + (6 \times \,\square\,)$

   $\square + \square = \square$

2. $7 \times 3 = (7 \times 1) + (\square \times 2)$

   $\square + \square = \square$

3. $9 \times 5 = (9 \times 1) + (9 \times \square)$

   $\square + \square = \square$

Do you UNDERSTAND?

4. In Exercise 2, what is another way to break apart the 7 in 7 × 3?

5. On Friday, Darnel received a box of skateboard wheels from the factory. The box contained 12 sets of 4 wheels. How many wheels were there in all?

 Break apart 12 into 10 + 2.

Independent Practice

Leveled Practice In **6** through **24**, use breaking apart to find each product.

6. $5 \times 10 = (5 \times 5) + (5 \times \square)$

7. $1 \times 3 = (1 \times \square) + (1 \times 2)$

8. $7 \times 11 = (7 \times 1) + (7 \times \square)$

9. $4 \times \square = (4 \times 3) + (4 \times 9)$

10. 9 × 9   **11.** 6 × 7   **12.** 3 × 5   **13.** 7 × 6   **14.** 4 × 7

15. 4 × 9   **16.** 9 × 7   **17.** 6 × 3   **18.** 7 × 8   **19.** 8 × 8

20. 6 × 4   **21.** 6 × 9   **22.** 9 × 3   **23.** 8 × 6   **24.** 7 × 12

In **25** through **28**, copy and complete by filling in with 6, 7, or 8.

25. $(8 \times 2) + (8 \times 4) = 8 \times \boxed{}$

26. $(7 \times 3) + (7 \times 5) = 7 \times \boxed{}$

27. $(6 \times 3) + (6 \times 4) = 6 \times \boxed{}$

28. $(9 \times 5) + (9 \times 3) = 9 \times \boxed{}$

In **29** through **34**, compare using $<$, $>$, or $=$ to fill in each $\bigcirc$.

29. $8 \times 4 \bigcirc 6 \times 4$

30. $3 \times 7 \bigcirc 4 \times 7$

31. $3 \times 6 \bigcirc 9 \times 2$

32. $11 \times 5 \bigcirc 12 \times 4$

33. $2 \times 12 \bigcirc 4 \times 6$

34. $9 \times 9 \bigcirc 8 \times 10$

Problem Solving

35. Reasoning How many eggs are in

  a 2 dozen?   **b** 6 dozen?   **c** 10 dozen?

 Remember 1 dozen = 12.

For **36** and **37**, use the table at the right.

36. In the Aztec calendar, each year has a number from 1 to 13. It also has one of 4 signs, as shown in the table. It takes 4×13 years to go through one complete cycle of the years. How many years is this?

 Break apart 13 into 10 + 3.

Aztec Year Names (first 16 years)			
2-House	3-Rabbit	4-Reed	5-Flint
6-House	7-Rabbit	8-Reed	9-Flint
10-House	11-Rabbit	12-Reed	13-Flint
1-House	2-Rabbit	3-Reed	4-Flint

37. The year 2006 is 7-Rabbit in the Aztec calendar. In what year will 11-Rabbit occur?

38. Jamal, Vera, and Tanya took a vacation. They traveled the distances shown in the table at the right. Who walked the farthest?

  A Jamal   **C** Vera

  B Tanya   **D** They all walked the same distance.

Hiker	Distance walked
Jamal	9 miles each day for 8 days
Vera	8 miles per day for 4 days and 4 miles a day for 8 days.
Tanya	7 miles each day for 5 days then 5 miles a day for 7 days.

39. The California Speedway in Fontana, California, opened in 1997. Tickets for the Historic Sports Car Festival cost $24 each. How can you use what you know about multiples of 12 to find the cost of three tickets?

40. Reasonableness Jillian says that the product of 11 × 12 is 1,212. Is this reasonable? Why or why not?

Use the diagram and table at the right to answer **41** through **43**.

41. Damian makes five shots from beyond the arc. How many points are scored?

42. Writing to Explain Vicki scores six baskets inside the arc and six free throws. Li scores six baskets from beyond the arc. Without multiplying, explain why each girl scores the same total.

43. In his last basketball game, Andrew scored 15 points. Which of the following is **NOT** a way he could have scored his points?

   A Five 3-point shots

   B Three 3-point shots in the first half and two 3-point shots in the second half

   C Three 2-point shots

   D Five 2-point shots, Five foul shots and two foul shots

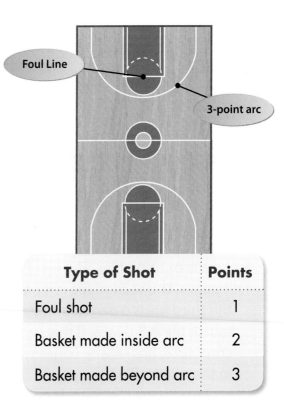

Type of Shot	Points
Foul shot	1
Basket made inside arc	2
Basket made beyond arc	3

For **44** through **47**, use the diagram at the right.

Write a multiplication sentence to find the total number of

44. white pieces

45. squares with pieces

46. white squares

47. Write two different addition sentences to find the number of squares on a chessboard.

MR 1.1 Analyze problems by identifying relationships, distinguishing relevant from irrelevant information, sequencing and prioritizing information, and observing patterns. **Also MR 1.0, NS 2.2, Grade 3** ⚷ .

Problem Solving

Look for a Pattern

Ella is learning how to play a waltz on the piano. Her teacher gives her a beginner's exercise for her left hand.

The music shows 4 measures. If this pattern continues, how many notes will she play in 8 measures?

3, 6, 9, 12, ▧, ▧, ▧, ▧

measure

Guided Practice*

Do you know HOW?

Solve. Find a pattern.

1. Julia is printing files. The first file is 2 pages, the second file is 4 pages, the third file is 6 pages, and the fourth file is 8 pages. If this pattern continues, how many pages will be in the eighth file?

Do you UNDERSTAND?

2. What multiplication facts can you use to help find the answer to Problem 1? Why?

3. **Write a Problem** Write a problem that uses a pattern for multiples of 5. Then answer your question.

Independent Practice

Look for a pattern. Use the pattern to find the missing numbers.

4. 5, 10, 15, 20, ▧, ▧, ▧, ▧

5. 9, 18, 27, ▧, ▧, ▧, ▧

Look for a pattern, Draw the next two shapes.

6.

7.

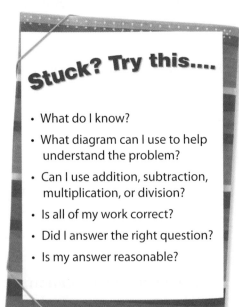

Stuck? Try this.....

- What do I know?
- What diagram can I use to help understand the problem?
- Can I use addition, subtraction, multiplication, or division?
- Is all of my work correct?
- Did I answer the right question?
- Is my answer reasonable?

Read and Understand

What do I know? The pattern for the first 4 measures is: **3, 6, 9, and 12.**

What am I asked to find? The number of notes she will play in 8 measures

Plan and Solve

Find a pattern. Skip count by 3s.

3, 6, 9, 12,...

What are the next four numbers?

3, 6, 9, 12, 15, 18, 21, 24

Ella plays 24 notes in 8 measures.

Look Back and Check

Is the answer reasonable?

There are 12 notes in 4 measures.

The number of notes in 8 measures is double the number in 4 measures.

The answer is reasonable.

Look for a pattern. Copy and complete each number sentence.

8. 30 + 5 = 35
300 + 5 = 305
3,000 + 5 = ▨
30,000 + 5 = ▨

9. 50 + 5 = 55
505 + 50 = 555
5,005 + 550 = ▨
50,505 + 5,050 = ▨

10. 60 + 8 = 68
608 + 60 = 668
6,008 + 660 = ▨
60,008 + 6,660 = ▨

11. Kaylee delivers invitations to everyone on her floor of her apartment building. There are 10 apartments on her floor. The numbers of the first four apartments are 2, 4, 6, and 8. If the pattern continues, what are the rest of the apartment numbers?

12. Look for a pattern in the table below to find the missing numbers.

300	320	340	▨	380
400	▨	440	460	▨
500	520	▨	560	580

13. Kerry has a newspaper route. The first four houses she delivers to are numbered 322, 326, 330, and 334. If this pattern continues, what will the next four numbers be?

14. Marvin is looking for a radio station on the AM dial. He tries these three stations: 1040, 1080, and 1120. If this pattern continues, what will be the next three numbers?

15. Jonas saves coins in his piggy bank. He drops in these groups of coins: 1 penny, 2 nickels, 3 dimes, 4 quarters, 5 pennies, 6 nickels, 7 dimes, and 8 quarters. If this pattern continues, what are the next four groups of coins?

16. Writing to Explain Suppose there are 18 bowls arranged in this pattern: big bowl, little bowl, big bowl, little bowl, and so on. Is the last bowl a big bowl or a little bowl? Explain.

NS 3.0 Solve problems involving addition, subtraction, multiplication, and division of whole numbers and understand the relationships among the operations. Also **MR 2.3**.

Meanings of Division

When do you divide?

A museum wants to display a collection of 24 gems on four shelves, placing the same number of gems on each shelf. How many gems will be on each shelf?

Choose an Operation Think about sharing. Divide to find the number in each group.

24 gems on 4 shelves

Another Example ## How can you divide to find the number of groups?

You have learned subtraction facts. Now you will use them to help you divide.

Terri has 24 gems. She wants to display them on shelves. She decides to display 4 gems on each shelf. How many shelves does she need?

Choose an Operation Think about repeated subtraction. Divide to find the number of groups.

What You Show

To find the number of shelves, put 4 gems in each group. How many groups are there?

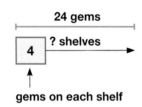

gems on each shelf

Terri needs 6 shelves.

What You Write

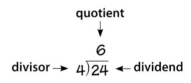

Explain It

1. How can repeated subtraction be used to find the number of shelves needed to hold 24 gems if each shelf holds 6 gems?

2. Explain what the quotient represents in each of the examples above.

What You Show

Think of sharing the gems equally among the 4 shelves. How many gems are on each shelf?

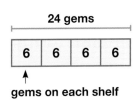

24 gems

6	6	6	6

↑
gems on each shelf

What You Write

divisor
↓
$24 \div 4 = 6$
↑   ↑
dividend   quotient

Each shelf should have 6 gems.

Guided Practice*

Do you know HOW?

In **1** and **2**, draw pictures to help you divide.

1. You put 18 people into 3 rows. How many people are in each row?

2. Rocco is putting 14 drawings into 2 art binders. How many drawings are in each binder?

Do you UNDERSTAND?

3. Explain how you could use repeated addition to check the answer to the example above.

4. Sixteen players came to soccer practice. They formed four teams with the same number of players per team. How many players were on each team?

Independent Practice

Leveled Practice In **5** through **7**, copy and complete the diagrams to help you divide.

5. Kevin is arranging 12 chairs in 3 equal groups. How many chairs are in each group?

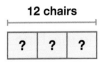

12 chairs

?	?	?

6. Meg has 36 beads. Each bracelet has 9 beads. How many bracelets does she have?

36 beads

9	? bracelets →

7. A farmer has 15 fruit trees. He plants 3 trees in each row. How many rows are there?

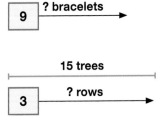

15 trees

3	? rows →

---

*For another example, see Set F on page 87.

In **8** through **11**, draw pictures to solve each problem.

8. Jeff puts 25 quarters into 5 equal groups. How many quarters are in each group?

9. Sally has 12 flower bulbs and divides them into 4 equal groups. How many flower bulbs are in each group?

10. Jena is making apple pies. She has 33 apples. She's putting 11 in each pie. How many pies will Jena make?

11. There are 30 stuffed bears in a gift shop arranged in 5 equal rows. How many bears are in each row?

Problem Solving

In **12** through **15**, use the table at the right.

12. How many students will be in each row for Mrs. Raymond's class photo?

13. How many more students will be in each row for Mr. Peterson's class than for Mr. Chen's class?

14. In which class will there be 7 students in each row?

Class Picture Day	
Each class must be arranged into three equal rows.	
Name of Teacher	**Number of Students**
Mrs. Raymond	24
Mr. Chen	18
Miss Clifford	21
Mr. Peterson	27

15. If 3 students were absent from Miss Clifford's class on picture day, how many fewer students would be in each row?

16. Kissing gouramis do not get enough oxygen using their gills underwater, so they come to the surface to breath. A fish store tells you that you need 3 gallons of water for each gourami. How many gouramis can you keep in a 15 gallon tank?

17. Ray collects toy cars. He stores them in special boxes that fit 6 cars each. He had a total of 48 cars. Today he got 12 more cars. How many boxes will Ray need to store all of his cars now?

  A 2 boxes

  B 6 boxes

  C 8 boxes

  D 10 boxes

18. **Think** About the **Process** The drama club collects 242 bottles and 320 cans in a fundraiser. Each is worth a nickel. However, the recycling machine rejects 48 cans. Which expression shows how many nickels they raised?

  A $(242 + 320) - 48$

  B $242 + 320 + 48$

  C $(320 - 242) + 48$

  D $(320 - 242) - 48$

Algebra Connections

Properties and Number Sentences

Remember multiplication properties can be used to help you solve multiplication problems:

- Commutative Property
  $3 \times 2 = 2 \times 3$
- Associative Property
  $(5 \times 2) \times 4 = 5 \times (2 \times 4)$
- Identity Property
  $9 \times 1 = 9$
- Zero Property
  $8 \times 0 = 0$

Example: $8 \times 5 = \boxed{} \times 8$

 Think *The Commutative Property of Multiplication means you can multiply numbers in any order.*

Since $8 \times 5 = 5 \times 8$, the value of $\boxed{}$ must be 5.

Copy and complete. Check your answers.

1. $39 \times \boxed{} = 39$

2. $\boxed{} \times 12 = 12$

3. $(8 \times 5) \times 2 = \boxed{} \times (5 \times 2)$

4. $20 \times 4 = 4 \times \boxed{}$

5. $6 \times \boxed{} = 5 \times 6$

6. $15 \times 3 = \boxed{} \times 15$

7. $\boxed{} \times 8 = 8 \times 9$

8. $1 \times \boxed{} = 24$

9. $\boxed{} \times 25 = 0$

10. $0 = \boxed{} \times 9$

11. $16 \times \boxed{} = 16$

12. $\boxed{} \times 5 = 6 \times (4 \times 5)$

13. $12 \times 0 = \boxed{}$

14. $7 \times \boxed{} = 0$

15. $7 \times (1 \times \boxed{}) = (7 \times 1) \times 3$

For **16** through **18**, use the information in the table to find the answer.

16. Write two number sentences to represent the number of seats in 6 rows.

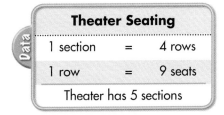

Theater Seating

1 section	=	4 rows
1 row	=	9 seats
Theater has 5 sections		

17. No one is sitting in the last row of the theater that is otherwise filled. How many seats are being used?

18. How many rows of seats does the theater have?

NS 3.0 ⚷ Solve problems involving addition, subtraction, multiplication, and division of whole numbers and understand the relationships among the operations.

Relating Multiplication and Division

<u>Operations that undo each other are</u> inverse operations. Multiplying by 3 and dividing by 3 are inverse operations.

Each trading card sheet has 3 rows with 2 pockets in each row. How many pockets are on each sheet?

3 rows of 2

Guided Practice*

Do you know HOW?

In **1** and **2**, copy and complete each fact family.

1. $8 \times \blacksquare = 32$

$32 \div \blacksquare = 4$

$32 \div \blacksquare = \blacksquare$

$\blacksquare \times \blacksquare = 32$

2. $6 \times 9 = \blacksquare$

$54 \div \blacksquare = 9$

$54 \div 9 = \blacksquare$

$9 \times \blacksquare = \blacksquare$

In **3** and **4**, write the fact family for each set of numbers.

3. 3, 6, 18

4. 5, 7, 35

Do you UNDERSTAND?

5. Why are there four number sentences in the example above?

6. Is $2 \times 6 = 12$ part of the fact family from the example above?

7. Why is $3 + 3 = 6$ **NOT** in the fact family of 2, 3, and 6?

8. If you know $7 \times 9 = 63$, what division facts do you know?

Independent Practice

Leveled Practice In **9** through **12**, copy and complete each fact family.

9. $5 \times \blacksquare = 35$

$35 \div 7 = \blacksquare$

$\blacksquare \times \blacksquare = 35$

$35 \div \blacksquare = \blacksquare$

10. $9 \times \blacksquare = 72$

$72 \div 8 = \blacksquare$

$\blacksquare \times \blacksquare = 72$

$72 \div \blacksquare = \blacksquare$

11. $3 \times \blacksquare = 18$

$18 \div 6 = \blacksquare$

$\blacksquare \times \blacksquare = 18$

$18 \div \blacksquare = \blacksquare$

12. $2 \times \blacksquare = 24$

$24 \div 12 = \blacksquare$

$\blacksquare \times \blacksquare = 24$

$24 \div \blacksquare = \blacksquare$

DIGITAL

Animated Glossary
www.pearsonsuccessnet.com

*For another example, see Set G on page 87.

A fact family <u>shows all the related multiplication and division facts for a set of numbers</u>. You can use fact families to help you remember division facts.

This is the fact family for 2, 3, and 6:

$2 \times 3 = 6$ $6 \div 2 = 3$

$3 \times 2 = 6$ $6 \div 3 = 2$

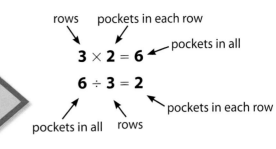

rows   pockets in each row

$3 \times 2 = 6$ ← pockets in all

$6 \div 3 = 2$

pockets in all   rows   pockets in each row

Each has 6 pockets.

In **13** through **20**, write a fact family for each set of numbers.

13. 7, 8, 56

14. 2, 8, 16

15. 6, 7, 42

16. 6, 6, 36

17. 3, 8, 24

18. 7, 10, 70

19. 6, 5, 30

20. 5, 8, 40

Problem Solving

21. How many years will it take to release all 50 quarters? Write a division fact you can use to find this quotient.

State Quarters	
First quarters released	1999
Number of new quarters each year	Text
California quarter released	2005

22. In the fact family for the numbers 5, 6, 30, which term does **NOT** describe 5 or 6?

  A factor   **C** product

  B divisor   **D** quotient

23. Josh practiced his drums two hours before dinner and three hours after dinner. How many hours did he practice in all?

  A 3 hours   **C** 5 hours

  B 4 hours   **D** 6 hours

24. Write the fact family that has 9 as a factor and 45 as a product.

25. **Number Sense** Why does the fact family for 64 and 8 have only two number sentences?

NS 2.3, Grade 3
Use the inverse relationship of multiplication and division to compare and check results. Also, **NS 3.0**.

Special Quotients

How can you divide with 1 and 0?

A sandwich is cut into 8 pieces. How many people can have 1 piece each? Find $8 \div 1$.

1 group of 8

8 people can have 1 piece of sandwich

Dividing by 1

Think What number times 1 equals 8?

$1 \times 8 = 8$

So, $8 \div 1 = 8$.

Rule: Any number divided by 1 is itself.

Guided Practice*

Do you know HOW?

In **1** through **8**, use multiplication facts to help you divide.

1. $9 \div 9$ **2.** $5 \div 1$

3. $0 \div 4$ **4.** $7 \div 1$

5. $3 \overline{)0}$ **6.** $1 \overline{)1}$

7. $1 \overline{)2}$ **8.** $6 \overline{)6}$

Do you UNDERSTAND?

9. What multiplication sentence can help you find $0 \div 8$?

10. What multiplication sentence can help you find $8 \div 8$?

11. Writing to Explain If none of the sandwich is left, how many pieces can 4 people have?

Independent Practice

Use multiplication facts to help you divide.

12. $1 \overline{)3}$ **13.** $8 \overline{)0}$ **14.** $2 \overline{)0}$ **15.** $4 \overline{)4}$

Copy and complete by writing >, <, or = for each $\bigcirc$.

16. $7 \div 7 \bigcirc 2 \div 2$ **17.** $0 \div 5 \bigcirc 3 \div 1$ **18.** $4 \div 1 \bigcirc 4 \div 4$

19. $6 \div 6 \bigcirc 0 \div 4$ **20.** $9 \div 1 \bigcirc 4 \div 1$ **21.** $3 \div 3 \bigcirc 6 \div 1$

22. $0 \div 3 \bigcirc 0 \div 8$ **23.** $0 \div 5 \bigcirc 5 \div 5$ **24.** $8 \div 1 \bigcirc 6 \div 1$

25. $0 \div 9 \bigcirc 0 \div 7$ **26.** $0 \div 1 \bigcirc 1 \div 1$ **27.** $7 \div 1 \bigcirc 0 \div 6$

*For another example, see Set F on page 87.

1 as a Quotient

To find $8 \div 8$, think 8 times what number equals 8?

$$8 \times 1 = 8$$
So, $8 \div 8 = 1$.

Rule: Any number (except 0) divided by itself is 1.

Dividing 0 by a Number

To find $0 \div 8$, think 8 times what number equals 0?

$$8 \times 0 = 0$$
So, $0 \div 8 = 0$.

Rule: 0 divided by any number (except 0) is 0.

Dividing by 0

To find $8 \div 0$, think 0 times what number equals 8?

There is no such number.

Rule: You cannot divide by 0.

Problem Solving

28. Three friends decided to buy lunch. Anne spent $3.42, Saul spent $4.41, and Ryan spent $4.24. Write these numbers from least to greatest.

29. Tony's family is driving 70 miles to a fair. They have already traveled 30 miles. They are traveling at a speed of 40 miles per hour. How many hours will it take them to complete the trip?

30. On a trip to the beach, the Torrez family brings 5 beach balls for their 5 children.

  a If the beach balls are divided evenly, how many beach balls will each child get?

  b If the children give the 5 balls to 1 parent, how many balls will the parent have?

31. Algebra If $\square \div \triangle = 0$, what do you know about $\square$?

  A $\square$ cannot equal 0.

  B $\square$ must equal 0.

  C $\square$ must equal 1.

  D $\square$ must equal $\triangle$.

32. Write a Problem Write a word problem in which 5 is divided by 5 and another problem in which 5 is divided by 1.

33. In one season, a baseball team will practice 3 times a week. If there are 24 practices, how many weeks will the team practice in the season?

34. Number Sense Write a fact family for 3, 3, and 9.

NS 2.3, Grade 3
☞ Use the inverse relationship of multiplication and division to compare and check results. Also, NS 3.0 ☞

Using Multiplication Facts to Find Division Facts

How does multiplication help you divide?

Matt wants to buy 28 super bouncy balls to give as prizes. How many packs does Matt need to buy?

7 balls in each pack.

Choose an Operation Divide to find the number of equal groups.

Guided Practice*

Do you know HOW?

In **1** through **6**, use multiplication facts to help you divide.

1. $27 \div 9$ **2.** $40 \div 5$

3. $24 \div 4$ **4.** $66 \div 6$

5. $9\overline{)63}$ **6.** $9\overline{)81}$

Do you UNDERSTAND?

7. What multiplication fact could you use to help you find $72 \div 9$?

8. Matt has 40 super bouncy balls to put in 10 bags. He puts the same number in each bag. What multiplication fact can you use to find the number of balls in each bag?

Independent Practice

Leveled Practice In **9** through **27**, use multiplication facts to help you find the quotient.

9. ▢ $\times 3 = 27$ $27 \div 3 =$ ▢   **10.** ▢ $\times 8 = 40$ $40 \div 8 =$ ▢

11. ▢ $\times 6 = 42$ $42 \div 6 =$ ▢   **12.** ▢ $\times 7 = 63$ $63 \div 7 =$ ▢

13. $7\overline{)49}$ **14.** $3\overline{)27}$ **15.** $6\overline{)48}$ **16.** $7\overline{)21}$ **17.** $4\overline{)16}$

18. $9\overline{)36}$ **19.** $5\overline{)15}$ **20.** $12\overline{)60}$ **21.** $6\overline{)36}$ **22.** $2\overline{)14}$

23. $3\overline{)24}$ **24.** $4\overline{)32}$ **25.** $2\overline{)18}$ **26.** $7\overline{)35}$ **27.** $7\overline{)56}$

How many groups of 7 are in 28?

Change this to a multiplication sentence:

What number times 7 equals 28?

☐ × 7 = 28   4 × 7 = 28

There are two ways to write division facts.

$$28 \div 7 = 4$$

or

$$7\overline{)28}^{\,4}$$

Matt needs to buy 4 packs of bouncy balls.

Problem Solving

For **28** and **29**, use the table at the right.

28. On a field trip to the aquarium, Shana spends $24 in the gift shop. Which item can Shana buy the most of? Explain.

Price List	
Postcard packs	$3
Mini-flags	$6
Sea lion toy	$8

29. How many mini-flags can Shana buy if she uses all of her money?

For **30**, use the diagram at the right.

30. People started riding carousels in the United States in 1835. The carousel drawing at the right has a total of 36 horses with an equal number of horses on each circle. Write a division fact you can use to find the number of horses on the outer circle.

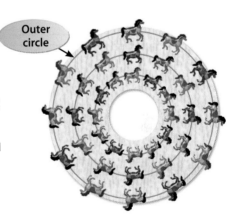

Outer circle

31. Carson plays a card word game. She gives the same number of cards to each of 4 players. If there are 20 cards in all, how many cards does each player get?

32. The total lunch bill for six people is $52. They add an $8 tip and split the bill evenly. How much is each person's equal share of the total bill?

A $6   **C** $10

B $8   **D** $12

MR 2.3 Use a variety of methods, such as words, numbers, symbols, charts, graphs, tables, diagrams, and models, to explain mathematical reasoning. Also **MR 2.4, NS 3.0** ⚬══⚬ .

Problem Solving

Draw a Picture and Write an Equation

Ruben's scout troop is making 4 milk-jug birdfeeders. Each birdfeeder will use the same number of wooden dowels. If they have 24 dowels in all, how many dowels will be used for each feeder?

24 dowels

Guided Practice*

Do you know HOW?

Solve. Write an equation to help you.

1. Tina put 32 flowers into eight bouquets. How many flowers were in each bouquet if each had the same number of flowers?

32 flowers in all

?	?	?	?	?	?	?	?

↑
Flowers in
each bouquet

Do you UNDERSTAND?

2. How did the picture in Problem 1 help you to write an equation?

3. How many birdfeeders could Ruben make with 36 dowels?

4. **Write a Problem** Write a problem about sharing items that you can solve by drawing a picture. Then solve.

Independent Practice

Solve.

5. Kylie bought a bag of 30 beads to make bracelets. Each bracelet requires 5 beads. How many bracelets can Kylie make?

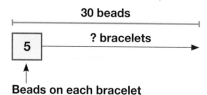

30 beads

| 5 | ? bracelets →

↑
Beads on each bracelet

6. In Exercise 5, what equation can you write to answer the problem?

Stuck? Try this....

- What do I know?
- What diagram can I use to help understand the problem?
- Can I use addition, subtraction, multiplication, or division?
- Is all of my work correct?
- Did I answer the right question?
- Is my answer reasonable?

*For another example, see Set G on page 87.

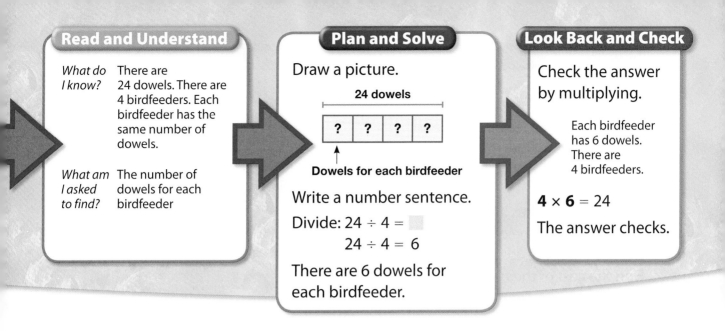

Read and Understand

What do I know? There are 24 dowels. There are 4 birdfeeders. Each birdfeeder has the same number of dowels.

What am I asked to find? The number of dowels for each birdfeeder

Plan and Solve

Draw a picture.

24 dowels

| ? | ? | ? | ? |

↑
Dowels for each birdfeeder

Write a number sentence.

Divide: $24 \div 4 = \square$

$24 \div 4 = 6$

There are 6 dowels for each birdfeeder.

Look Back and Check

Check the answer by multiplying.

Each birdfeeder has 6 dowels. There are 4 birdfeeders.

$4 \times 6 = 24$

The answer checks.

---

7. Sheena is packing 18 paperweights in boxes. She packs them in 6 boxes with the same number of paperweights in each box. How many paperweights are in each box?

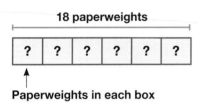

18 paperweights

| ? | ? | ? | ? | ? | ? |

↑
Paperweights in each box

8. Jodi is bundling newspapers. She has 66 newspapers and puts 6 newspapers in each bundle. How many bundles does Jodi make?

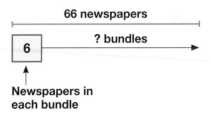

66 newspapers

? bundles

| 6 |

↑
Newspapers in each bundle

Use the bar graph at the right for **9** and **10**.

9. How much more money did Katie save in September than in October?

10. Katie used the money she saved in November and December to buy her mother a present. How much did she spend?

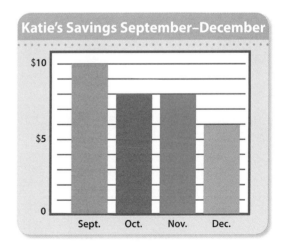

Katie's Savings September–December

---

11. Draw It Manny is going camping with his friends. He packed 60 sandwiches. How many sandwiches can Manny and his friends eat each day if they go camping for 5 days and eat the same number of sandwiches each day?

12. Draw It Jenna bought 36 pencils to give to her friends before the first day of school. If each friend received 6 pencils, how many friends did Jenna buy pencils for?

Use the table at the right for **13** and **14**.

13. Everett bought a leash, collar, and bed at the sale. How much did Everett spend in all?

14. Draw It Everett has his dog groomed at the pet shop. The cost of grooming is three times the cost of a dog bowl. Find the cost of the grooming.

Dog Supplies Sale	
Leash	$8
Collar	$6
Bowls	$7
Medium Beds	$15

15. Rena has 16 scarves. If 4 of her scarves are blue and one half of her scarves are red, how many are **NOT** red or blue?

16. Frank, Chuck, Bob and Dan arranged their exercise mats in a row. Bob's mat is next to only one other mat. Dan is on the third mat. Chuck is not next to Dan. Who is on which mat?

17. Emma is fencing a square garden with 52 feet of fencing. How many feet of fencing will Emma use on each side? Draw a bar diagram and write a number sentence to solve the problem.

18. Oliver has 75 apple slices that he distributes to 15 students in his gymnastics class. How many slices does each student get?

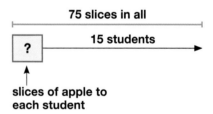

Think About the Process

19. Sandy spent $36 on pet toys. Each toy cost $12. Which number sentence can be used to find how many toys she bought?

   A $12 + 24 = $ ▢

   B $36 \div 12 = $ ▢

   C $6 \times 6 = $ ▢

   D $36 \div 6 = $ ▢

20. Three groups of 24 students each competed in the junior mathematics relay. What two simpler problems can you use to find the total number of students in the three groups?

   A $(3 + 24) - (12 + 4)$

   B $(3 \times 12) + (20 + 2)$

   C $(3 \times 20) + (3 \times 4)$

   D $(4 \times 12) + (32 + 4)$

Find the product.

1. 7×2 **2.** 4×5 **3.** 6×8 **4.** 9×7

5. 4×8 **6.** 0×1 **7.** 3×6 **8.** 8×8

9. 3×3 **10.** 6×7 **11.** 5×7 **12.** 9×4

Find the quotient.

13. $81 \div 9$ **14.** $4\overline{)12}$ **15.** $56 \div 7$ **16.** $2\overline{)10}$ **17.** $54 \div 6$

18. $5\overline{)20}$ **19.** $0 \div 8$ **20.** $3\overline{)21}$ **21.** $24 \div 6$ **22.** $9\overline{)27}$

23. $63 \div 9$ **24.** $8\overline{)64}$ **25.** $18 \div 3$ **26.** $5\overline{)5}$ **27.** $81 \div 9$

Error Search Find each product or quotient that is not correct. Write it correctly and explain the error.

28. $8 \div 1 = 8$ **29.** $4 \times 4 = 16$ **30.** $0 \div 5 = 5$ **31.** $9 \times 6 = 53$

32. $12 \div 2 = 6$ **33.** $25 \div 5 = 5$ **34.** $5 \times 3 = 15$ **35.** $24 \div 3 = 6$

36. $7 \times 7 = 42$ **37.** $18 \div 2 = 8$ **38.** $12 \div 6 = 2$ **39.** $28 \div 7 = 4$

Number Sense

Estimating and Reasoning Write whether each statement is true or false. Explain your answer.

40. The product of 1 and 34,654 is 34,654.

41. The quotient of 8 divided by 0 is not possible.

42. The sum of 52,128 and 21,179 is less than 70,000.

43. The difference of $8,853 - 1,978$ is greater than 8,000.

44. The product of 2 and a number will always be even.

45. The product of 6 and 7 is 6 less than 36.

1. Which has the same value as 3×5? (3-1)

   A $5 + 3$

   B $5 + 5 + 5$

   C $5 + 5 + 5 + 3$

   D $3 + 3 + 3 + 3$

2. Grant made 4 California state flags for the school play. Each flag had 1 bear. How many bears did Grant need? (3-3)

   A 0

   B 1

   C 4

   D 5

3. Which is a way to find 7×8? (3-4)

   A $32 + 32$

   B $35 + 14$

   C $35 + 8$

   D $35 + 21$

4. Alfonzo applies numbers on the back of football jerseys. Below are the first five numbers he applied. If the pattern continues, what are the next three numbers he will apply? (3-5)

   9, 18, 27, 36, 45, ▢, ▢, ▢

   A 54, 63, 72

   B 54, 63, 71

   C 63, 64, 72

   D 63, 72, 81

5. Three friends have 27 water balloons to share equally. How many water balloons will each friend get? (3-6)

27 water balloons

| ? | ? | ? |

↑
Water balloons
each friend gets

   A 9

   B 8

   C 7

   D 6

6. What is $35 \div 7$? (3-9)

   A 7

   B 6

   C 5

   D 4

7. Each flower has 5 petals.

If Stephanie counted the petals in groups of 5, which list shows numbers she could have named? (3-2)

   A 15, 20, 25, 30

   B 15, 20, 30, 40

   C 12, 15, 18, 30

   D 10, 12, 14, 16

8. Which number sentence is true? (3-8)

    A $4 \div 4 = 0$

    B $7 \div 1 = 1$

    C $2 \div 0 = 0$

    D $0 \div 8 = 0$

9. Diego wanted to paint his fence. It takes him 7 minutes to paint one section of a fence. How many minutes would it take him to paint 3 sections? (3-4)

    A 18

    B 21

    C 24

    D 28

10. Olivia has 48 daisies. She bought 6 vases to put her daisies into. Which number sentence shows how many daisies she can put in each vase if she puts the same number in each vase? (3-10)

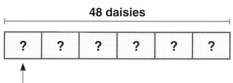

48 daisies

| ? | ? | ? | ? | ? | ? |

↑
Daisies in each vase

    A $48 \div 6 = 8$

    B $48 + 6 = 54$

    C $48 - 6 = 42$

    D $6 \times 48 = 288$

11. Which number makes the number sentence true? (3-3)

$7 \times 5 = \boxed{} \times 7$

    A 0

    B 1

    C 5

    D 7

12. Which is a way to find 6×10? (3-4)

    A $(3 \times 5) + (3 \times 5)$

    B $(3 \times 6) + (3 \times 4)$

    C $(6 \times 10) + (6 \times 10)$

    D $(3 \times 10) + (3 \times 10)$

13. Which numeral makes both number sentences true? (3-9)

$4 \times \boxed{} = 32$
$32 \div 4 = \boxed{}$

    A 9

    B 8

    C 7

    D 6

14. Which number sentence is in the same fact family as $63 \div 9 = \boxed{}$? (3-7)

    A $63 \times 9 = \boxed{}$

    B $9 + \boxed{} = 63$

    C $\boxed{} - 9 = 63$

    D $\boxed{} \times 9 = 63$

Set A, pages 56–58

Write an addition sentence and a multiplication sentence.

$5 + 5 + 5 = 15$

$3 \times 5 = 15$

Remember multiplying is the same as adding the same number over and over.

1.  2.

Set B, pages 60–63

When you multiply any number by 0, the product is 0.

$9 \times 0 = 0$

When you multiply a number by 2, the product is always even.

$2 \times 8 = 16$

Remember you can change the order of factors when you multiply.

1. 10×0 2. 9×2

3. 12×3 4. 5×7

Set C, pages 64–67

Use the Distributive Property to break apart a problem into two simpler problems.

Find 4×6.

Break apart 6 into $3 + 3$.

$(4 \times 3) + (4 \times 3)$

$12 \; + \; 12 \; = \; 24$

So, $4 \times 6 = 24$

Remember any number multiplied by 0 is 0.

Use breaking apart to find each product.

1. 4×3 2. 6×5

3. 9×9 4. 8×3

Set D, pages 68–69

Look for a pattern. Tell the missing numbers.

1, 5, 9, 13, ☐ , ☐

Find the pattern.

$1 + 4 = 5$

$5 + 4 = 9$

$9 + 4 = 13$

Finish the pattern.

$13 + 4 = 17$

$17 + 4 = 21$

The missing numbers are 17 and 21.

Remember that in some patterns you do not add the same number each time.

1. 2, 10, 18, 26, ☐ , ☐ , ☐

2. 1, 2, 4, 7, 11, 16, 22, ☐ , ☐ , ☐

3. 3, 6, 9, 12, ☐ , ☐ , ☐

4. 5, 11, 17, 23, ☐ , ☐ , ☐

Set E, pages 70–72 and 74–75

Katherine is making 6 lunches. She has 30 carrot sticks. How many carrot sticks go in each lunch?

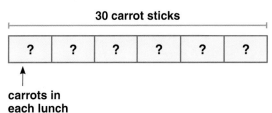

30 carrot sticks

| ? | ? | ? | ? | ? | ? |

↑
carrots in
each lunch

There are 5 carrot sticks in each lunch when 30 are shared equally in 6 lunches.

Remember a fact family shows all of the related facts for a set of numbers.

Copy and complete each fact family.

1. $5 \times \square = 40$

$\square \div 5 = 8$

$8 \times 5 = \square$

$\square \div 8 = \square$

2. $7 \times 9 = \square$

$\square \div 7 = 9$

$9 \times \square = 63$

$63 \div \square = 7$

Set F, pages 76–79

Find $36 \div 4$.

What number times 4 equals 36?

$\square \times 4 = 36$

$9 \times 4 = 36$

So, $36 \div 4 = 9$

Remember zero divided by any number is zero.

1. $4\overline{)4}$ **2.** $2\overline{)18}$

3. $7\overline{)28}$ **4.** $2\overline{)0}$

5. $8\overline{)56}$ **6.** $8\overline{)48}$

Set G, pages 80–82

What do I know?   Mrs. Collins has 24 pairs of scissors. She puts the same number of each in 6 drawers. How many pairs of scissors are in each drawer?

What am I asked to find?   The number of scissors in each drawer

Draw a picture.

24 scissors in all

| ? | ? | ? | ? | ? | ? |

↑
Scissors in each drawer

Divide to find the number of scissors in each drawer.

$24 \div 6 = \square$

$24 \div 6 = 4$

There are 4 pairs of scissors in each drawer.

Remember to draw a picture to help you solve the problem.

Solve.

1. Winifred buys 20 bookmarks for her and three of her friends. Each person received the same number of bookmarks. How many bookmarks did each friend receive?

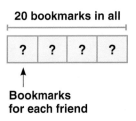

20 bookmarks in all

| ? | ? | ? | ? |

↑
Bookmarks
for each friend

Topic 4

Multiplying by 1-Digit Numbers

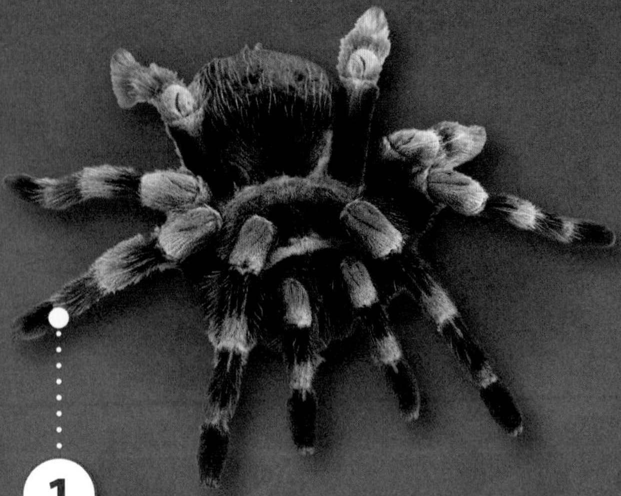

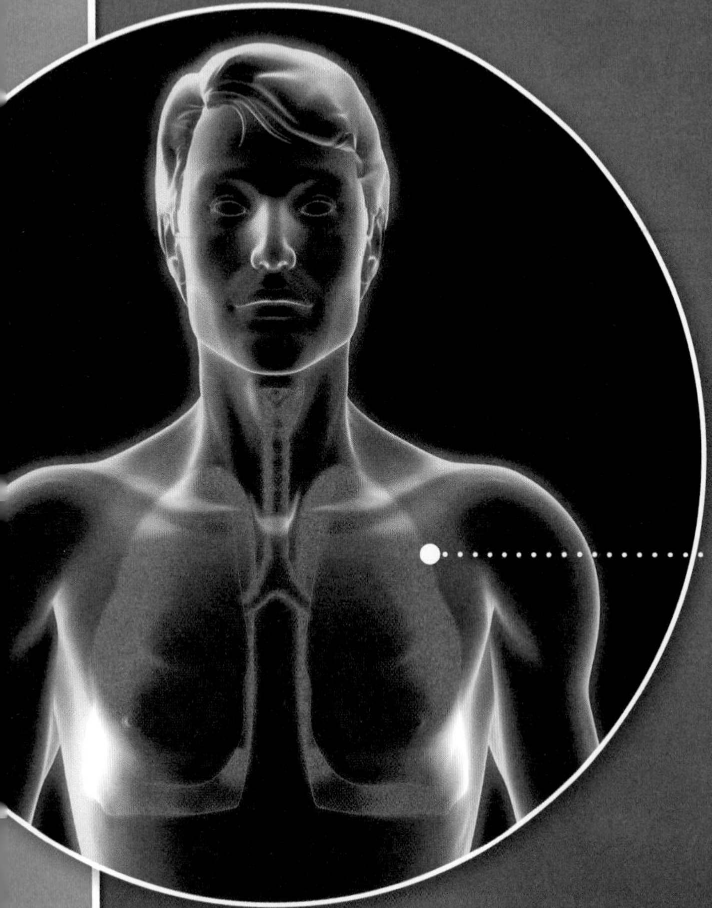

1 About how many eggs can a red-kneed tarantula lay at one time? You will find out in Lesson 4-3.

2 How many gallons of air does a student breathe each school day? You will find out in Lesson 4–1.

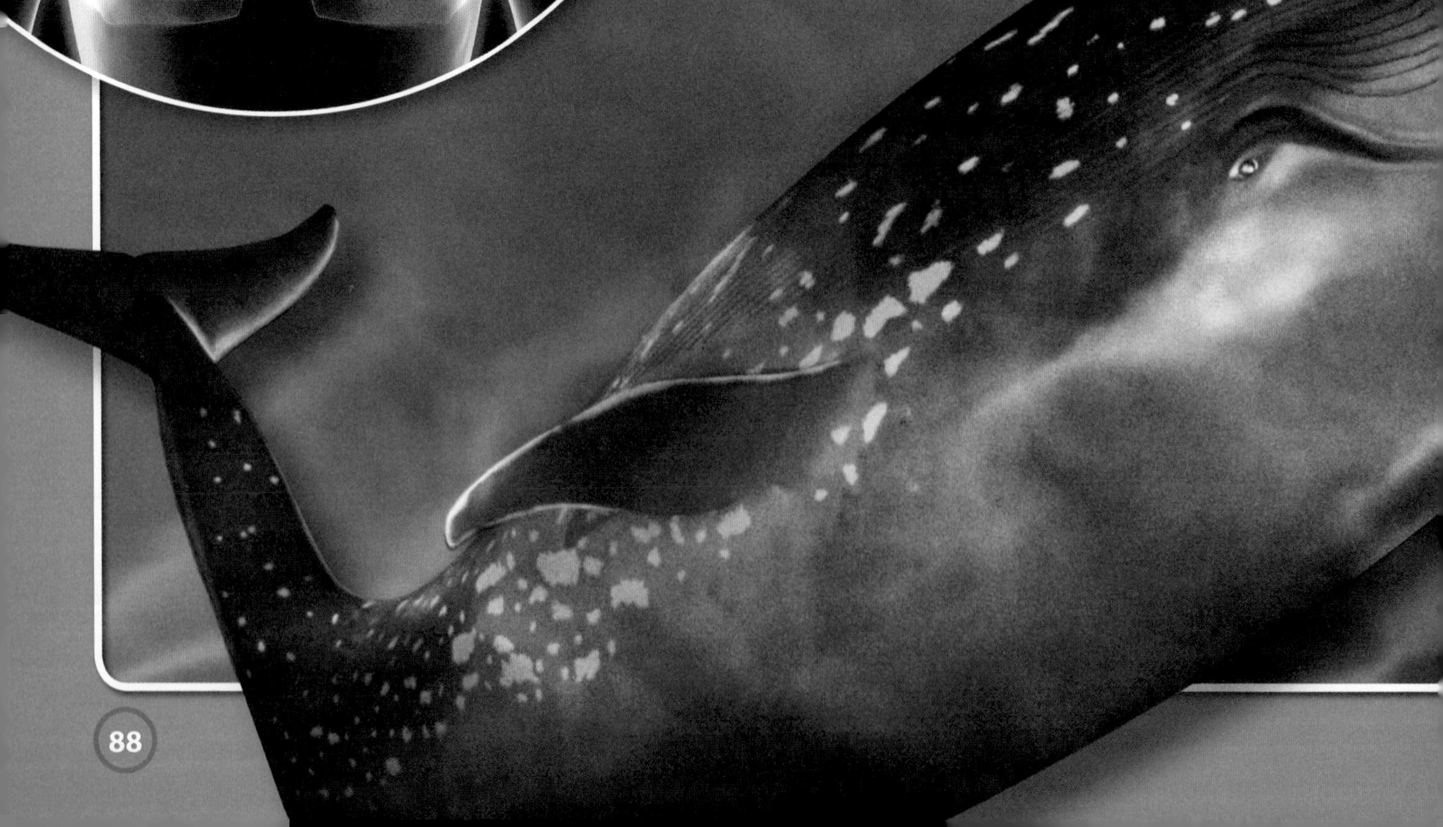

3

How many floors does the U.S. Bank Tower in Los Angeles have? You will find out in Lesson 4–5.

Review What You Know!

1. You multiply numbers to find a ? .

2. In the number sentence $8 \times 6 = 48$, 8 is a ? .

3. When you estimate to the nearest 10 or 100, you may use ? .

Multiplication Facts

Find each product.

4. 5×6 **5.** 7×3

6. 9×5 **7.** 6×8

8. 6×4 **9.** 12×3

10. 8×5 **11.** 9×9

Rounding

Round each number to the nearest ten.

12. 16   **13.** 82   **14.** 35

15. 52   **16.** 24   **17.** 96

18. 78   **19.** 472   **20.** 119

Round each number to the nearest hundred.

21. 868   **22.** 499   **23.** 625

24. 167   **25.** 772   **26.** 341

27. 1,372   **28.** 9,009   **29.** 919

30. Writing to Explain Explain how to round 743 to the nearest hundred.

4

How long was the longest blue whale? You will find out in Lesson 4–2.

NS 2.4, Grade 3
Solve simple problems
involving multiplication
of multi-digit numbers
by one-digit numbers.

Multiplying by Multiples of 10 and 100

What is the rule when you multiply by multiples of 10 and 100?

You can use basic multiplication facts to multiply by multiples of 10 and 100. Find 3×50.

? in all

Guided Practice*

Do you know HOW?

In **1** through **6**, use basic facts to help you multiply.

1. 7×10 **2.** 2×100

3. 3×20 **4.** 9×800

5. 6×10 **6.** 8×500

Do you UNDERSTAND?

7. How many zeros will be in the product for 5×200? Explain how you know.

8. Reasonableness Peter said the product of 4×500 is 2,000. Bob said it is 200. Who is correct?

Independent Practice

Leveled Practice In **9** through **32**, find each product.

9. $3 \times 7 = $ ▨   **10.** $6 \times 4 = $ ▨   **11.** $8 \times 5 = $ ▨   **12.** $2 \times 8 = $ ▨

$3 \times 70 = $ ▨ $6 \times 40 = $ ▨ $8 \times 50 = $ ▨ $2 \times 80 = $ ▨

$3 \times 700 = $ ▨ $6 \times 400 = $ ▨ $8 \times 500 = $ ▨ $2 \times 800 = $ ▨

13. 4×20 **14.** 7×40 **15.** 70×2 **16.** 8×60 **17.** 3×70

18. 5×500 **19.** 3×600 **20.** 9×700 **21.** 600×6 **22.** 100×9

23. 5×40 **24.** 200×6 **25.** 9×50 **26.** 900×4 **27.** 80×3

28. 8×70 **29.** 2×90 **30.** 300×4 **31.** 7×100 **32.** 800×5

For another example, see Set A on page 114.

Find 3 × 50.	Find 3 × 500.	When the product of a basic fact ends in zero, the answer will have an extra zero.
Think 3 × 50 = 3 × 5 × 10	**Think** 3 × 500 = 3 × 5 × 100	
Multiply: 3 × 5 = 15	Multiply: 3 × 5 = 15	6 × 5 = 30
Write one zero after 15.	Write two zeros after 15.	6 × 50 = 300
3 × 5<u>0</u> = 15<u>0</u>	3 × 5<u>00</u> = 1,5<u>00</u>	6 × 500 = 3,000
So, 3 × 50 = 150.	So, 3 × 500 = 1,500.	

Problem Solving

In **33** and **34**, use the table to the right.

33. Tina visited Funland with her mom and a friend. They chose Plan C. How much did they save on the two children's tickets by buying combined tickets instead of buying separate tickets?

Data

Funland Ticket Prices	Adult	Child
Plan A Waterpark	$30	$20
Plan B Amusement Park	$40	$30
Plan C Combined A + B	$60	$40

34. Aimee's scout troop has 8 girls and 4 adults. How much did the troop pay for tickets to the amusement park?

35. A fourth grader breathes about 50 gallons of air per hour. Shana, a fourth grader, arrives at school at 8:00 A.M. and leaves at 3:00 P.M. How many gallons of air does she breathe at school?

36. Number Sense Without calculating the answer, tell which has the greater product, 4 × 80 or 8 × 400. Explain how you know.

37. Last year, the fourth graders at Summit School collected 500 cans of food for the food drive. This year's fourth graders want to collect two times as many cans. How many cans do this year's fourth graders hope to collect?

   A 250 cans   **C** 1,000 cans

   B 500 cans   **D** 10,000 cans

38. Ted, Jason, and Angelina are trying to raise 200 dollars for a local shelter. Ted raised 30 dollars. Jason raised 90 dollars. How much money does Angelina need to raise in order to reach their goal?

	$200
Goal	

Amount raised	$30	$90	?

Lesson

4-2

NS 2.4, Grade 3 🔑
Solve simple problems
involving multiplication
of multi-digit numbers by
one-digit numbers. Also,
AF1.1.

Using Mental Math to Multiply

What are some ways to multiply mentally?

Evan rode his bicycle for 18 miles each day for 3 days.
How many miles did he ride his bicycle in all?

Find 3 × 18 mentally.

18 miles
per day

| DAY 1 | DAY 2 | DAY 3 |

Guided Practice*

Do you know HOW?

In **1** and **2**, use the breaking apart
method to find each product mentally.

1. 6 × 37   **2.** 51 × 3

In **3** and **4**, use compatible numbers
to find each product mentally.

3. 33 × 4   **4.** 9 × 83

Do you UNDERSTAND?

5. Explain how to use mental math
to multiply 56 × 4.

6. How could place-value blocks
be used to model the breaking
apart method in the example at
the top?

 *You can draw place-value blocks to
help you visualize the model.*

Independent Practice

Leveled Practice In **7** through **20**, use mental math to find each product.

7. 4 × 36   Breaking apart: (4 × ▢) + (4 × ▢) = ▢

8. 6 × 42   Breaking apart: (6 × ▢) + (6 × ▢) = ▢

9. 5 × 17   Compatible numbers: 5 × ▢ = 100   ▢ − 15 = ▢

10. 7 × 29   Compatible numbers: 7 × ▢ = 210   ▢ − 7 = ▢

11. 7 × 28   **12.** 61 × 8   **13.** 14 × 5   **14.** 64 × 3   **15.** 2 × 58

16. 4 × 23   **17.** 3 × 27   **18.** 44 × 6   **19.** 5 × 35   **20.** 9 × 52

DIGITAL   Animated Glossary
www.pearsonsuccessnet.com

One Way

Find 3 × 18.

Break apart 18 into 10 and 8.

Think of 3 × 18 as
(3 × 10) + (3 × 8).

    30 + 24

Add to find the total.

30 + 24 = 54

So, 3 × 18 = 54.

Another Way

Compatible numbers <u>are numbers that are easy to work with mentally</u>. Substitute a number for 18 that is easy to multiply by 3.

    3 × 18
    ↓
    3 × 20 = 60

Now adjust. Subtract 2 groups of 3.

60 – 6 = 54   So, 3 × 18 = 54.

Evan rode his bicycle 54 miles in all.

Problem Solving

For **21** and **22**, use the table to the right.

21. To raise money, the high school band members sold items shown in the table. Use mental math to find how much money the band raised in all.

Item	Cost	Number Sold
Caps	$9	36
Mugs	$7	44
Pennants	$8	52

22. How much more do 10 caps cost than 10 pennants?

23. Writing to Explain Ashley and 3 friends took a bus to Sacramento. The cost of the trip was 43 dollars per person. How much did the trip cost in all? Explain how you found the answer.

Total Cost

$43	$43	$43	$43

↑ Cost per person

24. **Think** About the Process Helen walked 5 miles every day for 37 days. Which choice shows how to find how many miles Helen walked?

A 35 × 5

B (40 × 5) + (3 × 5)

C (5 × 30) + (5 × 7)

D (30 × 5) – (3 × 5)

25. The height of one scuba diver is about 6 feet. The longest blue whale on record was about 18 scuba divers in length. Use breaking apart to estimate the length of the blue whale.

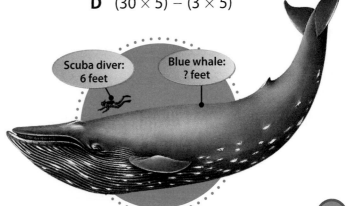

Scuba diver: 6 feet

Blue whale: ? feet

Lesson

4-3

MR 2.1 Use estimation
to verify the
reasonableness of
calculated results.

Using Rounding to Estimate

How can you use rounding to estimate when you multiply?

Hoover School is holding a Read-a-thon. Any student who raises more than $500 earns a prize. Hector has pledges totaling $4 per page read. Alan has pledges totaling $3 per page read. Both want to know if they will earn a prize.

Hector reads
153 pages

Alan reads
115 pages

Guided Practice*

Do you know HOW?

In **1** through **8**, estimate each product.

1. 6×125

2. 39×5

3. 538×3

4. 7×314

5. 2×97

6. 4×261

7. 63×6

8. 9×48

Do you UNDERSTAND?

9. Is the estimate in Exercise 1 more or less than the actual answer? Explain how you know.

10. Alan collects pledges for 70 more pages. Estimate to see if he will now get a prize.

Independent Practice

Leveled Practice In **11** through **34**, estimate each product.

11. 7×34 is close to $7 \times$ ▢

12. 6×291 is close to $6 \times$ ▢

13. 41×9 is close to ▢ $\times 9$

14. 814×3 is close to ▢ $\times 3$

15. 117×4

16. 3×86

17. 9×476

18. 34×6

19. 7×77

20. 52×9

21. 46×5

22. 3×287

23. 6×131

24. 602×9

25. 354×2

26. 77×8

27. 2×863

28. 44×8

29. 303×5

30. 486×7

31. 719×5

32. 6×609

33. 249×4

34. 54×9

For another example, see Set B on page 114.

Estimate 4 × 153 using rounding.

4 × 153
↓ Round 153 to 150
4 × 150 = 600

Two 150s is 300. Four 150s is 600.
So, 4 × 153 is about 600.

Hector raised more than 500 dollars.

He has earned a prize.

Estimate 3 × 115 using rounding.

3 × 115
↓ Round 115 to 100.
3 × 100 = 300

Alan has raised about 300 dollars.
This is not enough to earn a prize.

Problem Solving

35. Sam and his 2 brothers want to fly to San Francisco. One airline offers a round trip fare of $319. Another airline has a round trip fare of $389. About how much will Sam and his brothers save by buying the less expensive fare?

36. A Chilean Rose tarantula can lay about 500 eggs at one time. A red-kneed tarantula can lay 500 more eggs than this at one time. About how many eggs can a red-kneed tarantula lay at one time?

37. Reasonableness Ellie estimates that the product of 211 and 6 is 1,800. Is this estimate reasonable? Why or why not?

38. Number Sense Which has more pencils, 3 packs with 40 pencils or 40 packs with 3 pencils? Explain.

39. The students at Spring Elementary voted on a school mascot. The bar graph at the right shows the results of the vote.

Which mascot has about 4 times as many votes as the unicorn?

A Lion   **C** Dragon

B Owl   **D** Bear

40. Which mascot had the least amount of votes?

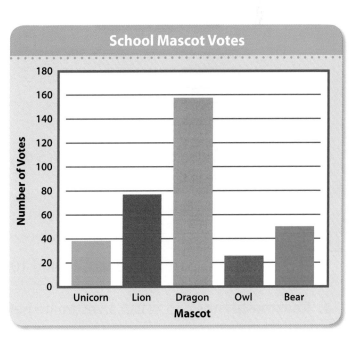

School Mascot Votes

Number of Votes — Mascot: Unicorn, Lion, Dragon, Owl, Bear

4-4

NS 2.4 Grade 3
Solve simple problems involving multiplication of multidigit numbers by a one-digit number (3,671 × 3 = __).

Using an Expanded Algorithm

How can you record multiplication?

A video game comes with 2 controllers in the box. How many controllers are in 16 boxes of this video game?

Choose an Operation Multiply to join equal groups.

Each box contains 2 controllers

Another Example **How do you record multiplication when the product has three digits?**

Gene played his new video game 23 times each day for 5 days. How many times did he play his video game in 5 days?

A 18

B 28

C 115

D 145

Choose an Operation Since 5 equal groups of 23 are being joined, you will multiply. Find 5 × 23.

What You Show

What You Write

$$
\begin{array}{r}
23 \\
\times \quad 5 \\
\hline
15 \\
+ \ 100 \\
\hline
115
\end{array}
$$

Gene played his video game 115 times in 5 days. The correct choice is **C**.

Explain It

1. Explain how the partial products, 15 and 100, were found in the work above.

2. Reasonableness How can an estimate help you eliminate choices above?

What You Show

Build an array to show 2 × 16.

$2 \times 10 = 20$ $2 \times 6 = 12$

$20 + 12 = 32$

What You Write

Here is one way to record multiplication.

```
    16
  ×  2
    12  ← Partial
  + 20  ← Products
    32
```

There are 32 controllers in the boxes.

Guided Practice*

Do you know HOW?

In **1** and **2**, use place-value blocks or draw pictures to build an array for each. Copy and complete the calculation.

1. $2 \times 34 = $

```
    34
  ×  2

  +
```

2. $3 \times 18 = $

```
    18
  ×  3

  +
```

Do you UNDERSTAND?

Use the array and the calculation shown for Exercise 3.

```
    14
  ×  3
    12
  + 30
    42
```

3. What calculation was used to give the partial product 12? 30? What is the product of 3×14?

Independent Practice

Leveled Practice In **4** and **5**, use place-value blocks or draw pictures to build an array for each. Copy and complete the calculation.

4.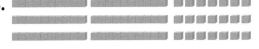

```
    27
  ×  3

  +
```

5.

```
    22
  ×  4

  +
```

For another example, Set D on page 115.

Leveled Practice In **6** through **15**, copy and complete the calculation.
Draw a picture to help.

6.   26
      × 5
   ▯▯▯
  + ▯▯▯
   ▯▯▯

7.   18
      × 3
   ▯▯▯
  + ▯▯▯
   ▯▯▯

8.   24
      × 2
   ▯▯▯
  + ▯▯▯
   ▯▯▯

9.   21
      × 4
   ▯▯
  + ▯▯▯
   ▯▯▯

10.   24
      × 3
   ▯▯▯
  + ▯▯▯
   ▯▯▯

11.   22
      × 8

12.   17
      × 3

13.   24
      × 8

14.   16
      × 5

15.   23
      × 7

Problem Solving

16. Geometry The sides of each of the shapes below are the same whole-number length. Which figure has a perimeter of 64 units? How long is each side?

17. Algebra Copy and complete each number sentence.

a ▯ × 14 = A where A is greater than 100.

b ▯ × 24 = B where B is less than 100.

18. Large tables in the library have 8 chairs and small tables have 4 chairs. How many students can sit at 3 large tables and 5 small tables if each seat is filled?

A 20 students   **C** 44 students

B 36 students   **D** 52 students

20. Writing to Explain Tim called 3 × 20 and 3 × 4 *simple calculations*. Explain what he meant.

19. Estimation Emma wants to put 3 smiley stickers on each of her note cards. Use estimation to decide if a roll of smileys has enough stickers for 42 note cards.

Type of Sticker	Number of Stickers per Roll
★	50
🐕	75
🙂	100
🌼	125

100 stickers

Mixed Problem Solving

Magnets have two poles (north and south). Like poles repel each other and unlike poles attract each other. Maglev trains use this for two purposes. First, like poles allow the train to hover above the tracks. Second, by switching between like and unlike poles, the train is propelled quickly down the tracks.

Data

Facts about Maglev Trains

The Shanghai maglev train travels at about 267 mph when going full speed.

The Shanghai maglev train travels about 19 miles from the Shanghai Lujiazui Financial district to the Pudong Shanghai airport.

The California-Nevada Interstate Maglev is a proposed project to build a maglev train from Anaheim, California to Las Vegas, Nevada.

1. Use rounding to find the distance of a round trip drive from the Shanghai Lujiazui, financial district, to the airport, and back.

2. Round the distance from the Shanghai Lujiazui financial district to the main Shanghai airport to the nearest ten.

3. Round the speed of the Shanghai maglev train to the nearest ten mph.

There are other maglev projects that some people want to build. To the right is a list of the projects and the approximate distances they would cover.

Data

Proposed Maglev Trains

Project	Distance
California-Nevada	269 miles
Baltimore-Washington, D.C.	39 miles
Munich	23 miles
Shanghai-Hangzhou	99 miles

4. How much farther will the Shanghai-Hangzhou train travel than the Baltimore-Washington train on a one-way trip?

5. How much farther is the California-Nevada maglev train than the other 3 maglev trains combined?

6. How far will 3 round trip tickets on the Munich maglev train be able to take a passenger?

7. Jenny rounded all of the distances in the table to the nearest ten. She found the distance for the California-Nevada maglev train was 300 miles. Is she correct? Explain.

8. Under the proposal, the California-Nevada maglev train will carry about 12,000 passengers per hour. How many passengers can it carry in 3 hours?

NS 2.4, Grade 3
Solve simple problems
involving multiplication
of multidigit numbers
by one-digit numbers
$(3,671 \times 3 = \_\_)$.

Multiplying 2-Digit by 1-Digit Numbers

What is a common way to record multiplication?

How many T-shirts with the saying, *and your point is...* are in 3 boxes?

Choose an Operation Multiply to join equal groups.

Saying on T-shirt	Number of T-shirts per Box
Trust Me	30 T-shirts
and your point is...	26 T-shirts
I'm the princess that's why	24 T-shirts
Because I said so	12 T-shirts

Another Example **Does the common way to record multiplication work for larger products?**

Mrs. Stockton ordered 8 boxes of T-shirts with the saying, *I'm the princess that's why.* How many of the T-shirts did she order?

Choose an Operation Since you are joining 8 groups of 24, you will multiply. Find 8×24.

Step 1 Multiply the ones. Regroup if necessary.

$$
\begin{array}{r}
\overset{3}{2}4 \\
\times\ \ 8 \\
\hline
2
\end{array}
$$

$8 \times 4 = 32$ ones
Regroup 32 ones as 3 tens 2 ones

Step 2 Multiply the tens. Add any extra tens.

$$
\begin{array}{r}
\overset{3}{2}4 \\
\times\ \ 8 \\
\hline
192
\end{array}
$$

8×2 tens $= 16$ tens
16 tens $+ 3$ tens $= 19$ tens
or 1 hundred 9 tens

Mrs. Stockton ordered 192 T-shirts.

Explain It

1. **Reasonableness** How can you use estimation to decide if 192 is a reasonable answer?

2. In the example above, is it 8×2 or 8×20? Explain.

Remember, one way to multiply is to find partial products.

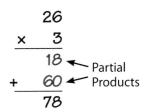

A shortcut for the partial products method is shown at the right.

Multiply the ones. Regroup if necessary.

$$
\begin{array}{r}
\overset{1}{2}6 \\
\times 3 \\
\hline
8
\end{array}
$$

Multiply the tens. Add any extra tens.

$$
\begin{array}{r}
\overset{1}{2}6 \\
\times 3 \\
\hline
78
\end{array}
$$

There are 78 T-shirts in 3 boxes.

Guided Practice*

Do you know HOW?

Find each product. Estimate to check reasonableness.

1. $\begin{array}{r} 15 \\ \times\ 5 \\ \hline \end{array}$
　　　2. $\begin{array}{r} 28 \\ \times\ 3 \\ \hline \end{array}$

3. $\begin{array}{r} 34 \\ \times\ 7 \\ \hline \end{array}$
　　　4. $\begin{array}{r} 43 \\ \times\ 4 \\ \hline \end{array}$

5. 5×70
　　　6. 5×78

7. 3×24
　　　8. 3×79

Do you UNDERSTAND?

9. Explain how you would estimate the answer in Exercise 3.

10. Carrie bought 8 boxes of T-shirts with the saying *Because I said so.* How many T-shirts did Carrie buy?

11. Writing to Explain Explain how the answer to Exercise 5 can be used to find the answer to Exercise 6.

Independent Practice

Find each product. Estimate to check reasonableness.

12. $\begin{array}{r} 12 \\ \times\ 6 \\ \hline \end{array}$
　　13. $\begin{array}{r} 18 \\ \times\ 7 \\ \hline \end{array}$
　　14. $\begin{array}{r} 72 \\ \times\ 5 \\ \hline \end{array}$
　　15. $\begin{array}{r} 49 \\ \times\ 8 \\ \hline \end{array}$

16. $\begin{array}{r} 31 \\ \times\ 4 \\ \hline \end{array}$
　　17. $\begin{array}{r} 52 \\ \times\ 6 \\ \hline \end{array}$
　　18. $\begin{array}{r} 79 \\ \times\ 7 \\ \hline \end{array}$
　　19. $\begin{array}{r} 87 \\ \times\ 7 \\ \hline \end{array}$

Independent Practice

Find each product. Estimate to check reasonableness.

20. 9×23 **21.** 6×51 **22.** 4×29 **23.** 8×42

24. 3×64 **25.** 5×56 **26.** 6×83 **27.** 4×47

28. 3×25 **29.** 2×43 **30.** 2×73 **31.** 9×26

Problem Solving

32. Use the diagram to the right. How many floors does the U.S. Bank Tower have if it has 4 times as many floors as an 18-story office building?

A 42 **B** 72 **C** 122 **D** 432

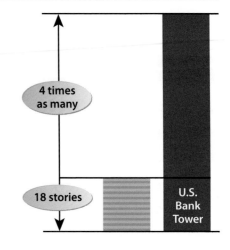

4 times as many

18 stories

U.S. Bank Tower

33. Estimation It takes 286 rolls of tape to make a car sculpture made of boxes. What is this number rounded to the nearest hundred?

A 200 **C** 300

B 280 **D** 380

34. **Think About the Process** Katie made 24 rag dolls. She gave away 8 of them as gifts. Which expression gives the number of rag dolls Katie had left?

A $24 + 8$

B 24×8

C $24 - 8$

D $24 \div 8$

35. A skateboard speed record of almost 63 miles per hour (about 92 feet per second) was set in 1998. At that speed about how many feet would the skateboarder travel in 6 seconds?

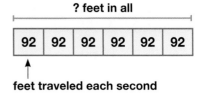

? feet in all

| 92 | 92 | 92 | 92 | 92 | 92 |

feet traveled each second

For **36** and **37**, use the table to the right.

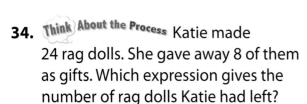

36. What is the average length fingernails will grow in one year?

A 60 mm **C** 40 mm

B 50 mm **D** 5 mm

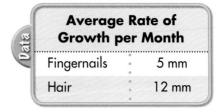

Average Rate of Growth per Month

Fingernails	5 mm
Hair	12 mm

37. How much longer will hair grow than fingernails in one year?

Algebra Connections

Multiplication and Number Sentences

Remember that a number sentence has two numbers or expressions connected by <, >, or =. Estimation or reasoning can help you tell if the left side or right side is greater.

Copy and complete. Write <, >, or = in the circle. Check your answers.

 Tip *Remember*
> is greater than   < is less than   = is equal to

Example: $7 \times 52 \bigcirc 7 \times 60$

Think *Is 7 groups of 52 more than 7 groups of 60?*

Since 52 is less than 60, the left side is less. Write "<".

$7 \times 52 \underset{<}{\bigcirc} 7 \times 60$

1. $5 \times 71 \bigcirc 5 \times 70$
2. $8 \times 30 \bigcirc 8 \times 35$
3. $2 \times 90 \bigcirc 89 + 89$

4. $4 \times 56 \bigcirc 200$
5. $6 \times 37 \bigcirc 37 \times 6$
6. $190 \bigcirc 9 \times 25$

7. $3 \times 33 \bigcirc 100$
8. $80 \bigcirc 4 \times 19$
9. $10 \times 10 \bigcirc 9 \times 8$

10. $1 \times 67 \bigcirc 1 + 67$
11. $2 + 34 \bigcirc 2 \times 34$
12. $6 \times 18 \bigcirc 7 \times 20$

. . . .

For **13** and **14**, copy and complete the number sentence below each problem. Use it to help explain your answer.

13. A red tray holds 7 rows of oranges with 8 oranges in each row. A blue tray holds 8 rows of oranges with 5 oranges in each row. Which tray holds more oranges?

____ × ____ ◯ ____ × ____

14. Look at the hats below. Mr. Fox bought 2 brown hats. Mrs. Lee bought 3 green hats. Who paid more for their hats?

____ × ____ ◯ ____ × ____

15. **Write a Problem** Write a problem using one of the number sentences in Exercises 1 to 6.

$30
$60
$10
$40

NS 2.4, Grade 3
Solve simple problems
involving multiplication
of multidigit numbers
by one-digit numbers
(3,671 × 3 = __).

Multiplying 3-Digit by 1-Digit Numbers

How do you multiply larger numbers?

Juan guessed that the large bottle had 3 times as many pennies as the small bottle. What was Juan's guess?

Choose an Operation Multiply to find "3 times as many."

264 pennies

Guided Practice*

Do you know HOW?

In **1** through **4**, find each product. Estimate to decide if the answer is reasonable.

1. 519
    × 4

2. 337
    × 2

3. 181 × 9

4. 6 × 268

Do you UNDERSTAND?

5. **Number Sense** In the example at the top, 3 × 6 tens is how many tens?

6. Sue guessed the large bottle had 8 times as many pennies as the small bottle. What was Sue's guess?

Independent Practice

Find each product. Estimate to check reasonableness.

7. 423
    × 2

8. 506
    × 4

9. 821
    × 3

10. 159
    × 5

11. 624
    × 7

12. 124
    × 6

13. 281
    × 9

14. 114
    × 7

15. 2 × 423

16. 3 × 300

17. 3 × 821

18. 5 × 410

19. 2 × 125

20. 3 × 310

21. 4 × 265

22. 5 × 412

*For another example, see Set E on page 115.

Step 1	**Step 2**	**Step 3**

Step 1

Multiply the ones.
Regroup if needed.

$$\begin{array}{r} \overset{1}{26\overset{}{4}} \\ \times\ \ 3 \\ \hline 2 \end{array}$$

3 × 4 ones = 12 ones
or 1 ten 2 ones

Step 2

Multiply the tens.
Add any extra tens.
Regroup if needed.

$$\begin{array}{r} \overset{1\ 1}{264} \\ \times\ \ 3 \\ \hline 92 \end{array}$$

(3 × 6 tens) + 1 ten = 19 tens
or 1 hundred 9 tens

Step 3

Multiply the hundreds.
Add any extra hundreds.

$$\begin{array}{r} \overset{1\ 1}{264} \\ \times\ \ 3 \\ \hline 792 \end{array}$$

(3 × 2 hundreds) + 1 hundred
= 7 hundreds

Juan's guess was 792 pennies.

Problem Solving

In **23** through **25**, find the weight of the animal.

23. Horse

24. Rhino

25. Elephant

Elephant: Weighs 9 times as much as the bear

Horse: Weighs 2 times as much as the bear

Rhino: Weighs 5 times as much as the bear

Bear: Weighs 836 pounds

26. Algebra What did Mr. Sims buy at the electronics sale if (3 × $129) + $180 stands for the total price?

27. Number Sense Which costs more—2 laptop computers or 4 picture phones? Use number sense to decide.

28. **Think About the Process** Which tells how to find the total cost of a laptop computer and 5 digital cameras?

A 5 × $420 × $295 **C** $420 + $295 + 5

B (5 × $420) + $295 **D** $420 + (5 × $295)

Electronics Sale

Data		
Digital Camera	$295
Laptop Computer	$420
DVD Player	$129
Picture Phone	$180

Multiplying Greater Numbers by 1-Digit Numbers

How do you multiply with four or more digits?

NS 2.4 ➝ Grade 3
Solve simple problems involving multiplication of multi-digit numbers by one-digit numbers.
Also **MR 2.1**

Mr. Singh has 5 acres of pistachio trees on his farm. The trees produced 3,210 pounds of nuts per acre. How many total pounds were produced?

Estimate: $3,000 \times 5 = 15,000$

5 acres

Other Examples

Multiplying by a multiple of 10,000

$$\begin{array}{r} 40,000 \\ \times 5 \\ \hline 200,000 \end{array}$$

Multiplying by a 5-digit number

$$\begin{array}{r} {}^{111} \\ 23,451 \\ \times 3 \\ \hline 70,353 \end{array}$$

Guided Practice*

Do you know HOW?

1. $\begin{array}{r} 90,000 \\ \times 3 \\ \hline \end{array}$

2. $\begin{array}{r} 3,062 \\ \times 2 \\ \hline \end{array}$

3. $\begin{array}{r} 2,842 \\ \times 5 \\ \hline \end{array}$

4. $\begin{array}{r} 4,962 \\ \times 7 \\ \hline \end{array}$

5. $1,627 \times 6$

6. $21,008 \times 3$

Do you UNDERSTAND?

7. Writing to Explain Why is it easier to multiply Excercise 1, a 5-digit number, than Exercise 5, a 4-digit number?

8. Mrs. Beach's farm has 8 acres of pistachio trees which produced 2,960 pounds of nuts per acre. How many total pounds were produced?

Independent Practice

In **9** through **23**, find each product. Estimate to decide if your answer is reasonable.

9. $\begin{array}{r} 3,367 \\ \times 3 \\ \hline \end{array}$

10. $\begin{array}{r} 7,054 \\ \times 8 \\ \hline \end{array}$

11. $\begin{array}{r} 6,041 \\ \times 6 \\ \hline \end{array}$

12. $\begin{array}{r} 12,345 \\ \times 4 \\ \hline \end{array}$

13. $\begin{array}{r} 4,326 \\ \times 5 \\ \hline \end{array}$

*For another example, see Set D on page 115.

Multiply the ones.	Multiply the tens.	Multiply the	Multiply the
Regroup if needed.	Add any extra tens. Regroup if needed.	hundreds. Add any extra hundreds. Regroup if needed.	thousands. Add any extra thousands. Regroup if needed.

$$\begin{array}{r} {\scriptstyle 1} \\ 3{,}212 \\ \times \quad 5 \\ \hline 0 \end{array}$$

$$\begin{array}{r} {\scriptstyle 1} \\ 3{,}212 \\ \times \quad 5 \\ \hline 60 \end{array}$$

$$\begin{array}{r} {\scriptstyle 1 \quad 1} \\ 3{,}212 \\ \times \quad 5 \\ \hline 060 \end{array}$$

$$\begin{array}{r} {\scriptstyle 1 \quad 1} \\ 3{,}212 \\ \times \quad 5 \\ \hline 16{,}060 \end{array}$$

So, 16,060 pounds of nuts were produced. The answer is reasonable because 16,060 is close to 15,000.

14. $5 \times 9{,}512$ **15.** $60{,}000 \times 9$ **16.** $7 \times 5{,}555$ **17.** $91{,}323 \times 2$ **18.** $14{,}332 \times 4$

19. $7 \times 7{,}639$ **20.** $12{,}054 \times 3$ **21.** $4{,}981 \times 2$ **22.** $2{,}976 \times 8$ **23.** $5 \times 10{,}000$

Problem Solving

For **24** through **26**, use the table at the right.

24. How much did the number of California bighorn sheep in Oregon increase from 2002 to 2003?

25. Was the 2003 sheep population more or less than twice the 2002 population?

26. One rancher predicted that the bighorn sheep population in Oregon will triple from 2003 to 2010. What is the predicted population in 2010?

27. Algebra Find the value of $6 \times a$ when a is 11,426.

28. A carpenter bought 8 boxes of 1 inch nails. Each box had 525 nails. How many nails did he buy in all?

  A 2,100 nails   **C** 4,000 nails

  B 2,625 nails   **D** 4,200 nails

525 nails in each box

MR 2.1 Use estimation to verify the reasonableness of calculated results. Also **MR 3.1, NS 2.4, Grade 3** ○——→ .

Reasonableness

Karen glued sequins onto her project. She used 7 rows with 28 sequins in each row. How many sequins did Karen glue in all?

After you solve a problem, check whether your answer is reasonable. Ask yourself: Did I answer the right question? Is the calculation reasonable?

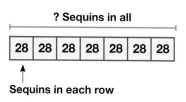

? Sequins in all

| 28 | 28 | 28 | 28 | 28 | 28 | 28 |

Sequins in each row

Guided Practice*

Do you know HOW?

Solve and make an estimate to show that your answer is reasonable.

1. A fish store has 8 empty tanks. After a delivery, they put 40 fish in each tank. How many fish were in the delivery?

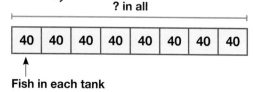

? in all

| 40 | 40 | 40 | 40 | 40 | 40 | 40 | 40 |

Fish in each tank

Do you UNDERSTAND?

2. In Problem 1, if your estimate was about 40 more than your actual answer, what would you do?

3. **Write a Problem** Write a problem about fish that would have an answer near 80. Then solve and use an estimate to show that your answer is reasonable.

Independent Practice

Use the problem below for **4** and **5**.

Dawn's Spanish teacher ordered 20 Spanish CDs for her class. If each CD costs $9.00, what will the total cost be?

4. Give an answer to the problem using complete sentences.

5. Check your answer. Did you answer the right question? Is your answer reasonable? How do you know?

Stuck? Try this....

- What do I know?
- What diagram can I use to help understand the problem?
- Can I use addition, subtraction, multiplication, or division?
- Is all of my work correct?
- Did I answer the right question?
- Is my answer reasonable?

Reasonable

There were 196 sequins in all.

Estimate: $7 \times 30 = 210$.

The answer is reasonable because 210 is close to 196.

The right question was answered and the calculation is reasonable.

Not reasonable

There were 140 sequins in all.

Estimate: $7 \times 20 = 140$.

The answer is not reasonable because 140 is not close to 196.

The right question was answered, but the calculation is not reasonable.

For **6** through **9**, use the chart at the right and the problem below.

A plane increases its height at a rate of 400 feet per second.

6. How high will the plane be after 5 seconds?

7. What number sentence did you use to solve the problem?

8. Did you answer the right question?

9. Is your answer reasonable? How do you know?

Data

Seconds	Increase in Height	Height
1 sec	400 ft	400 ft
1 sec	400 ft	800 ft
1 sec	400 ft	1,200 ft
1 sec	400 ft	1,600 ft
1 sec	400 ft	2,000 ft
1 sec	400 ft	2,400 ft

For **10** through **12**, use the chart at the right.

10. How much money does an American family spend in 20 weeks to feed a child who is 15 years old?

11. In four weeks, how much more money does a family spend to feed a child who is 8 years old than a child who is 3 years old?

12. Is your answer for Problem 11 reasonable? How do you know?

Data

Money spent by an American Family to Feed a Child

Age of Child	Weekly Amount
3–5 years	$20
6–8 years	$30
9–14 years	$35
15–17 years	$40

For **13** through **16**, use the chart at the right.

13. How many stickers does Mr. Richardson have on rolls?

14. How many more stickers on sheets does Mr. Richardson have than stickers in boxes?

15. Is your calculation for Problem 14 reasonable? How do you know?

16. How many stickers does Mr. Richardson have in all?

Mr. Richardson's Stickers

On sheets	♥ ♥ ♥
On roll	♥ ♥ ♥ ♥
In boxes	♥

1 ♥ = 10 stickers

17. The distance from Bethany's home to New York City is 180 miles. After Bethany drove 95 miles she said she had traveled over half the distance. Is Bethany correct?

180 miles to New York

| 95 miles | ? |

18. On her way from New York City, Bethany stopped for a break after driving 116 miles. How many miles does she have left to drive home?

180 miles to home

| 116 miles | ? |

Think About the Process

19. Which of the following uses the Distributive Property to solve the equation 4 × 9?

A 4 × 9 = (3 × 3) + (1 × 6)

B 4 × 9 = (4 × 9) + (4 × 9)

C 4 × 9 = (2 × 9) + (2 × 9)

D 4 × 9 = (2 × 3) + (2 × 6)

20. Louisa bought six boxes of trail mix packs. Each box had 15 packs. Which tells how to find the total number of trail mix packs?

A (6 × 2) × 15

B (6 × 15) × 2

C 6 × 15

D 15 × 3

Find each product. Estimate to check
if the answer is reasonable.

1.   21
    $\times$ 4

2.   843
    $\times$ 6

3.   6,318
    $\times$ 5

4.   5,008
    $\times$ 9

5.   40
    $\times$ 3

6.   17
    $\times$ 8

7.   92,075
    $\times$ 2

8.   796
    $\times$ 7

9.   24,927
    $\times$ 6

10.   1,234
    $\times$ 9

11.   700
    $\times$ 5

12.   99
    $\times$ 9

13.   50,000
    $\times$ 4

Find each difference. Estimate to check
if the answer is reasonable.

14. 3,427 − 648

15. 7,005 − 6,496

16. 502 − 89

Error Search Find each product that is not correct.
Write it correctly and explain the error.

17.   56,829
    $\times$ 5
    ———
    284,145

18.   408
    $\times$ 9
    ———
    3,602

19.   2,365
    $\times$ 3
    ———
    7,098

20.   45
    $\times$ 4
    ———
    49

21.   777
    $\times$ 7
    ———
    5,439

Number Sense

Estimating and Reasoning Write whether each
statement is true or false. Explain your answer.

22. The product of 6 and 39 is less than 240.

23. The sum of 3,721 and 1,273 is greater than 4,000 but less than 6,000.

24. The product of 5 and 286 is greater than 1,500.

25. The product of 4 and 3,103 is closer to 12,000 than 16,000.

26. The difference of 4,637 − 2,878 is greater than 3,000.

27. The quotient of 4 divided by 1 is 1.

1. Mrs. Henderson bought 4 boxes of facial tissues. Each box has 174 tissues. Which number sentence shows the best way to use rounding to estimate the total number of tissues? (4-3)

   A $4 + 100 = 104$

   B $4 + 200 = 204$

   C $4 \times 100 = 400$

   D $4 \times 200 = 800$

2. Part of the calculation for 26×3 is shown below. What partial product should replace ▮ ? (4-4)

   A 8

   B 18

   C 20

   D 60

   $$\begin{array}{r} 26 \\ \times\ \ 3 \\ \hline ▮ \\ +\ 60 \\ \hline 78 \end{array}$$

3. What is $5 \times 3,817$? (4-7)

   A 15,055

   B 19,055

   C 19,085

   D 19,805

4. Wally has 80 pennies. He put the pennies in stacks with the same number in each stack. Which arrangement is possible, if Wally used all of the pennies? (4-5)

   A 8 stacks of 8 pennies

   B 16 stacks of 5 pennies

   C 25 stacks of 4 pennies

   D 6 stacks of 15 pennies

5. A gallon of paint can cover about 400 square feet of wall space. How many square feet of wall space will 3 gallons cover? (4-1)

   A 12

   B 120

   C 1,200

   D 12,000

6. Which shows one way to use breaking apart to find 4×13? (4-2)

   A $(4 \times 10) + (4 \times 3)$

   B $(4 \times 10) \times (4 \times 3)$

   C $(4 \times 10) + (4 \times 13)$

   D $(2 \times 10) + (2 \times 3)$

7. A factory produced 275 cars in a week. At this rate, how many cars would the factory produce in 4 weeks? (4-6)

   A 8,300

   B 1,100

   C 1,000

   D 880

8. Each photo album can hold 248 photos. Andy has 3 full albums. Which number sentence shows the best way to use compatible numbers to estimate the total number of pictures Andy has? (4-3)

   A $3 \times 250 = 750$

   B $3 \times 200 = 600$

   C $3 \times 300 = 900$

   D $240 \div 3 = 80$

9. Quinn finished 32 math facts in a 1-minute drill. At this rate, about how many math facts will he finish in a 3-minute drill? (4-3)

A 60

B 70

C 90

D 120

10. Susanna's school has 5 grades with an average of 48 students in each grade. Which is a reasonable number of students in Susanna's school? (4-8)

A 205, because 5×48 is about $5 \times 40 = 200$.

B 240, because 5×48 is about $5 \times 50 = 250$.

C 285, because 5×48 is about $5 \times 60 = 300$.

D 315, because 5×48 is about $6 \times 50 = 300$.

11. One serving of Very Vanilla soy milk contains 16 grams of sugar. If Mary drank 5 servings of soy milk in one day, how many grams of sugar would she get just from soy milk? Use mental math to solve. (4-2)

A 80

B 75

C 50

D 21

12. The workers at the world's largest freshwater aquarium feed 33,300 worms each month to their various creatures. How many worms will be used in 8 months? (4-7)

A 244,400

B 246,400

C 264,400

D 266,400

13. Blane earned 230 points when he played a video game. Jane earned 7 times as many points as Blane. How many points did Jane earn? (4-6)

A 1,610

B 1,421

C 1,410

D 161

14. What is 5×48? (4-5)

A 340

B 240

C 140

D 60

15. Mrs. Ortiz can make 50 sopapillas out of one batch of dough. If she makes 4 batches of dough, how many sopapillas can she make? (4-1)

A 8

B 20

C 200

D 2,000

Reteaching

Set A, pages 90–91

Use basic multiplication facts to multiply by multiples of 10 and 100.

For a multiple of 10, multiply by the digit in the tens place. Then, write one zero in the product.

Find 4×60.
Multiply $4 \times 6 = 24$.

Write one zero after 24.
$4 \times 60 = 240$
So, $4 \times 60 = 240$.

For a multiple of 100, multiply by the digit in the hundreds place. Then, write two zeros in the product.

Find 4×600.
Multiply $4 \times 6 = 24$.

Write two zeros after 24.
$4 \times 600 = 2,400$
So, $4 \times 600 = 2,400$.

Remember when the product of a basic fact has a zero, the answer will have an extra zero.

Write the basic fact. Then find the product.

1. 8×60
2. 3×40
3. 6×50
4. 5×300
5. 700×4
6. 2×900
7. 300×7
8. 80×8
9. 100×4
10. 30×6
11. 20×9
12. 9×800
13. 5×70
14. 2×70
15. 4×800
16. 60×6
17. 900×3
18. 500×8

Set B, pages 92–95

Find 2×27 using compatible numbers.

Subtract 2 to make 25.
$2 \times 25 = 50$

Now adjust. Add 2 groups of 2.
$50 + 4 = 54$

So, $2 \times 27 = 54$.

Estimate 8×102 using rounding.

Round 102 to 100.
So, $8 \times 100 = 800$.

Remember when both rounded numbers are less than the factors they replace, their product will also be less than the product of the factors.

Find each product using mental math.

1. 6×13
2. 3×46
3. 7×63
4. 9×24

Estimate each product.

5. 2×72
6. 28×6
7. 61×9
8. 49×4
9. 5×299
10. 213×5

Set C, pages 96–98

Find 4 × 12.

Use blocks or draw a picture to build an array.

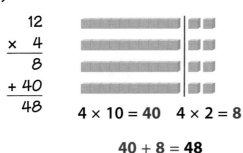

$$\begin{array}{r} 12 \\ \times\ \ 4 \\ \hline 8 \\ +\ 40 \\ \hline 48 \end{array}$$

4 × 10 = 40   4 × 2 = 8

40 + 8 = 48

Remember to check that your picture accurately shows the numbers that are being multiplied.

1. $\begin{array}{r}22\\\times\ 6\\\hline\end{array}$ **2.** $\begin{array}{r}28\\\times\ 3\\\hline\end{array}$

3. $\begin{array}{r}75\\\times\ 5\\\hline\end{array}$ **4.** $\begin{array}{r}53\\\times\ 4\\\hline\end{array}$

5. $\begin{array}{r}88\\\times\ 2\\\hline\end{array}$ **6.** $\begin{array}{r}21\\\times\ 6\\\hline\end{array}$

Set D, pages 100–102, 104–107

Find 768 × 6.

Step 1

Multiply the ones. Regroup if necessary.

$$\begin{array}{r} ^{4}\ \\ 768 \\ \times\ \ \ \ 6 \\ \hline 8 \end{array}$$

Step 2

Multiply the tens. Add any extra tens. Regroup if necessary.

$$\begin{array}{r} ^{4\ 4}\ \\ 768 \\ \times\ \ \ \ 6 \\ \hline 08 \end{array}$$

Step 3

Multiply the hundreds. Add any extra hundreds.

$$\begin{array}{r} ^{4\ 4}\ \\ 768 \\ \times\ \ \ \ 6 \\ \hline 4,608 \end{array}$$

Remember that you can use an array to help you multiply.

1. $\begin{array}{r}18\\\times\ 2\\\hline\end{array}$ **2.** $\begin{array}{r}48\\\times\ 5\\\hline\end{array}$

3. $\begin{array}{r}233\\\times\ 6\\\hline\end{array}$ **4.** $\begin{array}{r}907\\\times\ 7\\\hline\end{array}$

5. $\begin{array}{r}4,172\\\times\ 3\\\hline\end{array}$ **6.** $\begin{array}{r}42,252\\\times\ 6\\\hline\end{array}$

Set E, pages 108–110

Ty is making centerpieces for 12 tables at a school banquet. How many sheets of paper will be needed if each centerpiece uses 5 sheets of paper?

? sheets in all

12 tables

5

12 × 5 = 60 sheets of paper

Estimate to determine if the answer is reasonable.

12 rounds to 10
10 × 5 = 50

Compare the answer to the estimate.

Remember to check if your answer is reasonable

Solve.

1. Mitchell earns 8 dollars per hour delivering newspapers. How much will Mitchell earn if he works for 10 hours?

? dollars in all

| 8 | 8 | 8 | 8 | 8 | 8 | 8 | 8 | 8 | 8 |

hours in each box

Variables and Expressions

1 This air tanker is used to fight forest fires throughout California. How many tons of water can this plane carry? You will find out in Lesson 5-4.

C-FLSF

2 How could an ancient Mayan pyramid be a type of calendar? You will find out in Lesson 5-3.

Review What You Know!

3

The largest pumpkin grown in the United States weighed 1,502 pounds. How much did the largest pumpkin in California weigh? You will find out in Lesson 5-2.

Vocabulary

Choose the best term from the box.

- expression
- factors
- ordered pair
- multiple

1. A ? is the product of a whole number and any other whole number.

2. A(n) ? may include numbers and at least one operation.

3. A(n) ? is a pair of numbers used to name a point on a coordinate grid.

4. ? are numbers multiplied together to find a product.

Patterns

For each set of numbers, find the missing number.

5. 2, ▢, 4, 5, 6

6. ▢, 10, 15, 20

7. 3, 6, 9, ▢

8. 4, 8, ▢, 16

9. 17, ▢, 35, 44

10. 1.5, 2, ▢, 3

Multiplication

Solve.

11. 5 × 6

12. 12 × 4

13. 35 × 2

14. 9 × 8

15. 60 × 3

16. 125 × 4

17. In baseball, there are 6 outs in 1 full inning. Would you multiply or divide to find the number of outs in 2 innings?

18. **Writing to Explain** How would you describe the pattern for multiples of 2? multiples of 5?

AF 1.1 Use letters, boxes, or other symbols to stand for any number in simple expressions or equations (e.g., demonstrate and understanding and the use of the concept of a variable). Also AF 1.0

Variables and Expressions

How can you use expressions with variables?

A **variable** is a symbol that stands for a number.

A Tae Kwan Do class has 23 people. If *n* more people sign up, how many people will be taking the class?

n	$23 + n$
3	
5	
7	

Other Examples

An **algebraic expression** is a mathematical phrase that contains numbers or variables and at least one operation.

Word form	Expression
add 5	$n + 5$
multiply by 2	$2 \times n$

Guided Practice*

Do you know HOW?

In **1** through **3**, copy and complete the table.

c	$c + 8$
1. 4	
2. 9	
3. 13	

Do you UNDERSTAND?

4. **Writing to Explain** Could you use the variable *k* instead of *n* to represent more students signing up for the Tae Kwan Do class?

5. If *n* is 12, how many people will be taking the Tae Kwan Do class?

Independent Practice

For **6** through **8**, copy and complete the table for each problem.

6.

d	$d + 30$
3	
7	
12	

7.

g	$5 \times g$
6	
9	
15	

8.

m	$m \div 10$
350	
240	
120	

DIGITAL Animated Glossary
www.pearsonsuccessnet.com

For another example, see Set A on page 132.

What You Show

Use the expression, $23 + n$, to find the missing numbers.

$23 + n$
$\downarrow$
$23 + 3 = 26$

n	$23 + n$
3	$23 + 3$
5	$23 + 5$
7	$23 + 7$

What You Write

If 3 more people sign up, there will be 26 people in the class.

If 5 more people sign up, there will be 28 people in the class.

If 7 more people sign up, there will be 30 people in the class.

For **9** through **12**, fill in the missing numbers.

9.

z	152	128	112	88
$z \div 8$	19		14	11

10.

t	43	134	245	339
$t + 47$	90	181		386

11.

y	387	201	65	26
$y - 13$	374	188		

12.

x	5	7	10	20
$x \times 12$	60	84		

Problem Solving

13. The year 2020 will be the fifth leap year after the year 2000. Name the years between 2000 and 2020 that are leap years.

 A leap year will occur every 4 years between 2000 and 2020.

14. Which expression represents how many seconds are in 5 minutes?

A $s + 5$

B $s \div 5$

C $s \times 5$

D $s - 5$

15. A Ferris wheel has 12 cars. The operator needs to keep 2, 4, or 6 cars empty. Make a table to show how many people can ride if each car holds 4 people.

16. Write an expression to represent the cost of parking a car for n hours in a lot that charges $7.00 per hour. Find the cost of parking the car for 3 hours.

17. Reasonableness Edgar used $10 \times d$ to represent the number of pennies in d dollars. Is this reasonable?

18. Reasoning How could you make $36.32 with exactly 4 bills and 4 coins?

Equality

Why is equality important when you find values of expressions?

AF1.1 Use letters, boxes, or other symbols to stand for any number in simple expressions or equations (e.g., demonstrate an understanding and the use of the concept of a variable). Also **AF 1.0**

A bus was carrying 18 people. Suppose 12 people get on and *f* people get off the bus. The expression for the number of people on the bus now is 18 + 12 − *f*. If *f* = 4, how many people are on the bus?

12 people get on the bus

Guided Practice*

Do you know HOW?

Find the value of each expression for $x = 5$.

1. $9 - x$

2. $x + x - 3$

3. $13 + x$

4. $10 - x - x$

5. $2 + x - 7$

6. $14 + x - 17$

Do you UNDERSTAND?

7. In the example above, what does *f* represent?

8. If 14 people got off of the bus in the example above, how many people would be on the bus then?

Independent Practice

In **9** through **16**, find the value of each expression for $k = 8$.

9. $17 + k$

10. $k - 1 + 23$

11. $k + k$

12. $k - 8 + k$

13. $k + 40 + k$

14. $63 - k + k$

15. $100 + k$

16. $k - 1 - 2$

In **17** through **24**, find the value of each expression for $w = 7$.

17. $w + w - w$

18. $w - w + 1$

19. $w - 7$

20. $17 - w - w$

21. $w + 28$

22. $w + w + 17$

23. $1 + w + 1$

24. $74 + w - 45$

In **25** through **32**, find the value of each expression for $y = 11$.

25. $y + 1$

26. $y + 14 - y$

27. $y - 7 - 3$

28. $y + y - 22$

29. $y + 12 + 9$

30. $y + y$

31. $39 - y$

32. $90 - y + 82$

*For another example, see Set B on page 132.

If $f = 4$, find the value of $18 + 12 - f$.

$18 + 12 - f$

$18 + 12 - 4$ Substitute 4 for f.

$30 - 4$ Add 18 and 12.

26   Subtract 4 from 30.

There are 26 people on the bus.

If $f = 10$, find the value of $18 + 12 - f$.

$18 + 12 - f$

$18 + 12 - 10$ Substitute 10 for f.

$30 - 10$ Add 18 and 12.

20   Subtract 10 from 30.

There are 20 people on the bus.

Problem Solving

33. Reasoning Maria wrote two number sentences shown below. Then she covered some of the numbers with letter cards. The same letter stands for the same number. What number is covered up by the letter "R"? Explain how you found your answer.

$$\boxed{R} + \boxed{R} = 10$$

$$\boxed{R} - 2 = \boxed{S}$$

34. Jeremiah had $212 in his bank account yesterday. Today he bought a DVD for $23, two CDs which each cost $13, and x dollars worth of groceries. If he has only 98 dollars left in his account at the end of the day, how much did he spend on groceries?

$212				
$23	$13	$13	$x	$98

35. Neil is n years old. His sister Jackie is $n - 7$ years old. How old is Jackie if Neil is 17 years old?

A 7 years old   **C** 17 years old

B 10 years old   **D** 24 years old

36. George owns 186 books and 6 bookcases. If he puts an equal number of books on each bookcase, how many books are on each bookcase?

A 21 books   **C** 62 books

B 31 books   **D** 91 books

37. Writing to Explain Annie and some of her friends are going to a school basketball game. If each ticket costs $1, and together they spent $8, how would you find how many friends went to the game with Annie?

38. The largest pumpkin grown in the United States weighed 1,502 pounds. The largest pumpkin grown in California weighed about 221 pounds less. How much did the largest pumpkin grown in California weigh?

Expressions with Parentheses

How can you use parentheses when writing an expression?

Nia earned $11 for pulling weeds and $10 for cleaning windows. She spent $6 for a movie and $3 for snacks. She saved the rest of the money. How much money did Nia save?

AF 1.2
Interpret and evaluate mathematical expressions that now use parentheses.
Also AF 1.3,
AF 1.0.

Snacks: $3

Movie: $6

Guided Practice*

Do you know HOW?

Find the value of each expression below.

1. $(11 - 6) + (5 - 3)$ **2.** $(94 - 10) + 29$

3. $(6 - 3) + (15 + 3)$ **4.** $(45 - 16) + 11$

5. $16 + (33 - 18)$ **6.** $(16 + 33) - 18$

Do you UNDERSTAND?

7. Nia said she saved 18 dollars. What did Nia do wrong?

8. Explain why the answer to $(10 - 4) - 2$ and $10 - (4 - 2)$ are not the same.

Independent Practice

In **9** through **20**, find the value of each expression.

9. $(12 + 7) - 4$ **10.** $(9 - 8) - (3 - 2)$ **11.** $12 - (9 - 1)$ **12.** $(12 - 9) - 1$

13. $(1 - 1) + 1$ **14.** $(10 - 6) + 2$ **15.** $(21 - 8) + 3$ **16.** $(6 - 3) + (4 + 4)$

17. $(12 - 2) + (1 + 7)$ **18.** $4 + (9 - 7)$ **19.** $7 + (18 - 2)$ **20.** $(17 - 7) + (10 + 4)$

In **21** through **26**, choose where to place the parentheses to make the number sentence true.

21. $20 - 10 - 8 = 2$ **22.** $18 - 2 + 5 = 11$ **23.** $15 + 2 - 5 = 12$

24. $13 - 2 + 6 = 5$ **25.** $34 + 11 - 9 = 36$ **26.** $101 + 4 - 1 = 98$

Animated Glossary
www.pearsonsuccessnet.com

DIGITAL

Step 1

Write a number expression.

Group the amounts earned together and group the amounts spent together. Use parentheses ( ) to show the two groups.

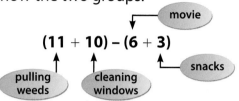

$(11 + 10) - (6 + 3)$

pulling weeds   cleaning windows   snacks   movie

Step 2

Find the value of the expression. Parentheses <u>tell which operation to do first in a number expression.</u>

$(11 + 10) - (6 + 3)$ Do the operations in parentheses first. Then subtract.

21 – 9

12

Nia saved $12.

Problem Solving

27. Jay is 50 inches tall. Sara is 5 inches shorter than Jay. Ted is 2 inches taller than Sara. Find the value of the expression $(50 - 5) + 2$ to find Ted's height.

A 43 inches **C** 53 inches

B 47 inches **D** 57 inches

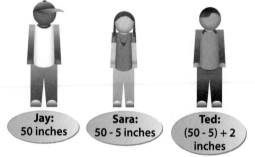

Jay: 50 inches   Sara: 50 - 5 inches   Ted: (50 - 5) + 2 inches

28. Which property of addition is shown below?

$3 + (4 + 5) = (3 + 4) + 5$

A Associative Property

B Commutative Property

C Zero Property

D None of the above

29. **Geometry** Write an expression to show the perimeter of this triangle. Then find the value of the expression.

3 + 10   16 − 11   12

30. It is believed that the Mayan pyramid of Kukulkan in Mexico was used as a calendar. It has 4 stairways leading to the top platform. Each stairway has 91 steps. In addition, there is one extra step at the top. Write an expression with parentheses that will help find the total number of steps.

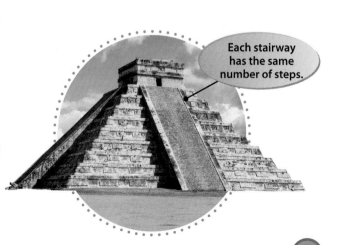

Each stairway has the same number of steps.

Lesson

5-4

AF 1.3
Use parentheses to
indicate which operation
to perform first when
writing expressions
containing more
than two terms and
different operations.
Also **AF 1.0, 1.2, 2.3**

Simplifying Expressions

What order should you use when you simplify an expression?

Jack evaluated $(7 \times 2) - 3 + 4 \times 1$.

To avoid getting more than one answer, he used the order of operations given at the right.

Order of Operations

1. Do the operations inside parentheses.

2. Multiply and divide from left to right.

3. Add and subtract from left to right.

Other Examples

Simplify expressions with a variable

First, substitute the value for the variable.
Then follow the order of operations to simplify.

Find the value of the expression:
$(19 + a) + 16 \div 4$ for $a = 12$.

(19 + 12) + 16 ÷ 4

31 + 16 ÷ 4

31 + 4 = 35

Find the value of the expression:
$(16 - b) + 2 \times 3$ for $b = 9$.

(16 − 9) + 2 × 3

7 + 2 × 3

7 + 6 = 13

Guided Practice*

Do you know HOW?

Use the order of operations to simplify
the following expressions.

1. $8 + 14 \div 2 - (3 - 1)$

2. $7 \times (6 - 1) + 4$

3. $17 + 4 \times 3$

4. $(8 + 1) + 9 \times 7$

5. $(4 \times 3) \div 2 + 1 + 2 \times 6$

Do you UNDERSTAND?

6. In the example above, what operation do you do first?

7. Writing to Explain Explain the steps involved in simplifying the expression $(4 + 2) - 1 \times 3$.

8. Which is greater, $1 \times 5 + 4$ or $1 + 5 \times 4$?

9. Would the value of $(15 - 3) \div 3 + 1$ change if the parentheses were removed?

For another example, see Set D on page 133.

First, do the operations inside parentheses.

$(7 \times 2) - 3 + 4 \times 1$
$\vee$
$14 \quad - \quad 3 + 4 \times 1$

Then, multiply and divide in order from left to right.

$14 - 3 + 4 \times 1$
$\vee$
$14 - 3 \quad + \quad 4$

Finally, add and subtract in order from left to right.

$14 - 3 + 4$
$\vee$
$11 + 4 = 15$

Independent Practice

In **10** through **15**, use the order of operations to simplify the expression.

10. $6 - 3 \times 2 + 4$

11. $(4 \times 8) \div 2 + 8$

12. $(18 + 7) \times (11 - 7)$

13. $2 + 3 \times 4 + 5 \times 6$

14. $17 \times 20 - (17 + 20)$

15. $90 - 5 \times 5 \times 2$

In **16** through **21**, find the value of each expression for $b = 3$.

16. $39 \times 8 - (b + 4)$

17. $22 \div (2 \times 7 - b) + 1$

18. $2 \times b - 3 + b \times 4$

19. $39 \div b + 7$

20. $4 + 5 \times 6 \div b$

21. $(5 \times 10) \times (2 \times b - 1)$

Problem Solving

22. To solve the equation $n + 20 = 25$, Darlene tested values for n until she found one that would work. She tested 5, 6, and 7. Which is correct?

23. Which operation should be used first in the the expression?

$6 \times 3 + 7 \div (2 - 1)$

A $\times$ **B** $+$ **C** $\div$ **D** $-$

24. An air tanker fights fires using lake water. The plane scoops up 2,000 pounds of water in each of its two tanks. Write an expression to find how much water the tanker carries when each tank is filled.

25. Use the operation signs $+$, $-$, $\times$, and $\div$ once each in the expression below to make the number sentence true. Explain how you found your answer.

$6 \quad (3 \quad 1) \quad 5 \quad 1 = 17$

MR 2.4 Express the solution clearly and logically by using the appropriate mathematical notation and terms and clear language; support solutions with evidence in both verbal and symbolic work. Also **MR 2.0, NS 3.0** .

Problem Solving

Act It Out and Use Logical Reasoning

Clark collected granite rocks, minerals, and gemstones. Use cubes to show the objects and solve the problem.

How many of each type of rock are in Clark's collection?

Hands-On
counters

Clark's Collection
....
2 granite rocks

3 times as many minerals as gemstones

6 rocks in all

2 granite rocks

Another Example Mr. Wilson collected rocks. How many granite rocks are there in Mr. Wilson's collection?

Data

Mr. Wilson's Collection
....
3 minerals

1 fewer gemstone than minerals

6 rocks in all

Step 1 There are 3 minerals.

There must be $3 - 1 = 2$ gemstones.

Step 2 Use counters to show 3 minerals and 2 gemstones.

Step 3 Find the number of granite rocks.

There are 6 rocks in all. If you add one red counter to show 1 granite rock, you will have 6 rocks in all.

$3 + 2 + 1 = 6$ rocks in all.

So, Mr. Wilson has 1 granite rock in his collection.

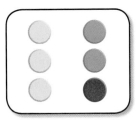

Explain It

1. What part of Mr. Wilson's collection is granite rocks?

2. **Reasoning** Suppose that one of the gemstones is an amethyst crystal. How could you show how many gemstones are amethyst crystals?

Use objects to show what you know. Use reasoning to make conclusions.

There are 6 rocks in all.
There are 2 granite rocks.

That leaves a total of 4 minerals and gemstones.

There are 4 minerals and gemstones.

There are 3 times as many minerals as gemstones.

There has to be 2 granite rocks, 3 minerals, and 1 gemstone.

$2 + 3 + 1 = 6$ so, the answer is reasonable.

Guided Practice*

Do you know HOW?

Use logical reasoning to find the amount in the collection.

1. Adam's collection:
   2 ladybugs
   1 more cricket than ladybug
   9 insects in all
   L = ▢ G = ▢ C = ▢

Do you UNDERSTAND?

2. In the example above, what is another way of checking if the answer is reasonable?

3. **Write a Problem** Write a problem in which you use logical reasoning to find how many gemstones there are in a collection.

Independent Practice

Use logical reasoning to find how many of each coin are in each collection.

4. Jack's collection:
   2 dimes
   Twice as many quarters as dimes
   9 coins in all
   Q = ▢ D = ▢ N = ▢

5. Larry's collection:
   14 coins in all
   6 quarters
   $\frac{1}{2}$ as many nickels as quarters
   Q = ▢ D = ▢ N = ▢

Stuck? Try this....

- What do I know?
- What diagram can I use to help understand the problem?
- Can I use addition, subtraction, multiplication, or division?
- Is all of my work correct?
- Did I answer the right question?
- Is my answer reasonable?

DIGITAL eTools
www.pearsonsuccessnet.com

Use logical reasoning to find how many of each coin are in each collection.

6. Kristie's collection:
13 coins in all
4 nickels
Twice as many dimes as nickels
Q = ⬜ D = ⬜ N = ⬜

7. Brian's collection:
4 nickels
1 more dime than nickels
11 coins in all
Q = ⬜ D = ⬜ N = ⬜

Problem Solving

8. Marley, Jon, and Bart swim a relay race. Jon swims two more laps than Marley. Bart swims twice as many laps as Marley. If Marley swims 3 laps, how many laps do they swim altogether?

9. Patty made a picnic lunch for her friends. She made 6 sandwiches. Three of the sandwiches were turkey. There is 1 fewer salami sandwich than roast beef. How many of each type of sandwich is there?

10. Leah's garden has tomatoes, peppers, and cucumbers. Each row contains one type of vegetable. Her garden has 11 rows of vegetables in all. There are 4 rows of tomatoes. There is 1 more row of cucumbers than tomatoes. How many rows of each type of vegetable are in Leah's garden?

11. Kenny, Jessica, Rebecca, and Quinn run every day. Kenny runs 4 miles every day. Jessica runs two more miles than Kenny. Rebecca runs half as many miles as Jessica. If the four of them run a total of 15 miles a day, how many miles does each of them run?

Think About the Process

12. Dale's dog is 10 inches longer than twice the length of his cat. If Dale's dog is 36 inches long, how could Dale find the length of his cat?

A $(36 - 10) \div 2$ **C** $(36 + 10) \div 2$

B $(36 - 10) \times 2$ **D** $(36 + 10) \times 2$

13. Michael and Jack work at the same store. Michael works 5 hours a day. Jack works twice as many hours as Michael. Which expression below shows how many hours Michael and Jack work together in one day?

A $2 - (5 \div 5)$ **C** $(5 \times 5) + 2$

B $5 + (2 + 5)$ **D** $5 + (2 \times 5)$

Find the value of each expression for $m = 6$.

1. $3 \times m$ **2.** $15 + m$ **3.** $36 - 12 - m$

4. $m + 17$ **5.** $m - 4 + 22$ **6.** $7 \times m + 3$

7. $20 - 2 \times m$ **8.** $8 + m - 2$ **9.** $(12 - m) \div 3 + 5$

Find the value of each expression.

10. $18 - (3 + 2)$ **11.** $(2 + 6) + 9$ **12.** $(29 - 4) + (12 + 13)$

13. $(17 - 9) + 7$ **14.** $5 - 2 \times 2 + 6$ **15.** $(9 \times 4) \div 6 + 14 \div 7$

16. $(30 - 2) \div 4$ **17.** $(2 \times 4) \times 9$ **18.** $(3 \times 4) \div (6 + 6)$

Find the quotient.

19. $56 \div 7$ **20.** $5 \div 1$ **21.** $24 \div 4$ **22.** $72 \div 8$ **23.** $64 \div 8$

Error Search Find each expression that is not correct.
Write it correctly and explain the error.

24. $12 - (8 - 4) = 0$ **25.** $10 - (4 \times 2) - 1 = 1$ **26.** $(10 + 5 \times 6) \div 5 = 8$

27. $5 + 2 \times 9 = 63$ **28.** $8 \times 8 - 2 \times 3 = 186$ **29.** $(12 - 4) \times 2 - 2 = 0$

Number Sense

Estimating and Reasoning Write whether each
statement is true or false. Explain your answer.

30. The expression $(3 + h) \times 0$ equals 0.

31. The product of 5 and 297 is closer to 1,000 than 1,500.

32. The sum of 3,810 and 8,609 is less than 13,000.

33. The difference of $593 - 202$ is 2 less than 393.

34. The product of 6 and 48 is 12 less than 300.

35. The expression $25 - (12 + 8)$ equals 21.

1. There are 24 dancers in Joy's recital. If n represents the number of jazz dancers, which expression represents the number of other types of dancers? (5-1)

A $24 + n$

B $24 - n$

C $24 \times n$

D $24 \div n$

2. Olivia had $24. She earned $12 babysitting. She then spent d dollars at the book store. If $d = \$19$, what is the value of $\$24 + \$12 - d$, the amount of money Olivia has now? (5-2)

A $36

B $27

C $19

D $17

3. Find $17 - (6 + 8)$. (5-3)

A 3

B 11

C 14

D 19

4. What is the value of the expression below? (5-4)

$8 \times (8 - 4) + 5$

A 72

B 65

C 37

D 32

5. What is the value of $s - 5 + s$, if $s = 15$. (5-2)

A 5

B 15

C 20

D 25

6. What is the value of the expression below if $w = 4$? (5-4)

$28 \div (w + 3) + 5$

A 8

B 9

C 12

D 15

7. Which shows the parentheses correctly placed to make the number sentence true? (5-3)

A $(22 - 6) + 8 = 16$

B $40 - (20 - 18) = 2$

C $14 - (3 + 4) = 7$

D $26 - (16 - 14) = 18$

8. Which number completes the table? (5-1)

w	108	90	72	42
$w \div 6$	18	15		7

A 12

B 13

C 66

D 576

9. Mrs. Chen purchased apples, kiwis, and mangos at the grocery store. She purchased a total of 24 pieces of fruit. Use the information in the table to find how many mangos Mrs. Chen purchased. (5-5)

Fruit	Number Purchased
Apples	4
Kiwis	4 times as many as mangos
Mangos	

A 16

B 5

C 4

D 3

10. What is the value of $1 + 3 \times 4 \div a$, if $a = 2$? (5-4)

A 6

B 7

C 8

D 12

11. Molly volunteers at her local community center. After 3 weeks, she has volunteered $14 + 12 + h$ hours. If $h = 19$, how many hours has Molly volunteered in all? (5-2)

A 35

B 36

C 45

D 315

12. After babysitting, Corrina will have $138 + x$, where x equals the amount she earns babysitting. If x is $25, how much money will she have after babysitting? (5-1)

A $163

B $162

C $153

D $113

13. Larry played 18 holes of golf. Use the information in the table to find how many holes Larry birdied. (5-5)

Score	Number of Holes
Birdie	
Bogey	5
Par	7 more than birdied

A 10

B 8

C 4

D 3

14. Zac made $20 mowing grass. He spent $16 on a DVD. Martina made $15 raking leaves. She spent $12 on a CD. Which expression shows how much more money Zac had left than Martina? (5-3)

A $20 - 16 - 15 - 12$

B $(20 - 16) + (15 - 12)$

C $(20 - 16) - (15 - 12)$

D $(20 - 15) - (16 - 12)$

Set A, pages 118–119

Each car on a ride holds 8 children. For c children, $c \div 8$ cars will be full on the ride. How many cars will be full if there are 16, 24, or 40 children?

Find the value of $c \div 8$ for each value of c.

c	$c \div 8$
16	2
24	3
40	5

If there are 16 children, 2 cars will be full.
If there are 24 children, 3 cars will be full.
If there are 40 children, 5 cars will be full.

Remember, to find unknown values, replace the variable with known values.

1.

e	16	25	36
$20 + e$			

2.

h	14	16	18
$h \times 4$			

3.

n	112	56	28
$n - 14$			

4.

f	96	36	144
$f \div 6$			

Set B, pages 120–121

Find the value of $17 + 14 - f$ for $f = 6$.

$17 + 14 - f$
$17 + 14 - 6$ Substitute 6 for f.

$31 - 6$ Add 17 and 14.

25 Subtract 6 from 31.

Remember to make sure that each step is equal to the step above it.

Find the value of each expression for $x = 7$.

1. $8 - x$ **2.** $x - x$

3. $x + x - 5$ **4.** $x + x + x$

Set C, pages 122–123

Find the value of the expression.

$(12 + 10) - (4 + 2)$ Do operations in parentheses first.

$22 - 6$ Then subtract.

16

Remember to do the operations in parentheses first.

Find the value of each expression.

1. $12 + (4 - 2)$

2. $(8 - 2) - (24 - 18)$

3. $(92 - 10) + 39$

4. $(15 - 4) - 9$

Set D, pages 124–125

Simplify $(6 \times 2) - 4 + 3 \times 2$.

Step 1

First, do the operations inside parentheses.

$(6 \times 2) - 4 + 3 \times 2$

$12 \quad - 4 + 3 \times 2$

Step 2

Then, multiply and divide in order from left to right.

$12 - 4 + 3 \times 2$

$12 - 4 + \quad 6$

Step 3

Finally, add and subtract in order from left to right.

$12 - 4 + 6$

$8 \quad + 6 = 14$

Remember to follow the order of operations.

Find the value of each expression.

1. $9 + 12 \div 2 + (4 - 1)$

2. $8 \times (5 - 2) + 6$

3. $19 + 3 \times 2$

4. $(5 + 4 \times 8) \times 3$

5. $(5 \times 6) - 5 + 2$

6. $8 \div 4 + 10 + (5 - 2)$

7. $(3 + 5) \times 4 - 3$

8. $9 - (2 + 6) - 1$

Set E, pages 126–128

Science classes collected different types of leaves. Every collection has some of each type. Use objects to solve the problem.

Mrs. Jackson's Class Collection

2 oak leaves
2 times as many poplar leaves as maple leaves
8 leaves in all

There are 2 oak leaves, 4 poplar leaves, and 2 maple leaves.

$2 + 4 + 2 = 8$, so the answer is reasonable.

Remember to act out the problem to help you solve it.

Use logical reasoning to find the amounts in the collection.

1. 3 ladybugs

3 more crickets than grasshoppers

10 insects in all

$L = \quad C = \quad G = $

Multiplying by 2-Digit Numbers

1 This Hollywood Bowl is one of the largest natural amphitheaters in the world. How many people sit in one of the middle sections? You will find out in Lesson 6–3.

2 The Pike's Peak Cog Railway is the highest cog railway in the world. How long is the train ride to the top? You will find out in Lesson 6-4.

Review What You Know!

3 The Queen Mary II is as tall as a 23-story building! How many feet high is this above the water? You will find out in Lesson 6–5.

4 In 1858, a telegraph cable connected Europe and America for the first time. How long was the cable? You will find out in Lesson 6-2.

Vocabulary

Choose the best term from the box.

> - rounding
> - Commutative Property
> - compatible
> - Distributive Property

1. __?__ numbers are easy to compute mentally.

2. When you break apart factors in different ways but get the same product, you are using the __?__ of Multiplication.

3. You can use __?__ when you do not need an exact answer.

Estimating Sums

Estimate each sum.

4. $16 + 3$

5. $688 + 95$

6. $1,511 + 269$

7. $3,246 + 6,423$

8. $283 + 178$

9. $1,999 + 421$

Multiplying by 1-Digit Numbers

Find each product.

10. 53×9

11. 172×7

12. 512×6

13. 711×4

14. $2,152 \times 3$

15. $1,914 \times 5$

Partial Products

16. **Writing to Explain** Explain why the array shown below represents 3×21.

Using Mental Math to Multiply 2-Digit Numbers

How can you multiply by multiples of 10 and 100?

NS 3.0 ⚬━➤ Solve problems involving addition, subtraction, multiplication, and division of whole numbers and understand the relationships among the operations.

How many adults under 65 visit the Sunny Day Amusement Park in 10 days? How many children visit the park in 100 days? How many adults 65 and over visit the park in 200 days?

Average Visitors Each Day

Adults under 65: **400**

Adults 65 and over: **50**

Children: **800**

Guided Practice*

Do you know HOW?

In **1** through **8**, use basic facts and patterns to find the product.

1. 30 × 100

2. 50 × 1,000

3. 25 × 10

4. 60 × 200

5. 20 × 20

6. 40 × 100

7. 400 × 50

8. 80 × 500

Do you UNDERSTAND?

9. When you multiply 60 × 500, how many zeros are in the product?

10. In cold weather, fewer people go to Sunny Day Amusement Park. November has 30 days. If the park sells 300 tickets each day in November, how many would they sell for the whole month?

Independent Practice

For **11** through **34**, multiply using mental math.

11. 30 × 10

12. 100 × 60

13. 50 × 10

14. 80 × 40

15. 20 × 1,000

16. 70 × 900

17. 40 × 20

18. 500 × 30

19. 250 × 40

20. 20 × 40

21. 300 × 40

22. 60 × 90

23. 70 × 800

24. 30 × 80

25. 60 × 500

26. 700 × 30

27. 600 × 50

28. 30 × 900

29. 25 × 400

30. 30 × 600

31. 400 × 30

32. 800 × 30

33. 500 × 80

34. 600 × 90

*For another example, see Set A on page 154.

Adults under 65 in 10 Days

To multiply 400 × 10, use a pattern.

$$4 \times 10 = 40$$
$$40 \times 10 = 400$$
$$400 \times 10 = 4{,}000$$

4,000 adults under 65 visit the park in 10 days.

Children in 100 Days

The number of zeros in the product is the total number of zeros in both factors.

$$800 \times 100 = 80{,}000$$

2 zeros   2 zeros   4 zeros

80,000 children visit the park in 100 days.

Adults 65 and over in 200 Days

If the product of a basic fact ends in zero, include that zero in the count.

$$5 \times 2 = 10$$
$$50 \times 200 = 10{,}000$$

10,000 adults 65 and over visit the park in 200 days.

Problem Solving

For **35** and **36**, use the table at the right.

35. What is the total distance traveled in one triathalon?

36. Susan has completed 10 triathalons. How far did she bicycle in the races?

Data

Parts of an Olympic-Distance Triathalon

Swimming	1,500 meters
Running	10,000 meters
Bicycling	40,000 meters

37. Writing to Explain Explain why the product of 50 and 800 has four zeros when 50 has one zero and 800 has two zeros.

38. Esther had 5 coins and two dollar bills to buy a snack at school. She paid $1.40 for her snack. She had exactly one dollar left. How did Esther pay for her snack?

39. For every 30 minutes of television air time, about 8 of the minutes are given to TV commercials. If 90 minutes of television is aired, how many minutes of commercials will be played?

   A 8 minutes   **C** 38 minutes

   B 24 minutes   **D** 128 minutes

40. If in one year a city recorded a total of 97 rainy days, how many of the days did it **NOT** rain?

365 days in one year

97	?

Lesson 6-2

Estimating Products

What are some ways to estimate?

NS 1.4 Decide when a rounded solution is called for and explain why such a solution may be appropriate.

In 1991, NASA launched the Upper Atmosphere Research Satellite (UARS). It orbits Earth about 105 times each week. There are 52 weeks in one year.

About how many orbits does it make in one year?

Orbits Earth about 105 times each week

Guided Practice*

Do you know HOW?

In **1** and **2**, use rounding to estimate each product.

1. 203×37 **2.** 177×14

In **3** and **4**, use compatible numbers to estimate each product.

3. 24×37 **4.** 15×27

Do you UNDERSTAND?

5. Writing to Explain In the example above, why are the estimates not the same?

6. About how many times does UARS orbit Earth in 3 weeks?

Independent Practice

For **7** through **30**, use rounding or compatible numbers to estimate each product.

 TIP *You can round just one number or round both to make compatible numbers.*

7. 32×83	**8.** 64×85	**9.** 31×46	**10.** 63×61
11. 42×703	**12.** 51×23	**13.** 27×41	**14.** 61×202
15. 62×20	**16.** 18×74	**17.** 12×89	**18.** 22×27
19. 79×43	**20.** 26×43	**21.** 346×18	**22.** 6×153
23. 602×43	**24.** 210×19	**25.** 79×79	**26.** 96×37
27. 840×49	**28.** 17×78	**29.** 35×45	**30.** 8×55

For another example, see Set B on page 154.

One Way

Use **rounding** to estimate the number of orbits in one year.

52 × 105

Round 105 to 100.

52 × 100 = 5,200

UARS orbits Earth about 5,200 times each year.

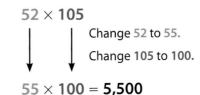

Another Way

Use **compatible numbers** to estimate the number of orbits in one year.

Compatible numbers are easy to multiply.

52 × 105

Change 52 to 55.

Change 105 to 100.

55 × 100 = 5,500

UARS orbits Earth about 5,500 times each year.

Problem Solving

31. A long-haul truck driver made 37 trips last year. If her average trip was 1,525 miles, about how far did she drive in all?

32. In one mission, an American astronaut spent more than 236 hours in space. About how many minutes did he spend in space?

 There are 60 minutes in 1 hour.

33. Estimate to decide which has a greater product, 39 × 21 or 32 × 32. Explain.

34. The Mars Orbiter circles the planet Mars every 25 hours. About how many hours does it take to make 125 orbits?

35. Use the diagram below. In 1858, two ships connected a telegraph cable across the Atlantic Ocean for the first time. One ship laid out 1,016 miles of cable. The other ship laid out 1,010 miles of cable. Estimate the total distance of cable used.

36. **Think About the Process** About 57 baseballs are used in a professional baseball game. What is the best way to estimate how many baseballs are used in a season of 162 games?

  A 6 × 100   **C** 60 × 1,000

  B 60 × 160   **D** 200 × 200

1,010 miles   1,016 miles

NS 3.2 ⊶ Demonstrate an understanding of, and the ability to use, standard algorithms for multiplying a multidigit number by a two-digit number and for dividing a multidigit number by a one-digit number; use relationships between them to simplify computations and to check results. Also NS 3.0 ⊶ .

Arrays and an Expanded Algorithm

Hands-On
grid paper

How can you multiply using an array?

There are 13 bobble-head dogs in each row of the carnival booth. There are 24 equal rows. How many dogs are there?

Choose an Operation
Multiply to join equal groups.

13 dogs per row

Another Example   **What is another way to show the partial products?**

There are 37 rows with 26 seats set up at the ring at the dog show. How many seats are there?

Estimate $40 \times 25 = 1,000$

Step 1   Draw a table. Separate each factor into tens and ones. $(30 + 7) \times (20 + 6)$

	30	7
20		
6		

Step 2   Multiply to find the partial products.

	30	7
20	600	140
6	180	42

Step 3   Add the partial products to find the total.

$$
\begin{array}{r}
42 \\
180 \\
140 \\
+\ 600 \\
\hline
962
\end{array}
$$

$26 \times 37 = 962$
There are 962 seats at the dog show ring.

Explain It

1. How is breaking apart the problem 37×26 like solving four simpler problems?

2. **Reasonableness** Explain why the answer 962 is reasonable.

Find 24 × 13.

Draw an array for 24 × 13.

Add each part of the array to find the product.

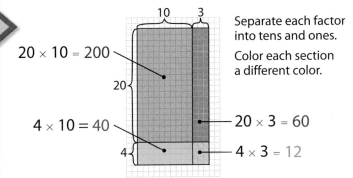

Separate each factor into tens and ones.

Color each section a different color.

$20 \times 10 = 200$

$4 \times 10 = 40$

$20 \times 3 = 60$

$4 \times 3 = 12$

Find the number of squares in each rectangle.

$$
\begin{array}{r}
12 \\
40 \\
60 \\
+ \ 200 \\
\hline
312
\end{array}
$$

partial products

In the booth, there are 312 bobble-head dogs.

Guided Practice*

Do you know HOW?

In **1** and **2**, copy and complete the calculation by finding the partial products.

1.
$$
\begin{array}{r}
13 \\
\times \ 17 \\
\hline
\end{array}
$$

2. 24 × 16

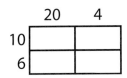

Do you UNDERSTAND?

3. In the example at the top, what four simpler multiplication problems were used to find 24 × 13?

4. At the dog show, the first 2 rows are reserved. How many people can sit in the remaining 35 rows?

Tip *There are 26 seats per row.*

Independent Practice

Leveled Practice Use grid paper to draw a rectangle. Then copy and complete the calculations.

Tip *You can solve the simpler problems in any order.*

5.
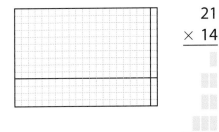
$$
\begin{array}{r}
21 \\
\times \ 14 \\
\hline
\end{array}
$$

6.
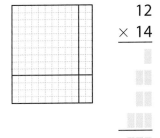
$$
\begin{array}{r}
12 \\
\times \ 14 \\
\hline
\end{array}
$$

eTools
www.pearsonsuccessnet.com
DIGITAL

Leveled Practice For **7** and **8**, use grid paper to draw a rectangle. Then copy and complete the calculations.

7.
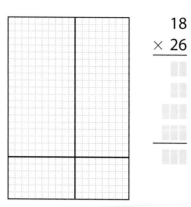
$$\begin{array}{r} 18 \\ \times\ 26 \\ \hline \end{array}$$

8.
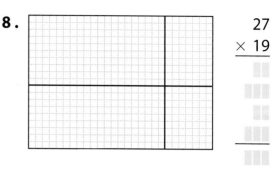
$$\begin{array}{r} 27 \\ \times\ 19 \\ \hline \end{array}$$

In **9** through **16**, copy and find the partial products. Then find the total.

9. 25×18

	20	5
10		
8		

10. 28×12

	20	8
10		
2		

11. 68×17

	60	8
10		
7		

12.
$$\begin{array}{r} 16 \\ \times\ 11 \\ \hline \end{array}$$

13.
$$\begin{array}{r} 21 \\ \times\ 31 \\ \hline \end{array}$$

14.
$$\begin{array}{r} 38 \\ \times\ 12 \\ \hline \end{array}$$

15.
$$\begin{array}{r} 29 \\ \times\ 17 \\ \hline \end{array}$$

16.
$$\begin{array}{r} 43 \\ \times\ 19 \\ \hline \end{array}$$

In **17** through **31**, find the products. Use partial products to help. Estimate to check for reasonableness.

17.
$$\begin{array}{r} 31 \\ \times\ 13 \\ \hline \end{array}$$

18.
$$\begin{array}{r} 21 \\ \times\ 33 \\ \hline \end{array}$$

19.
$$\begin{array}{r} 27 \\ \times\ 16 \\ \hline \end{array}$$

20.
$$\begin{array}{r} 59 \\ \times\ 41 \\ \hline \end{array}$$

21.
$$\begin{array}{r} 18 \\ \times\ 23 \\ \hline \end{array}$$

22.
$$\begin{array}{r} 28 \\ \times\ 29 \\ \hline \end{array}$$

23.
$$\begin{array}{r} 24 \\ \times\ 36 \\ \hline \end{array}$$

24.
$$\begin{array}{r} 43 \\ \times\ 39 \\ \hline \end{array}$$

25.
$$\begin{array}{r} 76 \\ \times\ 54 \\ \hline \end{array}$$

26.
$$\begin{array}{r} 88 \\ \times\ 22 \\ \hline \end{array}$$

27.
$$\begin{array}{r} 41 \\ \times\ 12 \\ \hline \end{array}$$

28.
$$\begin{array}{r} 38 \\ \times\ 27 \\ \hline \end{array}$$

29.
$$\begin{array}{r} 58 \\ \times\ 19 \\ \hline \end{array}$$

30.
$$\begin{array}{r} 29 \\ \times\ 15 \\ \hline \end{array}$$

31.
$$\begin{array}{r} 73 \\ \times\ 47 \\ \hline \end{array}$$

32. Writing to Explain Why is the product of 15 × 32 equal to the sum of 10 × 32 and 5 × 32?

33. The flagpole in front of City Hall in Luis's town is 35 feet tall. How many inches tall is the flagpole?

34. The prices at Nolan's Novelties store are shown at the right. If 27 boxes of neon keychains and 35 boxes of glow-in-the-dark pens were purchased, what is the total cost?

Item	Price per box
Neon Key-chains	$15
Glow-in-the-dark pens	$10

Data

35. The Hollywood Bowl can seat almost 18,000 people. Section G2 has 22 rows of benches which can seat 18 people. How many seats are in this section?

36. Algebra Elijah has *n* customers in his lawn-mowing business. He mows each lawn once a week. Which expression shows how many lawns he mows in 12 weeks?

A *n* + 12

C 12 − *n*

B *n* × 12

D 12 ÷ *n*

For **37** and **38**, use the diagram to the right.

37. Maggie is making a balloon game for the school fair. Kids will throw darts to try to pop the balloons. How many balloons are needed to set up the game?

38. Think About the Process Maggie knows that she will have to completely refill the balloon board about 15 times a day. Which expression shows how to find the number of balloons she will need?

A 15 × 13

C 15 × (13 × 14)

B 15 × 14

D 15 × (13 + 14)

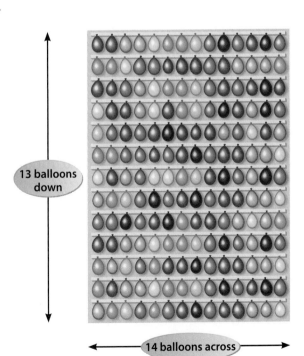

13 balloons down

14 balloons across

NS 3.2 ⚷ Demonstrate an understanding of, and the ability to use, standard algorithms for multiplying a multidigit number by a two-digit number and for dividing a multidigit number by a one-digit number; use relationships between them to simplify computations and to check results. Also NS 3.0 ⚷ .

Multiplying 2-Digit Numbers by Multiples of Ten

How can you find the product?

Mr. Jeffrey buys 20 rock identification kits for his science classes. If each kit has 28 rocks, how many rocks are there in all?

Choose an Operation

Multiply to find the number of rocks.

28 rocks per kit

Guided Practice*

Do you know HOW?

In **1** through **6**, multiply to find each product.

1.
$$
\begin{array}{r}
12 \\
\times\ 20 \\
\hline
0
\end{array}
$$

2.
$$
\begin{array}{r}
21 \\
\times\ 30 \\
\hline
0
\end{array}
$$

3. 35×20

4. 63×20

5. 27×60

6. 66×40

Do you UNDERSTAND?

7. Writing to Explain Why is there a zero in the ones place when you multiply by 20 in the example above?

8. What simpler multiplication problem can you solve to find 38×70?

9. Each year, Mr. Jeffrey's school orders 100 rock kits. How many rocks are in all of the kits?

Independent Practice

Leveled Practice In **10** through **30**, multiply to find each product.

10.
$$
\begin{array}{r}
12 \\
\times\ 30 \\
\hline
0
\end{array}
$$

11.
$$
\begin{array}{r}
24 \\
\times\ 10 \\
\hline
0
\end{array}
$$

12.
$$
\begin{array}{r}
33 \\
\times\ 20 \\
\hline
0
\end{array}
$$

13.
$$
\begin{array}{r}
71 \\
\times\ 30 \\
\hline
,0
\end{array}
$$

14.
$$
\begin{array}{r}
63 \\
\times\ 40 \\
\hline
,0
\end{array}
$$

15. 18×10

16. 20×51

17. 32×30

18. 40×22

19. 24×40

20. 34×50

21. 40×73

22. 88×30

23. 75×40

24. 22×60

25. 13×50

26. 60×23

27. 32×20

28. 82×80

29. 62×60

30. 52×50

*For another example, see Set D on page 155 .

One Way

Find 20 × 28.

Break 28 into tens and ones: 28 = 20 + 8.

Use a grid to find the partial products.

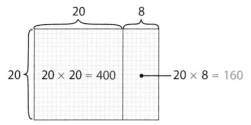

20 × 20 = 400   20 × 8 = 160

Add the partial products to find the total.
400 + 160 = 560

Another Way

Find 20 × 28.

Multiply 2 tens × 28.

$$\begin{array}{r} 1 \\ 28 \\ \times\ 20 \\ \hline 560 \end{array}$$

Record a 0 in the ones place of the answer. This shows how many tens are in the answer.

There are 560 rocks in all.

Problem Solving

31. Number Sense Rex's class raised frogs from tadpoles. The class has 21 students, and each raised 6 tadpoles. All but 6 of the tadpoles grew to be frogs. Write a number sentence to show how many frogs the class has.

32. How many fossil kits with 12 samples each have the same number of fossils as 30 fossil kits with 8 samples each?

A   20 fossil kits   C   200 fossil kits

B   24 fossil kits   D   240 fossil kits

33. A ride on the Pike's Peak Cog Railway takes 75 minutes. If the train's average speed is 100 feet per minute how long is the Pike's Peak Cog Railway?

34. In the United States, students spend about 900 hours per year in school. How many hours would a student spend in 12 years of school?

35. A roller coaster runs rides 50 times an hour and reaches speeds of 70 miles per hour. If each ride takes 8 rows of 4 people, how many people ride each hour?

A   160 people

B   1,500 people

C   1,600 people

D   2,240 people

8 rows of 4 people

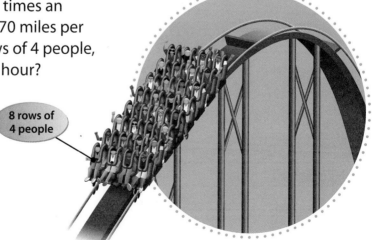

Multiplying 2-Digit by 2-Digit Numbers

What is a common way to record multiplication?

A ferry carried an average of 37 cars per trip on Saturday. If the ferry made 24 one-way trips, how many cars did it carry?

Choose an Operation Multiply to join equal groups.

NS 3.2 Demonstrate an understanding of, and the ability to use, standard algorithms for multiplying a multidigit number by a two-digit number and for dividing a multidigit number by a one-digit number; use relationships between them to simplify computations and to check results. Also NS 3.0 .

37 cars per trip

Guided Practice*

Do you know HOW?

In **1** through **6**, draw a diagram and fill it in with partial products. Then find the product.

1.   41
     × 23

2.   63
     × 31

3.   12
     × 27

4.   23
     × 36

5.   42
     × 18

6.   92
     × 34

Do you UNDERSTAND?

7. In the example above, is 888 a reasonable answer for 37 × 24?

8. Writing to Explain The ferry made 36 one-way trips on Sunday and carried an average of 21 cars on each trip.

   a How many cars were ferried on Sunday?

   b On which day were more cars ferried, Saturday or Sunday? Explain.

Independent Practice

Leveled Practice For **9** and **10**, copy each diagram and show the calculations for each partial product. Then find the product.

9. 18 × 33

	30	3
10	30 × 10 = 300	
8		3 × 8 = 24

10. 22 × 46

	40	6
20		
2		

For another example, see Set E on page 155.

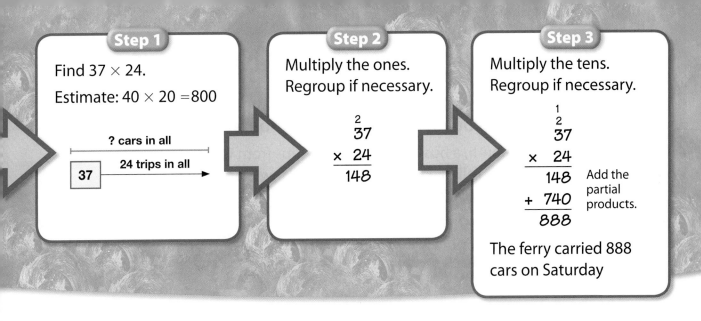

Step 1

Find 37 × 24.

Estimate: 40 × 20 = 800

? cars in all

| 37 | 24 trips in all → |

Step 2

Multiply the ones.
Regroup if necessary.

$$\begin{array}{r} \overset{2}{37} \\ \times\ 24 \\ \hline 148 \end{array}$$

Step 3

Multiply the tens.
Regroup if necessary.

$$\begin{array}{r} \overset{1}{\overset{2}{37}} \\ \times\ 24 \\ \hline 148 \\ +\ 740 \\ \hline 888 \end{array}$$

Add the partial products.

The ferry carried 888 cars on Saturday

In **11** through **20**, find the product.

11. $\begin{array}{r} 37 \\ \times\ 21 \\ \hline \end{array}$

12. $\begin{array}{r} 54 \\ \times\ 37 \\ \hline \end{array}$

13. $\begin{array}{r} 63 \\ \times\ 22 \\ \hline \end{array}$

14. $\begin{array}{r} 34 \\ \times\ 41 \\ \hline \end{array}$

15. $\begin{array}{r} 81 \\ \times\ 17 \\ \hline \end{array}$

16. 56 × 31   **17.** 53 × 17   **18.** 81 × 46   **19.** 15 × 16   **20.** 17 × 21

Problem Solving

21. Algebra Evaluate the expression $7 \times (15 + m)$ when $m = 31$.

A 136   C 322

B 232   D 682

22. Reasonableness Sara estimated 32 × 45 by using 30 × 40. How could Sara make a more accurate estimate?

23. Use the diagram to the right. The Queen Mary II's height above the water is the same as a 23-story building. If a single story is 11 feet tall, how high above the water is the Queen Mary II?

Each story is 11 feet tall.

23-story building   Queen Mary II

24. Mr. Morris bought sketch pads for 24 of his students. Each pad contained 50 sheets. How many sheets of paper were there altogether?

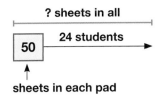

? sheets in all

| 50 | 24 students → |

sheets in each pad

25. Geometry Jon's backyard is a rectangle that measures 32 feet by 44 feet. How many square feet will the garden be?

Tip *The area of a rectangle is length × width.*

NS 3.2 🔑
Demonstrate an understanding of, and the ability to use, standard algorithms for multiplying a multidigit number by a two-digit number and for dividing a multidigit number by a one-digit number; use relationships between them to simplify computations and to check results. Also, NS 3.3 🔑, NS 3.0.

Multiplying Greater Numbers by 2-Digit Numbers

How do you multiply greater numbers?

Each month, a bus driver makes 22 trips from Woodbury to Carson Falls. Each trip is 132 miles. How many miles does the bus driver travel each month?

Choose an Operation Multiply to find the number of miles traveled monthly.

Woodbury

Each trip is 132 miles

Carson Falls

Other Examples

4-Digit by 2-Digit without regrouping

Find $3,232 \times 13$.
Estimate: $3,200 \times 10 = 32,000$

$$
\begin{array}{r}
3,232 \\
\times \quad 13 \\
\hline
9,696 \\
+ \ 32,320 \\
\hline
42,016
\end{array}
$$

4-Digit by 2-Digit with regrouping

Find $2,068 \times 74$.
Estimate: $2,000 \times 70 = 140,000$

$$
\begin{array}{r}
\overset{4\,5}{} \\
\overset{2\,3}{2,068} \\
\times \quad 74 \\
\hline
8,272 \\
144,760 \\
\hline
153,032
\end{array}
$$

Guided Practice*

Do you know HOW?

In **1** through **4**, multiply to find the product.

1. $\begin{array}{r} 134 \\ \times \ \ 12 \\ \hline \end{array}$

2. $\begin{array}{r} 219 \\ \times \ \ 13 \\ \hline \end{array}$

3. $\begin{array}{r} 4,000 \\ \times \quad 25 \\ \hline \end{array}$

4. $\begin{array}{r} 7,302 \\ \times \quad 49 \\ \hline \end{array}$

Do you UNDERSTAND?

5. Writing to Explain In the example at the top, the second partial product has a zero in the ones place. Explain why.

6. Suppose, a bus driver made 25 round trips from Woodbury to Carson Falls. How many miles were travelled in all?

Find 22 × 132.

Estimate: 20 × 100 = 2,000.

Multiply the ones.

$$\begin{array}{r} 132 \\ \times\ \ 22 \\ \hline 264 \end{array}$$

Multiply the tens.

$$\begin{array}{r} 132 \\ \times\ \ 22 \\ \hline 264 \\ 2,640 \end{array}$$

Add the partial products.

$$\begin{array}{r} 132 \\ \times\ \ 22 \\ \hline 264 \\ +\ 2,640 \\ \hline 2,904 \end{array}$$

The bus driver travels 2,904 miles each month

Independent Practice

Leveled Practice For **7** through **16**, find the partial products and the product.

7.
$$\begin{array}{r} 235 \\ \times\ \ 26 \end{array}$$

8.
$$\begin{array}{r} 306 \\ \times\ \ 19 \end{array}$$

9.
$$\begin{array}{r} 324 \\ \times\ \ 54 \end{array}$$

10.
$$\begin{array}{r} 2,619 \\ \times\ \ 27 \end{array}$$

11.
$$\begin{array}{r} 1,250 \\ \times\ \ 41 \end{array}$$

12.
$$\begin{array}{r} 425 \\ \times\ \ 71 \end{array}$$

13.
$$\begin{array}{r} 713 \\ \times\ \ 56 \end{array}$$

14.
$$\begin{array}{r} 1,567 \\ \times\ \ 13 \end{array}$$

15.
$$\begin{array}{r} 2,175 \\ \times\ \ 15 \end{array}$$

16.
$$\begin{array}{r} 7,956 \\ \times\ \ 36 \end{array}$$

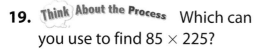

Problem Solving

For **17** and **18**, use the table at the right.

17. In 2004, how many DVDs were rented in 52 weeks?

18. How many more DVDs were purchased in 2005 than in 2004?

DVDs Rented and Purchased (Weekly Average)

Year	Rented	Purchased
2004	114	827
2005	126	1,015

19. **Think About the Process** Which can you use to find 85 × 225?

  A (80 × 225) + (5 × 225)

  B (85 × 225) + (85 × 1)

  C (80 × 200) + (80 × 25)

  D (80 × 220) + (5 × 220)

20. **Estimation** Bill played three dart games. His scores were 302, 186, and 297. What is the estimate of his total score for the three games?

MR 2.2 Apply strategies
and results from simpler
problems to more
complex problems.
Also MR 2.0,
NS 3.0.

Problem Solving

Two-Question Problems

Problem 1: Maya and Jose are preparing for a bike race. On Wednesday, they rode their bicycles 32 miles in the morning and 22 miles in the afternoon. How many miles did they ride in all?

Problem 2: Maya and Jose bicycled the same number of miles on Wednesday, Thursday, Friday, and Saturday. How far did they ride during the week?

Rode the same
distance 4 days
in a row

Guided Practice*

Do you know HOW?

Solve.

1. **Problem 1:** Julia used 3 rolls of film to take pictures on her vacation. There were 24 pictures on each roll. How many pictures did Julia take?

   Problem 2: It costs Julia 10¢ to print each picture. How much would it cost Julia to print every picture?

Do you UNDERSTAND?

2. Why do you need to know how many pictures Julia took to solve Problem 2?

3. **Write a Problem** Write a problem that uses the answer from Problem 1 below.

   Problem 1: Cal puts one vase on each of 5 tables. There are 6 flowers in each vase. How many flowers does Cal use?

Independent Practice

Solve. Use the answer from Problem 1 to solve Problem 2.

4. **Problem 1:** Martin buys a sandwich for $4, an apple for $1, and a drink for $2. How much did he pay altogether?

   ? Cost of Martin's lunch

$4	$1	$2

   Problem 2: How much change did Martin receive if he paid with a $20 bill?

   $20

Lunch	Change

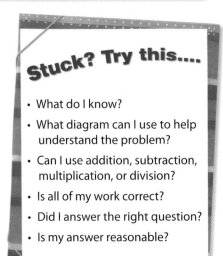

Stuck? Try this....

- What do I know?
- What diagram can I use to help understand the problem?
- Can I use addition, subtraction, multiplication, or division?
- Is all of my work correct?
- Did I answer the right question?
- Is my answer reasonable?

Sometimes you have to answer one problem to solve another problem.

? miles bicycled on Wednesday

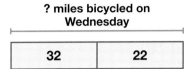

32	22

32 miles + 22 miles = 54 miles

Maya and Jose bicycled 54 miles on Wednesday.

Use the answer from Problem 1 to solve Problem 2.

? miles bicycled during the week

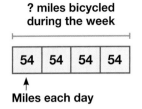

54	54	54	54

↑ Miles each day

4 × 54 miles = 216 miles

Maya and Jose rode 216 miles during the week.

---

5. Problem 1: Sally and Byron mow their neighbors' lawns in the summer. Sally mows 5 lawns each week. Byron mows three times as many lawns as Sally. How many lawns does Byron mow each week?

? Lawns mowed each week

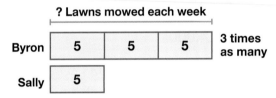

| Byron | 5 | 5 | 5 | 3 times as many |
| Sally | 5 | | | |

Problem 2: Byron gets paid $20 for each lawn he mows. How much does Byron get paid each week?

Amount Byron gets paid each week

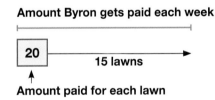

20 → 15 lawns

↑ Amount paid for each lawn

6. Problem 1: June's mom brought 3 bags of popcorn and 3 bottles of water to the park. How many bags of popcorn and bottles of water did June's mom take to the park?

? bags and bottles in all

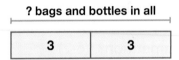

3	3

Problem 2: Each bag of popcorn that June's mom brought to the park contained 16 servings. How many servings of popcorn did June's mom bring to the park?

? servings in all

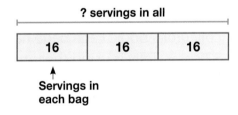

16	16	16

↑ Servings in each bag

---

7. Problem 1: Sydney made wooden penguins to sell at a fair. She used 5 pompoms and 4 beads for each penguin. How many pompoms and beads are there all together on each wooden penguin?

Problem 2: Sydney made 21 wooden penguins. How many pompoms and beads did she use for the wooden penguins altogether?

8. Problem 1: Dave's family plans to retile their porch floor. The measurements are 8 feet long by 6 feet wide. What is the area they plan to retile?

Problem 2: Each tile they plan to use is one square foot. Each tile costs 2 dollars. How much money will it cost to retile their porch floor?

1. Mr. Taylor installed 10 dozen ceramic tiles on his kitchen floor. Each tile costs $3. How many tiles did Mr. Taylor buy? How much did Mr. Taylor spend, before tax? (6-7)

   A 120 tiles; $360

   B 120 tiles; $390

   C 100 tiles; $300

   D 36 tiles; $108

2. Twenty-seven schools are participating in the regional band competition. Each school brought 38 band members. Which shows the best way to estimate how many band members are in the competition? (6-2)

   A 20×30

   B 20×40

   C 25×40

   D 30×30

3. Telly has 15 pages in her coin collector's book. Each page has 32 coins. Telly is using the table below to calculate how many coins she has in her book. Which number is missing from the table? (6-3)

   A 15

   B 150

   C 315

   D 480

	10	5
30	300	?
2	20	10

4. Which partial products can be used to find 35×64? (6-5)

   A 140 and 210

   B 140 and 2,100

   C 120 and 2,100

   D 140 and 1,800

5. There are 16 ounces in a pound. A grizzly bear at the city zoo weighs 723 pounds. Which is the best estimate of the number of ounces the grizzly bear weighs? (6-2)

   A 1,400

   B 7,000

   C 12,000

   D 14,000

6. The bank ordered 24 cases of computer paper. Each case had 10 reams. How many reams of computer paper did the bank order? (6-4)

   A 240

   B 250

   C 2,400

   D 2,500

7. To find 30×700, Scott first found $3 \times 7 = 21$. How many zeros should Scott include in the product? (6-1)

   A 1

   B 2

   C 3

   D 4

8. The school district bought 95 new 4th grade math books. Each book cost $52. How much did the district spend? (6-5)

A $4,945

B $4,930

C $4,240

D $655

9. What is $18 \times 1,642$? (6-6)

A 14,778

B 19,178

C 26,846

D 29,556

10. Which pair of numbers best completes the number sentence? (6-1)

 $ \times 1,000 = $

A 300 and 3,000

B 30 and 300,000

C 30 and 30,000

D 30 and 3,000

11. An amusement park sold 538 admission tickets. If the price of each ticket was $24, how much money did the park make from the sales? (6-6)

A $12,914

B $12,912

C $12,812

D $3,228

12. What is 15×29? (6-3)

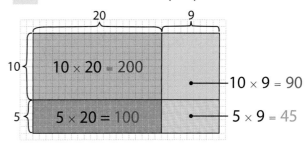

A 535

B 435

C 390

D 335

13. If 82 seats on a flight were sold for $189 each, about how much money did the airline make? (6-2)

A $16,000

B $18,000

C $19,000

D $20,000

14. Which shows one way to use partial products to find 60×78? (6-4)

A $(30 \times 70) + (30 \times 8)$

B $(60 \times 70) + (60 \times 80)$

C $(60 \times 70) + (60 \times 78)$

D $(60 \times 70) + (60 \times 8)$

15. Ray swims 40 laps each time he goes to the pool. He went 20 times this month. How many laps did he swim? (6-1)

A 8

B 80

C 800

D 8,000

Set A, pages 136–137

Use mental math to find 26 × 300.

You can think about the pattern.

26 × 3 = 78

26 × 30 =780

26 × 300 = 7,800

Remember that when a product of a basic fact ends in zero, there is one more zero in the answer.

1. 4 × 10   **2.** 7 × 1,000

3. 80 × 600   **4.** 50 × 4,000

5. 3 × 900   **6.** 600 × 10

Set B, pages 138–139

Use multiplication to estimate 16 × 24.

Round 24 to 20.

Round 16 to 20.

20 × 20 = 400

Remember you can also use compatible numbers to estimate.

1. 41 × 54   **2.** 79 × 32

3. 64 × 86   **4.** 32 × 71

5. 26 × 626   **6.** 53 × 200

Set C, pages 140–143

Find 14 × 12.

Draw a 14 × 12 array. Separate each factor into tens and ones. Color each section a different color. Add each part to find the product

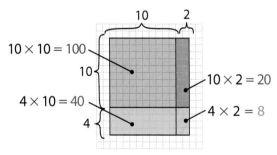

Remember you can solve the simpler problems in any order and the answer will remain the same.

Find the product. Use partial products to help.

1. 14 × 32   **2.** 64 × 12

3. 56 × 17   **4.** 72 × 15

5. 26 × 63   **6.** 47 × 27

7. 31 × 26   **8.** 43 × 19

9. 24 × 56   **10.** 68 × 22

Set D, pages 144–145

Find 16 × 30.

$$\begin{array}{r} \overset{1}{16} \\ \times\ 30 \\ \hline 480 \end{array}$$

Multiply 16 × 3 tens.

The 0 in the ones places shows how many tens are in the answer.

Remember to record a 0 in the ones place of the answer.

1. 39 × 10   **2.** 56 × 30

3. 41 × 20   **4.** 60 × 13

Set E, pages 146–149

Find 19 × 17.

Multiply the ones. Regroup if necessary.

$$\begin{array}{r} \overset{3}{19} \\ \times\ 14 \\ \hline 76 \end{array}$$

Multiply the tens. Regroup if necessary.

$$\begin{array}{r} 19 \\ \times\ 14 \\ \hline 76 \\ +\ 190 \\ \hline 266 \end{array}$$

Remember to regroup if necessary.

1. $\begin{array}{r} 53 \\ \times\ 36 \\ \hline \end{array}$ **2.** $\begin{array}{r} 23 \\ \times\ 18 \\ \hline \end{array}$

3. 56 × 64   **4.** 39 × 82

5. 2,912 × 82   **6.** 23 × 1,321

Set F, pages 150–151

When you solve two question problems, solve the first problem, and use that answer to help you solve the second problem.

Problem 1: It costs $3 for a ticket to the pool and $7 for a ticket to the water park. How much does it cost for 4 people to go to each?

Cost of 4 pool tickets:
4 × $3 = $12

Cost of 4 water park tickets:
4 × $7 = $28

Problem 2: How much more does it cost the group of 4 to go to the water park than to the pool?

28 − 12 = 16

It costs $16 more.

Remember to use the information from Problem 1 to answer Problem 2.

Solve.

1. Problem 1: Rose visited 14 cities on her vacation. She bought 3 souvenirs in each city to send to her friends. How many souvenirs did Rose buy on her vacation?

Problem 2: It costs Rose $2 to send each souvenir to her friends. How much did it cost Rose to send all of the souvenirs that she bought on vacation?

Dividing by 1-Digit Divisors

1

An ultralight plane tracks the trek of monarch butterflies from Canada, throught the United States, and into Mexico. About how many miles do the butterflies travel each day? You will find out in Lesson 7-3.

2

How many solar cells does it take to power a solar car? You will find out in Lesson 7–1.

Review What You Know!

Vocabulary

Choose the best term from the box.

- dividend
- divisor
- remainder
- quotient

1. In the number sentence 42 ÷ 6 = 7, 42 is the ?.

2. A ? is the answer to a division problem.

3. The number by which another number is divided is the ?.

Division Facts

Divide.

4. 15 ÷ 3 **5.** 64 ÷ 8 **6.** 24 ÷ 6

7. 72 ÷ 8 **8.** 35 ÷ 7 **9.** 12 ÷ 4

10. 36 ÷ 6 **11.** 14 ÷ 2 **12.** 45 ÷ 9

The California State Capitol is visited by over one million people every year. How many tours of the Capitol are run in one week? You will find out in Lesson 7-4.

Fact Families

Complete each fact family.

13. 7 × ■ = 28
■ × ■ = 28
■ ÷ 4 = 7
28 ÷ ■ = ■

14. ■ × 8 = 48
■ × ■ = 48
48 ÷ 6 = ■
■ ÷ ■ = 6

Multiplication and Division Stories

15. Each train coach can hold 40 people. How many people can ride in 3 coaches?

16. Writing to Explain A tennis pro buys 50 cans of tennis balls. There are 3 balls in every can. Explain how to find how many tennis balls the tennis pro bought.

NS 3.0 ⚬——⚬ Solve problems involving addition, subtraction, multiplication, and division of whole numbers and understand the relationships among the operations.

Using Mental Math to Divide

How can you use patterns to help you divide mentally?

Mr. Díaz ordered a supply of 320 pastels. He needs to divide them equally among four art classes. How many pastels does each class get?

320 pastels in all

Choose an Operation
Division is used to make equal groups.

Guided Practice*

Do you know HOW?

In **1** and **2**, use patterns to find each quotient.

1. $28 \div 7 = \square$

$280 \div 7 = \square$

$2,800 \div 7 = \square$

$28,000 \div 7 = \square$

2. $64 \div 8 = \square$

$640 \div 8 = \square$

$6,400 \div 8 = \square$

$64,000 \div 8 = \square$

Do you UNDERSTAND?

3. How is dividing 320 by 4 like dividing 32 by 4?

4. José orders 240 binders and divides them equally among the 4 classes. How many binders will each class get? What basic fact did you use?

Independent Practice

Leveled Practice In **5** through **8**, use patterns to find each quotient.

5. $36 \div 9 = \square$

$360 \div 9 = \square$

$3,600 \div 9 = \square$

$36,000 \div 9 = \square$

6. $10 \div 2 = \square$

$100 \div 2 = \square$

$1,000 \div 2 = \square$

$10,000 \div 2 = \square$

7. $45 \div 5 = \square$

$450 \div 5 = \square$

$4,500 \div 5 = \square$

$45,000 \div 5 = \square$

8. $24 \div 8 = \square$

$240 \div 8 = \square$

$2,400 \div 8 = \square$

$24,000 \div 8 = \square$

For **9** through **23**, use mental math to divide.

9. $200 \div 5$

10. $360 \div 4$

11. $540 \div 9$

12. $160 \div 4$

13. $160 \div 2$

14. $900 \div 3$

15. $320 \div 8$

16. $360 \div 6$

17. $180 \div 3$

18. $210 \div 7$

19. $720 \div 8$

20. $500 \div 5$

21. $350 \div 7$

22. $630 \div 9$

23. $480 \div 6$

*For another example, see Set A on page 188.

Find 320 ÷ 4.

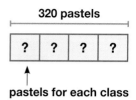
320 pastels

| ? | ? | ? | ? |

↑
pastels for each class

The basic fact is 32 ÷ 4 = 8.

32 tens ÷ 4 = 8 tens or 80.
320 ÷ 4 = 80

Each class will get 80 pastels.

Mr. Díaz wants to divide 400 erasers among 8 classes. How many erasers will each class get? Find 400 ÷ 8.

The basic fact is 40 ÷ 8.

40 tens ÷ 8 = 5 tens or 50.
400 ÷ 8 = 50

Each class will get 50 erasers.

Problem Solving

24. Number Sense Selena used a basic fact to help solve 180 ÷ 6. What basic fact did Selena use?

25. There are 52 weeks in 1 year. How many years are equivalent to 520 weeks?

26. At the North American Solar Challenge, teams use up to 1,000 solar cells to design and build solar cars for a race. If there are 810 solar cells in rows of 9, how many solar cells are in each row?

9 rows of solar cells

27. A bakery produced 37 loaves of bread an hour. How many loaves were produced in 4 hours?

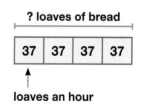
? loaves of bread

| 37 | 37 | 37 | 37 |

↑
loaves an hour

28. On Saturday afternoon, 350 people attended a play. The seating was arranged in 7 equal rows. How many people sat in each row? How do you know?

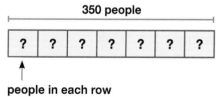
350 people

| ? | ? | ? | ? | ? | ? | ? |

↑
people in each row

29. Each row of seats in a stadium has 32 chairs. If the first 3 rows are completely filled, how many people are in the first 3 rows?

   A 9 people   **C** 96 people

   B 10 people   **D** 256 people

30. Writing to Explain If you know that 20 ÷ 5 = 4, how does that fact help you find 200 ÷ 5?

NS 1.4 ⚷ Decide when a rounded solution is called for and explain why such a solution may be appropriate.
Also MR 2.5

Estimating Quotients

When and how do you estimate quotients to solve problems?

700 rubber bands

Max wants to make 9 rubber-band balls. He bought a jar of 700 rubber bands. Estimate to find about how many rubber bands he can use for each ball.

Guided Practice*

Do you know HOW?

In **1** through **6**, estimate each quotient. Use rounding or compatible numbers.

1. 48 ÷ 5

2. 235 ÷ 8

3. 547 ÷ 6

4. 192 ÷ 5

5. 662 ÷ 8

6. 362 ÷ 3

Do you UNDERSTAND?

7. Writing to Explain Is an estimate or an exact answer needed for the problem below?

Max bought two jars of rubber bands for $4.65 each. How much did he spend?

8. Reasonableness Max decides to use the 700 rubber bands to make 8 balls. Is it reasonable to say that each ball would contain about 90 rubber bands?

Independent Practice

Leveled Practice In **9** through **28**, estimate the quotient.

 First round to the nearest ten. Then try multiples of ten that are near the rounded number.

9. 430 ÷ 9

10. 620 ÷ 7

11. 138 ÷ 5

12. 232 ÷ 6

13. 172 ÷ 3

14. 342 ÷ 8

15. 652 ÷ 6

16. 599 ÷ 9

17. 853 ÷ 6

18. 326 ÷ 4

19. 637 ÷ 6

20. 971 ÷ 2

21. 747 ÷ 8

22. 232 ÷ 9

23. 387 ÷ 4

24. 552 ÷ 7

25. 657 ÷ 4

26. 912 ÷ 4

27. 625 ÷ 3

28. 821 ÷ 3

For another example, see Set B on page 188.

One Way

Use compatible numbers.

What number close to 700 is easily divided by 9?

Try multiples of ten near 700.

710 is not easily divided by 9.

720 is 72 tens and can be divided by 9.

720 ÷ 9 = 80

A good estimate is about 80 rubber bands for each ball.

A rounded solution is all that is needed. Max does not need to know the exact number of rubber bands to use for each ball.

Another Way

Use multiplication.

9 times what number is about 700?

**9 × 8 = 72,
so 9 × 80 = 720.**

700 ÷ 9 is about 80.

Problem Solving

Use the chart at the right for **29** and **30.**

29. Ada sold her mugs in 3 weeks. About how many did she sell each week?

30. Ben sold his mugs in 4 weeks. About how many did he sell each week?

Mugs Sold in Fundraiser
Each Mug = 50 mugs

Ada

Ben

31. Tony's truck can safely carry 3,000 pounds. He has 21 televisions that he needs to deliver. Each television weighs 95 pounds.

  a Can Tony safely carry all of the televisions in his truck?

  b Is an exact answer needed or is an estimate needed? Explain.

32. Writing to Explain Copy and complete by filling in the circle with > or <. Without dividing, explain how you know which quotient is greater.

930 ÷ 4 ◯ 762 ÷ 4

33. Lexi bought 3 boxes of envelopes. Each box has 45 envelopes. How many envelopes did she buy?

  A 15 envelopes

  B 90 envelopes

  C 135 envelopes

  D 145 envelopes

34. If you jog about 26 miles in 6 days, about how many miles do you jog each day?

  A About 20 miles

  B About 10 miles

  C About 6 miles

  D About 4 miles

NS 3.2 Demonstrate an understanding of, and the ability to use, standard algorithms for multiplying a multidigit number by a two-digit number and for dividing a multidigit number by a one-digit number; use relationships between them to simplify computations and to check results. Also **NS 1.4** .

Dividing with Remainders

Hands-On
counters

3 rows of plants

What happens when some are left?

Maria has 20 pepper plants to place in 3 rows. She has to plant the same number in each row. How many plants will go in each row? How many are left over?

Guided Practice*

Do you know HOW?

In **1** through **4**, use counters or draw pictures. Tell how many items are in each group and how many are left over.

1. 26 pens
5 groups

2. 34 cars
7 boxes

3. 30 marbles
4 bags

4. 40 balls
6 bins

Do you UNDERSTAND?

5. Writing to Explain When you divide a number by 6 what remainders are possible?

6. Tia is planting her garden with 15 plants. She wants them planted in equal groups of 4. How many groups of 4 can she make? How many plants will she have left over?

Independent Practice

Leveled Practice In **7** through **14**, copy and then complete the calculations. Use counters or pictures to help.

 The remainder should always be less than the divisor.

7. R
$8)\overline{35}$

8. R
$3)\overline{17}$

9. R
$9)\overline{51}$

10. R
$5)\overline{48}$

11. R
$6)\overline{47}$

12. R
$7)\overline{65}$

13. R
$9)\overline{77}$

14. R
$4)\overline{30}$

DIGITAL
Animated Glosssary, eTools
www.pearsonsuccessnet.com

For another example, see Set C on page 189.

Divide 20 counters among 3 rows.

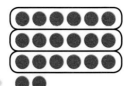

$3 \times 6 = 18$ counters

The part that is left after dividing is called the remainder.

There are 2 counters left over. This is not enough for another row, so the remainder is 2.

Check your answer.

$$\begin{array}{r} 6 \text{ R}2 \\ 3\overline{)20} \\ -18 \\ \hline 2 \end{array}$$

Divide: 3 groups of 6 in 20
Multiply: $3 \times 6 = 18$
Subtract: $20 - 18 = 2$
Compare: $2 < 3$

$3 \times 6 = 18$, and $18 + 2 = 20$

Maria can plant 6 plants in each row. She will have 2 plants left over.

In **15** through **24**, divide. You may use counters or pictures to help.

15. $3\overline{)29}$ **16.** $7\overline{)41}$ **17.** $9\overline{)55}$ **18.** $8\overline{)62}$ **19.** $5\overline{)37}$

20. $7\overline{)45}$ **21.** $4\overline{)22}$ **22.** $6\overline{)28}$ **23.** $8\overline{)33}$ **24.** $8\overline{)75}$

Problem Solving

25. In 2005, an ultra light airplane tracked Monarch butterflies migrating to Mexico. The plane followed the butterflies through Texas for 13 days. During this time, how many miles did the butterflies travel?

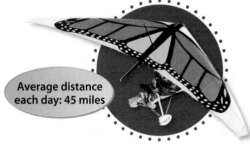

Average distance each day: 45 miles

26. Reasonableness Carl's teacher took 27 photos on their class trip. She wants to arrange them on the wall in 4 equal rows. Carl said if she does this, she will have 7 photos left over. Is this reasonable?

27. Writing to Explain Jim has 46 compact discs. He wants to buy 8 cases that hold 8 discs. Explain why Jim needs to buy 6 cases to hold his 46 compact discs.

28. Think About the Process Jack helped Mrs. Sanchez pack 61 books in 7 boxes. Each box held 8 books. Which expression shows how to find how many books he had left?

A $61 - 8$ **C** $61 - 7$

B $61 \div 8$ **D** $61 \div 7$

29. At the school concert, there were 560 people seated in 8 rows. If there were no empty seats, how many people were in each row?

A 553 people   **C** 70 people

B 480 people   **D** 60 people

Lesson

7-4

NS 3.4 Solve problems involving division of multidigit numbers by one-digit numbers.
Also **MR 2.3**

Connecting Models and Symbols

Hands-On
place-value blocks

57 student drawings

How can place-value help you divide?

Mrs. Lynch displayed 57 student drawings on 3 walls in her art classroom. If she divided the drawings equally, how many drawings are on each wall?

Estimate: 60 ÷ 3 = 20

↑
drawings on each wall

Another Example **How do you model remainders?**

Helen has 55 postcards. As an art project, she plans to glue 4 postcards onto sheets of colored paper.

How many pieces of paper can she fill?

Step 1 Divide the tens.

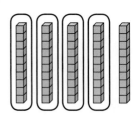

Division is used to find the number of equal groups.

$$\begin{array}{r} 1 \\ 4\overline{)55} \\ -4 \\ \hline 1 \end{array}$$

There is 1 ten in each group and 1 ten left over.

Step 2 Regroup the 1 ten as 10 ones and divide.

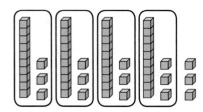

$$\begin{array}{r} 13\text{ R}3 \\ 4\overline{)55} \\ -4 \\ \hline 15 \\ -12 \\ \hline 3 \end{array}$$

Trade the extra ten for ten ones.

The 1 ten and 5 ones make 15.

There are 3 ones in each group and 3 left over.

Helen will fill 13 pieces of colored paper.

Explain It

1. In the first step above, what does the 1 in the quotient represent?

2. Reasonableness How can you check that the answer is correct?

Use place-value blocks to show 57.	Trade the extra tens for ones.	Divide the ones.

Use place-value blocks to show 57.

Divide the tens into three equal groups.

$$3\overline{)57} \quad \begin{array}{r} 1 \\ -3 \end{array} \quad \text{3 tens used}$$

Trade the extra tens for ones.

$$\begin{array}{r} 1 \\ 3\overline{)57} \\ -3 \\ \hline 27 \end{array} \quad \begin{array}{l} \text{3 tens used} \\ \text{27 ones left} \end{array}$$

Divide the ones.

$$\begin{array}{r} 19 \\ 3\overline{)57} \\ -3 \\ \hline 27 \\ -27 \\ \hline 0 \end{array} \quad \begin{array}{l} \\ \\ \text{27 ones used} \end{array}$$

There are 19 drawings on each wall.

Guided Practice*

Do you know HOW?

In **1** through **4**, use place-value blocks or draw pictures. Tell how many are in each group and how many are left over.

1. 76 magazines
5 boxes

2. 56 marbles
3 bags

3. 82 muffins
7 boxes

4. 72 photos
3 albums

Do you UNDERSTAND?

5. Describe another way to show 57 using place-value blocks.

6. Mrs. Lynch displayed 48 paintings in 3 sets. If each set had the same number of paintings, how many were in each set?

Independent Practice

Leveled Practice In **7** through **10**, use the model to complete each division sentence.

7. 71 ÷ ⬜ = ⬜ R2

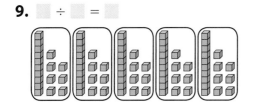

8. ⬜ ÷ 4 = ⬜

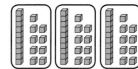

9. ⬜ ÷ ⬜ = ⬜

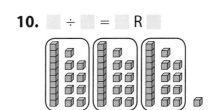

10. ⬜ ÷ ⬜ = ⬜ R ⬜

eTools
www.pearsonsuccessnet.com
DIGITAL

*For another example, see Set D on page 189.

Independent Practice

In **11** through **30**, use place-value blocks or draw pictures to solve.

11. 3)46   **12.** 8)96   **13.** 4)55   **14.** 2)51   **15.** 5)89

16. 6)76   **17.** 7)36   **18.** 3)72   **19.** 2)63   **20.** 4)92

21. 3)44   **22.** 4)67   **23.** 6)85   **24.** 3)56   **25.** 5)97

26. 2)39   **27.** 4)31   **28.** 5)87   **29.** 7)82   **30.** 5)22

Problem Solving

31. Maya used place-value blocks to divide 87. She made groups of 17 with 2 left over. Use place-value blocks or draw pictures to determine how many groups Maya made.

32. **Writing to Explain** Harold has 64 toy cars in 4 equal boxes. To find the number in each box, he divided 64 by 4. How many tens did he regroup as ones?

33. **Think About the Process** Jake walks dogs and delivers papers to earn money. This month, he earned $52 delivering papers and $43 walking dogs. Each month, he puts half of his money into the bank. Which shows how much Jake saved this month?

   A $(52 + 43) + 2$ **C** $(52 + 43) \div 2$

   B $(52 + 43) \times 2$ **D** $(52 + 43) - 2$

34. **Number Sense** Tina has 52 berries. She wants to have some each day for lunch. How many berries can she have each day if she wants to eat them in 5 days?

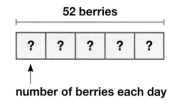

52 berries

| ? | ? | ? | ? | ? |

↑
number of berries each day

35. The 4 fourth-grade classes from Jameson Elementary School took a trip to the California State Capitol Building. Each class had 24 students. At the Capitol, the students were divided into 6 equal groups. How many students were in each group?

36. Every 4 weeks the California State Capitol runs about 224 tours. About how many tours do they run in one week?

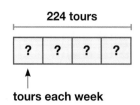

224 tours

| ? | ? | ? | ? |

↑
tours each week

Mixed Problem Solving

1. For about how many years was the California Trail in use?

2. How many years did the California Gold Rush span?

3. At the peak of the Gold Rush, how much could one miner earn in five days if he mined $2,000 of gold each day?

4. After the peak, a miner earned $6 to $10 a day. How many days would a miner have to work in order to earn $50?

5. In 1849 the population in California was about 15,000 people, and by 1850 the population had grown to about 20,000 people. What was the increase in the population?

California Gold Rush

The California Trail was a major overland emigrant route across the American West from the late 1840s until the late 1860s when railroads were introduced.

It was used by 250,000 gold-seekers.

Many of the people who traveled this route came with their possessions in a 9-foot long 4-foot wide covered wagon.

The California Gold Rush lasted from 1848 to 1859.

At the peak of the gold rush in 1849, it was not uncommon for a miner to dig $2,000 of gold a day.

Later, an average miner might earn $6 to $10 a day.

6. **Geometry** A California rancher is building a pen for his sheep. The pen is 65 feet long and 22 feet wide. How much fencing will be needed?

7. **Estimation** If a cook on a ranch trip was paid $75 a month, about how much did a cook earn in one week? One month is about four weeks.

8. During the California Gold Rush, the demand for cattle was so great that a steer worth $14 in Texas was worth $95 in California. How much more would you spend for 5 cattle in California than in Texas at that time? Show how you found your answer.

9. Tanya has a poster with pictures of cowboy hats on it. The pictures are in 4 rows with 6 hats in each row. How many hats are shown in all?

NS 3.2 ⌐
Demonstrate an
understanding of, and
ability to use standard
algorithms . . . for dividing
a multidigit number by a
one-digit number . . .
Also NS 3.4 ⌐

Dividing 2-Digit Numbers by 1-Digit Numbers

76 cans of soup in all

What is a common way to record division?

At the school food drive, Al needs to put the same number of soup cans into four boxes. How many soup cans will go in each box?

Choose an Operation Divide to find the number in each group.

Another Example **How do you divide with a remainder?**

Al collects 58 cans of vegetables. He puts the same number of cans in four boxes. How many cans of vegetables will go in each box? How many cans will be left over?

A 14 cans; 2 cans left over

B 15 cans; 2 cans left over

C 16 cans; 2 cans left over

D 18 cans; 2 cans left over

Step 1

Divide the tens.

Regroup the remaining ten as 10 ones.

$$
\begin{array}{r}
14 \\
4\overline{)58} \\
-4 \\
\hline
1
\end{array}
$$

Step 2

Divide the ones.

Subtract to find the remainder.

$$
\begin{array}{r}
14 \\
4\overline{)58} \\
-4 \\
\hline
18 \\
-16 \\
\hline
2
\end{array}
$$

Step 3

Check: $14 \times 4 = 56$ and $56 + 2 = 58$.

There will be 14 cans of vegetables in each box and 2 cans left over.

The correct choice is **A**.

Explain It

1. **Reasonableness** How can you use estimation to decide if 14 is reasonable?

2. Why is multiplication used to check division?

Step 1

Divide the tens.

$$4\overline{)76}$$
with quotient 1, -4, remainder 3

Think There is **1** ten in each group and **3** tens left over.

Step 2

Divide the ones.

$$4\overline{)76}$$
quotient 19, -4, 36, -36, 0

Think Trade the 3 tens for 30 ones.

30 ones and 6 ones make **36** ones.

There will be 19 soup cans in each box.

Step 3

Check by multiplying.

$$\begin{array}{r} \overset{3}{19} \\ \times\ 4 \\ \hline 76 \end{array}$$

The answer checks.

Guided Practice*

Do you know HOW?

In **1** and **2**, copy and complete each calculation.

1.
$$\begin{array}{r} 4\ \ \ \\ 2\overline{)94} \\ -\ \blacksquare \\ \hline 4 \\ -1\blacksquare \\ \hline 0 \end{array}$$

2.
$$\begin{array}{r} 6R\blacksquare \\ 5\overline{)82} \\ -\ 5 \\ \hline \blacksquare\blacksquare \\ -\ \blacksquare\blacksquare \\ \hline \blacksquare \end{array}$$

Do you UNDERSTAND?

3. Explain how you would estimate the answer in Exercise 2.

4. Al collects 85 cans of fruit. He puts the same number of fruit cans in 4 boxes. Will he have any cans left over? If so, how many cans?

Independent Practice

Leveled Practice In **5** through **8**, copy and complete each calculation. Estimate to check reasonableness.

5.
$$\begin{array}{r} \blacksquare\blacksquare \\ 7\overline{)84} \\ -\ 7 \\ \hline 4 \\ -\ \blacksquare\blacksquare \\ \hline 0 \end{array}$$

6.
$$\begin{array}{r} 6\ \ \\ 3\overline{)78} \\ -\ \blacksquare \\ \hline 8 \\ -1\blacksquare \\ \hline 0 \end{array}$$

7.
$$\begin{array}{r} \blacksquare R\blacksquare \\ 4\overline{)93} \\ -\ 8 \\ \hline \blacksquare\blacksquare \\ -1\blacksquare \\ \hline 1 \end{array}$$

8.
$$\begin{array}{r} 1\ R\blacksquare \\ 6\overline{)80} \\ -\ \blacksquare \\ \hline \blacksquare\blacksquare \\ -\ \blacksquare\blacksquare \\ \hline \blacksquare \end{array}$$

For **9** through **18**, find each quotient. Use multiplication to check.

9. $3\overline{)63}$ **10.** $7\overline{)88}$ **11.** $6\overline{)96}$ **12.** $4\overline{)52}$ **13.** $5\overline{)73}$

14. $5\overline{)93}$ **15.** $3\overline{)87}$ **16.** $4\overline{)72}$ **17.** $6\overline{)77}$ **18.** $2\overline{)37}$

In **19** through **28**, find each quotient. Use multiplication to check.

19. $3\overline{)46}$ **20.** $7\overline{)65}$ **21.** $8\overline{)27}$ **22.** $9\overline{)86}$ **23.** $4\overline{)66}$

24. $8\overline{)59}$ **25.** $4\overline{)92}$ **26.** $3\overline{)74}$ **27.** $5\overline{)68}$ **28.** $2\overline{)89}$

Problem Solving

29. Some of the tallest selenite crystals in a cave in Chihuahua, Mexico, are 50 feet tall. About how many times taller are the tallest crystals than a 4-foot-tall fourth grader?

30. **Geometry** Zelda has a piece of fabric that is 7 feet long and 4 feet wide. She wants to divide it into 2 equal pieces. What is the area of each piece?

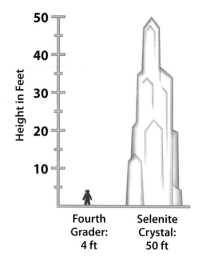

Use the recipe at the right for **31** and **32**.

31. How many ounces of Tasty Trail Mix are made following the recipe?

32. Maggie is making trail mix. She makes 4 batches of the recipe shown. Then she divides it into 3 equal sized bags. How many ounces are in each bag?

Tasty Trail Mix	
granola	8 oz
nuts	5 oz
raisins	2 oz
cranberries	3 oz

33. **Writing to Explain** Why does $51 \div 4$ have two digits in the quotient, while $51 \div 6$ has only one digit in the quotient?

34. **Write a Problem** Write a problem that could be solved by dividing 78 by 5.

35. **Estimation** Paulo has 78 cattle on his ranch. He needs to divide them equally among 3 pastures. Which shows the best way to estimate the number of cattle in each pasture?

  A $60 \div 3$ **C** $75 \div 3$

  B $66 \div 3$ **D** $90 \div 3$

36. Every year the city of San Marcos holds a Cinco de Mayo festival. If 60 students perform in 5 groups, how many students are in each group?

  A 10 students   **C** 25 students

  B 12 students   **D** 55 students

Algebra Connections

Simplifying Number Expressions

In order to simplify a number expression, you must follow the order of operations.

First, complete the operations inside the parentheses.

Then, multiply and divide in order from left to right.

Then, add and subtract in order from left to right.

> **Example:** $(5 + 3) \times 4$
>
> **Think** *Start with the operation inside the parentheses. What is 5 + 3?*
>
> $5 + 3 = 8$.
>
> *Then, multiply 8 × 4.*
>
> $8 \times 4 = 32$
>
> So, $(5 + 3) \times 4 = 32$

Simplify. Follow the order of operations.

1. $4 \times 8 - 6$
2. $12 + 8 \div 4$
3. $5 \times (8 - 2)$

4. $35 + (4 \times 6) - 7$
5. $7 \times 5 + 9$
6. $8 + 18 \div 3$

7. $6 + 4 + (12 \div 2)$
8. $(8 - 2) \div 3$
9. $(9 + 8) \times 2$

10. $10 + 4 \div (9 - 7)$
11. $(54 \div 9) + (6 \times 6)$
12. $(16 - 4) + (16 - 4)$

13. $(21 - 3) + 7$
14. $9 + (9 \div 3) \times 3$
15. $2 \div 2 + 2 - 1$

16. $3 \times 3 \div 3 + 6 - 3$
17. $5 + 4 \times 3 + 2 - 1$
18. $(6 \div 3) \times 2 + 7 - 5$

. . . .

For **19** through **24**, write the expression represented by each problem and then simplify the expression.

19. There are 2 teachers and 6 rows of 4 students in each a classroom.

20. Three cartons of a dozen eggs each, with 4 eggs broken in each carton.

21. Two groups of 10 students are in a room. Four students leave the room.

22. Six rows of 5 small toys and 1 row of 7 large toys.

23. 4 baskets of 10 apples, with 2 bruised apples in each basket.

24. Five groups of 4 tulips and 2 roses.

NS 3.4 🔑 Solve problems involving division of multidigit numbers by one-digit numbers.

Dividing 3-Digit by 1-Digit Numbers

How can you divide numbers in the hundreds?

A factory shipped 378 watches in 3 boxes. If the watches were equally divided, how many watches were there in each box?

Choose an Operation Divide to find the size of equal groups.

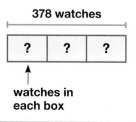

378 watches

| ? | ? | ? |

↑ watches in each box

Guided Practice*

Do you know HOW?

In **1** and **2**, copy and complete each calculation.

1.
```
      3▓▓
   2)658
   − ▓
   ───
     ▓
   − ▓
   ───
    ▓▓
   − ▓▓
   ───
     ▓
```

2.
```
    ▓▓▓ R▓
  4)954
  − 8
  ───
   ▓▓
  − ▓▓
  ───
   ▓▓
  − ▓▓
  ───
     2
```

Do you UNDERSTAND?

3. When you divide the hundreds in the first step above, what does the 1 in the quotient represent?

4. Jenny paid $195 to take violin lessons for 3 months. How much did 1 month of lessons cost?

$195

| ? | ? | ? |

↑ Cost for 1 month

Independent Practice

Leveled Practice In **5** through **13**, divide. You may draw a picture to help you.

5.
```
    1▓▓
  5)595
  − ▓
  ───
    ▓
  − ▓
  ───
    4▓
  − ▓▓
  ───
    ▓
```

6.
```
    ▓▓▓
  2)832
  − ▓
  ───
    3
  − ▓
  ───
    2▓
  − ▓▓
  ───
    ▓
```

7.
```
    2▓ R▓
  3)866
  − ▓
  ───
   ▓▓
  − ▓▓
  ───
   ▓▓
  − ▓▓
  ───
    ▓
```

8.
```
   ▓▓▓ R▓
  4)575
  − ▓
  ───
   ▓▓
  − ▓▓
  ───
   ▓▓
  − ▓▓
  ───
    ▓
```

9. 4)952

10. 3)761

11. 5)615

12. 2)871

13. 3)638

Estimate:

$360 \div 3 = 120$

Divide the hundreds.

$$\begin{array}{r} 1 \\ 3\overline{)378} \\ -3 \\ \hline 7 \end{array}$$

Divide the tens.

$$\begin{array}{r} 12 \\ 3\overline{)378} \\ -3 \\ \hline 7 \\ -6 \\ \hline 1 \end{array}$$

Divide the ones.

$$\begin{array}{r} 126 \\ 3\overline{)378} \\ -3 \\ \hline 7 \\ -6 \\ \hline 18 \\ -18 \\ \hline 0 \end{array}$$

There are 126 watches in each box.

The answer is reasonable because 126 is close to 120.

Problem Solving

14. Throughout the world, about 270 babies are born each minute. About how many babies are born in one hour?

15. During halftime at the football game, 81 band members will line up in 3 equal lines. How many band members will be in each line?

For **16** and **17**, use the table at the right.

16. There are 848 people getting on board the *Memphis Belle*. How many seats are needed for every person to sit?

17. Writing to Explain If 793 people are on the *Natchez Willie,* how many seats are needed for each person to sit?

Historic River Boat Tours

Natchez Willie	6 riders per seat
Memphis Belle	4 riders per seat

18. Algebra If $698 \div 4 = 174$ R ▢, what is the value of ▢?

19. The Galveston-Port Bolivar Ferry takes cars across Galveston Bay. One day, the ferry transported a total of 685 cars over a 5-hour period. If the ferry took the same number of cars each hour, how many cars did it take each hour?

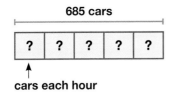

685 cars

?	?	?	?	?

cars each hour

20. Theo bought a T-shirt for $21 and a pair of shorts for $16. He paid with two $20 bills. How much money did Theo get back?

A $1.00

B $2.00

C $3.00

D $4.00

NS 3.2 ⚿
Demonstrate an
understanding of, and
ability to use standard
algorithms . . . for dividing
a multidigit number by a
one-digit number . . .
Also **NS 3.4** ⚿

Deciding Where to Start Dividing

What do you do when there aren't enough hundreds to divide?

Madison is making iguana key chains using pom-poms. She has 145 pink pom-poms. Are there enough pink pom-poms to make 36 key chains?

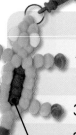

2 yellow pom-poms

4 pink pom-poms

7 blue pom-poms

31 green pom-poms

3 yards of plastic lace

4 pink
pom-poms

Guided Practice*

Do you know HOW?

In **1** and **2**, copy and complete each calculation.

1.
```
      6
  7)455
  -
  ─────
     5
  -
  ─────
```

2.
```
          R
  5)319
  - 3
  ─────
  -
  ─────
```

Do you UNDERSTAND?

3. Madison has 365 blue pom-poms. How many key chains can she make?

4. Explain how an estimated quotient can help you decide where to start.

Independent Practice

Leveled Practice In **5** through **13**, divide. You may draw a picture to help you.

5.
```
  6)444
  -
  ─────
  -
  ─────
```

6.
```
     1
  3)588
  -
  ─────
     8
  -
  ─────
     8
  -
  ─────
```

7.
```
     5  R
  8)417
  -
  ─────
  -
  ─────
```

8.
```
         R
  2)935
  - 8
  ─────
  -
  ─────
  -
  ─────
```

9. 8)526 **10.** 5)690 **11.** 3)769 **12.** 4)923 **13.** 6)342

There are not enough hundreds to put one in each group.

Start by dividing the tens.

$$\begin{array}{r} 3 \\ 4\overline{)145} \\ -12 \\ \hline 25 \end{array}$$

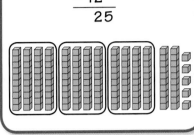

Divide the ones.

$$\begin{array}{r} 36 \text{ R1} \\ 4\overline{)145} \\ -12 \\ \hline 25 \\ -24 \\ \hline 1 \end{array}$$

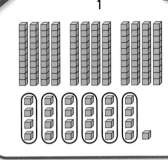

To check, multiply the quotient by the divisor and add the remainder.

$$\begin{array}{r} 2 \\ 36 \\ \times 4 \\ \hline 144 \end{array}$$

$144 + 1 = 145$

Madison has enough pink pom-poms to make 36 key chains.

In **14** through **23**, divide. Then check your answer.

14. $6\overline{)96}$ **15.** $5\overline{)295}$ **16.** $2\overline{)306}$ **17.** $9\overline{)517}$ **18.** $4\overline{)624}$

19. $7\overline{)430}$ **20.** $4\overline{)229}$ **21.** $5\overline{)655}$ **22.** $3\overline{)209}$ **23.** $6\overline{)438}$

Problem Solving

For **24** and **25**, use the bar graph at the right.

James is organizing his CDs. He plans to put them into stackable cubes that hold 8 CDs each.

24. How many cubes will James need for his entire collection?

25. If James decides to group his Rock and World Music CDs together, how many cubes would he need for them?

26. Number Sense How can you tell without dividing that $479 \div 6$ will have a 2-digit quotient?

27. A family is going on a trip for 3 days. The total cost for the hotel is $336. They budgeted $100 a day for food. How much will each day of the trip cost?

    A $33   **B** $112   **C** $145   **D** $212

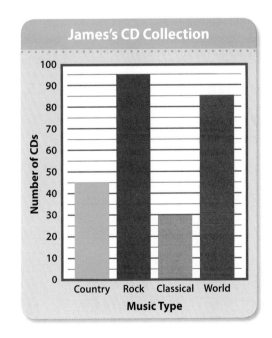

NS 3.2
Demonstrate an
understanding of, and
ability to use standard
algorithms . . . for dividing
a multidigit number by a
one-digit number . . .
Also NS 3.4

Zeros in the Quotient
Do zeros matter?

Liam has 326 nails that he wants to store in 3 containers. He wants to put the same number in each container. How many nails will go in each container?

326 nails

Estimate: $330 \div 3 = 110$

? nails in
each container

Guided Practice*

Do you know HOW?

In **1** through **4**, divide. Then check your answer.

1. $4\overline{)816}$ **2.** $2\overline{)608}$

3. $2\overline{)213}$ **4.** $3\overline{)619}$

Do you UNDERSTAND?

5. How can you check the answer in the problem above?

6. Liam sold some hammers at a market and made $212. If he sold each hammer for $2, how many hammers did he sell?

Independent Practice

Leveled Practice In **7** through **25**, divide. Then check your answer.

7. $3\overline{)309}$

8. $7\overline{)749}$

9. $5\overline{)508}$ R

10. $4\overline{)834}$ R

11. $7\overline{)763}$ **12.** $4\overline{)830}$ **13.** $2\overline{)818}$ **14.** $5\overline{)530}$ **15.** $8\overline{)823}$

16. $3\overline{)326}$ **17.** $6\overline{)658}$ **18.** $3\overline{)922}$ **19.** $8\overline{)482}$ **20.** $9\overline{)970}$

21. $9\overline{)927}$ **22.** $2\overline{)412}$ **23.** $5\overline{)525}$ **24.** $2\overline{)217}$ **25.** $7\overline{)717}$

For another example, see Set H on page 190.

Divide the hundreds.

$$\begin{array}{r} 1 \\ 3\overline{)326} \\ -3 \\ \hline \end{array}$$

Divide the tens.

$$\begin{array}{r} 10 \\ 3\overline{)326} \\ -3 \\ \hline 2 \\ -0 \\ \hline 26 \end{array}$$

Since 3 > 2, there are not enough tens to put any in each group.

Place a zero in the quotient and bring down the 6.

Divide the ones.

$$\begin{array}{r} 108 \text{ R2} \\ 3\overline{)326} \\ -3 \\ \hline 2 \\ -0 \\ \hline 26 \\ -24 \\ \hline 2 \end{array}$$

There will be 108 nails in each container with 2 left over.

Problem Solving

For **26** through **28**, use the information at right.

26. Writing to Explain A zookeeper has 540 pounds of hay. Is this enough hay to feed one elephant for 5 days?

27. Another zookeeper has 324 pounds of meat. Is this enough to feed 3 lions for a full week? Explain.

28. Is 654 pounds of fish enough to feed 5 sea lions for 6 days? Explain.

29. Reasoning What digit belongs in the number sentence below?

8 ▢ 7 ÷ 4 = 206 R3

Elephant: Eats 120 pounds of hay daily

Lion: Eats 15 pounds of meat daily

Sea Lion: Eats 30 pounds of fish daily

30. Claire divided 415 ÷ 2 and got a quotient of 27 R1. What mistake did Claire make?

  A She divided the hundreds incorrectly.

  B She forgot to record that there were not enough tens to divide.

  C She regrouped the hundreds incorrectly.

  D She wrote the wrong remainder.

31. The school band needs to raise money for 3 parades. They need $276 for each parade. The band plans to hold 4 fundraisers. If they raise an equal amount at each fundraiser, what is the least amount they can make at each fundraiser to reach their goal?

Lesson

7-9

NS 4.1 Understand that many whole numbers break down in different ways. Also NS 4.0.

Factors

Hands-On
counters

How can you use multiplication to find all the factors of a number?

Jean has 16 action figures. She wants to arrange them in equal sized groupings around her room. What are the ways that Jean can arrange the action figures? Jean needs to think of all the factors of 16.

16 action figures

Guided Practice*

Do you know HOW?

In **1** through **4**, write each number as a product of two factors in two different ways.

1. 36   **2.** 42

3. 50   **4.** 64

In **5** through **8**, find all the factors of each number. Use counters to help.

5. 12   **6.** 20

7. 28   **8.** 54

Do you UNDERSTAND?

9. What factor does every even number have?

10. Writing to Explain Is 5 a factor of 16?

11. Jean got 2 more action figures. What are all the different groupings she can make now?

12. Jean's brother has 100 action figures. What are all of the factors for 100?

Independent Practice

In **13** through **32**, find all the factors of each number. Use counters to help.

Tip For even numbers, remember 2 is always a factor.

13. 6   **14.** 32   **15.** 45   **16.** 11   **17.** 36

18. 25   **19.** 63   **20.** 22   **21.** 51   **22.** 30

23. 14   **24.** 18   **25.** 27   **26.** 21   **27.** 40

28. 55   **29.** 39   **30.** 35   **31.** 29   **32.** 48

DIGITAL

eTools
www.pearsonsuccessnet.com

16 = 1 × 16

Jean can arrange
16 figures in 1 group
or
16 groups of 1 figure.

So, 1 and 16 are
factors of 16.

16 = 2 × 8

Jean can arrange
2 figures in 8 groups
or
2 groups of 8 figures.

So, 2 and 8 are
factors of 16.

16 = 4 × 4

Jean can arrange
4 figures in 4 groups.

4 is a factor of 16.

The factors of 16 are
1, 2, 4, 8, and 16.

Problem Solving

33. As part of her science project, Shay is making a model of a California wind farm. She wants to put 24 turbines in her model. What arrays can she make using 24 turbines?

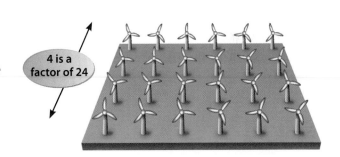

4 is a factor of 24

34. Anita wants to include an array of 15 photos on her web site. Describe the arrays that she can make.

35. Which lists all the factors of 38?

   A 1, 38   **C** 1, 2, 38

   B 1, 2, 14, 38   **D** 1, 2, 19, 38

36. Number Sense Any number that has 9 as a factor also has 3 as a factor. Why is this?

37. Writing to Explain Which is greater, $\frac{4}{5}$ or 0.75?

38. The manatee is an endangered sea mammal. A mother manatee, pictured to the right, is three times as long as her baby. How long is the baby manatee?

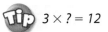 $3 \times ? = 12$

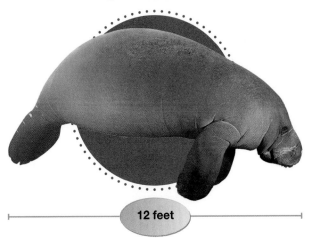

12 feet

Lesson

7-10

NS 4.2 Know that numbers such as 2, 3, 5, 7 and 11 do not have any factors except 1 and themselves and that such numbers are called prime numbers. Also NS 4.0.

Prime and Composite Numbers

A prime number <u>is a whole number greater than 1 that has exactly two factors, 1 and itself.</u>

A composite number <u>is a whole number greater than 1 that has more than two factors.</u>

Numbers	Factors
2	1, 2
3	1, 3
4	1, 2, 4
5	1, 5
6	1, 2, 3, 6

Guided Practice*

Do you know HOW?

In **1** through **6**, tell whether each number is prime or composite.

1. 32   **2.** 41

3. 57   **4.** 21

5. 95   **6.** 103

Do you UNDERSTAND?

7. What is the only even prime number?

8. Writing to Explain Give an example of an odd number that is not prime. What makes it a composite number?

9. Roger has 47 cars. Can he group the cars in more than 2 ways?

Independent Practice

Leveled Practice In **10** through **31**, write whether each number is prime or composite.

10. 7 ☐☐☐☐☐☐☐

11. 9 ☐☐☐☐☐☐☐☐☐ ☐☐☐/☐☐☐/☐☐☐

12. 23   **13.** 33   **14.** 56   **15.** 67   **16.** 38

17. 58   **18.** 75   **19.** 101   **20.** 51   **21.** 300

22. 9   **23.** 2   **24.** 97   **25.** 1,900   **26.** 37

27. 11   **28.** 44   **29.** 1,204   **30.** 10   **31.** 59

DIGITAL   Animated Glossary
www.pearsonsuccessnet.com

For another example, see Set J on page 191.

Prime Numbers

The number 5 is a prime number. It has only two factors, 1 and itself.

There is only one way to make an array to represent 5.

 $1 \times 5 = 5$

Composite Numbers

The number 6 is a composite number. Its factors are 1, 2, 3 and 6.

There is more than one way to make an array to represent 6.

$1 \times 6 = 6$

$2 \times 3 = 6$

The number 1 is a special number. It is neither prime nor composite.

Problem Solving

For **32** through **34**, use the pictograph at the right.

32. Which types of flowers did a prime number of people vote for?

33. How many people are represented by the pictograph?

34. What was the favorite flower according to the pictograph?

35. How many people liked roses or daisies?

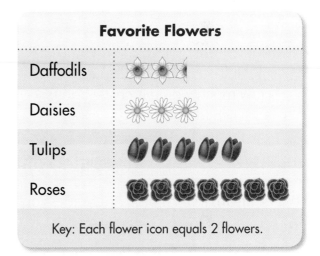

Favorite Flowers

Daffodils

Daisies

Tulips

Roses

Key: Each flower icon equals 2 flowers.

36. Which set of numbers below are all prime?

A 1, 2, 7, 11, 25   **C** 3, 5, 13, 19

B 1, 3, 5, 7, 9   **D** 15, 21, 27, 31

37. A scuba diver is 17 feet below water. He swims three times deeper. How deep is the scuba diver now?

38. Writing to Explain Greta said that the product of two prime numbers must also be a prime number. Joan disagreed. Who is correct?

39. Derrick ran 28.2 feet. Krystal ran 32.1 feet. How much further did Krystal run?

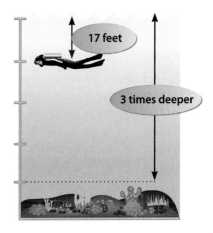

17 feet

3 times deeper

Lesson
7-11

MR 3.2 Note the method of deriving the solution and demonstrate a conceptual understanding of the derivation by solving similar problems.
Also NS 3.0 ⟐ .

Problem Solving

Multiple-Step Problems

Paul and Libby sold some sock monkeys for a total of $72. Libby sold 5 monkeys from her collection. Paul sold 3 monkeys from his collection. If they sold each sock monkey for the same amount, how much did they sell each monkey for?

Paul sold 3 monkeys.

Libby sold 5 monkeys.

Guided Practice*

Do you know HOW?

Solve.

1. Adult admission to the town fair is $7. Child admission to the fair is $3. How much would it cost 2 adults and 4 children to enter the fair?

Do you UNDERSTAND?

2. What is the hidden question or questions?

3. **Write a Problem** Write a problem that contains a hidden question.

Independent Practice

Write the answer to the hidden question or questions. Then solve the problem. Write your answer in a complete sentence.

4. Charlie and Lola like to walk around the perimeter of their town park. The perimeter is 2 miles long. Last week Charlie walked around the perimeter 4 times and Lola walked around it 5 times. How many more miles did Lola walk than Charlie last week?

5. Abby buys 15 sunflower plants and 12 petunia plants to plant in her garden. She plans to plant the flowers in rows of 3. How many rows of flowers will Abby plant?

6. What is the hidden question in Problem 5?

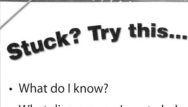

Stuck? Try this....

- What do I know?
- What diagram can I use to help understand the problem?
- Can I use addition, subtraction, multiplication, or division?
- Is all of my work correct?
- Did I answer the right question?
- Is my answer reasonable?

Find the hidden question. How many monkeys did Paul and Libby sell in all?

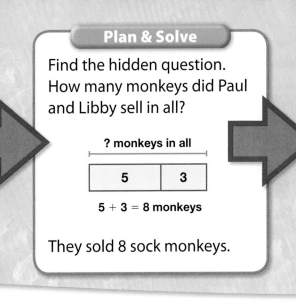

? monkeys in all

5	3

5 + 3 = 8 monkeys

They sold 8 sock monkeys.

Use the answer to the hidden question to solve the problem.

If they sold each sock monkey for the same amount, how much did they sell each sock monkey for?

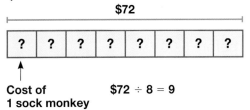

$72

?	?	?	?	?	?	?	?

Cost of 1 sock monkey

$72 ÷ 8 = 9

Paul and Libby sold each sock monkey for $9.

For **7** through **9**, use the table to the right.

7. Terrence and Jennifer went to Al's Discount Music Store. Terrence bought 4 CDs and two 3-packs of blank CDs. Jennifer bought 8 DVDs, 3 CDs, and one 3-pack of blank CDs. Together, how much did they spend?

8. Give an example of a hidden question in Problem 10.

9. In one hour, Al's Discount Music Store sold 22 DVDs, 36 CDs, and six 3-packs of blank CDs. How much was sold in one hour?

Al's Discount Music Store	
3-pack blank CD's	$7
DVDs	$5
CDs	$10

For **10** through **12**, tell whether an exact answer is needed or if an estimate is enough. Use the data at the right and solve.

10. Carlos' family bought 3 hamburgers and 2 salads from Diner Delight. They paid with a $20 bill. How much change should they receive?

11. Amber and her family bought 3 chicken sandwiches, 2 salads, and 1 baked potato. They spent $4 on drinks. How much did they spend in all?

12. In one hour, Diner Delight sold 46 hamburgers and 23 salads. How many items did the diner sell?

Diner Delight	
Hamburger	$4
Chicken Sandwich	$5
Baked Potato	$2
Salad	$3

Use the data to the right for **13** through **16**.

Samir and Maya are both under 12 years old. They are trying to find out how much they would save by going to a movie before 6:00 P.M.

Metro Movies Ticket Prices			
	Children under 12	Adults under 65	65 and over
Before 6:00 P.M.	$4	$6	$3
Evening	$6	$7	$6

13. Look at Samir's work. What are the hidden questions Samir solved?

Samir's Work

$2 \times \$4 = \$8$

$2 \times \$6 = \$12$

$\$12 - \$8 = \$4$

14. Look at Maya's work. What is the hidden question Maya solved?

Maya's Work

$\$6 - \$4 = \$2$

15. What should Maya's next step be to find out how much money she and Samir would save?

16. What is the difference in the cost of 5 adult tickets for a movie before 6:00 P.M. and after 6:00 P.M.?

17. Algebra In $b \times c = 134$, b is a one-digit number and c is a two-digit number. What numbers could b and c represent?

18. A tractor-trailer is also known as an 18-wheeler because it has 18 wheels. How many more wheels are on 2 tractor-trailers than on 5 cars?

Think About the Process

19. Justine's plant stand has 6 shelves. Each shelf holds 4 plants. Justine has already placed 16 plants on her stand. Which number sentence will answer the hidden question, "How many more plants can Justine's plant stand hold?"

  A 4×16

  B 6×16

  C $24 - 16$

  D $24 - 20$

20. Justine decided to buy more plants. She paid with two $20 bills. She received $12 in change. What must you find first before you can find the cost of each plant?

  A The number of plants that she bought

  B The amount Justine received in change

  C The cost of each plant

  D The amount Justine paid

Find the quotient. Estimate to check
if the answer is reasonable.

1. 480 ÷ 8   **2.** 29 ÷ 3   **3.** 749 ÷ 8   **4.** 304 ÷ 3

5. 4)‾608   **6.** 5)‾528   **7.** 515 ÷ 3   **8.** 6)‾87

9. 95 ÷ 5   **10.** 888 ÷ 9   **11.** 54 ÷ 4   **12.** 210 ÷ 3

13. 8)‾807   **14.** 465 ÷ 2   **15.** 5)‾64   **16.** 964 ÷ 4

Find the sum. Estimate to check if the answer is reasonable.

17.   46,037
   + 12,750

18.   9,979
   + 2,956

19.   73,678
   + 26,321

20.   2,873
   +   49

21.   21,165
   + 15,375

22. 54,893 + 3,746   **23.** 23,963 + 12 + 3,987   **24.** 48 + 40,287 + 834

Error Search Find each quotient that is not correct.
Write it correctly and explain the error.

25. 19 ÷ 2 = 9 R1   **26.** 808 ÷ 4 = 22   **27.** 354 ÷ 5 = 70 R4

28. 74 ÷ 6 = 12 R2   **29.** 377 ÷ 3 = 125   **30.** 940 ÷ 7 = 140

Number Sense

Estimating and Reasoning Write whether each
statement is true or false. Explain your answer.

31. The quotient of 398 ÷ 4 is closer to 100 than 90.

32. The product of 9 and 32 is greater than the product of 3 and 92.

33. The quotient of 154 ÷ 5 is less than 30.

34. The quotient of 1,500 ÷ 30 is 30.

35. The difference of 4,321 − 2,028 is less than 1,000.

36. The sum of 2,243 and 5,809 is greater than 7,000 but less than 9,000.

1. A stadium has 30,000 seats and 6 main gates. How many seats are served by each gate if each gate serves the same number of seats? (7-1)

   A 50

   B 500

   C 5,000

   D 50,000

2. What is the quotient? (7-3)

   A 3 R8

   B 4 R2

   C 4 R3

   D 5 R2

$$7\overline{)30}$$ R

3. Two boxes contain a total of 576 pencils. How many pencils are in each box? (7-6)

   A 1,152

   B 328

   C 288

   D 238

4. Rachel found bracelets on sale for 3 for $15. How much would she spend on 5 bracelets? (7-11)

   A $5

   B $20

   C $25

   D $30

5. Nelly has 74 bricks to outline 5 different flower beds. How many bricks will she use for each flower bed if she uses the same number around each? (7-4)

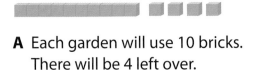

   A Each garden will use 10 bricks. There will be 4 left over.

   B Each garden will use 13 bricks. There will be 9 left over.

   C Each garden will use 14 bricks. There will be 0 left over.

   D Each garden will use 14 bricks. There will be 4 left over.

6. What is 318 ÷ 4? (7-6)

   A 78 R2

   B 78

   C 79 R2

   D 79

7. Harold earned $196 by mowing 5 lawns. Which number sentence shows the best way to estimate the amount he earned for each lawn? (7-2)

   A $200 ÷ 5 = $40

   B $150 ÷ 5 = $30

   C $200 ÷ 10 = $20

   D 5 × $200 = $1,000

8. What is 537 ÷ 5? (7-8)

  A 107 R2

  B 107

  C 101 R2

  D 17 R2

9. Each costume requires 2 yards of material. How many costumes can Sara make out of 35 yards? How much material will she have left? (7-5)

  A She can make 17 costumes with 1 yard left.

  B She can make 17 costumes with 0 yards left.

  C She can make 16 costumes with 3 yards left.

  D She can make 16 costumes with 1 yard left.

10. Which shows all the factors of 24? (7-9)

  A 2, 3, 4, 6, 8, 12

  B 1, 2, 3, 4, 6, 8, 12, 24

  C 1, 2, 3, 4, 12, 24

  D 1, 2, 3, 4, 6, 12, 24

11. Which number is prime? (7-10)

  A 88

  B 65

  C 51

  D 17

12. Holly uses 7 sheets of tissue paper to make one flower. If she bought a package with 500 sheets of tissue paper, about how many tissue flowers will she be able to make? (7-2)

  A 80

  B 70

  C 60

  D 7

13. The baker made 52 rolls. He put an equal amount in each of the 4 baskets in the display case. How many rolls did he put in each basket? (7-5)

  A 14

  B 13

  C 12

  D 9

14. Which statement is true? (7-10)

  A The only factors of 3 are 3 and 1.

  B The only factors of 4 are 4 and 1.

  C The only factors of 6 are 6 and 1.

  D The only factors of 8 are 8 and 1.

15. What can you tell about 427 ÷ 7 just by looking at the problem? (7-7)

  A It will have a three-digit quotient.

  B It will have a two-digit quotient.

  C It will have a one-digit quotient.

  D It will have a remainder.

Set A, pages 158–159

A class shares 270 pens equally among 3 groups of students.

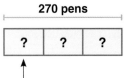

270 pens

?	?	?

pens for each group of students

Find 270 ÷ 3.

The basic fact is 27 ÷ 3 = 9.

27 tens ÷ 3 = 9 tens

So, 270 ÷ 3 = 90 pens.

Remember to check your division by multiplying.

1. 250 ÷ 5   **2.** 81,000 ÷ 9

3. 3,200 ÷ 4   **4.** 42,000 ÷ 7

5. 1,000 ÷ 2   **6.** 240 ÷ 4

7. 450 ÷ 5   **8.** 72,000 ÷ 9

9. 3,600 ÷ 4   **10.** 49,000 ÷ 7

11. 2,000 ÷ 2   **12.** 280 ÷ 4

Set B, pages 160–161

Use estimation to find about how many objects are shared equally.

130

?	?	?	?	?	?	?

How many in each group?

What number close to 130 is easily divided by 7?

Try multiples of ten near 130:

140 is 14 tens and can be divided by 7.

140 ÷ 7 = 20

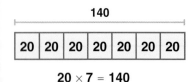

140

20	20	20	20	20	20	20

20 × 7 = 140

Since 140 > 130, the estimate is too high.

So, the estimate of 20 is greater than the exact answer.

Remember to try rounding the dividend to the nearest ten.

Estimate each quotient.

1. 718 ÷ 8   **2.** 156 ÷ 4

3. 482 ÷ 8   **4.** 117 ÷ 4

5. 843 ÷ 7   **6.** 321 ÷ 2

7. 428 ÷ 6   **8.** 811 ÷ 9

9. 561 ÷ 8   **10.** 723 ÷ 8

11. 632 ÷ 9   **12.** 362 ÷ 9

13. 402 ÷ 2   **14.** 122 ÷ 6

15. 251 ÷ 5   **16.** 362 ÷ 6

Reteaching

Set C, pages 162–163

A group of 56 students needed to sign up for a recess activity. There were 9 choices. How many students will be signed up for each activity? How many will be left over?

$$\begin{array}{r} 6 \text{ R2} \\ 9\overline{)56} \\ -\ 54 \\ \hline 2 \end{array}$$

Divide: 6 groups of 9 in 56
Multiply: $6 \times 9 = 54$
Subtract: $56 - 54 = 2$
Compare $2 < 9$

Check: $9 \times 6 = 54$ and $54 + 2 = 56$

$56 \div 9 = 6$ R2

Remember that you can use counters or pictures to help.

1. $3\overline{)41}$ **2.** $2\overline{)75}$

3. $5\overline{)63}$ **4.** $3\overline{)92}$

5. $3\overline{)68}$ **6.** $4\overline{)47}$

7. $7\overline{)79}$ **8.** $6\overline{)87}$

Set D, pages 164–166

Tom divides 54 pennies equally among 4 stacks. How many pennies are in each stack? How many are left over?

Use place-value blocks.

Each stack has 13 pennies. Two pennies are left over.

Remember to divide the tens and then the ones.

Divide. You may use place-value blocks or pictures to help.

1. 38 CDs
5 stacks

2. 42 nickels
3 stacks

3. 62 dimes
4 stacks

4. 77 nickels
6 stacks

Set E, pages 168–170 and 172–173

Find $67 \div 4$.

$$\begin{array}{r} 1 \\ 4\overline{)67} \\ -\ 4 \\ \hline 2 \end{array}$$
Divide.
Multiply.
Subtract.

$$\begin{array}{r} 16 \text{ R3} \\ 4\overline{)67} \\ -\ 4 \\ \hline 27 \\ -\ 24 \\ \hline 3 \end{array}$$
Bring down the 7.
Divide.
Multiply.
Subtract.

Check:

$$\begin{array}{r} 16 \\ \times\ 4 \\ \hline 64 \end{array} \qquad \begin{array}{r} 64 \\ +\ 3 \\ \hline 67 \end{array}$$
The answer checks.

Remember that the remainder must be less than the divisor.

Divide. Check your answer.

1. $434 \div 7$ **2.** $329 \div 2$

3. $9 \div 5$ **4.** $53 \div 2$

5. $869 \div 7$ **6.** $275 \div 3$

7. $977 \div 4$ **8.** $161 \div 6$

Set F, pages 174–175

Find 915 ÷ 6.

Estimate: 900 ÷ 6 = 150

The estimate is more than 100, so you can divide hundreds.

```
      152 R3
   6)915      Divide the hundreds.
    - 6
     ───
      31       Divide the tens.
    - 30
     ───
      15       Divide the ones.
    - 12
     ───
       3       Include the remainder.
```

Remember that an estimate can tell you where to start dividing.

Tell whether you will start dividing the hundreds or the tens.

1. 524 ÷ 4   **2.** 601 ÷ 5

3. 398 ÷ 8   **4.** 265 ÷ 3

5. 710 ÷ 9   **6.** 429 ÷ 2

7. 820 ÷ 8   **8.** 372 ÷ 5

Set G, pages 176–177

Find 626 ÷ 6.

```
     104 R2
  6)626        Divide the hundreds.
   - 6
    ───
     2         There are not enough tens to divide.
   - 0         Put a 0 in the quotient.
    ───
    26         Bring down the ones and divide.
  - 24
    ───
     2
```

Remember to write zeros in the quotient when needed.

1   815 ÷ 8   **2.** 218 ÷ 2

3. 417 ÷ 2   **4.** 428 ÷ 4

5. 423 ÷ 4   **6.** 619 ÷ 3

Set H, pages 178–179

Find the factors of 12.

Start with 1 group of 12.
12 = **1 × 12**

Then 2 groups of 6.
12 = **2 × 6**

Then 3 groups of 4.
12 = **3 × 4**

Since the factor pairs have started to repeat, these are all the possible factors of 12: **1, 2, 3, 4, 6, 12**

Remember you can use counters to help find ways to multiply.

Write each number two different ways using multiplication.

1. 45   **2.** 40

3. 56   **4.** 63

5. 36   **6.** 16

Set J, pages 180–181

Is 49 prime or composite?

Find factors other than 1 and 49.

49 is composite because it is divisible by 7.

49 = 7 × 7
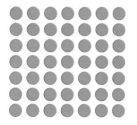

Remember that you can use counters to help find ways to multiply.

Write whether each number is prime or composite.

1. 13   **2.** 25

3. 355   **4.** 2

5. 29   **6.** 2232

Set K, pages 182–184

Answer the hidden question first. Then solve the problem.

Admission Cost	
Adults	$6.00
Children	$3.00

Brett and his family went to the county fair. They bought 2 adult passes and 3 children passes. How much more money did Brett's family spend on the adult passes?

2 × $6 = $12

3 × $3 = $9

Brett's family spent $12 on the adult passes and $9 on the children passes.

Use the hidden question to solve the problem.

$12 − $9 = $3

Brett's family spent $3 more on the adult passes.

Remember to find a hidden question to help you solve the problem.

1. Angelique works at a store at the mall. She earns a wage of $8 an hour, and earns $10 an hour if she works on weekends and holidays. Last week, she worked 24 hours during the week and 16 hours during the weekend. How much did Angelique earn last week?

2. Robby bought 4 packages of favors and 3 packages of balloons. There are 10 favors and 12 balloons in each package. How many more favors did Robby buy?

Lines, Angles, Shapes, and Solids

1

The Headquarters for the United States Department of Defense is named after the polygon it resembles. Which polygon does it look like? You will find out in Lesson 8-3.

2

The Great Pyramid of Giza was built by the ancient Egyptians. What is the length of one of its sides? You will find out in Lesson 8-7.

3

How could you describe the state of California in geometric terms? You will find out in Lesson 8-2.

4

There are three muscles in your neck that are critical for breathing and singing. They are named after a type of triangle that has a similar shape. What kind of triangle is it? You will find out in Lesson 8-4.

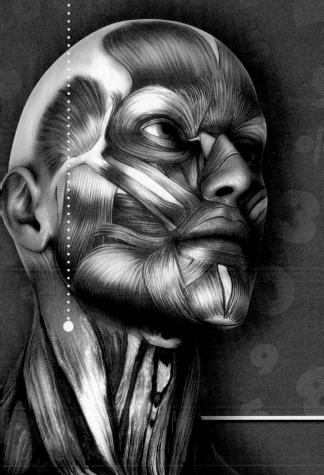

Review What You Know!

Vocabulary

Choose the best term from the box.

> - triangle
> - plane figure
> - quadrilateral
> - line

1. A polygon with four sides is a ?.

2. A polygon with three sides is a ?.

3. A ? is a straight path of points that goes on forever in two directions.

4. A figure with only two dimensions is a ?.

Solids

Name what each figure looks like.

5.

6.

7.

8.

Addition

Solve.

9. 35 + 39 **10.** 72 + 109 **11.** 44 + 12

12. 145 + 238 **13.** 642 + 8 **14.** 99 + 41

15. 984 + 984 **16.** 22 + 888 **17.** 72 + 391

18. **Writing to Explain** To find the sum of 438 + 385, how many times will you need to regroup? Explain.

MG 3.1: Identify lines that are parallel and perpendicular.

Points, Lines, and Planes

What are some important geometric terms?

A point is an exact location in space.

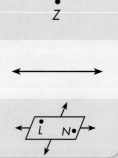

A line is a straight path of points that goes on and on in two directions.

A plane is an endless flat surface.

Guided Practice*

Do you know HOW?

For **1–4**, use the diagram at the right.

1. Name four points.

2. Name four lines.

3. Name two pairs of parallel lines.

4. Name two pairs of perpendicular lines.

Do you UNDERSTAND?

5. What geometric term could you use to describe the top and bottom sides of a chalkboard? Why?

6. What geometric term could you use to describe a chalkboard?

7. What geometric term could you use to describe the tip of your pencil?

Independent Practice

In **8** through **14**, use geometric terms to describe what is shown.

8.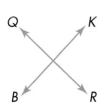

9.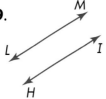

10.

11. • A

12.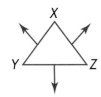

13.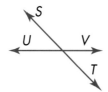

14.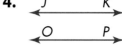

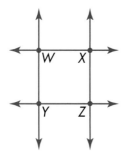

*For another example, see Set A on page 218.

Pairs of lines are given special names depending on their relationship.

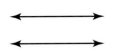

Parallel lines
never intersect.

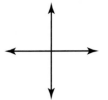

Intersecting lines
pass through the
same point.

Perpendicular lines
are lines that form
square corners.

For **15** through **17**, describe each image shown using a geometric term.

15.

16.

17.

Problem Solving

18. Estimation Georgia purchased items to make dinner. She bought chicken for $5.29, salad items for $8.73, and rice for $1.99. Estimate how much Georgia spent in all.

19. I have 6 square faces and 8 vertices. What am I?

  A Cube   **C** Pyramid

  B Square   **D** Circle

For **20**, use the diagram at the right.

20. Reasoning Line *AB* is parallel to line *CD* and line *CD* is perpendicular to line *EF*. What can you conclude about *AB* and *EF*?

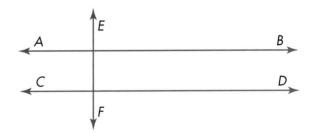

21. The website of a company that sells sports equipment averages 850 visitors a day. How many visitors would the website average in 7 days?

22. Which geometric term below best describes the surface of a desk?

  A Point   **C** Line

  B Plane   **D** Parallel

23. Writing to Explain If all perpendicular lines are also intersecting lines, are all intersecting lines also perpendicular? Explain.

24. If $40 \times 8 = 320$, how many zeros will there be in the product $4,000 \times 8$?

Line Segments, Rays, and Angles

What geometric terms are used to describe parts of lines and types of angles?

MG 3.5 Know the definitions of a right angle, an acute angle, and an obtuse angle. Understand that 90°, 180°, 270°, and 360° are associated, respectively, with $\frac{1}{4}, \frac{1}{2}, \frac{3}{4}$, and full turns. Also **MG 3.1.**

A line segment <u>is a part of a line with two endpoints.</u>

A ray <u>is a part of a line that has one endpoint and continues on forever in one direction.</u>

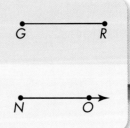

Guided Practice*

Do you know HOW?

In **1** through **4**, use geometric terms to describe what is shown.

1.   P   X

2.

3.  B   Y

4.  L   M   N

Do you UNDERSTAND?

5. What geometric term describes a line that has only one endpoint?

6. What geometric term describes a line that has two endpoints?

7. Which geometric term describes what two edges of a book make when a corner is formed?

Independent Practice

In **8** through **11**, use geometric terms to describe what is shown.

8. H   O   S

9. B ———— D

10. X ———→ Y

11. P   S   T

For **12** through **14**, use the figure shown to the right.

12. Name four line segments.

13. Name four rays.

14. Name 2 right angles.

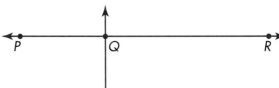
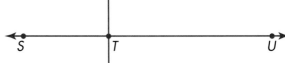

For another example, see Set B on page 218.

An angle is a figure formed by two rays that have the same endpoint. Angles are given special names depending upon their size.

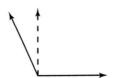

A right angle is a square corner.

An acute angle is less than a right angle.

An obtuse angle is greater than a right angle.

A straight angle forms a straight line.

Problem Solving

15. Writing to Explain Is the figure shown below formed by two rays with a common endpoint? If so, is it an angle? Explain.

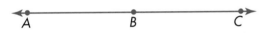

16. Which choice names the figure shown below?

G   H

A   Ray *GH*   C   Line segment *GH*

B   Line *GH*   D   Angle *GH*

17. What three capital letters can be written by drawing two parallel line segments and then one line segment that is perpendicular to the line segments you already drew?

18. Lexi said that two lines can both intersect a line and form perpendicular lines. Draw a picture to explain what she means.

For **19** through **21**, use the map of California to the right.

19. In geometric terms, how would you describe the route between 2 cities?

20. How would you describe the cities?

21. How would you describe the map of the state of California?

22. Draw It Randy used 96 sticks to build a model project. Bryan used 3 times as many. Draw a diagram showing how many sticks Bryan used.

DIGITAL

Animated Glossary
www.pearsonsuccessnet.com

MG 3.0 Demonstrate an understanding of plane and solid geometric objects and use this knowledge to show relationships and solve problems.

Polygons

How do you identify polygons?

A polygon is a closed plane figure made up of line segments. Each line segment is a side. The point where the two sides meet is called a vertex.

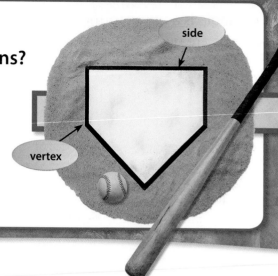

Guided Practice*

Do you know HOW?

Draw an example of each polygon. Write the number of sides and vertices it has.

1. pentagon

2. triangle

3. octagon

4. quadrilateral

Do you UNDERSTAND?

5. Is a circle a polygon? Why or why not?

6. **Writing to Explain** Does every hexagon have the same shape?

Independent Practice

In **7** through **18**, name each polygon.
Write the number of sides and vertices it has.

7.

8.

9.

10.

11.

12.

13.

14.

15.

16.

17.

18.

Animated Glossary
www.pearsonsuccessnet.com

*For another example, see Set C on page 218.

Here are some examples of polygons.

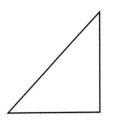

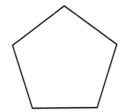

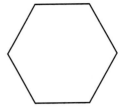

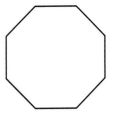

| Triangle | Quadrilateral | Pentagon | Hexagon | Octagon |
| 3 sides | 4 sides | 5 sides | 6 sides | 8 sides |

Problem Solving

19. The building to the right is named for the polygon it looks like. What is the name of the polygon?

    A Quadrilateral   C Hexagon

    B Pentagon   D Octagon

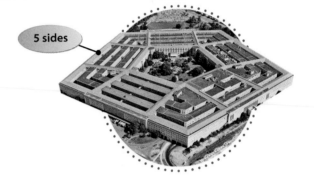

5 sides

20. What rule could be used to sort these polygons?

Group A

Group B

21. **Draw It** Tim and Peter both are on a swimming team. In one week, Tim swam 244 meters and Peter swam 196 meters. Draw a bar diagram to show how many more meters Tim swam than Peter.

22. Carla gathered a total of 124 seashells. How many seashells would she have if she gathered 4 times that amount?

23. Tasha is hosting a party for 216 people. If 6 people can sit at each table, how many tables will Tasha need to set up?

24. **Writing to Explain** What do you notice about the number of sides and the number of vertices a polygon has? How many vertices would a 20-sided polygon have?

25. Which polygon does **NOT** have at least 4 sides?

    A Octagon   C Quadrilateral

    B Hexagon   D Triangle

MG 3.7 Know the definitions of different triangles (e.g., equilateral, isosceles, scalene) and identify their attributes.

Triangles

How can you classify triangles?

Triangles can be classified by their sides.

Equilateral Triangle
3 equal sides

Isosceles Triangle
2 equal sides

Scalene Triangle
0 equal sides

Guided Practice*

Do you know HOW?

In **1** through **4**, classify each triangle by its sides and then by its angles.

1. 　　**2.**

3. 　　**4.**

Do you UNDERSTAND?

5. Can a triangle have more than one obtuse angle? Explain.

6. Is it possible to draw a right isosceles triangle? If so, draw an example.

7. Can a triangle have more than one right angle? If so, draw an example.

Independent Practice

In **8** through **16,** classify each triangle by its sides and then by its angles.

8. 　　**9.** 　　**10.**

11. 　　**12.** 　　**13.**

14. 　　**15.** 　　**16.**

DIGITAL

Animated Glossary
www.pearsonsuccessnet.com

For another example, see Set D on page 219.

Triangles also can be classified by their angles.

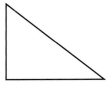

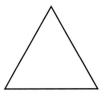

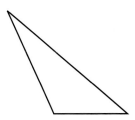

A right triangle <u>has one right angle</u>.

An acute triangle <u>has three acute angles.</u> All of its angles measure less than 90°.

An obtuse triangle <u>has one obtuse angle.</u> One angle has a measure greater than 90°.

In **17** through **19**, classify each triangle by its sides and then by its angles.

17.

18.

19.

Problem Solving

20. Reasoning Use the diagram below. If the backyard is an equilateral triangle, what do you know about the lengths of the other two sides?

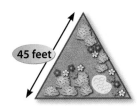

45 feet

21. If Chris uses a third line to make a triangle, what kind of triangle will it be?

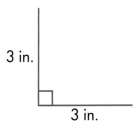

3 in.

3 in.

22. Writing to Explain Is an equilateral triangle always an isosceles triangle?

23. When you multiply any number by 1, what is the product?

Use the diagram at the right for **24**.

24. Which is the best name for this muscle group shown at the right?

   A Right muscle group

   B Scalene muscle group

   C Isosceles muscle group

   D Equilateral muscle group

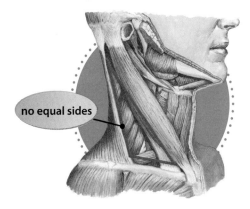

no equal sides

Lesson

8-5

MG 3.8 Know the definition of different quadrilaterals (e.g., rhombus, square, rectangle, parallelogram, trapezoid).

Quadrilaterals

How can you classify quadrilaterals?

Quadrilaterals can be classified by their angles or pairs of sides.

 Square

Rectangle

Other Examples

A rhombus is a quadrilateral that has opposite sides that are parallel and all of its sides are the same length.

A trapezoid is a quadrilateral with only one pair of parallel sides.

Guided Practice*

Do you know HOW?

In **1** through **4**, write all the names you can use for each quadrilateral.

1.

2.

3.

4.

Do you UNDERSTAND?

5. What is true about all quadrilaterals?

6. Why is a trapezoid not a parallelogram?

7. What is the difference between a square and a rhombus?

Independent Practice

In **8** through **15**, write all the names you can use for each quadrilateral.

8.

9.

10.

11.

DIGITAL

Animated Glossary
www.pearsonsuccessnet.com

*For another example, see Set E on page 219.

A parallelogram has
2 pairs of parallel sides.

A rectangle has
4 right angles. It is
also a parallelogram.

A square has 4 right angles and
all sides are the same length.
It is a parallelogram, rectangle,
and rhombus.

12.

13.

14.

15.

Problem Solving

16. A quadrilateral has two pairs of parallel sides and exactly 4 right angles. What quadrilateral is being described?

17. Reasoning Is it possible for a quadrilateral to be both a rhombus and a parallelogram?

18. Algebra What number comes next in the pattern?

4, 16, 64, 256,

19. Writing to Explain All the sides of an equilateral triangle are congruent. Is an equilateral triangle also a rhombus? Explain.

20. Valley Ridge Elementary has 108 fourth-grade students and 4 fourth-grade teachers. If split equally, how many students should be in each class?

21. If a theater can hold 235 people for one showing of a movie and they show the movie 5 times a day, how many people could view the movie in one day?

22. In math class, Mr. Meyer drew a quadrilateral on the board. It had just one set of parallel sides and no right angles. What shape was it?

   A Square   **C** Rectangle

   B Rhombus   **D** Trapezoid

23. Jamie went to exercise at a swimming pool. The length of the pool was 25 yards. If she swam a total of 6 laps, how many yards did Jamie swim?

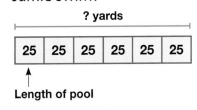

Circles

How do you describe a circle and the sets of points related to a circle?

A circle is the set of all points in a plane that are the same distance from a point called the center.

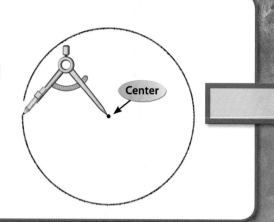

Center

Guided Practice*

Do you know HOW?

Use geometric terms to describe what is shown in red.

1.

2.

3.

4.

Do you UNDERSTAND?

5. If you know the diameter of the circle, explain how to find the radius.

6. If the radius of a circle is 7 inches, how long is its diameter?

7. **Writing to Explain** In any circle, which is lager, the radius or diameter?

Independent Practice

For **8** through **11**, use geometric terms to describe what is shown in red.

8.

9.

10.

11.

For **12** through **15**, find the diameter of each circle.

12.
4 in.

13.
3 cm

14.
6 ft

15.
11 cm

*For another example, see Set F on page 219.

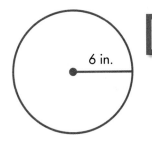

A radius is any line that connects the center to a point on a circle.

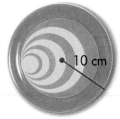

6 in.

A diameter is any line segment that connects two points through the center of the circle.

The diameter is two times the radius.

radius = 6 inches

diameter = 2 × 6 inches = 12 inches

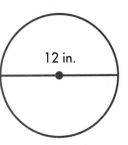

12 in.

For **16** through **18**, find the length of the diameter of each object.

16.

10 cm

a frisbee

17.

5 in.

a dinner plate

18.

1 ft

a bike tire

19. Geometry What will be the next figure in the pattern to below? Explain how you know

20. Which multiplication sentence is shown by the array to the below?

21. Writing to Explain If you know the diameter of a circle, how would you find the radius?

22. A diameter of a circle is ▨ as long as its radius.

    A Four times   **C** Twice

    B Three times   **D** Half

23. Isaac said that since a chord can be the diameter of a circle then a chord could also be the radius of a circle. Is he right?

24. Evaluate the expression below when $z = 45$.

$$4 + z + 16 - z$$

MG 3.6 Visualize, describe, and make models of geometric solids (e.g., prisms, pyramids) in terms of the number and shape of faces, edges, and vertices; interpret two-dimensional representations of three-dimensional objects; and draw patterns (of faces) for a solid that, when cut and folded, will make a model of the solid. Also MG 3.0.

Solids

How can you describe and classify solids?

A solid figure <u>has three dimensions</u>: <u>length, width, and height.</u>

Solids can have curved surfaces.

Sphere   Cylinder   Cone

Another Example **How can you build a solid figure?**

A **net** <u>is a pattern that can be used to make a solid.</u>

This is a net for a cube. Each of the faces is connected to at least one other face.

This is a net for a triangular prism.

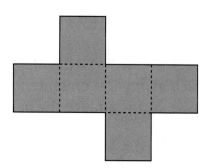

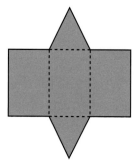

Explain It

1. Explain why the net for a cube has six squares.

2. Why does the net for a triangular prism have two triangles and three rectangles?

Some solids have all flat surfaces. They are named by referring to their faces.

face-flat surface of a solid

vertex-point where 3 or more edges meet. (plural: vertices)

edge-line segment where 2 faces meet.

rectangular prism
4 rectangular faces
2 square faces

cube
6 square faces

triangular prism
2 triangular faces
3 rectangular faces

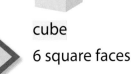

rectangular pyramid
1 rectangular face
4 triangular faces

square pyramid
1 square face
4 triangular faces

Guided Practice*

Do you know HOW?

For **1** through **4**, identify each solid.

1.

2.

3.

4.

Do you UNDERSTAND?

5. Which solid figure has four triangular faces and one square face?

6. Why is a cube a special kind of rectangular prism?

7. Does a sphere have any edges or vertices? Explain.

Independent Practice

Leveled Practice For **8** through **10**, copy and complete the table.

	Solid Figure	Faces	Edges	Vertices	Shape(s) of Faces
8.	Rectangular prism	▢	▢	▢	4 rectangles and 2 squares
9.	Cube	6	▢	▢	▢
10.	Rectangular pyramid	▢	8	▢	▢

*For another example, see Set G on page 220.

In **11** through **14**, trace each net, and cut it out. Fold and tape together to make a solid. The dotted lines shown are fold lines.

11.

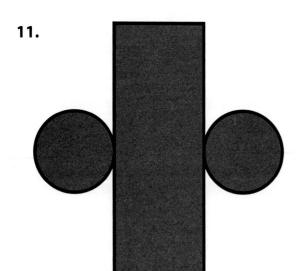

12.

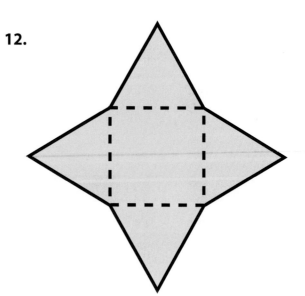

13.

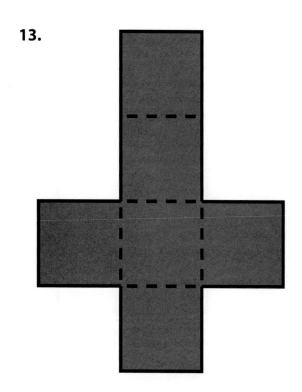

14.

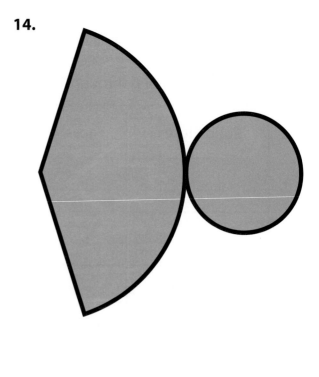

For **15** through **18**, tell what solid figure best represents each object.

15.

16.

17.

18.

19. Todd's father offered to drive some members of the soccer team to a game. His car can fit 4 players. He drives 10 players from his home to the game. How many one-way trips must he make if he stays to watch the game?

 Draw a picture to show each one-way trip.

20. Writing to Explain The length of the base of each side of the Great Pyramid of Giza is 756 feet long. If the Great Pyramid of Giza is a square pyramid, what is the distance around the base of the pyramid?

For **21** and **22**, use the rectangular pyramid shown at the right.

21. How many edges does the rectangular pyramid have?

22. How many vertices does the rectangular pyramid have?

23. A square pyramid is a special kind of rectangular pyramid. It has 1 square face and 5 vertices. How many triangular faces does a square pyramid have?

24. Which number is **NOT** between 0.5 and $\frac{3}{4}$ on a number line?

A $\frac{5}{8}$ **C** $\frac{13}{16}$

B 0.6 **D** 0.7

25. How many edges does this cube have?

A 6 edges **C** 8 edges

B 10 edges **D** 12 edges

26. In one soccer season, the Cougars scored six times as many goals as Jason made all season. Jason scored 12 goals. How many goals did the Cougars score throughout the season?

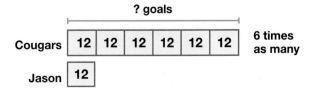

Views of Solids: Nets

How can you use a two-dimensional shape to represent a three-dimensional solid?

You can open up a three-dimensional solid to show a pattern. This pattern is called a net. The faces or <u>flat surfaces of a solid figure</u> are shown by a net.

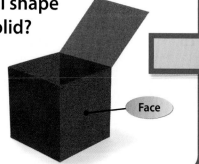

Face

MG 3.6 Visualize, describe, and make models of geometric solids (e.g., prisms, pyramids) in terms of the number and shape of faces, edges, and vertices; interpret two-dimensional representations of three-dimensional objects; and draw patterns (of faces) for a solid that, when cut and folded, will make a model of the solid.

Guided Practice*

Do you know HOW?

For **1** through **4**, identify how many faces each solid has.

1.

2.

3.

4.

Do you UNDERSTAND?

5. How is a cube like a rectangular prism?

6. Name a solid that has exactly 3 rectangular faces.

7. Draw a different net for the cube in the example above.

Independent Practice

For **8** through **14**, name the solid figure that can be made.

8.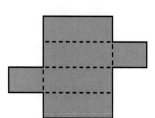

9.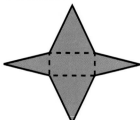

10.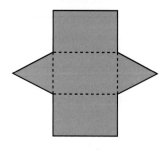

11.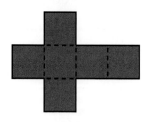

DIGITAL
Animated Glossary
www.pearsonsuccessnet.com

For another example, see Set H on page 220.

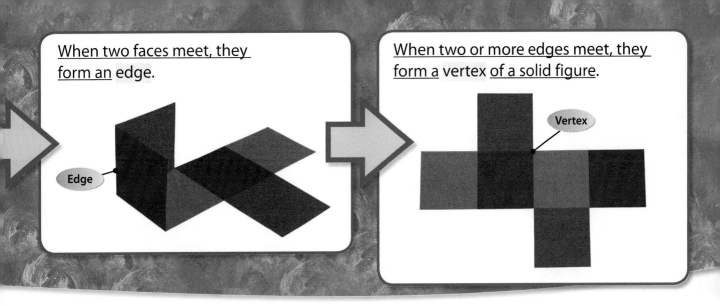

When two faces meet, they form an **edge**.

Edge

When two or more edges meet, they form a **vertex** of a solid figure.

Vertex

For **12** through **14**, name the solid figure that can be made.

12.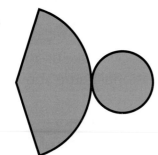

13.

14.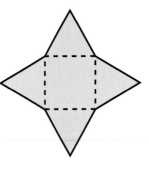

Problem Solving

15. Helga has baseball pennants hanging on all 4 walls of her bedroom. There are 7 pennants on each wall. How many pennants is this?

16. The net of what figure is shown below?

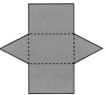

17. Draw a net for the figure below.

18. A jet plane travels at 450 miles per hour. It takes about 4 hours to fly from San Francisco to Wichita. What is the approximate distance between the two cities?

19. What is the name of the quadrilateral shown to the right?

    A parallelogram **C** rhombus

    B rectangle   **D** all of the above

Lesson

8-9

MG 3.6 Visualize, describe, and make models of geometric solids (e.g., prisms, pyramids) in terms of the number and shape of faces, edges, and vertices; interpret two-dimensional representations of three-dimensional objects; and draw patterns (of faces) for a solid that, when cut and folded, will make a model of the solid.

Views of Solids—Perspective

How can you get information about a solid from different perspectives?

You can think about solids from different perspectives. What would this solid look like from the front? From the side? From the top?

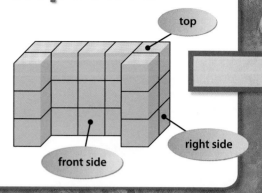

top

right side

front side

Guided Practice*

Do you know HOW?

front

1. Draw the top view of the solid figure.

2. Draw a side view of the solid figure.

3. Draw a front view of the solid figure.

Do you UNDERSTAND?

4. How many blocks make up the three-dimensional figure above?

5. How many blocks are not visible from the top view of the three-dimensional figure above?

6. In Exercise 1, how many blocks are not visible in the front view of the three-dimensional figure?

Independent Practice

For **7** through **12**, draw front, right, and top views of each stack of unit blocks.

7.

front

8.

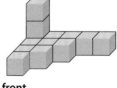

front

9.

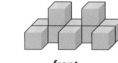

front

10.

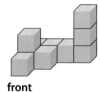

front

11.

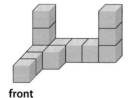

front

12.

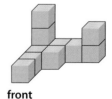

front

*For another example, see Set I on page 221.

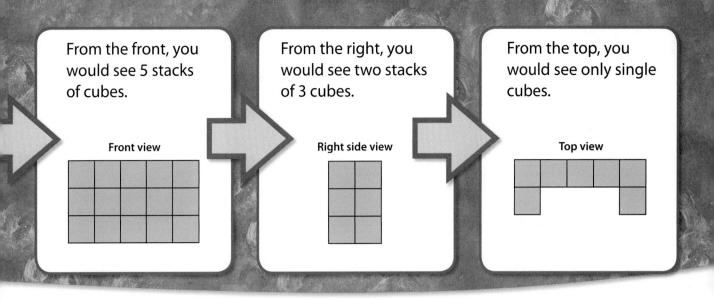

From the front, you would see 5 stacks of cubes.

Front view

From the right, you would see two stacks of 3 cubes.

Right side view

From the top, you would see only single cubes.

Top view

Problem Solving

13. How many edges does this retangular prism have?

A 4 edges
C 8 edges
B 6 edges
D 12 edges

14. The net of what figure is shown below?

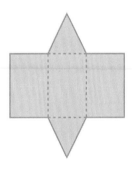

15. Explain why the net of a cube has six squares.

16. What would the top view of a cylinder look like?

17. Which choice below gives the number of faces, edges, and vertices of a cube?

A 6, 12, 8
C 4, 5, 6
B 6, 8, 12
D None of the above.

18. Number Sense Without dividing, tell whether $320 \div 4$ has a two-digit or a three-digit quotient. Explain how you know.

19. The image to the right is of the Great Pyramid in Egypt. What shape do you see from a side view?

MR 3.3 Develop generalizations of the results obtained and apply them in other circumstances.
Also **MR 3.0, MG 3.0.**

Problem Solving

Make and Test Generalizations

What is true about all of these shapes?

Guided Practice*

Do you know HOW?

1. Look at each group of three letters below. Give a generalization for each group of letters that does not apply to the other group of three letters.

E F T   **C O S**

Do you UNDERSTAND?

2. **Writing to Explain** Is the generalization that every four sided polygon has at least one right angle correct? If not, draw a picture to show why not.

3. **Write a Problem** Select 3 items and make two correct generalizations about them.

Independent Practice

Solve.

4. Look at each group of numbers below. Compare the size of the factors to each product. What generalization can you make about factors and products for whole numbers?

   $6 \times 8 = 48$ $46 \times 5 = 230$ $1 \times 243 = 243$

5. Write the factors for 8, 16, and 20. What generalization can you make about all multiples of 4?

Stuck? Try this....

- What do I know?
- What diagram can I use to help understand the problem?
- Can I use addition, subtraction, multiplication, or division?
- Is all of my work correct?
- Did I answer the right question?
- Is my answer reasonable?

*For another example, see Set K on page 221.

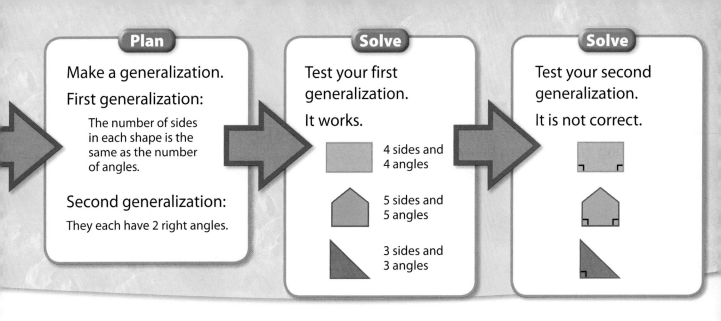

Plan

Make a generalization.

First generalization:

The number of sides in each shape is the same as the number of angles.

Second generalization:

They each have 2 right angles.

Solve

Test your first generalization.

It works.

4 sides and 4 angles

5 sides and 5 angles

3 sides and 3 angles

Solve

Test your second generalization.

It is not correct.

6. What generalization can you make about each of the polygons at the right?

   A All sides of each polygon are the same length.

   B All polygons have 5 sides.

   C All polygons have 4 angles.

   D All polygons have 3 angles.

7. The factors for 3 and 6 are shown in the table to the right. Jan concluded if you double a number, then you double the number of factors. Is Jan correct? Why or why not?

Number	3	6
Factors	1, 3	1, 2, 3, 6

8. How many faces does a rectangular pyramid have?

9. How many acute angles can an isosceles triangle have?

10. Look at the pattern below. Draw the shape that would come next.

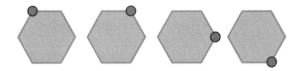

11. What generalization could be made about the triangles below?

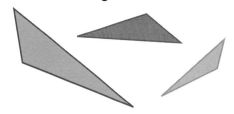

12. **Writing to Explain** Susan said that all squares are rectangles and therefore all rectangles are squares. Is Susan correct? Why or why not?

13. Michael lives on the 21st floor of a 25 story building. If each floor is 12 feet in height, how many feet above ground level is Michael's apartment?

1. During a game, some of the sticks landed in the pattern below. Which line is parallel to line S? (8-1)

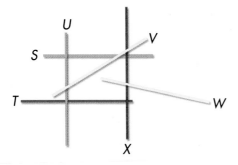

A Line *T*

B Line *U*

C Line *W*

D Line *X*

2. Circle *R* is shown below.

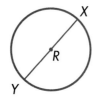

What does line segment *YR* appear to be? (8-6)

A A diameter

B A center

C A radius

D A chord

3. Which polygon has 8 edges? (8-3)

A Pentagon

B Octagon

C Triangle

D Hexgon

4. Which type of angle is angle *A*? (8-2)

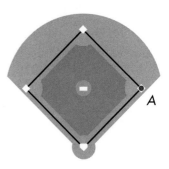

A Acute

B Obtuse

C Right

D Straight

5. Thomas chose these shapes.

He said the following shapes did not belong with the ones he chose.

Which is the best description of the shapes Thomas chose? (8-10)

A Polygons with more than 4 sides

B Polygons with parallel sides

C Polygons with all sides congruent

D Polygons with a right angle

6. Which polygon has more than 5 vertices? (8-3)

A Pentagon

B Quadrilateral

C Triangle

D Hexagon

7. Which view is shown of this solid? (8-9)

Solid   View

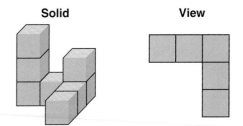

A Front view

B Top view

C Side view

D The view is not from this solid.

8. What solid figure can be made from the net shown below? (8-8)

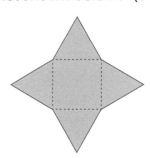

A Triangular pyramid

B Square pyramid

C Rectangular pyramid

D Rectangular prism

9. Which geometric terms best describe the triangle? (8-4)

A Isosceles, acute

B Isosceles, right

C Equilateral, obtuse

D Scalene, acute

10. Which best describes the tissue box? (8-7)

A 5 faces and 12 edges

B 6 faces and 8 edges

C 6 faces and 12 edges

D 12 faces and 6 edges

11. Which statement is true about the quadrilaterals shown below? (8-5)

A They are all rhombuses.

B They are all squares.

C They are all rectangles.

D They are all parallelograms.

Set A, pages 194–195

Pairs of lines are given special names.

Line DE and FG are parallel lines.

Remember that perpendicular lines intersect.

Match each term on the left with the correct image on the right.

1. _____ parallel lines   **a**

2. _____ point   **b**

3. _____ intersecting lines   **c**

Set B, pages 196–197

Geometric terms are used to describe figures.

A ray has one endpoint and continues on forever in one direction.

An angle is formed by two rays or line segments with a common endpoint.

Remember that a line segment does not continue beyond its endpoints.

Use geometric terms to describe what is shown.

1.   2.

3.   4.

Set C, pages 198–199

A polygon is a closed figure made up of line segments called sides. Each side meets at a point called a vertex.

Count the number of sides and vertices to identify the polygon.

The polygon is a hexagon.

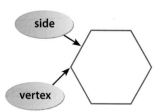

Remember that a polygon has the same number of sides and vertices .

Write the number of sides and vertices of each polygon.

1. octagon   2. square

3. pentagon   4. trapezoid

Set D, pages 200–201

Triangles can be classified by their sides and angles.

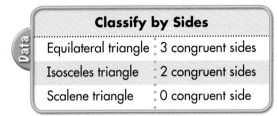

Classify by Sides	
Equilateral triangle	3 congruent sides
Isosceles triangle	2 congruent sides
Scalene triangle	0 congruent side

Classify by Angles	
Right triangle	one right angle
Acute triangle	all acute angles
Obtuse triangle	one obtuse anlge

Remember that an acute angle has a measure less than 90°. An obtuse angle has a measure greater than 90°.

Classify each triangle by its sides and angles.

1.  2.

3.   4.

Set E, pages 202–203

Name the quadrilateral.

Opposite sides are parallel and the same length. There are no right angles.

It is a parallelogram.

Remember that a quadrilateral can be a rectangle, square, trapezoid, parallelogram, or rhombus.

Classify each quadrilateral.

1.   2.

Set F, pages 204–205

- A radius connects the center of a circle with any point on the circle.

- A diameter is a line segment that connects two points on the circle that passes through the center of the circle.

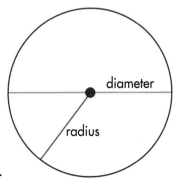

diameter

radius

Remember, on a circle all points are the same distance from the center. Use geometric terms to describe what is shown in red.

1.   2.

3.   4.

5.   6.

Set G, pages 206–209

Name the solid figure.

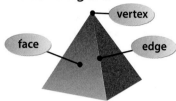

Identify what plane figures form the faces of the figure.

How many faces, edges, and vertices does this figure have?

The figure has 5 faces, 8 edges, and 5 vertices.

The solid figure is a square pyramid. Four of the faces are triangles, and one face is a square.

Remember that some solid figures have curved surfaces.

1. How many faces does a rectangular prism have?

2. How many edges does a cube have?

3. How many vertices does a cylinder have?

4. What plane figure is a face of both a cylinder and a cone?

Name the figures shown.

5.    6.

Set H, pages 210–211

Tell which solid figure can be made from the net below.

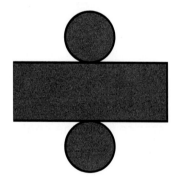

- When two or more faces meet, they form an edge.

- When two or more edges meet, they form a vertex of a solid figure.

When folded and taped together, the net would form a cylinder.

Remember, you can use a net to show all the faces of a solid figure. Copy and complete the table.

		Faces	Edges	Vertices
1.	Triangular prism	5		
2.	Square prism			5
3.	Cube		12	
4.	Rectangular prism	6		
5.	Triangular pyramid			4

Set I, pages 212–213

Draw front, right, and top views of this solid.

Remember to consider blocks that might be hidden from your view in the drawings.

Draw the top, right side, and front views of each solid figures.

Here is a front view of the solid.

Here is a right side view of the solid.

Here is a top view of the solid.

1.

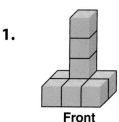

Front

2.

Front

3.

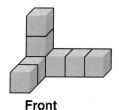

Front

Set J, pages 214–215

What is the same in all of these shapes?

What do I know? The picture shows a square, a right isosceles triangle, and a rectangle.

What am I asked to find? What is the same in all of these shapes?

The number of sides in each is the same as the number of angles. Test your generalization.

| 4 sides, 4 angles | 3 sides, 3 angles | 4 sides, 4 angles |

Remember to test your generalizations.

1. Look at each group of numbers below. Give a generalization for each group of numbers that does not apply to the other group of three numbers.

Fraction Meanings and Concepts

1 Who designed the California state flag? You will find out in Lesson 9-1.

CALIFORNIA REPUBLIC

2 How many gallons of milk does an average milk cow produce each day? You will find out in Lesson 9-5.

3 Only 180 pandas are living in captivity. What fraction of pandas living in captivity were born in 2005? You will find out in Lesson 9-4.

4 The world's largest pumpkin pie was made in 2005. How much did the pumpkin pie weigh? You will find out in Lesson 9-3.

Vocabulary

Choose the best term from the box.

- fraction
- thirds
- denominator
- numerator

1. Three equal parts of a shape are called ? .

2. A ? can name a part of a whole.

3. The number below the fraction bar in a fraction is the ? .

Division Facts

Divide.

4. $20 \div 4$ 5. $48 \div 8$ 6. $36 \div 9$

7. $54 \div 6$ 8. $30 \div 6$ 9. $18 \div 6$

10. $42 \div 7$ 11. $21 \div 3$ 12. $40 \div 8$

13. Amelia hiked 12 miles in 6 hours. How many miles did Amelia hike each hour?

Fraction Concepts

Name the number of equal parts in each figure.

14.   15.   16.

17.   18.   19.

20. **Writing to Explain** Is $\frac{1}{4}$ of the figure below red? Explain why or why not.

NS 1.5 Explain different interpretations of fractions, for example, parts of a whole, parts of a set, and division of whole numbers by whole numbers; explain equivalence of fractions. Also **NS 1.7**.

Regions and Sets

How can you name and show parts of a region and parts of a set?

A fraction is a symbol, such as $\frac{2}{3}$ or $\frac{5}{1}$, used to name a part of a whole, a part of a set, a location on a number line, or a division of whole numbers.

What fraction of the Nigerian flag is green?

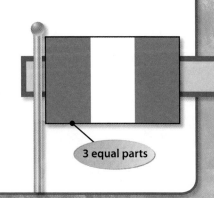

3 equal parts

Another Example **How can you draw parts of a region and parts of a set?**

Draw Parts of a Region

Draw a flag that is $\frac{3}{5}$ green.

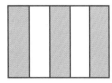

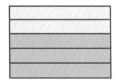

In both flags, there are 5 equal parts, and 3 of the parts are green. Both flags are $\frac{3}{5}$ green.

Draw Parts of a Set

Draw a set of shapes in which $\frac{4}{10}$ of the shapes are small triangles.

There are 4 small triangles out of 10 shapes. So, $\frac{4}{10}$, or four tenths, of the shapes are small triangles.

Explain It

1. Draw a flag that is $\frac{3}{6}$ green. How does this flag compare to a flag of the same size that is $\frac{3}{5}$ green?

2. What fraction of the set of shapes above is orange? What fraction of the shapes are squares? What is the same about these two fractions?

Parts of a region

The numerator <u>tells how many equal parts are described</u>. The denominator <u>tells how many equal parts there are in all</u>.

$$\frac{2}{3}$$ ← Numerator
← Denominator

In the Nigerian flag, $\frac{2}{3}$ of the flag is green.

Parts of a set

These flags show the first 4 letters in the International Code of Signals:

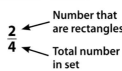

What fraction of these flags are rectangles?

$$\frac{2}{4}$$ ← Number that are rectangles
← Total number in set

In this set of 4 flags, $\frac{2}{4}$ are rectangles.

Guided Practice*

Do you know HOW?

In **1** and **2**, write a fraction to describe the part of each region or set that is green.

1.

2.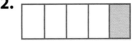

In **3** and **4**, draw a model for each fraction.

3. $\frac{4}{5}$ of a region   4. $\frac{2}{9}$ of a set

Do you UNDERSTAND?

5. **Writing to Explain** What fraction of the signal flags at the top contain blue? What fraction of the flags contain yellow? Why do these fractions both have the same denominator?

6. What fraction of the squares below contain a red circle? What fraction of the circles are red?

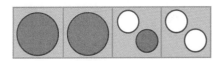

Independent Practice

In **7** and **8**, write a fraction to describe the part of each region or set that is green.

7.    8.

*For another example, see Set A on page 248.

Independent Practice

In **9** and **10**, write a fraction to describe the part of each region or set that is blue.

9.

10. ▲ ▲ ▲ ▲ ▲ ▲

In **11** through **18**, draw a model for each fraction.

11. $\frac{7}{10}$ of a region   **12.** $\frac{2}{8}$ of a region   **13.** $\frac{1}{6}$ of a region   **14.** $\frac{3}{9}$ of a region

15. $\frac{1}{8}$ of a set   **16.** $\frac{5}{6}$ of a set   **17.** $\frac{3}{7}$ of a set   **18.** $\frac{1}{10}$ of a set

Problem Solving

19. Maya tried a skateboard trick 12 times. She got it to work 3 times. What fraction describes the number of times the trick did **NOT** work?

20. Jane has a fish tank. Draw a model to show that $\frac{3}{10}$ of the fish are black and the rest of the fish are orange.

21. Students arranged 32 chairs in equal rows for a school concert. Describe two ways the students could have arranged the chairs.

22. When the numerator is the same as the denominator, what do you know about the fraction?

23. **Geometry** In the signal flag shown below, is $\frac{1}{3}$ of the flag red? Explain why or why not.

24. Alan's grandfather made 10 pancakes. Alan ate 3 pancakes. His sister ate 2 pancakes. What fraction of the pancakes did Alan eat?

A $\frac{3}{10}$ C $\frac{5}{10}$

B $\frac{2}{5}$ D $\frac{3}{5}$

Use the diagram at the right for **25**.

25. What fraction of the California state flag is the red stripe at the bottom?

A $\frac{1}{2}$ B $\frac{1}{3}$ C $\frac{1}{6}$ D $\frac{1}{10}$

Mixed Problem Solving

Some poems are written in a patterned form.
Below are examples of two types of poems.

Pattern 1	Pattern 2
A-A-B-C-C-B	A-A-B-B-C-C
Example: Old Mother Hubbard (A) Went to the cupboard (A) To fetch her poor dog a bone; (B) But when she came there (C) The cupboard was bare, (C) And so the poor dog had none. (B)	Example: Little Boy Blue, come blow your horn, (A) The sheep's in the meadow, the cow's in the corn; (A) Where is the boy who looks after the sheep? (B) He's under a haycock, fast asleep. (B) Will you wake him? No, not I, (C) For if I do, he's sure to cry. (C)

1. If Pattern 2 has 6 lines, which line will also rhyme with the fifth line?

2. What pattern do you notice in Pattern 2?

3. If you knew the first three lines of a poem, would you be able to tell if it follows Pattern 1 or Pattern 2.

4. Is there a difference in the number of lines that rhyme in Pattern 1 than in Pattern 2?

5. Which of the patterns described above does this poem follow?

> Jack and Jill
> Went up the hill
> To fetch a pail of water.
> Jack fell down
> And broke his crown
> And Jill came tumbling after.

6. One type of poem is called a limerick. Below is an example of a limerick:

> Hickory, dickory, dock,
> The mouse ran up the clock.
> The clock struck one,
> And down he run,
> Hickory, dickory, dock.

What is the rhyming pattern of the limerick?

7. A book contains 25 poems with 15 poems that follow Pattern 2 and 10 poems that follow Pattern 1. How many sets of rhyming lines are there?

    A 65   **C** 150

    B 75   **D** 250

8. How many lines will you read if a book contains 12 poems that follow Pattern 1 and 6 poems that follow Pattern 2?

Lesson

9-2

NS 1.5 Explain different interpretations of fractions, for example, parts of a whole, parts of a set, and division of whole numbers by whole numbers; explain equivalence of fractions.

Fractions and Division

How can you share items?

Tom, Joe, and Sam made clay pots using two rolls of clay. If they shared the clay equally, what fraction of the clay did each friend use?

3 friends share 2 rolls of clay

Choose an Operation
Divide to find a fraction of the total.

Guided Practice*

Do you know HOW?

Tell what fraction each person gets.

1. Three people share 2 cans of paint.

2. Two students share 1 sheet of paper.

3. Four friends share 3 apples.

4. Five friends share 5 bagels.

Do you UNDERSTAND?

5. How do you write 3 ÷ 5 as a fraction?

6. In Exercises 1 through 4, did you use the number of items as the denominator or as the numerator?

7. If 6 people equally shared 3 rolls of clay to make pots, how much clay did each person use?

Independent Practice

In **8** through **13**, tell what fraction each person gets when they share equally.

 The number of items shared is the numerator and the number of people is the denominator.

8. Four students share 3 breakfast bars.

9. Ten friends share 7 dollars.

10. Five women each run an equal part of a 3-mile relay.

11. Ten students share 1 hour to give their reports.

12. Six soccer players share 5 oranges.

13. Five friends pay for a 4 dollar gift.

For another example, see Set B on page 248.

Step 1

Think about sharing 2 rolls of clay among 3 people. Divide each roll into 3 equal parts.

Each part is $1 \div 3$ or $\frac{1}{3}$.

Step 2

The parts were shared equally.

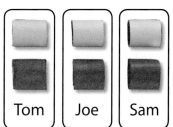

Tom   Joe   Sam

Each person used one part from each roll of clay for a total of 2 parts.

This is the same as $\frac{2}{3}$ of one roll of clay.

You can write division as a fraction. So, $2 \div 3 = \frac{2}{3}$.

Problem Solving

14. Eight friends divide 3 pizzas equally. How much pizza does each friend get?

15. Algebra Find the missing numbers in the following pattern:

1, 3, 9, ▢, 81, ▢

16. Reasoning A group of friends went to the movies. They shared 2 bags of popcorn equally. If each person got $\frac{2}{3}$ of a bag of popcorn, how many people were in the group?

17. When Sharon's reading group took turns reading aloud, every student had a chance to read. They finished a 12 page story. If each student read 3 pages, how many students were in the reading group?

18. There were 16 teams at a gymnastics meet. Each team had 12 members. How many gymnasts participated in the meet?

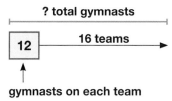

? total gymnasts

12   16 teams

gymnasts on each team

19. Twenty-one soccer players were put into 3 equal teams. How many players were on each team?

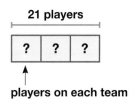

21 players

? ? ?

players on each team

20. **Think** **About the Process** Four friends are baking bread. They equally share 3 sticks of butter. Which number sentence can be used to find the fraction of a stick of butter that each friend uses?

A $3 \div 12 = ▢$ **C** $3 \div 4 = ▢$

B $5 \div 12 = ▢$ **D** $3 \div 5 = ▢$

3 sticks of butter

NS 1.5 Explain different interpretations of fractions, for example, parts of a whole, parts of a set, and division of whole numbers by whole numbers; explain equivalence of fractions.

Equivalent Fractions

Hands-On
fraction strips

$\frac{1}{8}$

How can you find two fractions that name the same part of a whole?

Lee ate $\frac{1}{4}$ of a pizza. Write another fraction that is equivalent to $\frac{1}{4}$.

Equivalent fractions <u>name the same part of a whole</u>.

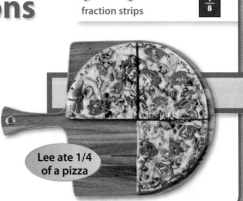

Lee ate 1/4 of a pizza

Another Example How can you divide to find an equivalent fraction?

Sara ate $\frac{6}{8}$ of a small mushroom pizza. Which fraction is equivalent to $\frac{6}{8}$?

Divide the numerator and denominator by the same number to find an equivalent fraction.

$$\frac{6}{8} \overset{\div 2}{\underset{\div 2}{=}} \frac{3}{4}$$ So, $\frac{3}{4}$ is equivalent to $\frac{6}{8}$.

Check your answer using fractions strips.

Find $\frac{6}{8}$ by counting 6 of the $\frac{1}{8}$ strips.

Find $\frac{3}{4}$ by counting 3 of the $\frac{1}{4}$ strips.

Both $\frac{6}{8}$ and $\frac{3}{4}$ name the same part of a whole.

1											
$\frac{1}{2}$						$\frac{1}{2}$					
$\frac{1}{3}$				$\frac{1}{3}$				$\frac{1}{3}$			
$\frac{1}{4}$			$\frac{1}{4}$			$\frac{1}{4}$			$\frac{1}{4}$		
$\frac{1}{5}$		$\frac{1}{5}$		$\frac{1}{5}$		$\frac{1}{5}$		$\frac{1}{5}$			
$\frac{1}{6}$		$\frac{1}{6}$		$\frac{1}{6}$		$\frac{1}{6}$		$\frac{1}{6}$		$\frac{1}{6}$	
$\frac{1}{8}$	$\frac{1}{8}$	$\frac{1}{8}$	$\frac{1}{8}$	$\frac{1}{8}$	$\frac{1}{8}$	$\frac{1}{8}$	$\frac{1}{8}$				
$\frac{1}{10}$	$\frac{1}{10}$	$\frac{1}{10}$	$\frac{1}{10}$	$\frac{1}{10}$	$\frac{1}{10}$	$\frac{1}{10}$	$\frac{1}{10}$	$\frac{1}{10}$	$\frac{1}{10}$		
$\frac{1}{12}$	$\frac{1}{12}$	$\frac{1}{12}$	$\frac{1}{12}$	$\frac{1}{12}$	$\frac{1}{12}$	$\frac{1}{12}$	$\frac{1}{12}$	$\frac{1}{12}$	$\frac{1}{12}$	$\frac{1}{12}$	$\frac{1}{12}$

Explain It

1. Can you divide 6 and 8 by any number to find an equivalent fraction? Explain.

2. Using fraction strips, find two fractions that are equivalent to $\frac{9}{12}$.

You can multiply the numerator and the denominator by the same number to find an equivalent fraction.

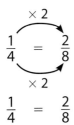

$$\frac{1}{4} = \frac{2}{8}$$

Use fractions strips to find equivalent fractions.

Both $\frac{1}{4}$ and $\frac{2}{8}$ name the same part of a whole.

So, $\frac{1}{4}$ and $\frac{2}{8}$ are equivalent fractions.

Guided Practice*

Do you know HOW?

In **1** through **6**, multiply or divide to find an equivalent fraction.

1. $\overset{\times 3}{\underset{\times 3}{\frac{2}{3}}} = \frac{\square}{\square}$

2. $\overset{\div 5}{\underset{\div 5}{\frac{10}{15}}} = \frac{\square}{\square}$

3. $\frac{1}{4} = \frac{\square}{16}$

4. $\frac{10}{12} = \frac{5}{\square}$

5. $\frac{15}{20} = \frac{\square}{4}$

6. $\frac{3}{8} = \frac{9}{\square}$

Do you UNDERSTAND?

7. Suppose Lee's pizza had 12 equal slices instead of 4. How many slices are gone if he ate $\frac{1}{4}$ of the pizza? Explain.

8. **Reasoning** Josh, Lisa, and Vicki each ate $\frac{1}{2}$ of a pizza. The pizzas were the same size, but Josh ate 1 slice, Lisa ate 3 slices, and Vicki ate 4 slices. How is this possible?

Independent Practice

Leveled Practice For **9** through **16**, multiply or divide to find equivalent fractions.

Tip You can check your answers using fractions strips.

9. $\overset{\times 5}{\underset{\times 5}{\frac{4}{9}}} = \frac{\square}{\square}$

10. $\overset{\div 3}{\underset{\div 3}{\frac{9}{15}}} = \frac{\square}{\square}$

11. $\overset{\times 2}{\underset{\times 2}{\frac{5}{7}}} = \frac{\square}{\square}$

12. $\overset{\div 2}{\underset{\div 2}{\frac{2}{4}}} = \frac{\square}{\square}$

13. $\frac{10}{10} = \frac{1}{\square}$

14. $\frac{3}{4} = \frac{12}{\square}$

15. $\frac{10}{20} = \frac{\square}{4}$

16. $\frac{30}{40} = \frac{6}{\square}$

 DIGITAL Animated Glossary, eTools
www.pearsonsuccessnet.com

In **17** through **26**, find an equivalent fraction for each.

17. $\frac{8}{18}$ **18.** $\frac{2}{10}$ **19.** $\frac{1}{3}$ **20.** $\frac{3}{5}$ **21.** $\frac{24}{30}$

22. $\frac{60}{80}$ **23.** $\frac{2}{15}$ **24.** $\frac{21}{28}$ **25.** $\frac{12}{15}$ **26.** $\frac{12}{20}$

Problem Solving

For **27** through **29**, use the fraction strips at the right.

27. Name 10 pairs of equivalent fractions.

28. **Reasoning** How can you show that $\frac{6}{8}$ and $\frac{9}{12}$ are equivalent by multiplying and dividing?

 Tip *First, divide the numerator and denominator of $\frac{9}{12}$ by 3. Then multiply.*

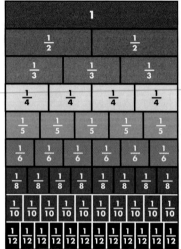

29. The world's largest pumpkin pie weighed 2,020 pounds. The pie was $12\frac{1}{3}$ feet across and $\frac{1}{3}$ foot thick. Write a fraction equivalent to $\frac{1}{3}$.

30. In a school poetry contest, 15 out of 45 students who entered will win a small prize. Half of the remaining students receive a certificate. How many students get a certificate?

31. **Algebra** James has 18 mystery books and 12 sports books. Rich has twice as many mystery books and three times as many sports books. How many books does Rich have?

32. **Writing to Explain** In the United States, $\frac{1}{5}$ of all states start with the letters M, A, or N. How can you use equivalent fractions to find out how many states this is?

33. Look at the model. Name three equivalent fractions for the area that is red.

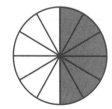

34. Where would the parentheses go for the following expression to be true?

$7 + 5 - 8 - 3 = 7$

A $(7 + 5) - 8 - 3$

B $7 + (5 - 8) - 3$

C $7 + 5 - (8 - 3)$

D $(7 + 5 - 8 - 3)$

Algebra Connections

Missing Numbers and Operations

Often there is more than one way to connect two numbers when a number and the operation is missing.

Here are some rules:

- If the number that appears first is less than the second number, try using addition and multiplication.

- If the number that appears first is greater than the second number, try using subtraction and division.

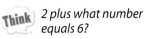

Example: 2 ☐ ▨ = 6

Use addition:

 2 plus what number equals 6?

2 + 4 = 6

Use multiplication:

 2 times what number equals 6?

2 × 3 = 6

Find the missing operation for each ☐ and the missing number for each ▨.

1. 4 ☐ ▨ = 8

4 ☐ ▨ = 8

2. 45 ☐ ▨ = 9

45 ☐ ▨ = 9

3. 80 ☐ ▨ = 8

80 ☐ ▨ = 8

4. 6 ☐ ▨ = 30

6 ☐ ▨ = 30

5. 8 ☐ ▨ = 56

8 ☐ ▨ = 56

6. 54 ☐ ▨ = 6

54 ☐ ▨ = 6

7. 3 ☐ ▨ = 21

3 ☐ ▨ = 21

8. 64 ☐ ▨ = 8

64 ☐ ▨ = 8

9. 28 ☐ ▨ = 4

28 ☐ ▨ = 4

10. 6 ☐ ▨ = 36

6 ☐ ▨ = 36

11. 5 ☐ ▨ = 40

5 ☐ ▨ = 40

12. 34 ☐ ▨ = 17

34 ☐ ▨ = 17

· ·

For **13** through **16**, find the missing operation and number. Then find the answer.

13. Cassie has $4. She wants to buy a blouse that costs $16. How much more money does Cassie need?

$4 ☐ $▨ = $16

14. Doug had 42 patio blocks. He stacked them in equal groups of 7 blocks. How many stacks were there?

42 ☐ ▨ = 7

15. Lesley had 37 postcards. She mailed some to her friends. If 25 postcards were left, how many stamps did she use?

37 ☐ ▨ = 25

16. There were 4 rabbits in each litter. Gerta's pet rabbit was mother to 20 rabbits. How many litters of rabbits were there?

4 ☐ ▨ = 20

NS 1.5 Explain different
interpretations of
fractions, for example,
parts of a whole, parts
of a set, and division
of whole numbers by
whole numbers; explain
equivalence of fractions

Fractions in Simplest Form

How do you write a fraction in simplest form?

Jason ran $\frac{4}{12}$ of the way around the track. Write $\frac{4}{12}$ in simplest form.

Since 4 is a factor of 12, it is a common factor of 4 and 12.

A fraction is in **simplest form** <u>when the numerator and denominator have no common factor other than 1.</u>

$\frac{4}{12}$ of the way around the track

Guided Practice*

Do you know HOW?

For **1** through **6**, write each fraction in simplest form.

1. $\frac{6}{8}$ **2.** $\frac{15}{45}$

3. $\frac{10}{100}$ **4.** $\frac{16}{80}$

5. $\frac{21}{33}$ **6.** $\frac{12}{14}$

Do you UNDERSTAND?

7. Writing to Explain Explain how you can tell $\frac{4}{9}$ is in simplest form.

8. Jamal ran $\frac{8}{12}$ of the way around a track. Write this fraction in simplest form.

 If the numerator and denominator are even numbers, they have 2 as a common factor.

Independent Practice

In **9** through **33**, write each fraction in simplest form.
If it is in simplest form, write simplest form.

9. $\frac{3}{12}$ **10.** $\frac{2}{10}$ **11.** $\frac{4}{8}$ **12.** $\frac{12}{16}$ **13.** $\frac{4}{6}$

14. $\frac{2}{5}$ **15.** $\frac{2}{6}$ **16.** $\frac{3}{16}$ **17.** $\frac{8}{10}$ **18.** $\frac{5}{12}$

19. $\frac{3}{7}$ **20.** $\frac{8}{20}$ **21.** $\frac{9}{10}$ **22.** $\frac{9}{15}$ **23.** $\frac{12}{20}$

24. $\frac{5}{6}$ **25.** $\frac{3}{9}$ **26.** $\frac{15}{18}$ **27.** $\frac{30}{40}$ **28.** $\frac{30}{35}$

29. $\frac{2}{3}$ **30.** $\frac{7}{14}$ **31.** $\frac{9}{16}$ **32.** $\frac{4}{12}$ **33.** $\frac{5}{15}$

DIGITAL Animated Glossary
www.pearsonsuccessnet.com

Write $\frac{4}{12}$ in simplest form by dividing twice.

4 and 12 are both even. Two is a common factor.

2 and 6 are both even. Two is a common factor.

Write $\frac{4}{12}$ in simplest form by dividing by 4.

$$\overset{\div 4}{\frac{4}{12}} = \underset{\div 4}{\frac{1}{3}}$$

In simplest form, $\frac{4}{12} = \frac{1}{3}$.

Problem Solving

34. Reasoning If the numerator and the denominator of a fraction are both prime numbers and not equal to each other, can the fraction be simplified?

35. Estimation About what fraction of this model is red?

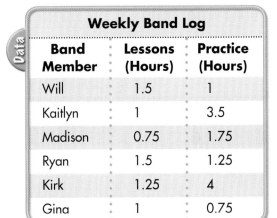

Use the table at the right for **36** and **37**.

36. What fraction of the band members practice for more than 2 hours a week? Write your answer in simplest form.

37. What fraction of the band members spend more time on lessons than on practice? Write your answer in simplest form.

Data

Weekly Band Log		
Band Member	Lessons (Hours)	Practice (Hours)
Will	1.5	1
Kaitlyn	1	3.5
Madison	0.75	1.75
Ryan	1.5	1.25
Kirk	1.25	4
Gina	1	0.75

38. **Think About the Process** Which of the following helps you find the simplest form of $\frac{4}{8}$?

  A Subtract 4 from 8

  B Divide 4 by 8

  C Compare fraction strips for fourths and eighths

  D Compare fraction strips for eighths and halves

39. The year 2005 was a record year for panda births. In that year, 16 pandas were born in captivity. If a total of 180 pandas are living in captivity, what fraction of pandas were born in 2005? Write your answer in simplest form.

NS 1.5 Explain different interpretations of fractions, for example, parts of a whole, parts of a set, and division of whole numbers by whole numbers; explain equivalence of fractions. Also **NS 1.7**.

Improper Fractions and Mixed Numbers

fraction strips

$\frac{1}{8}$

How can you name an amount in two different ways?

How many times will Matt need to fill his $\frac{1}{4}$-cup container to make $2\frac{1}{4}$ cups of punch?

$2\frac{1}{4}$ is a mixed number. A mixed number <u>has a whole number part and a fraction part</u>.

$2\frac{1}{4}$ cups

Other Examples

Write a mixed number as an improper fraction.

$3\frac{1}{3}$ Multiply the whole number by the denominator. Then, add the numerator.

$3 \times 3 = 9$
$9 + 1 = 10$

$\frac{10}{3}$ Write the sum as the numerator. The denominator stays the same.

Write an improper fraction as a mixed number.

$\frac{17}{4}$ Divide the numerator by the denominator.

$$4\overline{)17} \quad \begin{array}{r} 4\ R1 \\ \hline -16 \\ \hline 1 \end{array}$$

$4\frac{1}{4}$ Write the quotient as the whole number. Write the remainder as the numerator. The denominator stays the same.

Guided Practice*

Do you know HOW?

Write the mixed number as an improper fraction. Write the improper fraction as a mixed number or whole number.

1. $1\frac{3}{8}$
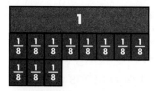

2. $\frac{4}{3}$
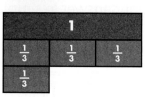

Do you UNDERSTAND?

3. If Matt filled a $3\frac{1}{4}$ cup container, how many $\frac{1}{4}$ cups would he need to use?

4. Nancy bought $7\frac{1}{2}$ gallons of milk. She bought only half-gallon containers. How many half-gallon containers did she buy?

DIGITAL   Animated Glossary, eTools
www.pearsonsuccessnet.com

Use fraction strips to write $2\frac{1}{4}$ as an improper fraction.

An improper fraction <u>has a numerator greater than or equal to its denominator.</u>

There are 9 fourths or $\frac{9}{4}$ shaded. So, $2\frac{1}{4} = \frac{9}{4}$.

Matt needs to fill the $\frac{1}{4}$-cup container 9 times.

1			
$\frac{1}{4}$	$\frac{1}{4}$	$\frac{1}{4}$	$\frac{1}{4}$
$\frac{1}{4}$	$\frac{1}{4}$	$\frac{1}{4}$	$\frac{1}{4}$
$\frac{1}{4}$			

Use fraction strips to write $\frac{3}{2}$ as a mixed number.

1	
$\frac{1}{2}$	$\frac{1}{2}$
$\frac{1}{2}$	

There is 1 whole and 1 half left over. So, $\frac{3}{2} = 1\frac{1}{2}$.

Independent Practice

For **5** through **9**, change each mixed number to an improper fraction.

5. $5\frac{1}{3}$
6. $2\frac{7}{8}$
7. $3\frac{2}{3}$
8. $6\frac{1}{4}$
9. $4\frac{4}{5}$

For **10** through **14**, change each improper fraction to a mixed number or whole number.

10. $\frac{12}{3}$
11. $\frac{9}{2}$
12. $\frac{37}{5}$
13. $\frac{48}{9}$
14. $\frac{41}{7}$

Problem Solving

15. Julia bought $3\frac{1}{4}$ yards of fabric. How many $\frac{1}{4}$ yards of fabric did Julia buy?

16. In one week Nate drank $\frac{17}{3}$ cups of milk. Write $\frac{17}{3}$ as a mixed number.

17. Sara bought a box of 6 granola bars. The total weight was $7\frac{1}{3}$ ounces. Write $7\frac{1}{3}$ as an improper fraction.

18. Kathy wrote the mixed number for $\frac{35}{5}$ as $\frac{7}{5}$. Is she correct? Why or why not?

19. Chris finished eating his lunch in 11 minutes. His brother took 3 times as long. How many minutes did it take his brother to finish his lunch?

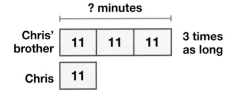

20. The average milk cow produces $4\frac{1}{2}$ gallons of milk a day. How much milk is this amount as an improper fraction?

A $\frac{11}{9}$ gallons   **C** $\frac{9}{2}$ gallons

B $\frac{19}{9}$ gallons   **D** $\frac{19}{2}$ gallon

Lesson

9-6

NS 1.5 Explain different interpretations of fractions, for example, parts of a whole, parts of a set, and division of whole numbers by whole numbers; explain equivalence of fractions.

fraction strips

$\frac{1}{8}$

Comparing Fractions

How can you compare fractions?

Isabella's father is building a model dinosaur with spare pieces of wood that measure $\frac{1}{4}$ of an inch and $\frac{5}{8}$ of an inch.

Which are longer, the $\frac{1}{4}$ inch pieces or the $\frac{5}{8}$ inch pieces?

$\frac{1}{4}$ of an inch

Guided Practice*

Do you know HOW?

Compare. Write >, <, or = for each ◯.
Use fraction strips or drawings to help.

1. $\frac{3}{4} \bigcirc \frac{6}{8}$ **2.** $\frac{1}{4} \bigcirc \frac{1}{10}$

3. $\frac{3}{5} \bigcirc \frac{7}{12}$ **4.** $\frac{1}{2} \bigcirc \frac{4}{5}$

Do you UNDERSTAND?

5. Mary says that $\frac{1}{8}$ is greater than $\frac{1}{4}$ because 8 is greater than 4. Is she right? Explain your answer.

6. Mr. Arnold used wood measuring $\frac{2}{5}$ foot, $\frac{1}{3}$ foot, and $\frac{3}{8}$ foot to build a birdhouse. Compare these lengths of wood.

Independent Practice

For **7** through **38**, compare, and then write >, <, or = for each ◯.
Use fraction strips or benchmark fractions to help.

7. $\frac{5}{6} \bigcirc \frac{10}{12}$ **8.** $\frac{3}{10} \bigcirc \frac{7}{8}$ **9.** $\frac{5}{12} \bigcirc \frac{1}{2}$ **10.** $\frac{7}{8} \bigcirc \frac{3}{4}$

11. $\frac{1}{3} \bigcirc \frac{2}{8}$ **12.** $\frac{1}{4} \bigcirc \frac{2}{3}$ **13.** $\frac{7}{12} \bigcirc \frac{3}{4}$ **14.** $\frac{2}{3} \bigcirc \frac{2}{12}$

15. $\frac{3}{8} \bigcirc \frac{2}{3}$ **16.** $\frac{3}{4} \bigcirc \frac{1}{8}$ **17.** $\frac{2}{3} \bigcirc \frac{5}{12}$ **18.** $\frac{1}{2} \bigcirc \frac{3}{4}$

19. $\frac{7}{10} \bigcirc \frac{11}{12}$ **20.** $\frac{7}{12} \bigcirc \frac{4}{10}$ **21.** $\frac{5}{12} \bigcirc \frac{4}{5}$ **22.** $\frac{2}{6} \bigcirc \frac{3}{12}$

23. $\frac{8}{10} \bigcirc \frac{3}{4}$ **24.** $\frac{3}{8} \bigcirc \frac{11}{12}$ **25.** $\frac{2}{3} \bigcirc \frac{10}{12}$ **26.** $\frac{7}{8} \bigcirc \frac{1}{6}$

DIGITAL   eTools
www.pearsonsuccessnet.com

Use benchmark fractions.

Compare $\frac{1}{4}$ and $\frac{5}{8}$.

You can use fraction strips to compare both fractions to $\frac{1}{2}$.

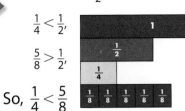

$\frac{1}{4} < \frac{1}{2}$,

$\frac{5}{8} > \frac{1}{2}$,

So, $\frac{1}{4} < \frac{5}{8}$

The $\frac{5}{8}$ inch pieces are longer.

Compare $\frac{1}{4}$ and $\frac{3}{4}$.

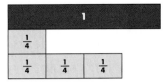

When the two fractions have the same denominators, you compare the numerators.

$$3 > 1$$

So, $\frac{3}{4} > \frac{1}{4}$.

---

27. $\frac{3}{8} \bigcirc \frac{7}{8}$

28. $\frac{2}{4} \bigcirc \frac{4}{8}$

29. $\frac{6}{8} \bigcirc \frac{8}{12}$

30. $\frac{1}{3} \bigcirc \frac{4}{9}$

31. $\frac{6}{8} \bigcirc \frac{8}{10}$

32. $\frac{3}{5} \bigcirc \frac{3}{6}$

33. $\frac{2}{12} \bigcirc \frac{2}{10}$

34. $\frac{5}{6} \bigcirc \frac{4}{5}$

35. $\frac{4}{4} \bigcirc \frac{1}{1}$

36. $\frac{2}{4} \bigcirc \frac{8}{10}$

37. $\frac{7}{8} \bigcirc \frac{3}{5}$

38. $\frac{3}{9} \bigcirc \frac{1}{3}$

Problem Solving

39. Number Sense Felicia drew the picture at the right to show that $\frac{3}{8}$ is greater than $\frac{3}{4}$. What was Felicia's mistake?

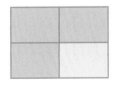

40. Writing to Explain Why can you compare two fractions with the same denominator by only comparing the numerators?

41. What can you conclude about $\frac{3}{5}$ and $\frac{12}{20}$ if you know that $\frac{3}{5} = \frac{6}{10}$ and that $\frac{6}{10} = \frac{12}{20}$?

42. Reasoning Which is longer, $\frac{1}{4}$ foot or $\frac{1}{4}$ yard? Explain.

43. If $34 \times 20 = 680$ then $34 \times 200 = $ ▢

44. A melon was divided into 8 equal slices. Juan ate three slices. Tom and Stacy ate the remaining slices. What fraction of the melon did Tom and Stacy eat?

   A $\frac{1}{4}$ **B** $\frac{2}{8}$ **C** $\frac{2}{3}$ **D** $\frac{5}{8}$

45. Neil is setting up for a dinner party. He has 6 tables each seating 5 guests and another table seating the left over 3 guests. How many people are coming to Neil's dinner party?

NS 1.5 Explain different interpretations of fractions, for example, parts of a whole, parts of a set, and division of whole numbers by whole numbers; explain equivalence of fractions.

Ordering Fractions

Hands-On
fraction strips $\frac{1}{8}$

How can you order fractions?

Three students made sculptures for a school project. Jeff's sculpture is $\frac{9}{12}$ foot tall, Scott's sculpture is $\frac{1}{3}$ foot tall, and Kristen's sculpture is $\frac{3}{6}$ foot tall. List the heights of the sculptures in order from least to greatest.

$\frac{9}{12}$ foot tall

Guided Practice*

Do you know HOW?

For **1** through **6**, order the fractions from least to greatest. Use fraction strips or drawings to help.

1. $\frac{2}{3}, \frac{1}{2}, \frac{5}{12}$

2. $\frac{5}{6}, \frac{1}{3}, \frac{1}{6}$

3. $\frac{7}{8}, \frac{3}{8}, \frac{3}{4}$

4. $\frac{2}{3}, \frac{3}{12}, \frac{3}{4}$

5. $\frac{7}{9}, \frac{2}{3}, \frac{4}{9}$

6. $\frac{2}{3}, \frac{1}{4}, \frac{1}{6}$

Do you UNDERSTAND?

7. What denominator would you use to find equivalent fractions when comparing $\frac{2}{3}, \frac{2}{4}, \frac{2}{12}$?

8. Three other students made sculptures with these heights: $\frac{2}{3}$ foot, $\frac{5}{6}$ foot, and $\frac{2}{12}$ foot. Write these heights in order from least to greatest.

Independent Practice

For **9** through **20**, find equivalent fractions with a common denominator and order from least to greatest. Use drawings or fraction strips to help.

9. $\frac{1}{4}, \frac{1}{6}, \frac{1}{2}$

10. $\frac{2}{4}, \frac{2}{6}, \frac{2}{12}$

11. $\frac{2}{3}, \frac{5}{6}, \frac{7}{12}$

12. $\frac{5}{12}, \frac{2}{3}, \frac{1}{4}$

13. $\frac{3}{5}, \frac{4}{10}, \frac{1}{2}$

14. $\frac{1}{2}, \frac{3}{5}, \frac{2}{10}$

15. $\frac{5}{6}, \frac{3}{4}, \frac{8}{12}$

16. $\frac{8}{12}, \frac{1}{2}, \frac{3}{4}$

17. $\frac{6}{8}, \frac{1}{2}, \frac{3}{8}$

18. $\frac{2}{5}, \frac{3}{10}, \frac{3}{5}$

19. $\frac{10}{12}, \frac{1}{2}, \frac{3}{4}$

20. $\frac{2}{4}, \frac{3}{12}, \frac{2}{3}$

eTools
www.pearsonsuccessnet.com

*For another example, see Set E on page 249.

Step 1

Find equivalent fractions with a common denominator.

$$\frac{3}{6} = \frac{6}{12}$$

$$\frac{1}{3} = \frac{4}{12}$$

Step 2

Compare the numerators.

$$\frac{4}{12} < \frac{6}{12} < \frac{9}{12}$$

Order the fractions from least to greatest.

So, $\frac{1}{3} < \frac{3}{6} < \frac{9}{12}$.

The heights of the sculptures in order from least to greatest are $\frac{1}{3}$ foot, $\frac{3}{6}$ foot, $\frac{9}{12}$ foot.

Problem Solving

21. Writing to Explain Sandy's sculpture is taller than Jason's. Becca's sculpture is taller than Sandy's sculpture. If Sandy's sculpture is $\frac{2}{3}$ foot tall, how tall could Jason's and Becca's sculpture be?

22. Estimation The fraction $\frac{2}{3}$ is $\frac{1}{3}$ less than 1 whole. Without finding equivalent fractions, order the fractions $\frac{7}{8}, \frac{2}{3},$ and $\frac{5}{6}$ from least to greatest.

23. The table at the right shows the number of pages four students read. Which lists the number of pages in order from least to greatest?

A 25, 69, 96, 64   **C** 64, 25, 69, 96

B 25, 64, 69, 96   **D** 25, 64, 96, 69

Students	Number of Pages
Francine	25
Ty	69
Greg	96
Vicki	64

24. Algebra Find the missing numbers in the pattern below.

▨ , **36, 54,** ▨ **,** ▨ **, 108,** ▨

25. Katie asked Kerry to name 3 fractions between 0 and 1. Kerry said $\frac{5}{12}, \frac{1}{4},$ and $\frac{2}{6}$. Order Kerry's fractions from least to greatest.

26. Geena had 6 pairs of earrings. Kiera had 3 times as many. How many pairs of earrings did Kiera have?

27. Each student in fourth grade had the same book to read. Charles read $\frac{2}{3}$ of the book, and Drew read $\frac{3}{5}$ of the book. Who read more?

MR 2.3 Use a variety of methods, such as words, numbers, symbols, charts, graphs, tables, diagrams, and models, to explain mathematical reasoning. Also **MR 2.4, NS 1.5**

Problem Solving

Writing to Explain

Jake found a piece of wood in the shape of an equilateral triangle. He cut off a section of the triangle as shown to the right.

Did Jake cut off $\frac{1}{3}$ of the triangle? Explain.

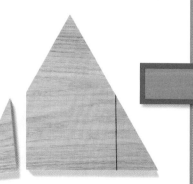

Section of wood cut off

Another Example

Eden says that $\frac{1}{2}$ is always the same amount as $\frac{2}{4}$. Matthew says that $\frac{1}{2}$ and $\frac{2}{4}$ are equivalent fractions, but they could be different amounts. Which student is correct? Explain.

The circles are the same size.

 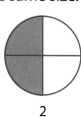

$\frac{1}{2}$ $\frac{2}{4}$

The amounts are the same.

The circles are not the same size.

$\frac{2}{4}$ $\frac{1}{2}$

The amounts are different.

Matthew is correct. $\frac{1}{2}$ and $\frac{2}{4}$ are equivalent fractions but they could represent different amounts.

Explain It

1. When will amounts of $\frac{1}{2}$ and $\frac{2}{4}$ be equal?

2. When are the fractional amounts $\frac{3}{6}$ and $\frac{2}{4}$ not equal?

What do I know?   The triangle is an equilateral triangle. One piece is cut off.

What am I asked to find?   Is the section that is cut off $\frac{1}{3}$ of the triangle?

| Plan |

Use words, pictures, numbers, or symbols to write a math explanation.

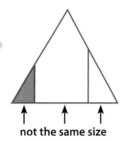

$\frac{1}{3}$ means that the whole has to be divided into 3 equal parts. The parts have to be the same size.

not the same size

The shaded section is not $\frac{1}{3}$ of the triangle.

Guided Practice*

Do you know HOW?

1. A board is cut into 12 equal pieces. How many pieces together represent $\frac{3}{4}$ of the board. Explain how you arrived at your answer.

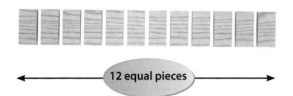

12 equal pieces

Do you UNDERSTAND?

2. Copy and draw the triangle above. Shade in $\frac{1}{3}$ of the triangle.

3. **Write a Problem** Write a problem that would use the figure below as part of its explanation.

Independent Practice

Write to explain.

4. Devon and Amanda knit the same size scarf. Devon's scarf is $\frac{3}{5}$ yellow. Amanda's scarf is $\frac{3}{4}$ yellow. How can you use a picture to show whose scarf is more yellow?

5. The school newspaper has a total of 18 articles and ads. There are 6 more articles than ads. How many articles and ads are there? Explain how you found your answer.

Stuck? Try this....

- What do I know?
- What diagram can I use to help understand the problem?
- Can I use addition, subtraction, multiplication, or division?
- Is all of my work correct?
- Did I answer the right question?
- Is my answer reasonable?

For another example, see Set H on page 249.

Lesson 9-8

6. Look at the cell pattern below. Explain how the number of cells changes as the number of divisions changes.

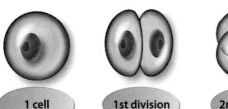

| 1 cell | 1st division | 2nd division | 3rd division |

7. Algebra Look at the number sentences in the chart below. What numbers replace ●, ▲, and ■? Explain your answer.

▲ + ■ = 18

● + ▲ = 20

■ + ■ = 14

8. Geometry Three streets intersect with one another. East Street runs horizontally, North Street runs vertically and Fourth Street runs diagonally and intersects both East Street and North Street. What geometric figure do the three streets form?

Use the data at the right for **9** and **10**.

9. How can you find the number of cards Linda has in her collection?

10. George has 100 rookie cards in his collection. How can you find the number of pictures in the pictograph that represent George's rookie cards?

Baseball Card Collections

Each ▨ = 25 cards

Think About the Process

11. Janet gets $25 a week to buy lunch at school. She spends $4 each day and saves the rest. How much money will Janet save at the end of the 5 days?

  A $(4 \times 5) + 25$ **C** $(25 - 5) + 4$

  B $25 + (5 - 4)$ **D** $25 - (5 \times 4)$

12. During recess, Rachel played on the bars and swings. She spent 10 minutes on the bars and twice as long on the swings. How much time did she play on the equipment?

  A $10 - (2 + 10)$ **C** $(10 + 2) - 10$

  B $10 + (2 \times 10)$ **D** $(10 \div 2) + 10$

Find each product. Estimate to check
if the answer is reasonable.

1.   923
    × 7

2.   2,202
    × 16

3.   16,204
    × 8

4.   32
    × 17

5.   6,060
    × 4

6.   451
    × 23

7.   4,972
    × 18

8.   51
    × 43

Find each difference. Estimate to check
if the answer is reasonable.

9.   9,000
    − 258

10.   6,932
    − 2,784

11.   485
    − 396

12.   4,001
    − 3,873

13.   6,249
    − 123

14. 2,060 − 793

15. 401 − 96

16. 6,920 − 760

17. 3,750 − 2,950

18. 888 − 599

19. 8,898 − 7,361

Error Search Find each answer that is not correct.
Write it correctly and explain the error.

20.   4,859
    + 745

    5,604

21.   262
    × 15

    1,572

22.   206
    × 4

    832

23.   7,502
    − 2,823

    10,325

24.   22,222
    × 5

    111,110

Number Sense

Estimating and Reasoning Write whether each
statement is true or false. Explain your answer.

25. The sum of 595 + 268 is 5 less than 868.

26. The product of 82 and 209 is less than 16,000.

27. The product of 3 and 206 is 18 more than 600.

28. The expression 2 × 4 + 12 ÷ 2 + 1 equals 11.

29. The quotient of 346 ÷ 5 has a remainder less than 5.

1. Tonya bought the fruit shown below. What fraction of the fruit are apples? (9-1)

   A $\frac{7}{10}$

   B $\frac{3}{7}$

   C $\frac{3}{10}$

   D $\frac{3}{12}$

2. Eight students share 5 yards of ribbon equally. What fraction does each student get? (9-2)

   A $\frac{8}{5}$ yard

   B $\frac{8}{8}$ yard

   C $\frac{5}{5}$ yard

   D $\frac{5}{8}$ yard

3. Jase completed 8 out of the 10 laps required to pass his swimming test. What fraction, in simplest form, of the laps did he complete? (9-4)

   A $\frac{8}{10}$

   B $\frac{4}{5}$

   C $\frac{3}{4}$

   D $\frac{2}{3}$

4. Javier and Mark drew straws to see who went down the waterslide first. Javier's straw was $\frac{5}{12}$ inch long and Mark's was $\frac{7}{12}$ inch long. Which symbol makes the comparison true? (9-6)

$$\frac{5}{12} \bigcirc \frac{7}{12}$$

   A $\times$

   B $=$

   C $<$

   D $>$

5. Sandy had 3 bottles of juice. She poured the bottles into 7 glasses for her friends to drink. Which number sentence can be used to find the fraction of a bottle of juice that each friend gets? (9-2)

   A $3 \times 7 = \square$

   B $3 \div 4 = \square$

   C $3 \div 7 = \square$

   D $7 \div 3 = \square$

6. Yao drank $\frac{11}{4}$ bottles of water during a soccer game. What is this number written as a mixed number? (9-5)

   A $3\frac{1}{4}$

   B $2\frac{3}{4}$

   C $2\frac{1}{2}$

   D $2\frac{1}{4}$

7. Which statement would be used in an explanation of how the drawing shows that $\frac{2}{3} = \frac{4}{6}$? (9-8)

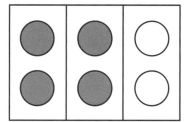

A 1 of the 3 rectangles are filled with shaded circles.

B 4 out of the 6 rectangles are shaded.

C Both $\frac{2}{3}$ and $\frac{4}{6}$ describe the part that is shaded.

D In the rectangles, 2 out of the 6 circles are shaded.

8. The student council ordered pizza for their meeting. Half of the members voted for cheese pizza, $\frac{1}{10}$ for hamburger, and $\frac{2}{5}$ for vegetable.

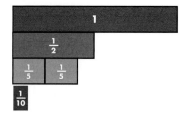

Which shows the fractions in order from least to greatest? (9-7)

A $\frac{1}{2}, \frac{1}{10}, \frac{2}{5}$

B $\frac{2}{5}, \frac{1}{10}, \frac{1}{2}$

C $\frac{1}{10}, \frac{1}{2}, \frac{2}{5}$

D $\frac{1}{10}, \frac{2}{5}, \frac{1}{2}$

9. What is the missing number which makes the fractions equivalent? (9-3)

$$\frac{3}{5} = \frac{9}{\square}$$

A 10

B 11

C 15

D 20

10. Which fraction is equivalent to the shaded area of the rectangle? (9-3)

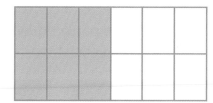

A $\frac{1}{4}$

B $\frac{3}{12}$

C $\frac{6}{12}$

D $\frac{2}{3}$

11. Mary weighed $7\frac{1}{2}$ pounds when she was born. What number makes the statement true? (9-5)

$$7\frac{1}{2} = \frac{\square}{2}$$

A 15

B 14

C 9

D 8

Set A, pages 224–226

You can write fractions to represent parts of a set. What part of the grapes are green?

$$\frac{\text{numerator}}{\text{denominator}} = \frac{\text{grapes}}{\text{parts in all}}$$

$\frac{3}{5}$ of the grapes are green.

Remember the numerator tells how many equal parts are described, and the denominator tells how many equal parts in all.

Write a fraction for the part of each set that is red.

1.  2.

Set B, pages 228–229

Four friends cut up 3 pieces of construction paper. If they shared the paper equally, what fraction of the paper did each friend use?

Each part is 1 ÷ 4, or $\frac{1}{4}$

Each person used 3 parts. Each part is $\frac{1}{4}$, so each person used $\frac{3}{4}$ of a piece of construction paper.

Remember you can draw a model to show each fraction amount.

Tell what fraction each person gets.

1. Five students share 1 hour to give their reports.

2. Two people share one sandwich.

3. Four friends share 3 cups of hot chocolate.

Set C, pages 230–232 and 234–235

Express $\frac{2}{6}$ in simplest form and find another equivalent fraction.

Divide the numerator and denominator by 2:

$2 \div 2 = 1$

$6 \div 2 = 3$

$\frac{2}{6}$ written in simplest form is $\frac{1}{3}$.

$$\overset{\times 2}{\underset{\times 2}{\frac{2}{6} = \frac{4}{12}}}$$

Multiply the numerator and the denominator by the same number to find an equivalent fraction.

$$\frac{1}{3} = \frac{2}{6} = \frac{4}{12}$$

Remember when you are finding the simplest form, start by dividing both by 2 if the numerator and denominator are even numbers.

Multiply or divide to find an equivalent fraction.

1. $\frac{8}{16} = \frac{\blacksquare}{8}$ 2. $\frac{6}{36} = \frac{54}{\blacksquare}$

Write each fraction in simplest form.

3. $\frac{8}{12}$ 4. $\frac{30}{40}$

5. $\frac{8}{72}$ 6. $\frac{14}{22}$

Set D, pages 236–237

Write an equivalent fraction for $\frac{1}{3}$.

Count how many $\frac{1}{6}$ that are equal to $\frac{1}{3}$.
Two of the sixths equal the same amount as $\frac{1}{3}$.

So, $\frac{1}{3} = \frac{2}{6}$.

Remember when you compare fractions strips, they are equivalent if the shaded areas are equal.

Use fraction strips to find an equivalent fraction.

1. $\frac{6}{10} = \dfrac{}{}$ 2. $\frac{3}{4} = \dfrac{}{}$

3. $\frac{4}{12} = \dfrac{}{}$ 4. $\frac{1}{5} = \dfrac{}{}$

Set E, pages 238–241

Compare $\frac{4}{6}$ and $\frac{3}{4}$.

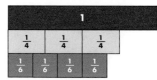

So, $\frac{4}{6} < \frac{3}{4}$.

Order $\frac{4}{6}$, $\frac{3}{4}$, and $\frac{1}{2}$ from least to greatest.

When the two fractions have the same denominators, compare the numerators.

To order fractions, find a common denominator.

$\frac{3}{6} < \frac{4}{6} < \frac{3}{4}$. So $\frac{1}{2}, \frac{4}{6}, \frac{3}{4}$.

Remember to use fraction strips, benchmark fractions, or equivalent fractions with common denominators when ordering fractions.

Compare. Write $<$, $>$, or $=$ for each $\bigcirc$.

1. $\frac{5}{10} \bigcirc \frac{1}{2}$ 2. $\frac{3}{4} \bigcirc \frac{5}{12}$

3. $\frac{7}{8} \bigcirc \frac{5}{8}$ 4. $\frac{7}{10} \bigcirc \frac{10}{12}$

Order from least to greatest.

5. $\frac{1}{2}, \frac{2}{3}, \frac{5}{12}$ 6. $\frac{7}{8}, \frac{3}{8}, \frac{3}{4}$

Set F, pages 242–244

Is each section $\frac{1}{4}$ of the square?

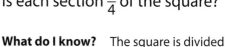

What do I know? The square is divided into 4 pieces.

What am I asked to find? Do all the sections represent $\frac{1}{4}$ of the square?

$\frac{1}{4}$ means that the whole is divided into 4 equal parts. The sections are not equal and cannot each represent $\frac{1}{4}$ of the square.

Remember to explain your answer.

1. Peter says that $\frac{3}{4}$ is always the same as $\frac{6}{8}$. Nadia says that while they are equivalent fractions, $\frac{3}{4}$ and $\frac{6}{8}$ could represent different amounts. Who is correct?

Addition and Subtraction of Fractions

1

The Metrodome in Minnesota has a sliding roof. What fraction of Major League baseball parks have a roof? You will find out in Lesson 10-3.

2

Mancala is one of the oldest games in the world. There are many names for this game which is played in different countries. How many stones are used in a game of Mancala? You will find out in Lesson 10-1.

3

Californium is a chemical element that was discovered in 1950. How many elements were named after California scientists? You will find out in Lesson 10-2.

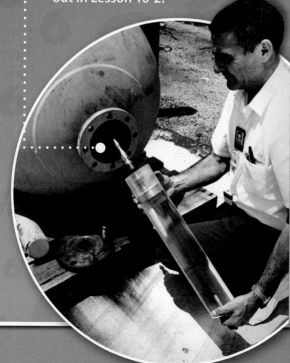

Vocabulary

Choose the best term from the box.

- common factor
- numerator
- denominator
- simplest form

1. The factor that two or more numbers have in common is called a(n) _?_.

2. A _?_ represents the total number of equal parts in all.

3. The number above the fraction bar in a fraction is known as the _?_.

Parts of a Region or Set

4. What fraction of the set below is red?

5. What fraction of the rectangle below is not green?

Fraction Concepts

Draw a model to show each fraction.

6. $\frac{4}{5}$ **7.** $\frac{1}{4}$ **8.** $\frac{2}{3}$

9. $\frac{1}{4}$ **10.** $\frac{6}{8}$ **11.** $\frac{3}{5}$

12. $\frac{6}{10}$ **13.** $\frac{11}{12}$ **14.** $\frac{5}{5}$

15. Writing to Explain Why are $\frac{3}{4}$ and $\frac{4}{8}$ not equivalent fractions?

NS 2.3 Grade 5
Solve simple problems,
including ones arising
in concrete situations,
involving the addition
and subtraction of
fractions and mixed
numbers (like and unlike
denominators of 20 or
less), and express answers
in the simplest form.

Adding and Subtracting Fractions with Like Denominators

How can you add fractions with like denominators?

Jimmy painted $\frac{1}{8}$ of a fence in the morning and $\frac{4}{8}$ of a fence in the afternoon. How much did he paint in all?

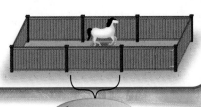

$\frac{1}{8}$ of the fence

Another Example **How can you subtract fractions with like denominators?**

Mandy planted $\frac{1}{6}$ of her garden with corn and $\frac{5}{6}$ of her garden with tomatoes. How much more of her garden is planted with tomatoes?

One Way

Subtract $\frac{5}{6} - \frac{1}{6}$ using fraction strips.

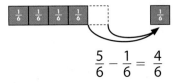

$$\frac{5}{6} - \frac{1}{6} = \frac{4}{6}$$

Simplify.

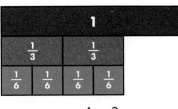

$$\frac{4}{6} = \frac{2}{3}$$

Mandy has $\frac{2}{3}$ more of her garden planted with tomatoes.

Another Way

Subtract $\frac{5}{6} - \frac{1}{6}$.

$$\frac{5}{6} - \frac{1}{6} = \frac{5-1}{6} = \frac{4}{6}$$

Simplify.

$$\frac{4}{6} \overset{\div 2}{\underset{\div 2}{=}} \frac{2}{3}$$

Mandy has $\frac{2}{3}$ more of her garden planted with tomatoes.

Explain It

1. If Mandy planted $\frac{2}{5}$ of her garden with carrots and $\frac{3}{5}$ with cucumbers, how much more of her garden is growing cucumbers?

252

One Way

Add $\frac{1}{8} + \frac{4}{8}$ using fraction strips.

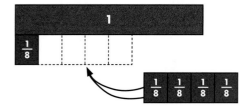

There are 5 eighths in all.
Jimmy painted $\frac{5}{8}$ of the fence.

Another Way

Add $\frac{1}{8} + \frac{4}{8}$.

The denominators are the same, so add the numerators.

$$\frac{1}{8} + \frac{4}{8} = \frac{1+4}{8} = \frac{5}{8}$$

Jimmy painted $\frac{5}{8}$ of the fence.

Guided Practice*

Do you know HOW?

Add or subtract the fractions. Write the answers in simplest form. You may use fraction strips to help.

1. $\frac{1}{5} + \frac{2}{5}$ **2.** $\frac{3}{12} + \frac{5}{12}$

3. $\frac{3}{6} - \frac{1}{6}$ **4.** $\frac{4}{10} - \frac{2}{10}$

Do you UNDERSTAND?

5. In the example above, how do you know that $\frac{5}{8}$ is in simplest form?

6. After painting $\frac{5}{8}$ of the fence, Jimmy painted another $\frac{2}{8}$ of the fence. How much had he painted in all?

Independent Practice

For **7** through **16**, add. Write the answer in simplest form. You may use fraction strips to help.

7. $\frac{1}{9}$
$+ \frac{3}{9}$

8. $\frac{2}{6}$
$+ \frac{1}{6}$

9. $\frac{4}{12}$
$+ \frac{4}{12}$

10. $\frac{1}{12}$
$+ \frac{9}{12}$

11. $\frac{3}{8}$
$+ \frac{3}{8}$

12. $\frac{1}{3}$
$+ \frac{1}{3}$

13. $\frac{2}{5}$
$+ \frac{1}{5}$

14. $\frac{1}{6}$
$+ \frac{3}{6}$

15. $\frac{1}{8}$
$+ \frac{3}{8}$

16. $\frac{1}{7}$
$+ \frac{4}{7}$

DIGITAL

eTools
www.pearsonsuccessnet.com

For **17** through **26**, subtract. Write the answer in simplest form.
You may use fraction strips to help.

17. $\frac{11}{12}$
$-\frac{2}{12}$

18. $\frac{5}{8}$
$-\frac{3}{8}$

19. $\frac{5}{9}$
$-\frac{2}{9}$

20. $\frac{10}{11}$
$-\frac{9}{11}$

21. $\frac{9}{12}$
$-\frac{3}{12}$

22. $\frac{3}{4}$
$-\frac{1}{4}$

23. $\frac{4}{5}$
$-\frac{2}{5}$

24. $\frac{5}{6}$
$-\frac{1}{6}$

25. $\frac{10}{12}$
$-\frac{6}{12}$

26. $\frac{6}{7}$
$-\frac{1}{7}$

For **27** through **36**, add or subtract. Write the answer in simplest form.
You may use fraction strips to help.

27. $\frac{1}{8} + \frac{2}{8}$

28. $\frac{5}{7} - \frac{2}{7}$

29. $\frac{1}{12} + \frac{3}{12}$

30. $\frac{7}{10} - \frac{3}{10}$

31. $\frac{1}{5} + \frac{3}{5}$

32. $\frac{2}{6} - \frac{1}{6}$

33. $\frac{2}{4} + \frac{1}{4}$

34. $\frac{8}{10} - \frac{3}{10}$

35. $\frac{7}{10} + \frac{1}{10}$

36. $\frac{3}{4} - \frac{2}{4}$

Problem Solving

37. Algebra All 4 sides of a rectangle have the same length. If the perimeter is 16 inches, what is the length of each side?

38. Stan makes a smoothie with $\frac{2}{8}$ cup of water and $\frac{3}{8}$ cup of milk. How much water and milk does he use in all?

For **39** and **40**, use the diagram at the right.

39. Harriet took 7 horses from the barn to the pasture when she cleaned their stalls. If there was a horse in every stall, what fraction of the horses were in the pasture?

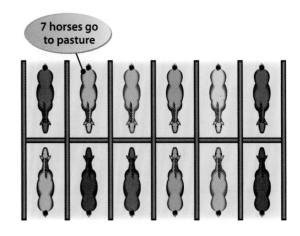

7 horses go to pasture

40. If Harriet took 3 more horses from the barn to the pasture, what fraction of the horses were then in the pasture? Write your answer in simplest form.

For **41** and **42**, use the picture to the right.

41. What fraction of the stained glass window is either green or purple?

42. What fraction of the stained glass window is either red or blue?

43. A new CD has 16 songs. If 4 of the songs are more than five minutes long and 7 of the songs are between three and five minutes long, then what fraction of the songs on the CD are shorter than three minutes long?

44. Sandy, Josh, and Jeremy are all decorating a banner. Sandy decorates $\frac{4}{8}$ of the banner, Josh decorates $\frac{3}{8}$ of the banner, and Jeremy decorates $\frac{1}{8}$ of the banner. How much more of the banner do they have to decorate?

45. Terri says since 80 has 8 as one of its factors, it will also have 4 and 2 as factors because 4 and 2 are factors of 8. Is she correct?

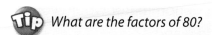 *What are the factors of 80?*

46. Austin walked $\frac{1}{6}$ mile to school. He then walked $\frac{2}{6}$ mile to the park. How far has Austin walked?

A $\frac{1}{2}$ mile   **C** $\frac{3}{4}$ mile

B $\frac{5}{8}$ mile   **D** $\frac{8}{6}$ miles

In the game, Mancala, there are 36 stones. When a stone is captured, it stays in one player's cala, or bin, for the rest of the game. The person who has the most captured stones at the end of the game wins.

47. Reasoning If Player 1 has captured $\frac{3}{36}$ of the stones and Player 2 has $\frac{7}{36}$ of the stones, what fraction of the stones have not been captured yet? Write your answer in simplest form.

Player 2's bin

Player 1's bin

Lesson
10-2

NS 2.3 Grade 5
Solve simple problems, including ones arising in concrete situations, involving the addition and subtraction of fractions and mixed numbers (like and unlike denominators of 20 or less), and express answers in the simplest form.

Adding Fractions with Unlike Denominators

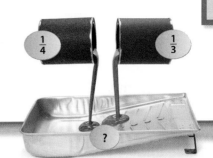

Hands-On
fraction strips

$\frac{1}{8}$

How can you add fractions with unlike denominators?

Terry mixed $\frac{1}{4}$ of a can of red paint and $\frac{1}{3}$ of a can of blue paint to make purple. What fraction of a can of purple paint does Terry have now?

$\frac{1}{4}$ $\frac{1}{3}$

?

Guided Practice*

Do you know HOW?

For **1** through **4**, write the answer in simplest form. You may use fraction strips or drawings to help.

1. $\frac{1}{3} + \frac{1}{6}$

2. $\frac{3}{8} + \frac{1}{4}$

3. $\frac{1}{6} + \frac{2}{4}$

4. $\frac{1}{5} + \frac{4}{10}$

Do you UNDERSTAND?

5. If Terry mixed $\frac{1}{4}$ can of red paint and $\frac{2}{12}$ can of yellow paint, how much orange paint would he have?

6. What denominator would you use to add $\frac{1}{3}$ and $\frac{3}{5}$?

Independent Practice

For **7** through **21**, write the answer in simplest form. You may use fraction strips or drawings to help.

7. $\begin{array}{r} \frac{3}{4} \\ + \frac{1}{8} \\ \hline \end{array}$

8. $\begin{array}{r} \frac{7}{10} \\ + \frac{1}{5} \\ \hline \end{array}$

9. $\begin{array}{r} \frac{3}{6} \\ + \frac{1}{3} \\ \hline \end{array}$

10. $\begin{array}{r} \frac{1}{5} \\ + \frac{1}{10} \\ \hline \end{array}$

11. $\begin{array}{r} \frac{7}{12} \\ + \frac{1}{3} \\ \hline \end{array}$

12. $\begin{array}{r} \frac{3}{10} \\ + \frac{2}{5} \\ \hline \end{array}$

13. $\begin{array}{r} \frac{1}{6} \\ + \frac{3}{4} \\ \hline \end{array}$

14. $\begin{array}{r} \frac{1}{5} \\ + \frac{1}{2} \\ \hline \end{array}$

15. $\begin{array}{r} \frac{1}{6} \\ + \frac{5}{12} \\ \hline \end{array}$

16. $\begin{array}{r} \frac{1}{4} \\ + \frac{1}{6} \\ \hline \end{array}$

17. $\frac{1}{8} + \frac{1}{4}$

18. $\frac{1}{12} + \frac{3}{4}$

19. $\frac{1}{10} + \frac{2}{5}$

20. $\frac{2}{4} + \frac{2}{8}$

21. $\frac{1}{5} + \frac{2}{10}$

DIGITAL

eTools
www.pearsonsuccessnet.com

For another example, see Set B on page 266.

One Way

Add $\frac{1}{4}$ and $\frac{1}{3}$ using fraction strips.

Both the $\frac{1}{4}$ and $\frac{1}{3}$ piece can be shown using twelfths.

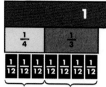

$$\frac{3}{12} + \frac{4}{12} = \frac{7}{12}$$

Terry has $\frac{7}{12}$ of a can of purple paint.

Another Way

Find $\frac{1}{4} + \frac{1}{3}$.

When you add fractions with unlike denominators, change the fractions to equivalent fractions that have a common denominator. Then add the numerators.

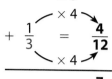

Think What number has 4 and 3 as factors?

Add the new fractions. Write the sum in simplest form.

$$\frac{7}{12}$$

Terry has $\frac{7}{12}$ of a can of purple paint.

Problem Solving

22. Reasoning To trim a child's costume, Nora needs $\frac{1}{2}$ yard of lace at the neck and $\frac{1}{5}$ yard for each wrist. How much lace does Nora need?

23. Francis read $\frac{1}{3}$ of his book yesterday and $\frac{1}{2}$ today. How much of the book has Francis read.

24. Add the two fractions represented by each circle. What is the sum in simplest form?

25. Number Sense Mary measures beads for a bracelet. Three clay beads are each $\frac{1}{8}$ inch long. Two glass beads are each $\frac{1}{4}$ inch long. What is the length of all five beads when strung together?

26. In all, 36 chemical elements were named after people or places. Of these, two were named for California scientists, and 2 were named for California places. What fraction of these 36 elements were named for California people and places? Write your answer in simplest form.

27. At the first stop, a trolley picks up $\frac{1}{6}$ of the number of passengers it can carry. At the second stop, it picks up $\frac{2}{3}$ of the number of passengers it can carry. Which sum is **NOT** the correct fraction of passengers that are on the bus after 2 stops?

A $\frac{5}{6}$ **B** $\frac{9}{12}$ **C** $\frac{15}{18}$ **D** $\frac{20}{24}$

Lesson
10-3

NS 2.3 Grade 5
Solve simple problems, including ones arising in concrete situations, involving the addition and subtraction of fractions and mixed numbers (like and unlike denominators of 20 or less), and express answers in the simplest form.

Hands-On
fraction strips

$\frac{1}{8}$

Subtracting Fractions with Unlike Denominators

How can you subtract fractions with unlike denominators?

Zoe and Frank are making macaroni and cheese. They bought $\frac{2}{3}$ pound of cheese. How much cheese will they have left if they use $\frac{1}{2}$ pound of cheese?

$\frac{2}{3}$ of a pound

$\frac{1}{2}$ of a pound

Guided Practice*

Do you know HOW?

For **1** through **4**, write the answer in simplest form. You may use fraction strips or drawings to help.

1. $\frac{2}{5} - \frac{2}{10}$ 2. $\frac{4}{6} - \frac{4}{8}$

3. $\frac{5}{6} - \frac{2}{12}$ 4. $\frac{7}{10} - \frac{2}{5}$

Do you UNDERSTAND?

5. How much cheese would Zoe and Frank have left if they used $\frac{1}{4}$ pound of cheese?

6. What denominator would you use to subtract $\frac{5}{6} - \frac{1}{5}$?

Independent Practice

For **7** through **21**, write the answer in simplest form. You may use fraction strips or drawings to help.

7. $\begin{array}{r} \frac{3}{4} \\ -\ \frac{3}{8} \\ \hline \end{array}$
8. $\begin{array}{r} \frac{7}{10} \\ -\ \frac{1}{5} \\ \hline \end{array}$
9. $\begin{array}{r} \frac{7}{9} \\ -\ \frac{2}{3} \\ \hline \end{array}$
10. $\begin{array}{r} \frac{5}{6} \\ -\ \frac{4}{12} \\ \hline \end{array}$
11. $\begin{array}{r} \frac{2}{3} \\ -\ \frac{2}{6} \\ \hline \end{array}$

12. $\begin{array}{r} \frac{5}{10} \\ -\ \frac{1}{5} \\ \hline \end{array}$
13. $\begin{array}{r} \frac{3}{4} \\ -\ \frac{4}{8} \\ \hline \end{array}$
14. $\begin{array}{r} \frac{7}{12} \\ -\ \frac{1}{3} \\ \hline \end{array}$
15. $\begin{array}{r} \frac{2}{5} \\ -\ \frac{3}{10} \\ \hline \end{array}$
16. $\begin{array}{r} \frac{5}{6} \\ -\ \frac{3}{4} \\ \hline \end{array}$

17. $\frac{4}{5} - \frac{1}{10}$
18. $\frac{1}{4} - \frac{1}{6}$
19. $\frac{11}{12} - \frac{2}{3}$
20. $\frac{5}{8} - \frac{1}{4}$
21. $\frac{1}{4} - \frac{1}{8}$

DIGITAL   eTools
www.pearsonsuccessnet.com

*For another example, see Set C on page 267.

One Way

Use fraction strips to subtract $\frac{2}{3} - \frac{1}{2}$.

Both $\frac{2}{3}$ and $\frac{1}{2}$ can be shown using sixths.

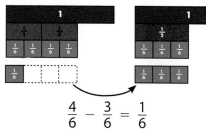

$$\frac{4}{6} - \frac{3}{6} = \frac{1}{6}$$

They have $\frac{1}{6}$ pound of cheese left.

Another Way

Find $\frac{2}{3} - \frac{1}{2}$.

Rewrite the fractions using the same denominator.

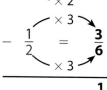

$$\frac{2}{3} \underset{\times 2}{\overset{\times 2}{=}} \frac{4}{6}$$

Think What number has 3 and 2 as factors?

$$-\frac{1}{2} \underset{\times 3}{\overset{\times 3}{=}} \frac{3}{6}$$

Subtract the new fractions. Write the difference in simplest form.

$$\frac{1}{6}$$

They have $\frac{1}{6}$ pound of cheese left.

Problem Solving

22. Algebra Write an expression to represent the cost of a pizza for *d* dollars with a coupon for $2 off.

23. The sum of two fractions is $\frac{8}{9}$. The difference is $\frac{2}{9}$. What are the two fractions?

24. Geometry Tim used 28 straws to make squares and hexagons. If he made 4 squares, how many hexagons could he make?

Each square uses 4 straws.

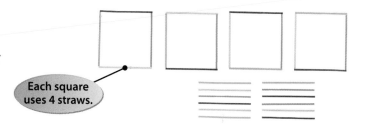

25. A banana bread recipe calls for $\frac{1}{4}$ cup of oil. A muffin recipe calls for $\frac{1}{2}$ cup of oil. How much more oil is needed to make the muffins?

26. Luke and Lydia ran for $\frac{3}{4}$ hour without stopping. This is $\frac{3}{16}$ hour more than Kevin and Sarah ran. How long did Kevin and Sarah run?

27. Of 30 Major League baseball teams, $\frac{7}{30}$ of the teams have a covered ballpark with a roof. If $\frac{1}{10}$ of the 30 ballparks are National League parks with a roof, what fraction of the ballparks are American League ballparks with a roof?

$\frac{7}{30}$ covered ballparks

$\frac{1}{10}$	?

28. Renee's pizza had 8 equal slices. She ate $\frac{3}{8}$ of her pizza. George's pizza had 12 equal slices. He ate $\frac{1}{4}$ of his pizza. If both pizzas were the same size, how much more pizza did Renee eat?

A $\frac{1}{8}$ more   **C** $\frac{1}{3}$ more

B $\frac{1}{4}$ more   **D** $\frac{5}{8}$ more

MR 2.3 Use a variety of methods, such as words, numbers, symbols, charts, graphs, tables, diagrams, and models, to explain mathematical reasoning. Also **AF 1.0**, **NS 2.3**, Grade 5.

Problem Solving

Draw a Picture and Write an Equation

Brad and his father hiked three trails. The Gadsen Trail is $\frac{9}{10}$ of a mile, the Rosebriar Trail is $\frac{1}{2}$ of a mile, and the Eureka Trail is $\frac{3}{5}$ of a mile. How far did they walk in all?

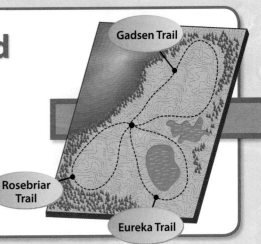

Another Example Sandra and Ron are hiking a trail. They have already hiked $\frac{1}{10}$ of a mile. How much further do they have to travel to reach the $\frac{3}{4}$ mile mark?

$\frac{3}{4}$ of a mile in all

| $\frac{1}{10}$ | ? |

One Way

$\frac{1}{10} + \boxed{} = \frac{3}{4}$

Find common denominators and add.

$\frac{1}{10} = \frac{2}{20}$ $\quad$ $\frac{3}{4} = \frac{15}{20}$

$\frac{2}{20} + \frac{13}{20} = \frac{15}{20}$

Sandra and Ron need to hike $\frac{13}{20}$ more of a mile to reach the $\frac{3}{4}$ mile mark.

Another Way

$\frac{3}{4} - \frac{1}{10} = \boxed{}$

Find common denominators and subtract.

$\frac{3}{4} = \frac{15}{20}$ $\quad$ $\frac{1}{10} = \frac{2}{20}$

$\frac{15}{20} - \frac{2}{20} = \frac{13}{20}$

Explain It

1. How could you find how much further Sandra and Ron will have to hike to reach one mile?

2. **Reasoning** If Sandra and Ron turn around and hike back $\frac{1}{10}$ of a mile, how can you find the difference between the length they traveled and $\frac{3}{4}$ of a mile?

What do I know?

Brad and his father hiked 3 trails.

Gadsen Trail = $\frac{9}{10}$ mi

Rosebriar Trail = $\frac{1}{2}$ mi

Eureka Trail = $\frac{3}{5}$ mi

What am I asked to find?

How far did Brad and his father walk in all?

Plan & Solve

Find a common denominator.

$$\frac{9}{10} = \frac{9}{10}$$
$$\frac{1}{2} = \frac{5}{10}$$
$$\frac{3}{5} = \frac{6}{10}$$

? miles in all

$\frac{9}{10}$	$\frac{5}{10}$	$\frac{6}{10}$

Then, add the fractions and simplify.

$$\frac{9}{10} + \frac{5}{10} + \frac{6}{10} = \frac{20}{10} \text{ or } \frac{10}{5} \text{ or 2 miles}$$

Brad and his father walked 2 miles in all.

Guided Practice*

Do you know HOW?

Draw a picture and write an equation to solve.

1. Hannah ran $\frac{1}{3}$ of a mile. David ran $\frac{1}{6}$ of a mile. How much farther did Hannah run than David?

Do you UNDERSTAND?

2. **Writing to Explain** If you were asked to find how far Brad and his father walked on the Rosebriar and Eureka Trails alone, would the common denominator be different?

3. **Write a Problem** Write a problem that you can solve by drawing a picture and writing an equation.

Independent Practice

Draw a picture and write an equation to solve.

4. Steve connected a wire extension that is $\frac{3}{8}$ feet long to another wire that is $\frac{1}{2}$ foot long. How long is the wire with the extension?

? feet

$\frac{3}{8}$	$\frac{1}{2}$

5. The wingspan of a ladybug is $\frac{1}{2}$ centimeters long and the wingspan of a bee is $\frac{1}{5}$ centimeter long. How much longer is the wingspan of a ladybug than a bee?

$\frac{1}{2}$ cm long

$\frac{1}{5}$	?

Stuck? Try this....

- What do I know?
- What diagram can I use to help understand the problem?
- Can I use addition, subtraction, multiplication, or division?
- Is all of my work correct?
- Did I answer the right question?
- Is my answer reasonable?

*For another example, see Set D on page 267.

6. A recipe calls for 3 times as many carrots as peas. If Carmen used 2 cups of peas, how many cups of carrots will she use?

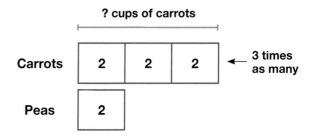

? cups of carrots

Carrots | 2 | 2 | 2 | ← 3 times as many

Peas | 2

7. Felix bought $\frac{5}{6}$ pounds of peanuts. He ate $\frac{3}{4}$ pounds of the peanuts with his friends. How much did Felix have left?

$\frac{5}{6}$ pounds of peanuts

| $\frac{3}{4}$ | ? |

8. Geometry Jack's dog has a rectangular pen. The length is two feet longer than the width. The width is 6 feet. What is the perimeter of the pen?

9. Writing to Explain Terrence has 8 comic books and 4 detective books. His sister says $\frac{2}{3}$ of his books are comic books. Terrence says that $\frac{8}{12}$ of his books are comic books. Who is correct?

10. Writing to Explain If the perimeter of the parallelogram below is 56 inches, and you know one side is 8 inches, will you be able to find the length of the other 3 sides? Why or why not?

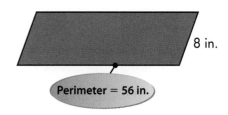

8 in.

Perimeter = 56 in.

Think About the Process

11. Four relay team members run an equal part of an 8-mile race. Which number sentence shows how far each member runs?

A $4 + 2 = 6$

B $8 \div 4 = 2$

C $2 + 2 + 2 = 6$

D $2 \times 4 = 8$

12. At an automobile dealership, there are 3 green cars, 4 blue cars, and 4 silver cars. Which number sentence tells how many cars are not silver?

A $7 + 4 = 11$

B $11 - 4 = 7$

C $3 + 4 + 4 = 11$

D $7 \times 4 = 28$

Mixed Problem Solving

Artists frequently mix base colors together to create different hues of paint for use in paintings. They often begin with three colors: blue, red, and yellow. The colors that are produced depend upon the fraction of paints that are combined.

Mr. McCrory is mixing paints together to create colors to use in some oil paintings.

Data				
Paint 1	$\frac{1}{4}$ blue	$\frac{1}{6}$ red	$\frac{5}{6}$ yellow
Paint 2	$\frac{3}{4}$ red	$\frac{1}{3}$ yellow	$\frac{5}{8}$ blue
Color	Light Purple	Orange	Deep Green

1. Use fraction strips to compare the fractions of color paint that were used to make the shade of deep green and the shade of light purple. Write the fractions from *greatest* to *least*.

2. Use fraction strips to order all the fractions of paint used from *least* to *greatest*.

3. Jared painted on a canvas using fractional amounts of colored paint. The chart at the right shows the fractional amount of each color that was used. Order each fraction from *least* to *greatest*.

Data				
Color of paint	Blue	Red	Yellow	White
Amount used	$\frac{2}{3}$	$\frac{6}{12}$	$\frac{8}{9}$	$\frac{4}{10}$

4. Elsie took a course on making stained glass at the community art center. She used $\frac{2}{6}$ of green colored glass, $\frac{1}{2}$ of yellow colored glass, and $\frac{1}{6}$ of red colored glass to make a sun catcher. Was more of her sun catcher made up of green or yellow colored glass? Draw a model to show your answer.

5. A flag is made up of fractional colors. $\frac{1}{3}$ of the flag is blue, and $\frac{1}{14}$ is white. The rest of the flag is made up of $\frac{2}{12}$ red and $\frac{1}{12}$ green. Order the fractions of color from *least* to *greatest*.

1. Mickie walked $\frac{1}{5}$ mile to her friend's house. Then they walked $\frac{3}{5}$ mile to the bus stop. How far did Mickie walk? (10-1)

A $\frac{5}{4}$ miles

B $\frac{4}{5}$ mile

C $\frac{2}{5}$ mile

D $\frac{4}{10}$ miles

2. Mrs. Garrison bought $\frac{7}{8}$ yard of fabric. She used $\frac{5}{8}$ yard to make a skirt for her daughter. How much fabric does she have left? (10-1)

A $\frac{1}{4}$ yard

B $\frac{1}{3}$ yard

C $\frac{3}{4}$ yard

D $\frac{4}{3}$ yards

3. What is $\frac{3}{10} + \frac{1}{5}$? (10-2)

A $\frac{4}{15}$

B $\frac{2}{5}$

C $\frac{4}{10}$

D $\frac{1}{2}$

4. Darrell bought $\frac{1}{4}$ pound of American cheese and $\frac{1}{8}$ pound of Swiss cheese at the deli. Which picture models how much cheese Darrell bought? (10-4)

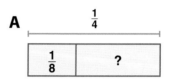

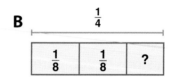

5. What is $\frac{5}{12} + \frac{1}{4}$ in simplest form? (10-2)

A $\frac{3}{4}$

B $\frac{9}{12}$

C $\frac{2}{3}$

D $\frac{3}{8}$

6. Joy bought $\frac{3}{4}$ of a quart of fruit salad and $\frac{1}{3}$ of a quart of three bean salad. How much more fruit salad did Joy buy? (10-3)

$\frac{1}{3}$ full

$\frac{3}{4}$ full

A $\frac{1}{3}$ quart

B $\frac{5}{12}$ quart

C $\frac{1}{2}$ quart

D $\frac{7}{12}$ quart

7. Bella used $\frac{1}{4}$ cup of white flour and $\frac{5}{8}$ cup of wheat flour in the bread recipe. How much more wheat flour did she use? (10-1)

A $\frac{1}{4}$

B $\frac{2}{4}$

C $\frac{3}{8}$

D $\frac{2}{8}$

8. Chen's mom bought $\frac{7}{8}$ pound of salmon. That night, the family ate $\frac{1}{4}$ pound. How much of the salmon was left? (10-3)

A $\frac{6}{4}$ pound

B $\frac{5}{8}$ pound

C $\frac{1}{3}$ pound

D $\frac{1}{4}$ pound

9. Walt ate $\frac{3}{10}$ of a pizza. Lakota also ate $\frac{3}{10}$ of the same pizza. How much of the pizza did they eat in all? (10-1)

A $\frac{1}{5}$

B $\frac{2}{5}$

C $\frac{1}{2}$

D $\frac{3}{5}$

10. Trent walked $\frac{3}{8}$ mile and jogged $\frac{1}{2}$ mile. How far did Trent go? (10-2)

A $\frac{7}{8}$ mile

B $\frac{3}{4}$ mile

C $\frac{2}{3}$ mile

D $\frac{2}{5}$ mile

11. A pitcher had $\frac{9}{10}$ gallon of juice. Manuella drank $\frac{2}{5}$ of a gallon of juice. Which number sentence can be used to find how much juice was left? (10-4)

A $\frac{9}{10} + \frac{2}{5} = \blacksquare$

B $\frac{9}{10} + \blacksquare = \frac{2}{5}$

C $\frac{9}{10} - \frac{2}{5} = \blacksquare$

D $\frac{2}{5} - \frac{9}{10} = \blacksquare$

12. What is $\frac{7}{12} - \frac{1}{3}$? (10-3)

A $\frac{1}{4}$

B $\frac{1}{3}$

C $\frac{5}{12}$

D $\frac{11}{12}$

Set A, pages 252–255

Find $\frac{1}{9} + \frac{5}{9}$.

Add the numerators. Write the sum over the like denominator.

$$\frac{1}{9} + \frac{5}{9} = \frac{6}{9}$$

Simplify if necessary.

$$\frac{6}{9} \overset{\div 3}{\underset{\div 3}{=}} \frac{2}{3}$$

So, $\frac{1}{9} + \frac{5}{9} = \frac{2}{3}$.

Find $\frac{7}{9} - \frac{5}{9}$.

Subtract the numerators. Write the difference over the like denominator.

$$\frac{7}{9} - \frac{5}{9} = \frac{2}{9}$$

Remember you can use fraction strips to add or subtract fractions with like denominators.

Add or subtract. Write each answer in simplest form.

1. $\frac{1}{7} + \frac{2}{7}$ **2.** $\frac{4}{15} + \frac{2}{15}$

3. $\frac{7}{8} - \frac{1}{8}$ **4.** $\frac{8}{10} - \frac{5}{10}$

5. $\frac{1}{4} + \frac{1}{4}$ **6.** $\frac{8}{9} - \frac{5}{9}$

7. $\frac{5}{12} + \frac{7}{12}$ **8.** $\frac{4}{13} - \frac{2}{13}$

Set B, pages 256–257

Add $\frac{1}{6} + \frac{1}{2}$ using fraction strips.

Find equivalent fractions with like denominators.

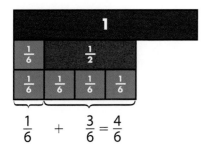

$$\frac{1}{6} \quad + \quad \frac{3}{6} = \frac{4}{6}$$

Simplify if necessary.

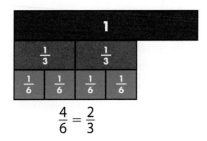

$$\frac{4}{6} = \frac{2}{3}$$

Remember to first find equivalent fractions to add fractions with unlike denominators.

Add the fractions. Write each answer in simplest form.

1. $\frac{2}{3} + \frac{1}{4}$ **2.** $\frac{3}{5} + \frac{1}{3}$

3. $\frac{1}{3} + \frac{1}{9}$ **4.** $\frac{1}{4} + \frac{1}{6}$

5. $\frac{3}{8} + \frac{1}{2}$ **6.** $\frac{2}{3} + \frac{1}{9}$

7. $\frac{2}{6} + \frac{2}{3}$ **8.** $\frac{2}{12} + \frac{4}{8}$

9. $\frac{1}{3} + \frac{3}{5}$ **10.** $\frac{2}{3} + \frac{1}{9}$

11. $\frac{2}{6} + \frac{1}{4}$ **12.** $\frac{3}{6} + \frac{1}{3}$

Set C, pages 258–259

Subtract $\frac{2}{3} - \frac{1}{4}$ using fraction strips.

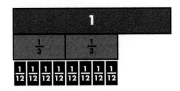
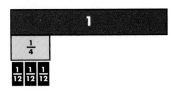

Both $\frac{2}{3}$ and $\frac{1}{4}$ can be shown using twelfths.

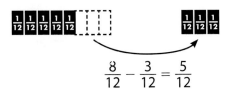

$$\frac{8}{12} - \frac{3}{12} = \frac{5}{12}$$

Remember to find equivalent fractions before subtracting fractions with unlike denominators.

Subtract the fractions. Write each answer in simplest form.

1. $\frac{3}{4} - \frac{3}{8}$ 2. $\frac{5}{12} - \frac{1}{6}$

3. $\frac{1}{2} - \frac{1}{3}$ 4. $\frac{7}{10} - \frac{1}{2}$

5. $\frac{4}{5} - \frac{1}{2}$ 6. $\frac{8}{9} - \frac{2}{9}$

7. $\frac{5}{6} - \frac{1}{12}$ 8. $\frac{7}{9} - \frac{1}{3}$

9. $\frac{4}{10} - \frac{1}{5}$ 10. $\frac{5}{6} - \frac{6}{8}$

Set D, pages 260–262

Tina and Andy are building a model airplane together. Tina built $\frac{1}{3}$ of the model, and Andy built $\frac{1}{5}$ of the model. How much more has Tina made than Andy?

$\frac{1}{3}$

| $\frac{1}{5}$ | ? |

Find a common denominator and subtract.

$$\frac{1}{3} = \frac{5}{15}$$
$$-\frac{1}{5} = \frac{3}{15}$$
$$\frac{2}{15}$$

Tina built $\frac{2}{15}$ more of the model than Andy.

Remember to identify the main idea before you write a number equation.

Draw a picture, and write an equation to solve.

1. Bonnie ran $\frac{1}{4}$ of a mile. Olga ran $\frac{1}{8}$ of a mile. How much farther did Bonnie run than Olga?

2. Linda's plant was $\frac{9}{12}$ foot tall. Macy's plant was $\frac{2}{3}$ foot tall. How much taller is Linda's plant than Macy's?

Topic 11

Fraction and Decimal Concepts

1 The Roman Colosseum is one of the best examples of Roman architecture. The arena is what fractional part of the Colosseum? You will find out in Lesson 11-3.

2 According to the Greek mathematician, Zeno, who lived in the fourth century B.C., this ball will never stop bouncing. You will find out why in Lesson 11-4.

3

The world's largest living thing, the General Sherman Giant Sequoia, is in Sequoia National Park in California. How tall is this tree? You will find out in Lesson 11–5.

Vocabulary

Choose the best term from the box.

> • greater   • tenth
> • hundredth   • decimal point

1. One of ten equal parts of a whole is one ? .

2. A dot used to separate dollars from cents or ones from tenths in a number is a ? .

3. One part of 100 equal parts of a whole is one ? .

4. The number 3,704 is ? than the number 3,407.

Comparing Numbers

Compare. Write >, <, or = for each ◯.

5. 801 ◯ 810   **6.** 1,909 ◯ 1,990

7. 455,311 ◯ 455,331   **8.** 505 ◯ 515

9. 629,348 ◯ 629,348   **10.** 43,627 ◯ 43,167

11. 101,101 ◯ 101,011   **12.** 95,559 ◯ 95,555

Ordering Numbers

Order the numbers from greatest to least.

13. 3,687   3,867   3,678   3,768

14. 108   118   801   811

15. 41,101   41,011   41,110   41,001

16. 4,593   4,395   4,595   4,359

17. Writing to Explain How would you order the numbers below from least to greatest? Explain.

15,420   154,200   1,542

GENERAL SHERMAN

Decimal Place Value

What are some ways to represent decimals?

A squirrel can weigh 1.64 pounds. There are different ways to represent 1.64.

1.64 pounds

NS 1.0 Understand the place value of whole numbers and decimals to two decimal places and how whole numbers and decimals relate to simple fractions.

Guided Practice*

Do you know HOW?

For **1** and **2**, write the expanded form for each number.

1. 3.91   **2.** 6.87

In **3** and **4**, draw and shade a grid for each number. Then, write the word form for each number.

3. 1.06   **4.** 2.36

Do you UNDERSTAND?

5. In Exercise 1, what digit is in the tenths place? in the hundredths place?

6. At the end of a basketball game, there are 3.29 seconds left on the clock. How would the referee say this number?

 When you read a number or write a number in word form, replace the decimal point with the word and.

Independent Practice

In **7** through **9**, write the decimal for each shaded part.

7.   **8.**   **9.**

In **10** through **12**, write the number in standard form.

10. four and thirty-six hundredths   **11.** $5 + 0.2 + 0.08$ **12.** $2 + 0.01$

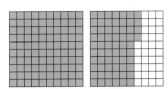

Expanded form: 1 + 0.6 + 0.04
Standard form: 1.64
Word form: one and sixty-four hundredths

Another Way

Use a place-value model.

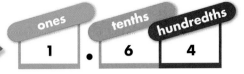

Expanded form: 1 + 0.6 + 0.04
Standard form: 1.64
Word form: one and sixty-four hundredths

In **13** through **17**, write the number in word form and give the value of the red digit for each number.

13. 2.47   **14.** 23.79   **15.** 1.85   **16.** 14.12   **17.** 9.05

In **18** through **22**, write each number in expanded form.

18. 3.19   **19.** 13.62   **20.** 0.78   **21.** 8.07   **22.** 17.2

Problem Solving

23. Reasoning Write a number that has a 4 in the tens place and a 6 in the hundredths place.

24. Mr. Cooper has 6 gallons of gas in his car. His car can hold 15 gallons in its gas tank. Will Mr. Cooper need more or less than 10 gallons to fill his tank?

25. Tisha wrote this amount: Five dollars and nine cents.

 a What is the decimal word form for this amount?

 b What is the decimal number?

26. Number Sense Write three numbers between 4.1 and 4.2.

 Use hundredths grids or money to help.

27. Writing to Explain Use the decimal model below to explain why 0.08 is less than 0.1.

28. What is the value of the 5 in 43.51?

 A five hundredths

 B five tenths

 C fifty-one hundredths

 D five

NS 1.2 ⟜ Order and compare whole numbers and decimals to two decimal places.

Comparing and Ordering Decimals

How do you compare decimals?

A penny made in 1982 weighs about 0.11 ounces. A penny made in 2006 weighs about 0.09 ounces. Which penny weighs more, a 1982 penny or a 2006 penny?

1982 penny
0.11 oz

2006 penny
0.09 oz

Another Example How do you order decimals?

Patrick has a 1982 penny, a 2006 penny, and a 2002 dime in his pocket. Order the weights of the coins from least to greatest.

Dime
0.10 oz

First compare the tenths place.　　　0.1̲1

　　　　　　　　　　　　　　　　　0.0̲9

　　　　　　　　　　　　　　　　　0.1̲0

The least number is 0.09 because it has 0 in the tenths place.

Compare the remaining numbers.　　0.1̲0
First compare the tenths. Both
decimals have a 1 in the tenths place.　0.1̲1

Compare the hundredths place.　　　0.10̲

　　　　　　　　　　　　　　　　　0.11̲

1 > 0, so 0.11 is the greatest decimal.

The order from least to greatest is 0.09, 0.10, 0.11.

Explain It

1. Order the numbers above from greatest to least.

2. Which place did you use to compare 0.10 and 0.11?

One Way

Use hundredths grids.

11 hundredths > 9 hundredths

0.11 > 0.09

Another Way

Use place value.

Start at the left. Look for the first place where the digits are different.

0.11   0.09

1 tenth > 0 tenths

0.11 > 0.09

A penny made in 1982 weighs more than a penny made in 2006.

Guided Practice*

Do you know HOW?

In **1** through **4**, write >, <, or = for each ◯. Use grids to help.

1. 0.7 ◯ 0.57

2. 0.23 ◯ 0.32

3. 1.01 ◯ 0.98

4. 0.2 ◯ 0.20

In **5** and **6**, order the numbers from least to greatest.

5. 0.65 0.6 0.71

6. 1.21 1.01 1.2

Do you UNDERSTAND?

7. Number Sense Which is greater, 2.02 or 0.22? Explain.

8. Maria told Patrick that her quarter weighs less than what a nickel weighs because 0.2 has less digits than 0.18. How can Patrick show Maria that 0.2 is greater than 0.18?

Independent Practice

For **9** through **16**, compare. Write >, <, or = for each. Use grids to help.

9. 0.01 ◯ 0.1

10. 7.31 ◯ 7.29

11. 6.56 ◯ 5.98

12. 1.1 ◯ 1.10

13. 3.22 ◯ 4.44

14. 9.01 ◯ 9.1

15. 2.01 ◯ 1.7

16. 0.01 ◯ 1.02

For **17** through **19**, order the numbers from least to greatest.

17. 1.2, 1.23, 1.1

18. 0.56, 4.56, 0.65

19. 0.21, 0.12, 0.22

---

20. Number Sense A bag of 500 nickels weighs 5.5 pounds. A bag of 200 half dollars weighs 5 pounds. Which bag weighs more?

21. Writing to Explain Evan said the numbers 7.37, 7.36, 2.59, and 2.95 were in order from greatest to least. Is he correct?

22. Number Sense Tell which coin is worth more.

 a 1 quarter or 1 half dollar

 b 1 dime or 1 penny

 c 1 dollar or 1 penny

23. Which number is **NOT** greater than 0.64?

 A 6.4

 B 4.6

 C 0.46

 D 0.66

For **24** and **25**, use the clocks at the right.

24. Which clock shows the earliest time?

25. Order the clock times from latest to earliest.

26. Which numbers are **NOT** in order from the least to the greatest?
 A 0.3, 0.7, 0.9

 B 0.04, 0.09, 0.12

 C 0.15, 0.19, 0.23

 D 0.24, 0.09, 0.18

27. Ms. Alvarez has $0.83 in her change purse. She has 7 coins. She has the same number of pennies as quarters. What coins does she have?

28. Which number has a 3 in the ten-thousands place?

 A 23,604   **C** 593,100

 B 32,671   **D** 694,392

29. Which number is between 6.7 and 7.3?

 A 6.07   **C** 6.83

 B 6.26   **D** 7.4

30. Fishing lures are sold by weight. A yellow minnow lure weighs 0.63 ounce and a green minnow lure weighs 0.5 ounce. Which lure weighs more?

31. Tom has one $10 bill, one $5 bill, 4 dollars, 3 quarters, and 2 dimes. Janet has three $5 bills, three $1 bills, and 8 quarters. Who has more money?

Algebra Connections

Number Patterns

Number patterns can help you predict the next number or numbers that follow.

Example: 10, 20, 30, 40, ▢

Think *How is each number in the number pattern related?*

Compare 10 and 20.

$10 + \underline{10} = 20$

Now, compare 20 and 30.

$20 + 10 = 30$

The pattern that best describes the list of numbers is: <u>add 10</u>.

The missing number in the number pattern is represented by a shaded box. Use the number pattern to find the missing number.

$40 + \underline{10} = 50$

The missing number is 50.

Fill in each shaded box with the number that best completes the number pattern. Then, tell how you completed the pattern.

1. 2, 4, 6, 8, ▢

2. 5, 10, 15, 20, ▢

3. 5, 8, 11, 14, ▢

4. 1, 3, 5, ▢, 9

5. 5, 15, ▢, 35, 45

6. 30, 23, ▢, 9, 2

7. 28, ▢, 18, 13, 8

8. 32, 36, ▢, 44, 48, ▢

9. 47, 56, ▢, 74, ▢, 92

10. 98, 91, ▢, 77, ▢

11. 75, 59, 43, ▢, ▢

12. 3, 5, 4, 6, 5, 7, 6, ▢

....

13. What are the missing numbers in the number pattern? Describe the number pattern.

48, ▢, ▢, 33, 28, 23

15. Write a Problem Write a problem using one of the number patterns in Exercises 1 to 12.

14. Complete the table. Describe the pattern.

A	B	C
4	6	10
5	8	13
6	▢	16
▢	11	19
15	▢	30
20	14	▢

NS1.6 🔑 ➞ Write tenths and hundredths in decimal and fraction notations and know the fraction and decimal equivalence for halves and fourths (e.g., $\frac{1}{2} = 0.5$ or 0.50; $\frac{7}{4} = 1\frac{3}{4} = 1.75$). Also **NS1.0**.

Fraction and Decimals

Hands-On
fraction strips

How can you write a fraction as a decimal and a decimal as a fraction?

On Kelsey Street, six out of 10 homes have swing sets in their backyards.

Write $\frac{6}{10}$ as a decimal.

6 of 10 houses have swing sets.

Other Examples

Write 2.1 as a mixed number.

Since $0.1 = \frac{1}{10}$, $2.1 = 2\frac{1}{10}$.

Write $2\frac{14}{100}$ as a decimal.

Since $\frac{14}{100} = 0.14$, $2\frac{14}{100} = 2.14$.

Guided Practice*

Do you know HOW?

For **1** and **2**, write a decimal and a fraction in simplest form for the part of each grid that is shaded.

1.   2.

Do you UNDERSTAND?

3. **Writing to Explain** Why is the fraction $\frac{6}{10}$ not written 0.06?

4. On Kelsey Street, what fraction of homes do **NOT** have swings? Write your answer as a fraction and a decimal.

Independent Practice

For **5** through **9**, write a decimal and a fraction in simplest form for the part of each grid that is shaded.

5.   6.   7.   8.   9.

For another example, see Set C on page 288.

Write $\frac{6}{10}$ as a decimal.

$\frac{6}{10}$ is six tenths, or 0.6.

$\frac{6}{10} = 0.6$

So, 0.6 of the houses have swing sets.

In Rolling Hills, 0.75 houses are two-story homes.

Write 0.75 as a fraction.

0.75 is seventy-five hundredths, or $\frac{75}{100}$.

$0.75 = \frac{75}{100}$

So, $\frac{75}{100}$, or $\frac{3}{4}$, of the houses are two-story homes.

For **10** through **19**, write an equivalent decimal, fraction, or mixed number in simplest form.

10. $9\frac{4}{10}$ **11.** $\frac{21}{100}$ **12.** 11.6 **13.** $1\frac{81}{100}$ **14.** 0.65

15. $\frac{50}{100}$ **16.** 0.48 **17.** $4\frac{7}{10}$ **18.** $\frac{20}{200}$ **19.** 1.45

Problem Solving

20. Estimation About what fraction of the rectangle to the right is shaded green?

21. The arena of the Colosseum in Rome was about $\frac{3}{20}$ of the entire Colosseum. Write this amount as a decimal.

 $\frac{1}{20} = \frac{5}{100}$

22. Which fraction is the same as 0.85?

A $\frac{85}{1,000}$ **C** $\frac{85}{1}$

B $\frac{85}{100}$ **D** $\frac{85}{10}$

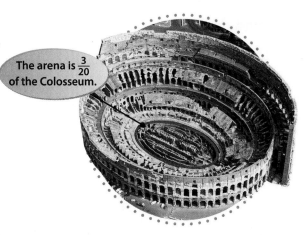

The arena is $\frac{3}{20}$ of the Colosseum.

23. Reasoning James, Vicki, Jaime, and Jill are in line for tickets for the basketball game. Jaime is first. Vicki is behind Jill. Jill is not last. James is in front of Jill. How are they ordered?

24. Algebra Find the missing numbers in the pattern below.

▨, 18, 27, ▨, ▨, 54, ▨

Lesson

11-4

NS 1.7 Write the fraction represented by a drawing of parts of a figure; represent a given fraction by using drawings; and relate a fraction to a simple decimal on a number line.

Locating Fractions and Decimals

How can you locate points on a number line?

In short-track speed skating, each lap is $\frac{1}{9}$ kilometer.
In long-track speed skating, each lap is 0.4 kilometer.
How can you use a number line to show these distances?

One lap = 0.4 km

One lap = $\frac{1}{9}$ km

Another Example **How can you name points on a number line?**

Naming fractions on a number line

What fraction is at point *P*?

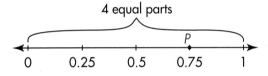

4 equal parts

| 0 | 0.25 | 0.5 | 0.75 | 1 |

There are 4 equal parts between 0 and 1. There are 3 equal
parts between 0 and point *P*. So, point *P* is at $\frac{3}{4}$.

Naming decimals on a number line

What number is at point *Q*?

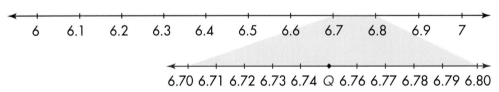

6   6.1   6.2   6.3   6.4   6.5   6.6   6.7   6.8   6.9   7

6.70 6.71 6.72 6.73 6.74 Q 6.76 6.77 6.78 6.79 6.80

There are 5 equal parts between 6.70 and
point *Q*. Each of these parts is 0.01, so point *Q* is at 6.75.

Explain It

1. Describe where you would place point *Q* on a number
line that shows only tenths.

2. What number is at point *R*?

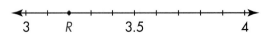

3   R   3.5   4

278

Locate $\frac{1}{9}$ on a number line.

Draw a number line, and label 0 and 1. Divide the distance from 0 to 1 into 9 equal parts.

Draw a point at $\frac{1}{9}$.

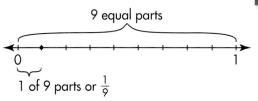

9 equal parts

0   1

1 of 9 parts or $\frac{1}{9}$

Locate 0.4 on a number line.

Draw a number line, and divide the distance from 0 to 1 into 10 equal parts to show tenths.

Draw a point at 0.4.

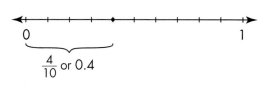

0   1

$\frac{4}{10}$ or 0.4

Guided Practice*

Do you know HOW?

For **1** and **2**, use the number line below to name the fraction.

1. *A*   **2.** *B*

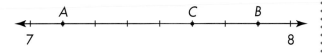

A   C   B

7   8

For **3** and **4**, name the point on the number line for each decimal.

3. 1.33   **4.** 1.39

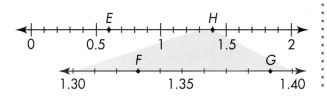

E   H

0   0.5   1   1.5   2

F   G

1.30   1.35   1.40

Do you UNDERSTAND?

5. Where would you locate 0.46 on the number line at the top?

6. In the number line for Exercises 1 and 2, what fraction is located at point *C*?

7. A 1,500-meter speed-skating race is $13\frac{1}{2}$ laps around a short track. Show $13\frac{1}{2}$ on a number line.

8. In the number line for Exercises 3 and 4, what point is at $\frac{6}{10}$?

Independent Practice

For **9** through **13**, use the number line below to name the decimal.

9. *J*   **10.** *K*   **11.** *L*   **12.** *M*   **13.** *N*

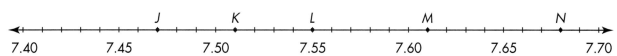

J   K   L   M   N

7.40   7.45   7.50   7.55   7.60   7.65   7.70

*For another example, see Set D on page 289.

For **14** through **18**, name the fraction that should be written at each point.

14. V **15.** Z **16.** X **17.** W **18.** Y

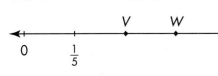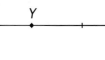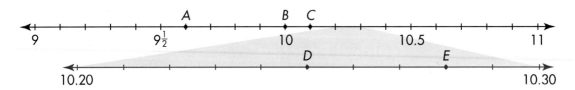

For **19** through **23**, name the point for each decimal or fraction.

19. $10\frac{1}{10}$ **20.** 10.28 **21.** 10.25 **22.** $9\frac{6}{10}$ **23.** 10.0

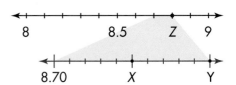

24. Writing to Explain Which two points on the number line to the right represent the same point?

25. Jack's distance in the shot-put throw was $8\frac{3}{4}$ meters. What is this distance as a decimal?

26. Write an expression that tells how to find the perimeter of a triangle with each side 2 inches long.

Use the diagram below for **27** and **28**.

According to the Greek mathematician Zeno, a ball will never stop bouncing because each bounce is half as high as the one before it.

27. Name the points at D and E for the next two bounces.

28. Writing to Explain Do you think it would be possible for the ball to reach zero by moving halfway closer at every step? Why or why not?

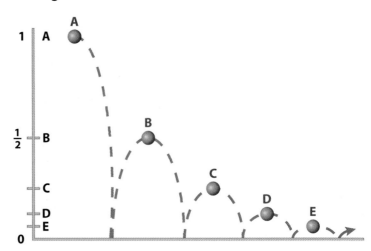

Algebra Connections

Divisibility

A number is divisible by another number when the quotient is a whole number and the remainder is 0.

Find which numbers in each list are divisible by the number shown.

1. 5
(5, 8, 10, 12, 15)

2. 8
(8, 14, 16, 19, 24)

3. 12
(12, 18, 25, 36, 48)

4. 14
(14, 27, 42, 56, 96)

5. 15
(15, 35, 45, 70, 90)

6. 16
(16, 32, 63, 80, 98)

7. 17
(17, 28, 34, 51, 69)

8. 22
(22, 33, 44, 55, 66)

9. 31
(31, 62, 83, 91, 124)

10. 4
(4, 8, 9, 12, 17)

11. 6
(6, 18, 21, 24, 35)

12. 7
(12, 14, 20, 28, 35)

13. 9
(18, 26, 36, 55, 63)

14. 18
(18, 35, 54, 72, 91)

Example:

Which of these numbers are divisible by 3?

(11, 14, 23, 42)

Use divisibility rules for 3s:

 Think *Is the sum of the digits of the number divisible by 3?*

Try 14.

1 + 4 = 5

5 is not divisible by 3, so 14 is not divisible by 3.

Now try 42.

4 + 2 = 6

6 is divisible by 3, so 3 is a factor of 42.

Check: **42 ÷ 3 = 14**

---

15. Bonnie has 64 packets of pepper. She wants to store the same amount of packets in bags so that each bag has the same number of packets. What are three different ways Bonnie can do this?

16. How many pieces of cloth 7 yards long could you cut from a piece of cloth that is 42 yards long? Explain.

42 yards in all

7 | ? pieces

NS 1.9 ⚷ Identify on a number line the relative position of positive fractions, positive mixed numbers, and positive decimals to two decimal places. Also NS 1.7 ⚷ .

Mixed Numbers and Decimals on the Number Line

How can you locate mixed numbers and decimals on a number line?

Laurie and Aaron went rollerblading. Laurie skated 1.6 miles, and Aaron skated $1\frac{3}{5}$ miles.

Who skated farther?

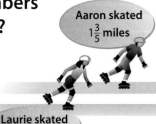

Aaron skated $1\frac{3}{5}$ miles

Laurie skated 1.6 miles

Other Examples

What fraction should be written at point *A*?

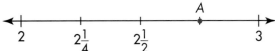

There are 4 equal parts between 2 and 3. Each part is $\frac{1}{4}$.
So, $2\frac{3}{4}$ should be written at *A*.

What decimal should be written at point *B*?

There are 10 equal parts between 1.40 and 1.50. There are 8 equal parts between 1.40 and point *B*. So, 1.48 should be written at *B*.

Guided Practice*

Do you know HOW?

For **1** through **6**, what decimal and fraction or mixed number should be written at each point?

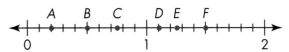

1. Point *A*
2. Point *B*
3. Point *C*
4. Point *D*
5. Point *E*
6. Point *F*

Do you UNDERSTAND?

7. The next day, Aaron skated 0.8 miles farther than the $1\frac{3}{5}$ miles he had skated the day before. Use a number line to show this distance as a decimal and as a mixed number.

Tip Convert 0.8 to a fraction.

8. If Lucy skated between 3.5 and 4.0 miles, what distances could she have skated?

Show $1\frac{3}{5}$ and 1.6 on the same number line.

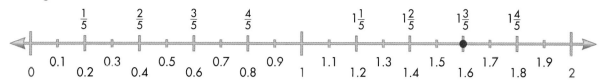

Draw a number line and label 0, 1, and 2.

Divide the distance between each whole number into 5 equal lengths.

Label the points $\frac{1}{5}, \frac{2}{5}$ and so on.

Then divide the distance between each whole number into 10 equal lengths. Label 0.1, 0.2, and so on.

Draw a point at $1\frac{3}{5}$ and 1.6.

Laurie and Aaron skated the same distance.

Independent Practice

For **9** through **13**, name the decimal for each point.

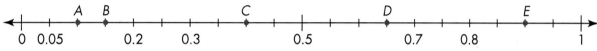

9. Point *A* **10.** Point *B* **11.** Point *C* **12.** Point *D* **13.** Point *E*

For **14** through **18**, name the mixed number that should be written at each point.

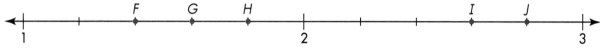

14. Point *F* **15.** Point *G* **16.** Point *H* **17.** Point *I* **18.** Point *J*

Problem Solving

19. The General Sherman Giant Sequoia in Sequoia National Park, east of Fresno, California, is the world's largest living tree. It is 83.8 meters high above its base. Write the height of the tree as a mixed number.

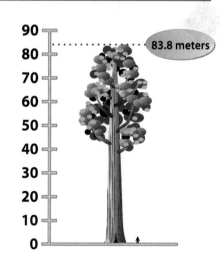

20. Jennifer lives $2\frac{1}{2}$ miles from school. Dorothy lives 2.4 miles from school. Does Dorothy or Jennifer live closer to the school? Use a number line to compare the two distances.

21. Renee and George are eating a pie they just baked. George cut himself a slice that was 0.2 of the pie. Renee cut herself a slice that was $\frac{2}{10}$ of the pie. How much of the pie did they eat together?

A $\frac{4}{15}$ **B** $\frac{1}{3}$ **C** $\frac{2}{5}$ **D** $\frac{1}{2}$

MR 2.3 Use a variety of methods, such as words, numbers, symbols, charts, graphs, tables, diagrams, and models, to explain mathematical reasoning. **Also MR 2.0, NS 1.5.**

Problem Solving

Use Objects and Make a Table

Hands-On
Cubes

Al has 12 containers of sand. One way to show $\frac{1}{2}$ is two groups of 6.

Using 12 or fewer cubes, how many other fractions can Al find that are equivalent to $\frac{1}{2}$?

$\frac{6}{12} = \frac{1}{2}$

Guided Practice*

Do you know HOW?

Solve. Use object to help.

1. One way to show $\frac{1}{3}$ using cubes is three groups of 4 cubes each. Using 12 or fewer cubes, how many other fractions can you find that are equivalent to $\frac{1}{3}$? Make a table to help.

Do you UNDERSTAND?

2. How many cubes are in each group to show $\frac{3}{6}$?

3. How many cubes are in each group to show $\frac{2}{4}$?

4. **Write a Problem** Write a word problem that uses the table you created in Problem 1 as an answer.

Independent Practice

Solve. Use objects or make a table or list to help.

5. Marianne has 12 cubes. She uses all 12 cubes and separates them into 4 groups. Then she uses 8 cubes and separates them into 4 groups. What fraction is Marianne trying to make?

6. Using 12 or fewer cubes, how many fractions can you find that are equivalent to $\frac{1}{5}$?

7. At a car wash, Jim washed 8 cars per hour, and David washed 6 cars per hour. How many cars did Jim wash if David washed 24 cars?

Stuck? Try this....

- What do I know?
- What diagram can I use to help understand the problem?
- Can I use addition, subtraction, multiplication, or division?
- Is all of my work correct?
- Did I answer the right question?
- Is my answer reasonable?

*For another example, see Set F on page 289.

Al can use cubes to solve this problem.

Using two groups of 7 gives $\frac{7}{14} = \frac{1}{2}$.

This uses more than 12 cubes.

Using two groups of 5 gives $\frac{5}{10} = \frac{1}{2}$.

This works. Al only used 10 cubes.

Make a table to show the other fractions equivalent to $\frac{1}{2}$.

First group	Second group	Fraction equivalent to $\frac{1}{2}$
4	4	$\frac{4}{8}$
3	3	$\frac{3}{6}$
2	2	$\frac{2}{4}$

Count all of the different ways to make $\frac{1}{2}$.

There are 4 other fractions that are equivalent to $\frac{1}{2}$ using 12 cubes or less.

8. Charlie had 12 cubes. He showed $\frac{8}{12}$ is equivalent to $\frac{2}{3}$ by making three groups of 4 and drawing a circle around two of the groups. Using 12 or fewer cubes, what is another fraction that is equivalent to $\frac{2}{3}$?

9. At Tara's Video Outlet, you can buy any 6 DVDs for 72 dollars. At Sam's DVD Palace, you can buy any 4 DVDs for 52 dollars. In which store do DVDs cost less? How much less?

10. Tyrone runs 4 miles each week. Francis runs 4 times as many miles each week. How many miles does Francis run each week?

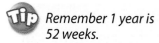

Miles each week

Francis	4	4	4	4	4 times as many

Tyrone	4

11. **Writing to Explain** If you know a person runs a certain number of miles every week, then how would you find out how many miles that person runs in one year?

Tip Remember 1 year is 52 weeks.

12. Jane has 24 pennies. She separated the pennies equally into 4 cups with 6 pennies in each cup. Complete the table at the right to show how many ways Jane can separate the pennies.

Number of cups	Number of pennies in each cup	Total number of pennies
4	▓	24
▓	12	24
3	▓	24

13. A store sells school-supply packs that contain 6 pencils and 4 pens. A customer bought enough packs to get 36 pencils. How many pens did the customer get?

eTools
www.pearsonsuccessnet.com

1. Quinton's frog leaped $2\frac{3}{4}$ feet on its first leap. Which point on the number line best represents the point where the frog landed? (11-5)

A L

B M

C N

D P

2. What decimal is shown in the grid below? (11-1)

A 6.12

B 2.61

C 1.62

D 1.26

3. Which shows the gymnastic scores in order from the least to the greatest? (11-2)

A 9.72, 9.8, 9.78, 9.87

B 9.78, 9.72, 9.87, 9.8

C 9.78, 9.8, 9.72, 9.87

D 9.72, 9.78, 9.8, 9.87

4. Which statement is true? (11-2)

0.14   0.09

A $0.14 > 0.09$

B $0.14 < 0.09$

C $0.09 = 0.14$

D $0.09 > 0.14$

5. What is 1.47 written as a fraction or mixed number? (11-3)

A $\frac{1}{147}$

B $\frac{47}{100}$

C $1\frac{47}{100}$

D $1\frac{47}{10}$

6. Which number is best represented by point R on the number line? (11-4)

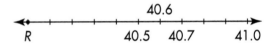

A 40.1

B 40.0

C 39.9

D 39.0

7. Which of the following is equal to $20 + 7 + 0.9 + 0.03$? (11-1)

A 20.79

B 20.93

C 27.39

D 27.93

8. Which fraction and decimal represent the part that is green? (11-3)

A $\frac{63}{100}$ and 0.63

B $\frac{63}{100}$ and 0.063

C $\frac{63}{100}$ and 6.3

D $\frac{63}{10}$ and 0.63

9. What fraction and decimal are best represented by point B on the number line? (11-5)

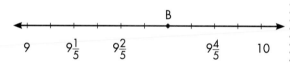

A $9\frac{3}{5}$ and 9.3

B $9\frac{3}{5}$ and 9.6

C $9\frac{3}{10}$ and 9.3

D $9\frac{3}{10}$ and 9.6

10. Which of the following has a 9 in the hundredths place? (11-1)

A 28.79

B 65.91

C 79.88

D 926.7

11. Which of the following has the least value? (11-2)

A 5.45

B 8.02

C 4.99

D 13.2

12. Use 15 or fewer cubes. Which fraction completes the table? (11-6)

Cubes in Group 1	Cubes in Group 2	Cubes in Group 3	Fraction Equivalent to $\frac{1}{3}$
2	2	2	$\frac{2}{6}$
3	3	3	$\frac{3}{9}$
4	4	4	$\frac{4}{12}$
5	5	5	

A $\frac{10}{15}$

B $\frac{3}{5}$

C $\frac{5}{10}$

D $\frac{5}{15}$

13. What fraction is best represented by point D on the number line? (11-4)

A $\frac{2}{5}$

B $\frac{3}{5}$

C $\frac{1}{2}$

D $\frac{3}{10}$

Set A, pages 270–271

Write the decimal shown in expanded, standard, and word form.

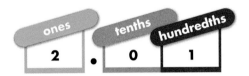

Expanded form: 2 + 0.01

Standard form: 2.01

Word form: Two and one hundredth

Remember to use the word *and* for the decimal point when you write a decimal in word form.

Write the following in word and expanded form.

1. 12.13

2. 1.09

3. 11.1

4. 88.08

Set B, pages 272–274

Compare 1.35 and 1.26 using place value.

Write the numbers, lining up the decimal points. Then compare digits by place value.

1.35

1.26

3 tenths > 2 tenths

So, 1.35 > 1.26.

Remember that zeros at the end of the decimal do not change its value.

Compare. Write >, <, or = for each ◯.

1. 1.82 ◯ 1.91

2. 6.95 ◯ 6.59

3. 26.30 ◯ 26.03

4. 1.1 ◯ 1.10

Set C, pages 276-277

Write $\frac{37}{100}$ as a decimal.

$\frac{37}{100}$ is 37 out of 100, or 0.37.

Write 1.7 as a mixed number.

Since 0.7 = $\frac{7}{10}$,

1.7 = $1\frac{7}{10}$.

Remember you can write a decimal and a fraction for the shaded part of each grid.

1.

2.

3.

4.

Set D, pages 278–280 and 282-283

Show $6\frac{1}{4}$ on a number line.

Divide the distance from 6 to 7 into 4 equal lengths. Label the tick marks and draw a point at $6\frac{1}{4}$.

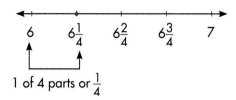

Show 7.7 on a number line.
Divide the distance from 7 to 8 into 10 equal lengths.

Label the tick marks, and draw a point at 7.7.

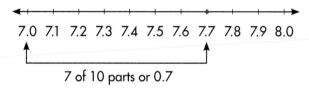

Remember that the distance between each tick mark is set evenly apart.

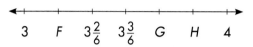

Name the fraction at each point.

1. G **2.** F **3.** H

J K L M N O
5.40 5.45 5.50 5.55 5.60 5.65 5.70

Name the decimal at each point.

4. K **5.** M **6.** O

Identify the point on the number line for each number.

7. $5\frac{3}{5}$ **8.** $5\frac{1}{2}$ **9.** 5.42

Set E, pages 284–285

You have 10 cubes. One way to show $\frac{1}{2}$ is two groups of 5. How many other fractions can you make with 10 or fewer cubes that are equivalent to $\frac{1}{2}$?

Make a table and count all the ways to make $\frac{1}{2}$.

Group 1	Group 2	Fraction
4	4	$\frac{4}{8} = \frac{1}{2}$
3	3	$\frac{3}{6} = \frac{1}{2}$
2	2	$\frac{2}{4} = \frac{1}{2}$
1	1	$\frac{1}{2} = \frac{1}{2}$

Remember you can act it out, use objects, or make a table.

1. You have 16 cubes. One way to show $\frac{1}{4}$ is four groups of 4. Using 16 or fewer cubes, what other fractions can you find that are equivalent to $\frac{1}{4}$?

2. You have 12 cubes. One way to show $\frac{1}{3}$ is three groups of 2. What other fractions can you make with 12 or fewer cubes that are equivalent to $\frac{1}{3}$?

Topic 12 Operations with Decimals

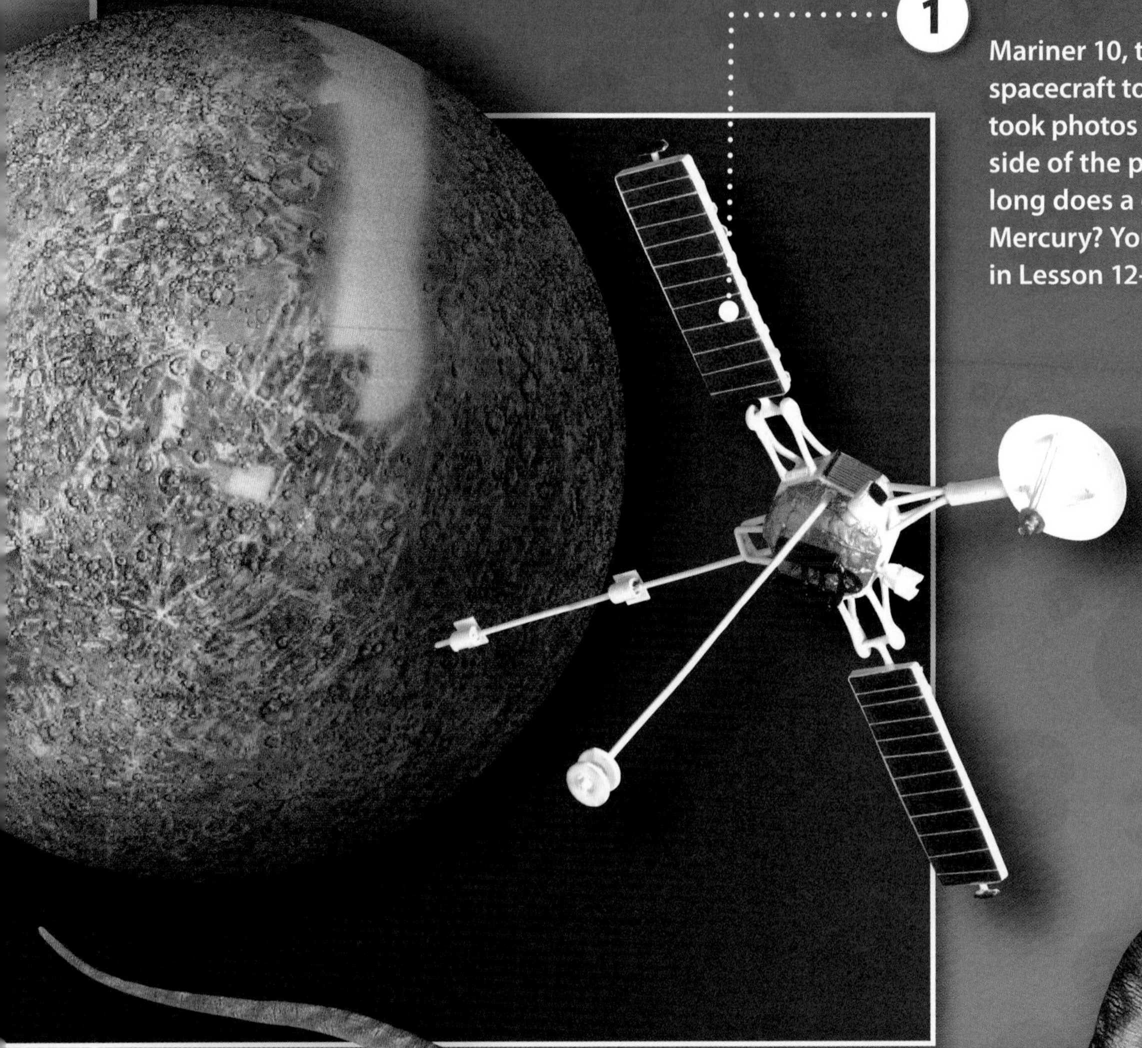

1 Mariner 10, the only spacecraft to visit Mercury, took photos of the daytime side of the planet. How long does a day last on Mercury? You will find out in Lesson 12-5.

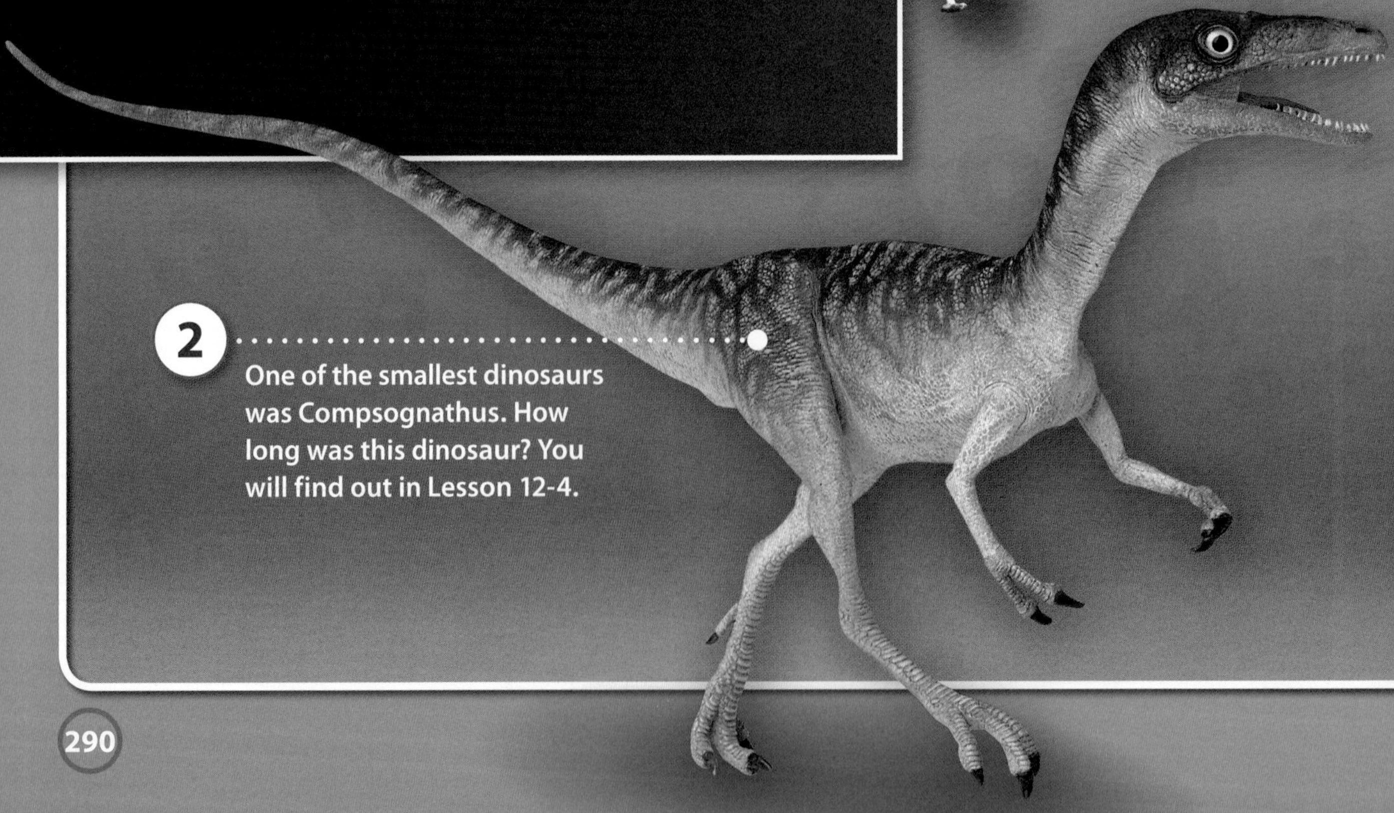

2 One of the smallest dinosaurs was Compsognathus. How long was this dinosaur? You will find out in Lesson 12-4.

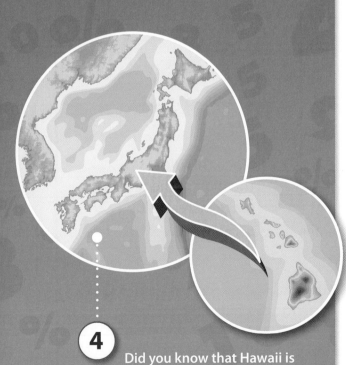

3 How much do tickets cost at the California Speedway? You will find out in Lesson 12-5.

4 Did you know that Hawaii is moving closer to Japan every year? Find out how much closer in Lesson 12-2.

Review What You Know!

Vocabulary

Choose the best term from the box.

> • fraction
> • decimal
> • mixed number
> • whole number

1. A ? names part of a whole.

2. A number that has a whole number and a fraction is a ? .

3. The ? equivalent of $\frac{1}{4}$ is 0.25.

Ordering Decimals

Order the numbers from least to greatest.

4. 0.4, 0.32, 0.25   5. 18.75, 18.7, 19.5

6. 2.4, 4.1, 1.5, 0.9   7. 3.5, 2.9, 4.6

Decimals and Fractions

Write each fraction as a decimal. Write each decimal as a fraction.

8. $\frac{2}{10}$ 9. 0.4   10. $\frac{41}{100}$

11. $\frac{6}{100}$ 12. 0.7   13. 0.75

Equivalent Fractions

Write each fraction in simplest form.

14. $\frac{2}{4}$ 15. $\frac{4}{10}$

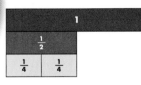

16. **Writing to Explain** How do you know that $\frac{3}{8}$ is in simplest form?

NS 2.2 Round two-place decimals to one decimal or to the nearest whole number and judge the reasonableness of the rounded answer.

Rounding Decimals

How can you round decimals?

A passenger train travels from Emeryville to Sparks. Sacramento is one of the stops along the route.

Rounded to the nearest whole number, what is the distance from Emeryville to Sparks?

Emeryville to Sacramento: 77.86 miles   Sacramento to Sparks: 134.12 miles

|← ———————————— 211.98 miles ———————————— →|

Another Example **How do you round to the nearest tenth?**

In Lesson 2-2 you learned how to round whole numbers. Now you will learn how to round decimals.

What is 211.98 rounded to the nearest tenth?

A 211.0

B 211.9

C 211.99

D 212.0

Step 1	**Step 2**	**Step 3**
Look at the tenths place	Look at the digit to the right.	**211.98** rounds to **212.0.** ↑
211.9̲8	**211.9̲8**	Since this digit is 8, the digit in the tenths place increases by 1.
	If the digit to the right is less than 5, round to 211.9. If the digit is 5 or greater than 5, round to 212.	

So, 211.98 rounded to the nearest tenth is 212.0. The correct choice is **D**.

Explain It

1. **Reasonableness** Why does the ones place change when you round 211.98 to the nearest tenth?

Look at the ones place.

211.98

Look at the digit to the right.

211.98

Since 9 > 5, round to the next whole number.

The distance from Emeryville to Sparks is about 212 miles.

A number line shows that the rounded answer is reasonable.

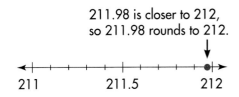

211.98 is closer to 212, so 211.98 rounds to 212.

211   211.5   212

Guided Practice*

Do you know HOW?

For **1** through **6**, round each decimal to the nearest whole number and to the nearest tenth.

1. 17.23

2. 19.80

3. 49.56

4. 67.59

5. 5.74

6. 82.19

Do you UNDERSTAND?

7. Writing to Explain In the example above, explain why the number line shows that 212 is a reasonable answer.

8. Round 77.86 to the nearest whole number.

9. Round 134.12 to the nearest whole number.

Independent Practice

For problems **10** through **24**, round each decimal to the nearest whole number.

10. 60.82

11. 88.3

12. 2.28

13. 0.69

14. 72.56

15. 41.48

16. 0.81

17. 7.61

18. 57.95

19. 63.66

20. 78.61

21. 4.10

22. 12.12

23. 91.95

24. 7.45

For problems **25** through **34**, round each decimal to the nearest tenth.

25. 3.78

26. 9.04

27. 23.97

28. 73.23

29. 99.94

30. 6.44

31. 0.32

32. 2.48

33. 44.54

34. 50.05

*For another example, see Set A on page 314.

35. Number Sense Name 3 decimals which, when rounded to the nearest tenth, round to 7.8.

36. Aaron filled his car with 8.53 gallons of gasoline. To the nearest tenth of a gallon, how much gasoline did Aaron purchase?

37. Which of these decimals when rounded to the nearest whole number does **NOT** round to 6?

   A 5.71   **C** 6.2

   B 5.91   **D** 6.82

38. What is 17.63 rounded to the nearest tenth?

   A 17   **C** 17.63

   B 17.6   **D** 18

39. Use a number line to explain why 0.28 rounded to the nearest whole number is 0.

40. Barbara's dog weighs 35.5 pounds. To the nearest whole number, how much does Barbara's dog weigh?

41. Reasonableness Danny had weighed two pieces of volcanic rock. The first piece had a weight of 4.99 grams and the second had a weight of 2.85 grams. Danny needs to record the combined weight of the two pieces of volcanic rock to the nearest gram. Is 4.0 + 2.9 a reasonable estimate of the weights to the nearest gram?

42. Dawn jogs 12 miles a week. How many miles does Dawn jog in 1 year?

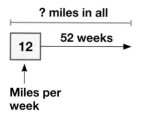

43. Reasoning Round 4.97 to the nearest tenth. Did the ones place change? Explain.

44. Writing to Explain What do the decimal numbers below have in common?

       3.6, 4.2, 4.1

45. Number Sense Marissa was asked to round 89.36 to the nearest tenth. She answered 89.3. Is she correct? Explain.

46. Geometry If a circle has a diameter of 86 centimeters, what is the radius of the circle?

47. According to Mica's rain gauge, it had rained 2.38 inches in 24 hours. What is 2.38 rounded to the nearest tenth? whole number?

48. The distance between Happy Valley and Rolling Meadow is 53.19 miles. What is this distance rounded to the nearest mile?

Mixed Problem Solving

The density of a material tells you how many grams are in a cubic centimeter. For example, the density of water is 1.0 gram per cubic centimeter. So, 1.0 cubic centimeter of water has a mass of 1.0 gram.

Use the table at the right for **1** through **4**.

Material	Density ($\frac{g}{cm^3}$)
Water	1.0
Ice	0.9
Aluminum	2.7
Iron	7.9
Balsa wood	0.13
Oak wood	0.79

Data

1. Order the densities in the table from least to greatest.

2. Materials with greater density than water sink in water. Which materials in the table will sink in water?

3. Which material has a density that is ten times greater than the density of oak wood?

4. Write an inequality to show which has a greater density, water or ice.

When you look closely at a rock, you may see different minerals. A mineral has properties you can measure, such as hardness or density.

Use the table at the right for **5** and **6**.

5. The density of a material equals its mass divided by its volume. What is the density of each mineral shown in the table?

Mineral Sample	Mass (grams)	Volume (cubic centimeters)	Density (grams per cubic centimeter)
#1	6	2	
#2	26	13	
#3	16	4	

6. Granite has a density of about 2.75 grams per cubic centimeter. If rounded to the nearest whole number, which of the samples could be granite?

7. Iron has a density of about 7.86 grams per cubic centimeter. What is this number rounded to the nearest tenth?

8. If a mineral has a mass of 33 grams and its density is 3 grams per cubic centimeter, what is its volume?

NS 2.1 ⚬━━ Estimate
and compute the sum
or difference of whole
numbers and positive
decimals to two places.
Also MR 2.5.

Estimating Sums and Differences of Decimals

How do you estimate when you add and subtract decimals?

In Beijing, China, it rained 5.82 inches in the first half of the year. In the second half of the year, it rained 18.63 inches. Estimate the rainfall for the whole year.

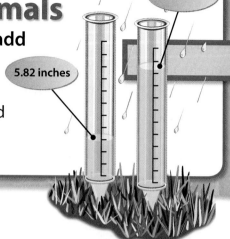

18.63 inches

5.82 inches

Guided Practice*

Do you know HOW?

In **1** through **4**, estimate each sum or difference.

1. 0.72 + 0.56

2. 18.54 − 1.99

3.   13.94
     +   4.72

4.   47.31
     − 11.25

Do you UNDERSTAND?

5. Explain why 1.4 and 0.75 both round to 1.

6. Reasonableness In the example above, explain why 2.5 inches is not a reasonable estimate of the rainfall for the whole year.

Independent Practice

In **7** through **22**, round to the nearest whole number to estimate each sum or difference.

 Tip *You can write rounded numbers in vertical format before adding or subtracting.*

7. 9.6 + 3.27

8. 9.51 + 8.61

9. 7.11 + 0.15

10. 1.45 + 6.85

11. 18.85 − 6.8

12. 4.31 − 1.28

13. 31.12 − 4.86

14. 0.66 − 0.34

15.   82.43
      −   3.90

16.   5.78
      −   3.86

17.   63.93
      +   3.31

18.   3.73
      +   0.81

19.   2.1
      +   7.5

20.   3.45
      −   2.44

21.   19.06
      +   1.99

22.   4.84
      +   0.73

For another example, see Set B on page 314.

Estimate 5.82 + 18.63.

Round each decimal to the nearest whole number. Then add.

$$
\begin{array}{r}
5.82 \longrightarrow 6 \\
+\ 18.63 \longrightarrow +\ 19 \\
\hline
25
\end{array}
$$

About 25 inches of rain fell in Beijing.

In August, 6.7 inches of rain fell in Beijing. In September, it rained 2.3 inches. About how much more did it rain in August than in September?

$$
\begin{array}{r}
6.7 \longrightarrow 7 \\
-\ 2.3 \longrightarrow -\ 2 \\
\hline
5
\end{array}
$$

Round each decimal to the nearest whole number. Then subtract the rounded numbers.

It rained about 5 inches more in August.

Problem Solving

In **23** and **24**, use the table at the right.

23. The table shows the weight of each type of vegetable Vanessa bought to make a large salad for her family picnic. About how much more did the cucumbers weigh than the lettuce?

24. About how much did all of the vegetables weigh altogether?

Vegetable	Weight (pounds)
	2.0
	2.6
	1.2
	3.5

25. Hawaii is moving toward Japan at a rate of approximately 2.8 inches per year. About how much closer will Hawaii be to Japan in 3 years?

26. Sunny has $50 to buy painting supplies. She wants to buy brushes for $7.33, paper for $14.97, and an easel for $38.19. Do you need to find the exact total, or an estimate?

27. Neil is installing 38 square yards of carpet in his home. He uses 12.2 square yards in one room and 10.5 square yards in another room. About how much carpet does he have left?

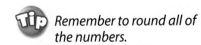 *Remember to round all of the numbers.*

    A about 13 square yards   **C** about 17 square yards

    B about 15 square yards   **D** about 20 square yards

Modeling Addition and Subtraction of Decimals

NS 2.0 Students extend their use and understanding of whole numbers to the addition and subtraction of simple decimals.

Hands-On
grid paper

How do you add decimals using grids?

Use the table at the right to find the total monthly cost of using the dishwasher and the DVD player.

Device	Cost/month
DVD player	$0.40
Microwave oven	$3.57
Ceiling light	$0.89
Dishwasher	$0.85

Another Example How do you subtract decimals with grids?

Find the difference between the cost per month to run the microwave oven and the ceiling light.

Use hundredths grids to subtract 3.57 − 0.89.

Shade three grids and 57 squares to show 3.57.

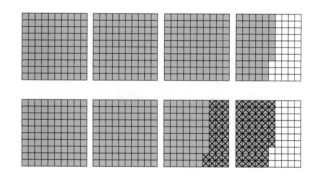

Cross out 8 columns and 9 squares of the shaded grid to show 0.89 being subtracted from 3.57.

Count the squares that are shaded but not crossed out to find the difference.
3.57 − 0.89 = 2.68

Explain It

1. **Reasonableness** How could you use the grids to check your answer above?

2. How would the grid above be different if the cost per month to run the microwave is $2.57?

Use hundredths grids to add $0.85 + $0.40.

It costs $0.85 to use the dishwasher per month.

Shade 85 squares to show $0.85.

It costs $0.40 to use the DVD player per month.

Use a different color and shade 40 more squares to show $0.40. Count all of the shaded squares to find the sum.

$0.85 + $0.40 = $1.25

The monthly cost of using the dishwasher and DVD player is $1.25.

Critical Thinking   **Guided Practice***

Do you know HOW?

In **1** through **6**, use hundredths grids to add or subtract.

1. 1.22 + 0.34   **2.** 0.63 + 0.41

3. 2.73 − 0.94   **4.** 1.38 − 0.73

5. 0.47 − 0.21   **6.** 2.02 + 0.8

Do you UNDERSTAND?

7. If you were to shade 40 squares first, and then shade 85 more, would the answer be the same as shading 85 squares and then 40 more?

8. Show the difference between the monthly cost of using the DVD player and the dishwasher.

Independent Practice

In **9** through **18**, add or subtract. Use hundredths grids to help.

9. 0.1 + 0.73

10. 0.37 + 0.47

11. 1.2 + 0.56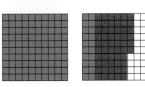

12. 1.33 − 0.35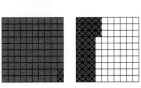

13. 3.0 − 1.47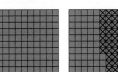

14. 1.11 + 0.89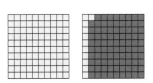

eTools
www.pearsonsuccessnet.com

15. 2.23 − 1.8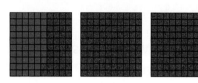

16. 0.4 − 0. 21

17. 0.58 + 2.4

18. 1.31 − 0.55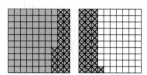

19. Writing to Explain How is adding 4.56 + 2.31 similar to adding $2.31 + $4.56?

20. Number Sense Do you think the difference of 1.4 − 0.95 is less than one or greater than one? Explain.

21. Number Sense Is the sum of 0.46 + 0.25 less than or greater than one? Explain.

22. Estimation Estimate to decide if the sum of 314 + 175 is more or less than 600.

23. Which choice represents the problem below?

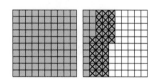

A 2.00 + 0.31 **C** 1.76 − 1.45

B 1.76 − 0.31 **D** 1.45 − 0.31

24. Geometry What kind of angle is made when two lines are perpendicular?

A acute angle

B right angle

C obtuse angle

D vertex

25. *Think* **About the Process** Which expression can be used to find the perimeter of the pool shown to the right?

A 50 + 25

B 25 + 25 + 25 + 25

C 50 + 50 + 25 + 25

D 50 + 50 + 50 + 50

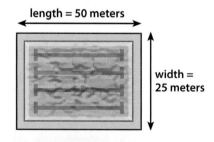

length = 50 meters

width = 25 meters

26. Write the number sentence that is shown by the hundredths grids to the right.

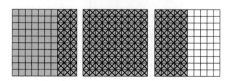

Find the sum. Write the answer in simplest form.

1. $\dfrac{3}{5}$
$+ \dfrac{1}{5}$

2. $\dfrac{1}{6}$
$+ \dfrac{7}{12}$

3. $\dfrac{1}{6}$
$+ \dfrac{1}{6}$

4. $\dfrac{1}{2}$
$+ \dfrac{1}{5}$

5. $\dfrac{2}{9}$
$+ \dfrac{4}{9}$

6. $\dfrac{4}{5}$
$+ \dfrac{1}{10}$

7. $\dfrac{7}{12}$
$+ \dfrac{1}{4}$

8. $\dfrac{1}{4}$
$+ \dfrac{1}{6}$

Find the difference. Write the answer in simplest form.

9. $\dfrac{5}{6}$
$- \dfrac{3}{4}$

10. $\dfrac{7}{10}$
$- \dfrac{3}{10}$

11. $\dfrac{2}{3}$
$- \dfrac{1}{2}$

12. $\dfrac{3}{4}$
$- \dfrac{1}{3}$

13. $\dfrac{5}{6}$
$- \dfrac{2}{3}$

14. $\dfrac{3}{4}$
$- \dfrac{1}{12}$

15. $\dfrac{7}{8}$
$- \dfrac{1}{2}$

16. $\dfrac{7}{12}$
$- \dfrac{1}{3}$

17. $\dfrac{8}{9}$
$- \dfrac{2}{3}$

18. $\dfrac{11}{12}$
$- \dfrac{2}{3}$

Error Search Find each answer that is not correct.
Write it correctly and explain the error.

19. $\dfrac{2}{5}$
$+ \dfrac{1}{5}$
$\overline{\dfrac{1}{5}}$

20. $\dfrac{5}{12}$
$+ \dfrac{1}{2}$
$\overline{\dfrac{11}{12}}$

21. $\dfrac{5}{6}$
$- \dfrac{1}{3}$
$\overline{\dfrac{4}{3}}$

22. $\dfrac{9}{10}$
$- \dfrac{3}{5}$
$\overline{\dfrac{3}{10}}$

23. $\dfrac{1}{6}$
$+ \dfrac{1}{3}$
$\overline{\dfrac{2}{9}}$

Number Sense

Estimating and Reasoning Write whether each
statement is true or false. Explain your answer.

24. The sum of 23,332 and 22,042 is less than 40,000.

25. The fraction $2\dfrac{1}{4}$ is greater than the decimal 3.5.

26. The product of 4 and 36 is 10 more than 120.

27. The expression $2 + 8 \times 4$ equals 40.

28. The quotient of $714 \div 7$ is greater than 100.

NS 2.1 Estimate and compute the sum or difference of whole numbers and positive decimals to two places. Also NS 2.2.

Adding and Subtracting Decimals

How can you add or subtract decimals?

The Patel family walked 14.35 kilometers from their cabin to Crystal River. Later, they walked 12.4 kilometers from Crystal River to Lake Dorrance. How far did they walk in all?

? km

14.35	12.4

Another Example **How can you subtract decimals?**

You know how to subtract whole numbers. In this lesson, you will learn how to subtract decimals.

23.23 kilograms

11.6	?

Roger's backpack weighed 23.23 kilograms. Marta's backpack weighed 11.6 kilograms. What is the difference in the weight of their backpacks?

Estimate 23.23 rounds to 23 and 11.6 rounds to 12. So the weight of the backpack is about 11 kg.

Step 1

Line up the decimal points. Write zeros as placeholders, if necessary.

```
  23.23
- 11.60
```

Step 2

Regroup, if necessary. Subtract hundredths.

```
  23.23
- 11.60
      3
```

Step 3

Regroup, if necessary. Subtract tenths.

```
   2 12
  23.23
- 11.60
    .63
```

Step 4

Subtract ones and tens, regrouping as necessary. Place the decimal point.

```
   2 12
  23.23
- 11.60
  11.63
```

Roger's backpack weighs 11.63 kilograms more than Marta's backpack.

Explain It

1. In Step 4, how do you know where to place the decimal point?

2. **Reasonableness** Is it reasonable to say that Roger's backpack weighs twice as much as Marta's backpack?

Step 1	Step 2	Step 3	Step 4
Line up the decimal points. Write zeros as place holders, if necessary.	Add the hundredths. Regroup if necessary.	Add the tenths. Regroup if necessary.	Add the ones, then the tens. Place the decimal point.

Step 1:
```
  14.35
+ 12.40
```

Step 2:
```
  14.35
+ 12.40
      5
```

Step 3:
```
  14.35
+ 12.40
     75
```

Step 4:
```
  14.35
+ 12.40
  26.75
```
The Patel family hiked 26.75 km in all.

*For another example, see Set D on page 315.

Guided Practice*

Do you know HOW?

For **1** through **6**, add or subtract.

1.
```
   8.24
+ 19.16
```

2.
```
  37.68
- 14.53
```

3.
```
   5.93
+ 87.82
```

4.
```
  62.53
- 43.75
```

5. 7.7 + 0.85

6. 0.6 − 0.42

Do you UNDERSTAND?

7. How many miles farther is the distance from the cabin to Crystal River than the distance from Crystal River to Lake Dorrance?

8. Is the answer in the example above reasonable?

Independent Practice

For **9** through **24**, add or subtract. Estimate to check the reasonableness of your answer.

9.
```
  2.73
+ 0.44
```

10.
```
  46.81
- 12.43
```

11.
```
  35.78
+ 70.71
```

12.
```
  17.15
-  2.38
```

13.
```
  4.83
- 0.56
```

14.
```
  12.55
+ 53.59
```

15.
```
  88.25
-  7.52
```

16.
```
  59.32
+  4.31
```

17. 70.1 − 65.81

18. 55.7 + 0.52

19. 89.82 − 46.3

20. 92.78 − 37.97

21. 9.12 + 82.4

22. 69.63 + 0.99

23. 39.65 − 17.69

24. 91.5 − 66.13

25. Number Sense Is 8.7 − 0.26 greater or less than 8? Explain.

26. Geometry Heather says an obtuse triangle always has no equal sides. Is she correct?

27. On Oak Street, 66.32 kilograms of trash was collected, and 31.21 kilograms of recyclables were collected in one week. How many kilograms were collected in all?

? kilograms	
66.32	31.21

28. Reasoning When Matt left his home in Redding, his odometer read 47,283.5 kilometers. By the time he had arrived in Los Angeles, his odometer read 48,163.7 kilometers. How many kilometers did Matt travel?

48,163.7 kilometers	
47,283.5 kilometers	?

29. One of the largest dinosaurs ever found, the *Puertasaurus,* measured 39.92 meters long. One of the smallest dinosaurs, the *Compsognathus,* measured 1.43 meters long. What was the difference in length of these dinosaurs?

30. Grace is following a recipe to make fruit punch. She wants to find how many quarts there are in 16 pints. Which could Grace use to solve this problem?

A 16 + 2   **C** 16 − 2

B 16 × 2   **D** 16 ÷ 2

31. **Think About the Process** The distance from Don's house to his school is twice the length of the distance from Don's house to the post office. The post office is 2.4 kilometers from the school. How would you find the distance from Don's house to the school?

A 2.4 + 2.4   **C** 2.4 + 1.2

B 2.4 − 1.2   **D** 2.4 − 0.2

32. In one week, Jessica spent 2.35 hours walking from her house to work. Together, Jessica and her friend, Constance, will spend 4.21 hours of their week walking from their homes to work. How many hours does Constance spend each week walking from home to work?

4.21 hours	
2.35	?

33. In a butterfly garden, there are 36 butterflies. Nine of them are yellow swallowtails. What fraction of the butterflies are yellow swallowtails?

Algebra Connections

Solving Equations

Remember that an equation is a number sentence which uses an equal sign to show that two expressions have the same value. You can use basic facts and mental math to help you find missing values in an equation.

Copy and complete. Check your answers.

1. 20 + ▢ = 34
2. 64 ÷ ▢ = 8
3. 5 × ▢ = 45
4. 54 − ▢ = 14

5. ▢ × 6 = 42
6. 36 ÷ ▢ = 4
7. ▢ + 15 = 31
8. ▢ − 8 = 6

9. 26 − ▢ = 18
10. 9 + ▢ = 20
11. 12 ÷ ▢ = 6
12. 4 × ▢ = 28

13. 72 ÷ ▢ = 8
14. ▢ × 9 = 54
15. ▢ − 5 = 7
16. ▢ + 7 = 29

17. ▢ + 32 = 46
18. 28 − ▢ = 9
19. ▢ ÷ 4 = 12
20. ▢ × 3 = 30

· ·

For **21** through **24**, copy and complete the equation using information from the problem. Then find the answer.

21. Jaina has $4. She needs $12 to buy a book. How much more money does Jaina need?

    4 + ▢ = 12

22. Harrison's allowance is $5 a week. How much money will he have if he saves his whole allowance for 4 weeks?

    ▢ × 5 = ▢

23. There are 49 fourth graders. The gym teacher needs to divide them into groups of 7. How many groups can be made?

    49 ÷ ▢ = ▢

24. **Write a Problem** Write a problem in which 4 is subtracted from 28 to find a difference. Write the number sentence and then solve.

Lesson

12-5

NS 2.1 Grade 5 ⚷
Add, subtract, multiply,
and divide with decimals;
add with negative
integers; subtract positive
integers from negative
integers; and verify the
reasonableness of the
results.

Multiplying and Dividing with Decimals

How can you multiply and divide money?

Ingrid bought 6 large rawhide bones for her dog, Lucky. Each bone cost $1.59. How much did Ingrid pay for the 6 bones?

$1.59 each

Another Example **How can you divide money amounts?**

Sam is buying new squeaky toys for his four dogs. The total came to $15.84. How much did each squeaky toy cost?

$15.84

| ? | ? | ? | ? |

↑
Cost of each toy

Step 1

Estimate.

$15.84 rounds to $16.

$16 ÷ 4 = $4

So, the cost for each toy should be about $4.

Step 2

Divide as you would with whole numbers.

```
      396
   4)$15.84
    - 12
      38
    - 36
      24
    - 24
       0
```

Step 3

Show the dollar sign and decimal point in the quotient.

```
     $3.96
   4)$15.84
    - 12
      38
    - 36
      24
    - 24
       0
```
Move the decimal point straight up.

Each squeaky toy costs $3.96. The answer is reasonable.

Explain It

1. How can you use multiplication to check your answer in Step 3?

2. Sam also bought 5 bags of dog food for $19.25. How much did each bag of dog food cost?

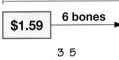

Step 1	Step 2	Step 3

Step 1

Estimate.

$1.59 rounds to $2.

$6 \times \$2 = \$12$

So the total cost should be about $12.

Step 2

Multiply with whole numbers.

? total cost

$1.59 — 6 bones →

$$\begin{array}{r} \scriptstyle 3\ 5 \\ \$1.59 \\ \times\ \ \ \ 6 \\ \hline \$954 \end{array}$$

Step 3

The number of decimal places in the product equals the total number of decimal places in the factors.

$$\begin{array}{rl} \scriptstyle 3\ 5 \\ \$1.59 & \text{2 decimal places} \\ \times\ \ \ \ 6 & \text{0 decimal places} \\ \hline \$9.54 & \text{2 decimal places} \end{array}$$

Ingrid bought 6 bones for $9.54.

Guided Practice*

Do you know HOW?

For **1** and **2**, multiply.

1. $\begin{array}{r} \$3.46 \\ \times\ \ \ 3 \\ \hline \end{array}$

2. $\begin{array}{r} \$62.58 \\ \times\ \ \ \ 6 \\ \hline \end{array}$

For **3** and **4**, divide.

3. $4\overline{)\$7.12}$

4. $9\overline{)\$2.88}$

Do you UNDERSTAND?

5. Ingrid bought 2 bottles of pet shampoo on sale for $3.48. How much did each bottle cost?

6. The store announces a special on dog food, 3 bones for $3.50. At the sale price, how much will Ingrid pay if she buys 9 bones?

Independent Practice

For **7** through **24**, multiply or divide.

7. $\begin{array}{r} \$3.83 \\ \times\ \ \ 4 \\ \hline \end{array}$

8. $\begin{array}{r} \$23.37 \\ \times\ \ \ \ 8 \\ \hline \end{array}$

9. $\begin{array}{r} \$17.99 \\ \times\ \ \ \ 6 \\ \hline \end{array}$

10. $\begin{array}{r} \$65.20 \\ \times\ \ \ \ 3 \\ \hline \end{array}$

11. $3\overline{)\$8.94}$

12. $6\overline{)\$4.62}$

13. $7\overline{)\$9.38}$

14. $5\overline{)\$7.65}$

15. $5\overline{)\$5.35}$

16. $\$6.44 \times 6$

17. $7\overline{)\$2.66}$

18. $2\overline{)\$8.32}$

19. $8 \times \$16.89$

20. $7 \times \$1.91$

21. $4\overline{)\$1.64}$

22. $8\overline{)\$8.24}$

23. $8\overline{)\$5.84}$

24. $\$5.76 \times 7$

*For another example, see Set E on page 315.

25. Amanda purchased 4 pounds of potatoes for $0.70 per pound. How much did Amanda pay for the potatoes?

26. **Writing to Explain** How can you tell that 3,100,899,005 is not a prime number?

27. **Geometry** Paul drew two lines. The first line, shown below, was 14.8 centimeters long. The second line was half the length of the first line. How long is the second line?

28. Erin made a telephone call to her cousin. Erin spent 9 minutes on the phone. The phone call cost $2.97. What was the price per minute of the call?

14.8 centimeters

29. Alice paid $1.92 for 6 cans of pet food for her cat, Sneakers. How much did each can cost?

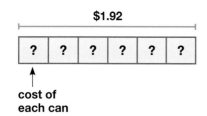

$1.92

| ? | ? | ? | ? | ? | ? |

↑
cost of
each can

30. Sheena bought five new CDs. Each CD cost $12.34. How much did the five CDs cost?

? total cost

| $12.34 | $12.34 | $12.34 | $12.34 | $12.34 |

31. Where do the parentheses need to go in the following expression?

$$7.5 + 9.5 - 6.4 + 3.1 = 7.5$$

32. Jonas has $22.45 in his bank account. Does he have enough money to buy a new CD for $13.72 and a movie ticket for $8.50?

33. **Think About the Process** One day on Mercury is the same as 59 days on Earth. It takes Mercury 1.49 days to revolve one time around the sun. Which expression can you use to find how many Earth days it takes Mercury to revolve around the sun one time?

A $59 \div 1.49$ **C** 59×1.49

B $1.49 \div 1$ **D** 365×1.49

34. Grandstand tickets at the California Speedway cost $20.00. If you buy tickets online, you pay $1.25 more per ticket. How much will 4 tickets cost?

A $21.25 **B** $84.00

C $81.25 **D** $85.00

Stop and Practice

Find the sum. Estimate to check
if the answer is reasonable.

| **1.** | 2.15
+ 3.97 | **2.** | 3.25
+ 1.56 | **3.** | 22.44
+ 18.59 | **4.** | 11.21
+ 0.09 |

Find the difference. Estimate to check
if the answer is reasonable.

| **5.** | 0.56
− 0.29 | **6.** | 27.21
− 3.19 | **7.** | 2.46
− 0.82 | **8.** | 3.06
− 1.98 |

Find the product. Estimate to check
if the answer is reasonable.

| **9.** | $5.13
× 4 | **10.** | $14.14
× 8 | **11.** | $2.86
× 7 | **12.** | $30.06
× 3 | **13.** | $5.26
× 8 |

Error Search Find each answer that is not correct.
Write it correctly and explain the error.

| **14.** | 27.58
− 13.49
41.07 | **15.** | 3.56
+ 9.71
13.26 | **16.** | $3.81
× 8
$24.48 | **17.** | $0.81
× 6
$4.86 | **18.** | $99.99
× 3
$299.97 |

Number Sense

Estimating and Reasoning Write whether each
statement is true or false. Explain your answer.

19. The number 23.68 is one tenth more than 23.67.

20. The sum of 32.83 and 27.91 is greater than 50 but less than 70.

21. The product of 5 and $6.12 is closer to $30 than $35.

22. The quotient of $1.72 ÷ 4 is less than $0.40.

23. The sum of 4.96 + 2.25 is 0.04 less than 7.25.

24. The quotient of $2.68 ÷ 3 is closer to $0.80 than $0.90.

Lesson
12-6

MR 2.6 Make precise
calculations and check
the validity of the results
from the context of the
problem. Also NS 3.0

Problem Solving

Try, Check, and Revise

Wilma bought supplies for her
dog at the pet store. She spent
a total of $26.18 not including
tax. She bought two of one item
in the chart and one other
item. What did she buy?

Dog Toy:
$7.98

Dog Supplies	
Leash	$11.50
Collar	$5.59
Bowls	$7.48
Medium Beds	$15.00
Toys	$7.98

Guided Practice*

Do you know HOW?

Use Try, Check, and Revise to solve
this problem. Write the answer in a
complete sentence.

1. Annie and Matt spent a total of $29
on a gift. Annie spent $7 more than
Matt. How much did each spend?

Do you UNDERSTAND?

2. How do you know that two beds
are too much?

3. Write a Problem Write a
problem using the Try, Check
and Revise strategy.

Independent Practice

Use Try, Check, and Revise to solve
this problem. Write the answer in
a complete sentence.

4. Lana's mom brought 27 cartons of orange
and grape juice to the park. There were
twice as many cartons of orange juice as
there were of grape juice. How many of
each kind did she bring?

5. In football, a team can score 2, 3, 6, 7, or
8 points. The terriers scored 3 times and
had 19 points. How did they score
their points?

Stuck? Try this....

- What do I know?
- What diagram can I use to help
  understand the problem?
- Can I use addition, subtraction,
  multiplication, or division?
- Is all of my work correct?
- Did I answer the right question?
- Is my answer reasonable?

Make a reasonable first try.

Two beds are too much.

Try one bed. Then try two of the smaller priced items, like the toy.

Check using the information given in the problem.

$7.98 + $7.98 + $15 = $30.96

That's too high but is close.

Revise. Use your first try to make a reasonable second try.

The first try was $4.78 too high. If you keep the bed, you need to come down $4.78 total or $ 2.39 for each item.

Try two collars.

$5.59 + $5.59 + $15 = $26.18

Wilma bought two collars and one medium bed.

For **6** through **8**, use the data at the right.

6. Trent spent $16.34, before tax, at Fun Town. He bought 3 different items. What did he buy?

7. Alicia spent $14.10, before tax, on 3 items at Fun Town. Two of her three items were the same. What did she buy?

8. Rich spent $30.80, before tax, at Fun Town. He bought two of one item and two of another item. What did Rich buy?

Fun Town	
Jump Rope	$2.35
Skateboard	$26.95
Basketball	$8.75
Football	$6.00
Baseball	$5.24
Bat	$9.40

Data

9. Mr. Mill took all of the tires off of the old bicycles and tricycles in his garage. He got 12 tires off of 5 cycles. How many of each type of cycle did he have?

10. Linda earned $8 per hour and Susan earned $10 per hour. Linda and Susan worked the same number of hours. Linda earned $72. How much did Susan earn?

11. If Chuck's Sports sold 12 fishing poles each week how many fishing poles would be sold in one month?

? fishing poles

12	12	12	12

↑
Fishing poles
sold each week

12. Lizzy bought six notebooks at the beginning of the school year. They were $2.19 each. How much did the six notebooks cost?

A $4.38　　　**C** $10.95

B $6.57　　　**D** $13.14

1. The distance across the widest part of a quarter is 24.26 millimeters. What is 24.26 rounded to the nearest tenth? (12-1)

A 24

B 24.2

C 24.3

D 25

2. Lee's turtle has a shell that is 14.42 centimeters long. Ty's turtle has a shell that is 12.14 centimeters long. Which is the best estimate of the difference? (12-2)

A 1 centimeter

B 2 centimeters

C 4 centimeters

D 6 centimeters

3. Larry spent $1.89 on a bottle of paint and $0.45 on a sponge brush. What was the total amount he spent? (12-3)

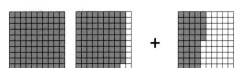

A $2.34

B $1.34

C $1.32

D $1.24

4. Tatum weighs 47.39 kilograms. What is her mass rounded to the nearest whole number? (12-1)

A 50 kilograms

B 48 kilograms

C 47.4 kilograms

D 47 kilograms

5. A penny has a mass of 2.5 grams. A quarter has a mass of 5.67 grams. What is the difference in their masses? (12-4)

A 2.17 grams

B 3.17 grams

C 5.42 grams

D 8.17 grams

6. Sale prices at the local market are shown below.

Type of Apple	Per Pound
Granny Smith	$1.69
Macintosh	$2.19
Red Delicious	$1.29

How much, before tax, did Minnie pay for 3 pounds of Granny Smith apples? (12-5)

A $3.87

B $4.97

C $5.07

D $6.57

7. Samantha rode her bicycle 6.79 miles on Saturday and 8.21 miles on Sunday. Which is the best estimate of the total miles she rode during the weekend? (12-2)

A 20 miles

B 15 miles

C 12 miles

D 1 mile

8. Mr. Leroy paid $9.48, before tax, for 3 plastic storage boxes. What was the price for each storage box? (12-5)

A $3.06

B $3.15

C $3.16

D $28.44

9. Mr. Treveses bought 2.72 kilograms of hamburger meat and 1.48 kilograms of turkey meat. How many kilograms of meat did he buy? (12-4)

A 1.24 kilograms

B 3.10 kilograms

C 4.10 kilograms

D 4.20 kilograms

10. What is 15.52 rounded to the nearest whole number? (12-1)

A 16

B 15.6

C 15.5

D 15

11. What is $6 \times \$19.37$? (12-5)

A $116.22

B $114.22

C $64.82

D $56.22

12. Which symbol makes the comparison true? (12-4)

$12.63 - 5.94 \bigcirc 3.8 + 2.88$

A $<$

B $=$

C $+$

D $>$

13. Jason spent $8.76, not including tax, on breakfast food. He bought 4 items. Two of the items were the same thing. What did he buy? (12-6)

Breakfast Food	
Bagel	$0.89
Box of Cereal	$2.79
Loaf of Bread	$1.59
Gallon of Juice	$3.19
Gallon of Milk	$3.79

A 2 bagels, a gallon of juice, and a gallon of milk

B 2 bagels, a box of cereal, and a gallon of milk

C 2 loaves of bread, a box of cereal, and a gallon of juice

D 2 boxes of cereal, a bagel, and a gallon of milk

Set A, pages 292–295

Round 306.87 to the nearest whole number.

Look at the ones place: 30**6**.87

Now look at the digit to the right: 306.87

If the digit to the right is less than 5, round to 306. If the digit is 5 or greater, round to 307.

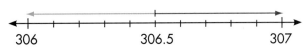

$8 > 5$
So, 306.87 rounds to 307.

Remember you must look at the digit to the right of the digit you are rounding.

Round each decimal to the nearest whole number and to the nearest tenth.

1. 18.34   **2.** 17.60

3. 68.58   **4.** 2.78

5. 6.83   **6.** 80.12

Set B, pages 296–297

Estimate $23.64 + 7.36$.

Round each decimal to the nearest whole number. Then add.

23.64 rounds to 24.
7.36 rounds to 7.

$24 + 7 = 31.$

Remember to compare the digit in the tenths place to 5 when you round to the nearest whole number.

1. $19.35 + 8.74$ **2.** $12.3 - 9.7$

3.   14.04   **4.**   7.48
       $+\ \ 9.33$ $+\ 3.92$

Set C, pages 298-300

Use hundredths grids to subtract $1.86 - 0.95$.

Shade one whole grid and 86 squares to show 1.86.

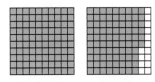

To subtract 0.95, cross out 9 columns and 5 squares of the shaded parts of the grid.

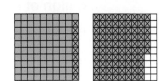

Count the squares that are shaded but not crossed out.

$1.86 - 0.95 = 0.91$

Remember to add decimals, shade the first number in one color and then continue on shading the second number with another color.

1. $0.2 + 0.89$

2. $0.67 - 0.31$

3. $0.34 + 0.34$

4. $0.81 - 0.78$

Set D, pages 302-304

Add 15.85 + 23.3.

Line up the decimal points.

Add the hundredths.	Add the tenths.	Add the ones, then the tens.
15.85 + 23.30 5	1 15.85 + 23.30 15	1 15.85 + 23.30 39.15

↑ Place the decimal in the answer.

Remember to use a zero as a placeholder.

Add or subtract.

1.　　6.32
　　+ 15.12

2.　　43.42
　　− 15.28

3.　　8.34
　　+ 97.25

4.　　71.35
　　− 67.82

5. 5.2 + 0.74

6. 0.8 + 0.56

Set E, pages 306-308

Find $2.78 mutiplied by 5.

Estimate.
$2.78 rounds to $3.

$5 \times \$3 = \$15$

3 4
2.78
× 　5
$13.90

Multiply the same way as with whole numbers. Count two decimal places in the factors. Place the decimal in the answer.

Remember you can use objects or draw pictures to multiply and divide decimals.

Multiply or divide.

1. $2.37
　× 　3

2. $65.88
　× 　6

3. 4)$5.12

4. 9)$4.68

Set F, pages 310–311

Dan spent $72.82 on 4 items at the store. Two of his items were the same. What did he buy?

Data	Kids Mart	
	Video games	$15.86
	Shoes	$32.96
	Sports hat	$12

Try two video games, one pair of shoes, and one hat.
　$31.72 + $32.96 + $12.00 = $76.68

That's too high but close.

Revise. Try two sports hats.
　$24.00 + $15.86 + $32.96 = $72.82

Dan bought 1 video game, 1 pair of sneakers, and 2 sports hats.

Remember to write the answer in a complete sentence.

Use Try, Check and Revise to solve the problem.

1. Terry, Corey, and Chris together made 20 baskets in a basketball game. Terry made 5 more baskets than Corey. Chris made 3 times more baskets than Corey. How many baskets did they each have?

Solving Equations

1

The United States Congress has 535 members that represent the country. How many members does California have in Congress? You will find out in Lesson 13-2.

2

How much faster than the wind can iceboats go? You will find out in Lesson 13-4.

3

How long does it take the International Space Station to orbit Earth one time? You will find out in Lesson 13-4.

Review What You Know!

Vocabulary

Choose the best term from the box.

- array
- factors
- solution
- equation

1. An arrangement of objects in rows and columns is called a(n) ? .

2. A number sentence that says two expressions are equal is a(n) ?.

3. The value of a variable that makes an equation true is the ? .

Multiplying

Find each product.

4. 83×6 **5.** 71×3 **6.** 49×8

7. 87×7 **8.** 66×9 **9.** 52×4

Number Patterns

Find the missing number in each pattern.

10. 3, 7, 11, 15, ▮

11. 16, 20, ▮, 28

12. 54, ▮, 36, 27

13. 63, 56, 49, ▮

Arrays

14. Write a multiplication fact for the array at the right.

15. Writing to Explain Is an array for 4×3 the same or different from the array shown above? Explain.

Lesson

13-1

AF 2.1 ○━━ Know and understand that equals added to equals are equal.
AF 2.2 ○━━ Know and understand that equals multiplied by equals are equal.
Also **AF 2.0**

Equal or Not Equal

How can you change both sides of an equation so that it stays true?

An equation is a number sentence stating that two expressions are equal.

Decide if these equations are true. Use the balance scale to the right.

Does 5 + 3 − 3 = 8 − 3?

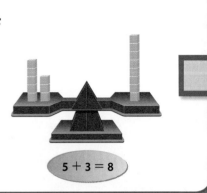

5 + 3 = 8

Guided Practice*

Do you know HOW?

For **1** through **4**, tell if the equation is true or false.

1. 8 + 6 + 2 = 14 + 2

2. 50 ÷ 5 ÷ 2 = 8 ÷ 2

3. 12 × 2 = 24 × 2

4. 15 − 5 = 10 − 5

Do you UNDERSTAND?

5. In the first example above, how can you tell that the equation is true using a pan balance?

6. Writing to Explain If 5 is being subtracted from different numbers on both sides of an equation, is the equation true?

Independent Practice

For **7** through **12**, tell if the equation is true or false.

7. 5 × 3 − 8 = 12 − 8

8. 8 ÷ 2 + 4 = 4 + 4

9. 4 + 7 − 2 = 11 − 9

10. 6 × 3 + 10 = 18 + 10

11. 2 × 3 + 6 = 6 + 6

12. 18 ÷ 3 − 2 = 6 − 2

For **13** through **18**, write the missing number that makes each equation true.

13. 4 × 6 = (2 × 2) × ▢

14. (14 − 2) ÷ 2 = ▢ ÷ 2

15. 6 + ▢ = (3 × 2) + 9

16. (6 + 8) ÷ ▢ = 14 ÷ 2

17. (4 + 5) ÷ 3 = ▢ ÷ 3

18. ▢ + (9 − 5) = 8 + (9 − 5)

DIGITAL · Animated Glossary
www.pearsonsuccessnet.com

For another example, see Set A on page 332.

Is this true?

$5 + 3 - 3 = 8 - 3$

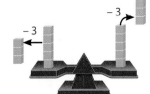

You can add or subtract the same number from both sides of an equation and the sides remain equal.

Check by finding the value of each side.

$5 + 3 - 3 = 8 - 3$
$8 - 3 = 5$
$5 = 5$

The equation is true.

Is this true?

$10 \div 2 = 5 \times 2 \div 5$

You can multiply both sides of an equation by the same number or divide both sides of an equation by the same number except 0 and the sides remain equal.

Check by finding the value of each side.

$10 \div 2 = 5 \times 2 \div 5$
$5 = 10 \div 5$
$5 \neq 2$

The equation is false.

Problem Solving

19. The equation $8 + 4 = 7 + 5$ shows that Hope and Cole have the same number of bookmarks. What equation would show how many bookmarks each has after giving away 3 bookmarks?

20. Rich delivers newspapers in his neighborhood. He started with 27 customers, 9 customers canceled their orders, and then he gained 9 new customers. How many customers does Rich now have?

21. Harry has 8 autographed baseballs. He gave 2 to his sister and half of what he had left to his brother. How many autographed baseballs does he have now?

22. Becky says $16 - 2 \times 7$ is equal to 14×7. Is Becky correct? Why or why not?

For **23** and **24**, use the table at the right.

A class was asked how many siblings each student had. The results are listed in the table.

23. What fraction of the students has more than 1 sibling?

24. What fraction of the class has fewer than 2 siblings?

Students' Siblings	
Number of Siblings	Fraction of Class
Zero	$\frac{2}{3}$
One	$\frac{1}{30}$
Two	$\frac{1}{5}$
Three or more	$\frac{1}{10}$

25. If ★ $+ 25 =$ ▲ $+ 25$ which statement is true?

    A ★ $=$ ▲

    C ★ $>$ ▲

    B ★ $=$ ▲ $- 25$

    D ★ $>$ ▲ $+ 25$

26. Writing to Explain Explain why $4 \times 3 + 6$ has a different value than $4 \times (3 + 6)$.

Lesson
13-2

AF 2.1 ●━━ Know and understand that equals added to equals are equal.
AF 2.0 Know how to manipulate equations.

Solving Addition and Subtraction Equations

How can you use addition and subtraction to solve equations?

Two operations that undo each other are called inverse operations. How many blocks should be removed from each side to get b by itself? Solve for b.

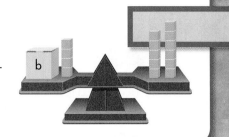

Guided Practice*

Do you know HOW?

1. $r + 3 = 12$

$r + 3 - \boxed{} = 12 - \boxed{}$

$r = \boxed{}$

2. $s - 5 = 9$

$s - 5 + \boxed{} = 9 + \boxed{}$

$s = \boxed{}$

3. $t + 23 = 61$

$t + 23 - \boxed{} = 61 - \boxed{}$

$t = \boxed{}$

Do you UNDERSTAND?

4. In the second example above, why do you add 10 to both sides?

5. Henry balanced box n and 12 blocks on one side of a pan balance and 16 blocks on the other side. How many blocks should he remove from both sides to find the weight of n?

Independent Practice

Leveled Practice   For **6** through **11**, solve for each $\boxed{}$.

6. $c - 4 = 16$

$c - 4 + \boxed{} = 16 + \boxed{}$

$c = \boxed{}$

7. $e + 7 = 19$

$e + 7 - \boxed{} = 19 - \boxed{}$

$e = \boxed{}$

8. $z - 6 = 21$

$z - 6 + \boxed{} = 21 + \boxed{}$

$z = \boxed{}$

9. $p + 8 = 18$

$p + 8 - \boxed{} = 18 - \boxed{}$

$p = \boxed{}$

10. $q - 5 = 17$

$q - 5 + \boxed{} = 17 + \boxed{}$

$q = \boxed{}$

11. $m + 1 = 8$

$m + 1 - \boxed{} = 8 - \boxed{}$

$m = \boxed{}$

DIGITAL   Animated Glossary
www.pearsonsuccessnet.com

Solve $b + 4 = 11$.

Undo adding 4 by subtracting 4 from each side.

$b + 4 - 4 = 11 - 4$

Simplify each side.

$b = 7$

The solution to $b + 4 = 11$ is 7.

Solve $n - 10 = 30$.

Undo subtracting 10 by adding 10 to each side.

$n - 10 + 10 = 30 + 10$

Simplify each side.

$n = 40$

The solution to $n - 10 = 30$ is 40.

For **12** through **19**, solve each equation.

12. $c - 4 = 23$ **13.** $e + 7 = 53$ **14.** $d - 6 = 3$ **15.** $4 + s = 17$

16. $x + 200 = 400$ **17.** $z - 8 = 3$ **18.** $y + 37 = 42$ **19.** $m - 51 = 29$

Problem Solving

20. The United States Congress includes 2 senators from each state plus the House of Representatives. The number of representatives, r, is based on a state's population. Write a rule for the total number of members each state has in Congress.

Number of Members of the United States Congress		
State	**House**	**Senate**
California	53	2
Missouri	9	2
New York	29	2

21. There are 3 bones in each finger and 2 bones in each thumb. How many bones are in two hands?

22. Reasonableness Debra solved the equation $f - 17 = 40$ and got 50. Is this solution reasonable? Explain.

23. **Think About the Process** A school is selling magazine subscriptions to raise money. The first week they sold 435 subscriptions. If their goal is to sell 640 subscriptions in two weeks, which equation would you use to find how many subscriptions need to be sold in the second week?

   A $s - 435 = 640$ **C** $s + 435 = 640$

   B $s - 640 = 435$ **D** $640 + 435 = s$

24. A factory can produce 30,000 pairs of sneakers each day. About how many days will it take to produce 600,000 pairs?

Solving Multiplication and Division Equations

n books in 7 groups

AF 2.2 ○━━ Know and understand that equals multiplied by equals are equal.
AF 2.0 Know how to manipulate equations.

How can you use multiplication and division to solve equations?

Jolene organized *n* books into 7 groups. Each group had 6 books. How many books did Jolene have? She wrote the equation $n \div 7 = 6$ to show the result. What is the value of *n*?

Guided Practice*

Do you know HOW?

1. $m \div 6 = 6$
$m \div 6 \times \boxed{} = 6 \times \boxed{}$
$m = \boxed{}$

2. $t \times 9 = 63$
$t \times 9 \div \boxed{} = 63 \div \boxed{}$
$t = \boxed{}$

3. $n \div 7 = 4$
$n \div 7 \times \boxed{} = 4 \times \boxed{}$
$n = \boxed{}$

Do you UNDERSTAND?

4. In the first example above, what is another way to describe the problem?

5. In the second example above, why must the solution to $w \times 4 = 32$ be less than 32?

6. Write an equation to show the following: Jolene had *g* groups of 16 books. Each group had 4 books. Find the value of *g*.

Independent Practice

Leveled Practice For **7** through **12**, solve for each $\boxed{}$.

7. $p \div 3 = 6$
$p \div 3 \times \boxed{} = 6 \times \boxed{}$
$p = \boxed{}$

8. $r \times 7 = 49$
$r \times 7 \div \boxed{} = 49 \div \boxed{}$
$r = \boxed{}$

9. $t \div 6 = 1$
$t \div 6 \times \boxed{} = 1 \times \boxed{}$
$t = \boxed{}$

10. $n \times 9 = 45$
$n \times 9 \div \boxed{} = 45 \div \boxed{}$
$n = \boxed{}$

11. $q \div 5 = 4$
$q \div 5 \times \boxed{} = 4 \times \boxed{}$
$q = \boxed{}$

12. $s \times 3 = 15$
$s \times 3 \div \boxed{} = 15 \div \boxed{}$
$s = \boxed{}$

For another example, see Set C on page 333.

Solve $n \div 7 = 6$ to find the number of books, n.

$n \div 7 = 6$

The inverse of dividing by 7 is multiplying by 7.

$n \div 7 \times 7 = 6 \times 7$

Simplify each side.

$n = 42$

The solution to $n \div 7 = 6$ is 42.

Jolene has 42 books.

Solve $w \times 4 = 32$.

The inverse of multiplying by 4 is dividing by 4.

$w \times 4 \div 4 = 32 \div 4$

Simplify each side.

$w = 8$

The solution to $w \times 4 = 32$ is 8.

For **13** through **24**, solve each equation.

13. $t \div 5 = 7$ **14.** $3 \times e = 18$ **15.** $j \div 4 = 8$ **16.** $d \div 3 = 3$ **17.** $c \div 5 = 4$

18. $2 \times r = 32$ **19.** $s \div 7 = 3$ **20.** $m \times 7 = 63$ **21.** $p \div 3 = 2$ **22.** $7 \times a = 49$

Problem Solving

23. Howard did homework from 5:05 P.M. until 6:23 P.M. Half of that time was spent studying for a science exam. How long did Howard study for the science exam?

24. Thomas spent 140 minutes every week practicing guitar. Write and solve an equation using multiplication to find out how many minutes Thomas practiced every day.

25. Algebra If the pattern below continues, what will the next three numbers be?

22, 23, 25, 28, 32, ☐ **,** ☐ **,** ☐

26. Writing to Explain Why must the solution to $6 \times k = 12$ be less than 12?

27. Geometry Which is the best name for this type of triangle?

A Equilateral   C Isosceles

B Scalene   D Right

28. A little league team is selling T-shirts. If their goal is to sell 90 T-shirts total and they average 15 T-shirts a week, which equation would you **NOT** use to find out how many weeks they will be selling T-shirts?

A $15 \times w = 90$ C $90 \div w = 15$

B $w \times 15 = 90$ D $w \div 90 = 15$

Translating Words to Equations

How can you write equations for situations?

Mandy is an adult golden retriever. If she weighs 65 pounds, write an equation that can be used to find the weight of Mandy's puppy, Tilly.

Combined weight: 73 pounds

AF 1.1 Use letters, boxes, or other symbols to stand for any number in simple expressions or equations (e.g., demonstrate an understanding and the use of the concept of a variable).
Also AF 1.0.

Another Example **How can you write equations for multiplication situations?**

In Lesson 5-1, you worked with expressions, such as $x + 3$. In this lesson, you will earn how to write equations.

Luis bought 4 bags of gourmet biscuits for his new puppy. There were 8 biscuits in each bag. Which equation can be used to find how many biscuits there were in all?

A $8 \div 4 = b$

B $b \div 4 = 8$

C $4 \times 8 = b$

D $b \times 4 = 8$

? Biscuits in all (*b*)

| 8 | 8 | 8 | 8 |

Biscuits in each bag

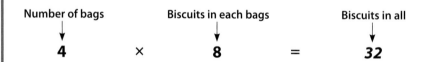

Number of bags → **4**   ×   Biscuits in each bags → **8**   =   Biscuits in all → **32**

The correct answer is **C**.

Explain It

1. In the example above, explain how you can tell that answer choices A and B are wrong.

2. Sam reads 80 pages every week during a summer reading program. Would you use multiplication or division to find how many pages he read over four weeks? Explain.

Let t = Tilly's weight.

Mandy's weight plus Tilly's weight is equal to 73 pounds.

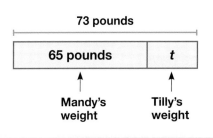

73 pounds

| 65 pounds | t |

↑ Mandy's weight ↑ Tilly's weight

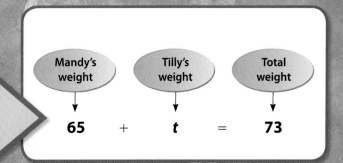

Mandy's weight		Tilly's weight		Total weight
65	+	t	=	73

Other Examples

Writing subtraction equations

A salad is weighed on plates weighing 3 ounces. The total weight of the salad and plate is 5 ounces. What is the weight of the salad?

$$5 - 3 = s$$

Writing division equations

One yard is 3 feet. A tree is 15 feet tall. How many yards tall is the tree?

$$15 \div 3 = y$$

Guided Practice*

Do you know HOW?

For **1** and **2**, write the expression for each word phrase.

1. the product of b and 5

2. the weight of an apple plus 4

For **3** and **4**, write the expression.

3. There are 9 T-shirts. How many T-shirts go in b boxes?

4. A decade is 10 years. How many years are in d decades?

Do you UNDERSTAND?

5. In the example above, why is the equation $65 + t = 73$ and not $65 \times t = 73$?

6. Write an equation using the diagram below.

s

| 20 | 20 | 20 | 20 |

7. The perimeter of a garden is g feet. Write an equation that can be used to find the perimeter of the garden in inches.

---

*For another example, see Set D on page 333.

For **8** through **11**, choose the equation that matches the situations.

8. Doug handed out 3 straws to each of 4 people. How many straws did Doug hand out altogether?

$4 \times 3 = s$ $\qquad$ $12 \div s = 4$

9. Andrea had 8 tickets and bought 12 more. How many tickets did Andrea have?

$8 \times t = 12$ $\qquad$ $8 + 12 = t$

10. There are 15 chairs in 1 row. How many chairs are there in 12 rows?

$15 \times 12 = c$ $\qquad$ $15 \div c = 12$

11. On a path, 12 joggers separated into 2 equal groups. How many joggers were in each group?

$12 \times 6 = h$ $\qquad$ $12 \div 2 = h$

Problem Solving

12. The unofficial speed record for iceboats is 143 miles per hour. At low wind speeds, ice boats can go 6 times faster than the wind speed. Write an expression for how fast an iceboat goes when the wind is blowing at w miles per hour.

13. Algebra Thomas saved $256. He used the money to buy 4 trains for his model railroad. Each train cost the same amount. Write a multiplication equation to find the cost of each train.

14. A theater has 358 seats on the main level and 122 seats in the balcony. If there are 6 shows a day, how many people can see the show in one day?

15. Number Sense How would you know that 3,200,910 is a composite number without having to divide?

16. The International Space Station takes 644 minutes to orbit Earth seven times. Which equation below would you use to find out how long one orbit takes?

A $s \div 7 = 644$ $\qquad$ **C** $s + 7 = 644$

B $s \times 7 = 644$ $\qquad$ **D** $s - 7 = 644$

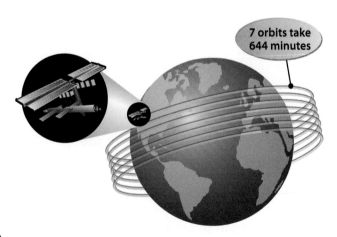

7 orbits take 644 minutes

17. **Think About the Process** If Francis is 6 years older than his sister, which expression can you use to find how old Francis will be when his sister, s, is 13?

A $s \times 6$ $\qquad$ **B** $s + 6$ $\qquad$ **C** $s \times 13$ $\qquad$ **D** $s + 13$

Stop and Practice

Solve each equation for z.

1. $z + 22 = 24$ **2.** $z - 19 = 24$ **3.** $z \times 4 = 32$

4. $z \div 9 = 4$ **5.** $15 + z = 24$ **6.** $z - 22 = 22$

7. $6 \times z = 6$ **8.** $z \div 5 = 1$ **9.** $3 \times z = 18$

Find the quotient. Estimate to check
if the answer is reasonable.

10. $\$9.64 \div 4$ **11.** $4\overline{)\$8.32}$ **12.** $3\overline{)\$8.85}$ **13.** $6\overline{)\$9.66}$ **14.** $\$7.04 \div 2$

Find the sum. Estimate to check
if the answer is reasonable.

15. $9 + 3{,}529 + 27 + 621$ **16.** $17{,}868 + 913 + 2{,}781$

17. $475 + 25 + 5{,}350 + 25{,}275$ **18.** $2 + 129 + 56 + 374$

Error Search Find each value of w that is not correct.
Write it correctly and explain the error.

19. $20 + w = 68$ **20.** $w - 12 = 50$ **21.** $w \div 2 = 9$ **22.** $w \times 6 = 42$
      $w = 88$ $w = 62$ $w = 11$ $w = 8$

Number Sense

Estimating and Reasoning Write whether each
statement is true or false. Explain your answer.

23. The expression $6 + 32 \div (2 \times 4)$ equals 76.

24. The product of 4 and $6.82 is closer to $24 than $28.

25. The sum of 25.11 and 17.32 is less than 42.

26. The quotient of 0 divided by 1 is 1.

27. The product of 5 and 45 is 25 more than 200.

28. The difference of 844 and 172 is greater than 600.

MR 1.1 Analyze problems by identifying relationships, distinguishing relevant from irrelevant information, sequencing and prioritizing information, and observing patterns. Also **NS 3.0** ⚷➤, **MR 3.2.**

Problem Solving

Work Backward

We can use operation trains to build numbers.
Here is one example:

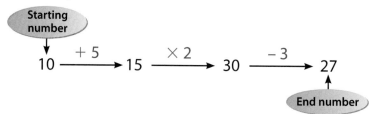

Starting number

$$10 \xrightarrow{\ +\,5\ } 15 \xrightarrow{\ \times\,2\ } 30 \xrightarrow{\ -\,3\ } 27$$

End number

Guided Practice*

Do you know HOW?

Solve by working backward. Use an operation train to find your answer.

1. Charlie picked some peppers from his garden. He gave 14 to his brother and 7 to his neighbor. He has 24 left. How many peppers did he pick from his garden?

Do you UNDERSTAND?

2. In the example above, how can you check the answer?

3. **Write a Problem** Write a problem that uses an operation train. Then work backward to answer your question.

Independent Practice

Work backward to solve each problem.
Write the answer in a complete sentence.

4. It took Wanda 25 minutes to walk from the shopping mall to the railroad station. She waited at the railroad station for 20 minutes. She boarded a train to Johnson City at 10:20 A.M. When did she leave the shopping mall?

5. Drew drove to Karen's house. He drove 2 miles west, then 4 miles south, and 1 mile east. How can Drew drive home from Karen's house using the same path?

Stuck? Try this....

- What do I know?
- What diagram can I use to help understand the problem?
- Can I use addition, subtraction, multiplication, or division?
- Is all of my work correct?
- Did I answer the right question?
- Is my answer reasonable?

Use the operation train below. Find the starting number, *x*.

If you know the end number and how the number was built, you can work backward to find the beginning number.

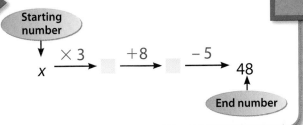

Do the inverse of the given operations and work backward.

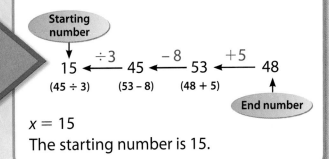

x = 15
The starting number is 15.

6. Nina walked 1 mile on Monday. She walked twice as far on Tuesday. On Wednesday, she walked three more miles than what she had walked on Monday. On Thursday, she walked one mile less than what she had walked on Wednesday. How many miles did Nina walk on Thursday?

7. Georgette bought some craft items at the store. The silk flowers cost three times as much as the ribbon. The ribbon cost double what the foam cost. The vase cost $12, which was three times as much as the foam. How much did the silk flowers cost?

8. Tara is 6 years older than Karen. Karen is 5 years younger than Dave. Dave is 3 years older than Luz. If Luz is 10 years old, how old is Tara?

9. Jason is thinking of a number. He adds 8, multiplies by 2, subtracts 4, and then divides by 2. The result is 24. What number is Jason thinking of?

10. Leslie has 3 boxes of tea. Each box contains 11 tea bags. Each tea bag uses 3 cups of hot water to make a mug of hot tea. How many cups of water will Leslie use if she makes all the tea?

11 tea bags in each box

11. The Declaration of Independence was signed in 1776. Three years earlier, the Boston Tea Party took place. Boston was settled 143 years before the Boston Tea Party. What year was Boston settled?

1776

3	143	?

12. Sylvia had $43 dollars left over after she went shopping. She spent $9 on pet food, $6 on salad items, $12 on soup, and $24 on vegetables. How much money did Sylvia have to start with?

? money Sylvia started with

$6	$9	$12	$24	$43

Lesson 13-5 **329**

1. Which equation is true? (13-1)

 A $36 \div 6 + 8 = 23 - 9 + 8$

 B $17 - 8 + 9 = 2 \times 5 + 9$

 C $20 \div 4 - 2 = 40 \div 5 - 2$

 D $11 + 3 - 5 = 2 \times 7 - 5$

2. How many counters equal the weight of box s? (13-2)

 A 3

 B 6

 C 9

 D 12

3. Mrs. Iverson bought 8 identical packages of pencils. She bought a total of 48 pencils. How many pencils did each package have? Let p equal the number of pencils in each package. Use the equation $8 \times p = 48$ to solve the problem. (13-3)

 A 384 pencils

 B 40 pencils

 C 6 pencils

 D 4 pencils

4. What value makes the equation true? (13-2)

 $w - 28 = 59$

 A 89

 B 87

 C 32

 D 31

5. Which number makes the equation true? (13-1)

 $12 \div \boxed{} = 6 + 6 \div 2$

 A 2

 B 3

 C 4

 D 6

6. Which equation is true? (13-1)

 A $45 \div 9 \times 9 = 5 + 9$

 B $45 \div 9 - 9 = 5 + 9$

 C $45 \div 9 + 9 = 5 + 9$

 D $45 \div 9 \div 5 = 5 \div 5$

7. Which equation would be used to solve the problem below?

 There are 32 fourth graders in art club. Mr. Willsborough put an equal number of students at 4 tables. How many tables did Mr. Willsborough use? (13-4)

 A $32 \times 4 = t$

 B $4 \div 32 = t$

 C $t \div 4 = 32$

 D $32 \div 4 = t$

8. Gentry has won a number of trophies. He put the trophies on 4 different shelves. Each shelf had 5 trophies. Gentry used the equation $t \div 4 = 5$ to find the number of trophies he had. What should Gentry do to find the value of t? (13-3)

A Divide each side by 4.

B Divide each side by 5.

C Multiply each side by 4.

D Multiply each side by 5.

9. The equation below shows that Joseph and Dillon both had some money, spent some of the money, and then earned more money.

┌─ Joseph ─┐   ┌─ Dillon ─┐
17 − 8 + 5 = 12 − ▢ **+ 12**

How much money did Dillon spend? (13-1)

A 14

B 13

C 12

D 10

10. If $n = 23$, then what is the value of m? (13-2)

$$n - 15 = m$$

A 38

B 37

C 8

D 7

11. Veronica bought a bouquet of 14 flowers for her mother. The bouquet had 8 daisies and some roses. Which equation would Veronica use to find how many roses, r, were in the bouquet? (13-4)

A $8 + r = 14$

B $8 \times r = 14$

C $r - 8 = 14$

D $8 + 14 = r$

12. If $a + 30 = b + 30$, which statement is true? (13-2)

A $a > b$

B $a = b$

C $a = b + 30$

D $b = a + 30$

13. What is the value of x in the diagram below? (13-5)

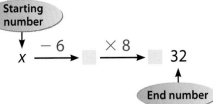

A 4

B 6

C 8

D 10

Set A, pages 318–319

Is this equation true?

$6 + 4 - 4 = 10 - 4$

When you perform the same operation on both sides of an equation, the equation is true.

$6 + 4 = 10$ Start with a true equation.

$6 + 4 - 4 = 10 - 4$ Subtract 4 from both sides.

The equation is true.

Is this equation true?

$12 \div 2 = 6 \times 2 \div 4$

The equation is false because both sides were not divided by the same number.

Remember that both sides of an equation must have the same value for the equation to be true.

Tell whether each equation is true or false.

1. $7 + 7 - 4 = 14 - 4$

2. $3 + 5 \times 8 = 8 \times 4$

3. $3 + 9 - 2 = 12 - 2$

4. $6 \times 8 + 12 = 48 + 12$

Write the number that makes each equation true.

5. $11 + 4 = 5 + \boxed{} + 4$

6. $18 - 9 - 2 = 3 \times 3 - \boxed{}$

7. $2 \times 2 \times 2 = \boxed{} \times 2$

Set B, pages 320–321

Solve $x + 7 = 41$.

Use subtraction to undo addition.

$x + 7 - 7 = 41 - 7$ Subtract 7 from each side.

$x = 34$ Simplify each side.

The solution to $7 + x = 41$ is 34.

Solve $y - 14 = 50$.

Use addition to undo subtraction.

$y - 14 + 14 = 50 + 14$ Add 14 to each side.

$y = 64$ Simplify each side.

The solution to $y - 14 = 50$ is 64.

Remember to add or subtract the same amount from both sides of the equation.

Solve each equation.

1. $y + 20 = 31$ **2.** $n - 10 = 36$

3. $r + 16 = 40$ **4.** $v - 25 = 25$

5. $l + 5 = 20$ **6.** $n - 8 = 17$

7. $x + 32 = 42$ **8.** $y - 18 = 13$

9. $p + 15 = 30$ **10.** $q - 11 = 19$

11. $s + 16 = 95$ **12.** $m - 15 = 0$

Set C, pages 322–323

Solve $n \div 6 = 5$.

Use multiplication to undo division.

$$n \div 6 \times 6 = 5 \times 6 \qquad \text{Multiply each side by 6.}$$

$$n = 30 \qquad \text{Simplify each side.}$$

The solution to $n \div 6 = 5$ is 30.

Remember to use division to undo multiplication.

1. $n \times 2 = 18$ 2. $y \div 10 = 36$

3. $m \times 12 = 36$ 4. $y \div 6 = 5$

5. $z \times 5 = 125$ 6. $t \div 7 = 4$

Set D , pages 324–326

Write an equation that matches the situation. There are 48 juice boxes in 4 cases. How many juice boxes are in each case?

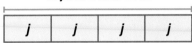

48 juice boxes in all

j	j	j	j

The equation $4 \times j = 48$ can be used to find how many juice boxes are in each case.

Remember there is more than one way to describe the same equation.

Write an equation.

1. Chan's soccer team has 8 girls. If there are 17 players in all, how many boys, b, are there?

2. Jane has 56 marbles. She puts an equal number of marbles in each of 7 bags. How many marbles, m, are in each bag.

Set E, pages 328–329

What is the value of x?

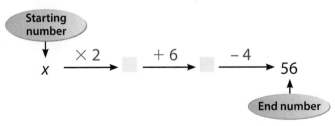

Start with the end number. Use inverse operations to work backward to find x.

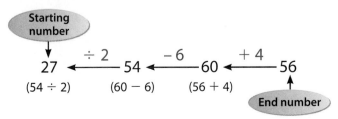

The value of x is 27.

Remember to identify all the steps in the process before working backward.

Work backward to solve.

1. For a school play, Juan sold 18 tickets, Teri sold 14 tickets, and Al sold 22 tickets. If they ended up with 45 unsold tickets, how many tickets did they start?

Integers

1 How deep can a person dive under water? You will find out in Lesson 14-2.

2 How hot does it get in Death Valley? You will find out in Lesson 14-3.

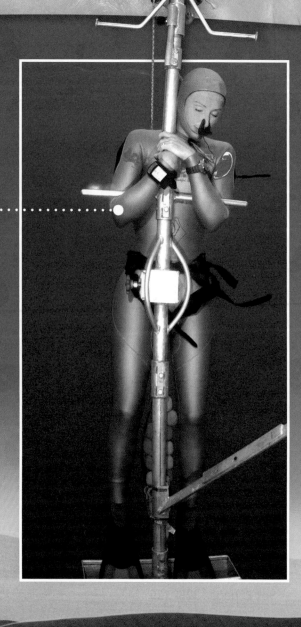

3

The Baltimore Light stands on an iron foundation in Baltimore's harbor. How deep is the foundation? You will find out in Lesson 14-3.

Review What You Know!

Vocabulary

Choose the best term from the box.

- array
- rounding
- factor
- product

1. In the number sentence $4 \times 7 = 28$, 4 is a ? and 28 is a ?.

2. An arrangement of objects in rows and columns is called a(n) ?.

3. When you estimate, you may use ?.

Multiplication Facts

Find each product.

4. 8×6 **5.** 7×5 **6.** 9×8

7. 8×8 **8.** 6×9 **9.** 5×8

10. 4×6 **11.** 6×5 **12.** 8×7

Adding Fractions

13. $\frac{1}{4} + \frac{1}{3}$ **14.** $\frac{6}{8} + \frac{1}{4}$ **15.** $\frac{1}{9} + \frac{3}{9}$

16 $\frac{1}{12} + \frac{2}{6}$ **17.** $\frac{2}{3} + \frac{1}{5}$ **18.** $\frac{5}{12} + \frac{1}{3}$

Arrays

19. Can you write a multiplication number sentence for the array below? Explain.

★ ★ ★ ★ ★ ★
★ ★ ★ ★ ★ ★

20. **Writing to Explain** Is an array for 7×4 the same or different than an array for 4×7? Explain.

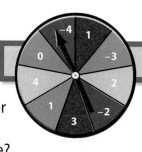
NS 1.8
Use concepts of
negative numbers
(e.g., on a number
line, in counting,
in temperature,
in "owing") . Also
NS 1.5, Grade 5

Understanding Integers

What are integers?

Integers <u>consist of whole numbers and
their opposites.</u>

Jill and Paul play a game using a spinner. They
begin with zero points. Jill gained 4 points with her
first spin. Paul lost 3 points with his first spin. How
are integers used to represent Jill's and Paul's score?

Other Examples

Positive Integers	
Word Description	Integer
22 feet above sea level	$^+22$
A deposit of $35	$^+35$
A temperature of 112°F	$^+112$
8 steps forward	$^+8$

Negative Integers	
Word Description	Integer
5 feet below sea level	$^-5$
$17 owed	$^-17$
65 degrees below 0	$^-65$
12 steps backwards	$^-12$

Guided Practice*

Do you know HOW?

For **1** through **4**, write an integer for
each word description.

1. 29 degrees below zero

2. 12 feet above sea level

3. 5 degrees Celsius

4. $18 owed

Do you UNDERSTAND?

5. On the number line in the example
above, what number is the opposite
of 4?

6. **Writing to Explain** On a number
line, how many units from 0 would
the points 8 and -8 be located?

DIGITAL

Animated Glossary
www.pearsonsuccessnet.com

For another example, see Set A on page 346.

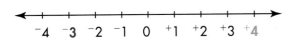

Negative integers are less than 0.
Negative 3 is written as −**3**. Paul
lost 3 points so his score was −3.

Positive integers are greater than 0.
Positive 4 is written as ⁺**4** or 4. Jill
gained 4 points, so her score was ⁺4.

Opposites are the same distance
from zero on a number line.

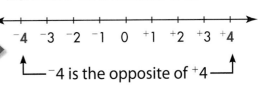

⁻4 is the opposite of ⁺4

Independent Practice

For **7** through **9**, write an integer for each word description.

7. 9 degrees below zero

8. A withdrawal of $45

9. 33 feet above sea level

For **10** through **14**, use the number line below.
Write the integer for each point.

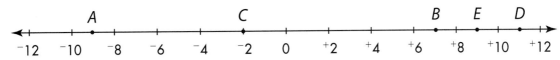

10. A   **11.** B   **12.** C   **13.** D   **14.** E

Problem Solving

15. Vostok, Antarctica, holds the world's record for the coldest temperature at about one hundred twenty-nine degrees below zero (°F). Express this temperature as an integer.

16. The numbers in the pattern increase the same amount each time. What are the next three numbers in this pattern?

⁻**9**, ⁻**6**, ⁻**3**, **0**, **3** ▢ , ▢ , ▢

17. In Newfoundland, Canada, when the wind is twenty knots or faster, it is called a stun breeze. Write an integer that could be the speed of a stun breeze.

18. Which integers come between ⁻7 and 3 on a number line?

A ⁻1, 4, ⁻7   **C** 5, ⁻8, 1

B 4, 5, 6   **D** ⁻3, ⁻5, 2

19. Reasonableness Does 0 have an opposite? Why or why not?

Lesson

14-2

NS 1.8 ⊶ Use
concepts of negative
numbers (e.g., on a
number line, in counting,
in temperature, in
"owing"). Also
NS 1.5 Grade 5 ⊶

Comparing Integers

How can you compare integers?

Each day, Amy records how
much money she has. She wrote
a negative number on Wednesday
and Thursday because she owed
money to her friends.

Which is greater, ⁺3 or ⁻4?

Day	Amount ($)
Monday	⁺3
Tuesday	0
Wednesday	⁻4
Thursday	⁻5

Guided Practice*

Do you know HOW?

For **1** through **8**, compare. Use >, <,
or = for ◯.

1. ⁺8 ◯ ⁻4   **2.** ⁻7 ◯ ⁺2

3. ⁻4 ◯ ⁻7   **4.** ⁺6 ◯ ⁺3

5. ⁻2 ◯ ⁺1   **6.** ⁻5 ◯ ⁻4

7. ⁻7 ◯ ⁺7   **8.** ⁺8 ◯ ⁺9

Do you UNDERSTAND?

9. Writing to Explain Use the
number line in the example above
to explain why ⁻5 is less than the
number ⁻3 even though 5 > 3?

10. If integer A is to the left of integer
B on a number line, is integer A
greater than or less than integer B?

Independent Practice

For **11** through **26**, write >, <, or = for ◯. Use a number line to help.

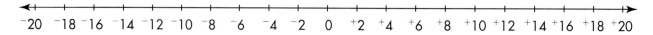

⁻20 ⁻18 ⁻16 ⁻14 ⁻12 ⁻10 ⁻8 ⁻6 ⁻4 ⁻2 0 ⁺2 ⁺4 ⁺6 ⁺8 ⁺10 ⁺12 ⁺14 ⁺16 ⁺18 ⁺20

11. ⁺4 ◯ ⁻6   **12.** ⁻15 ◯ ⁻8   **13.** ⁻12 ◯ ⁺5   **14.** ⁻17 ◯ ⁻12

15. ⁺7 ◯ ⁻18   **16.** ⁻2 ◯ ⁺6   **17.** ⁺10 ◯ ⁺12   **18.** ⁻14 ◯ ⁺14

19. ⁻2 ◯ ⁺8   **20.** ⁻13 ◯ ⁻4   **21.** ⁺7 ◯ ⁻9   **22.** ⁺18 ◯ ⁻14

23. ⁺12 ◯ ⁻19   **24.** ⁻13 ◯ ⁻10   **25.** ⁺19 ◯ ⁺12   **26.** ⁻11 ◯ ⁻20

Compare $^+3$ and $^-4$.

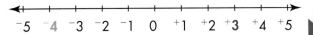

On a number line, values increase from left to right.

$^+3$ is to the right of $^-4$ on the number line.

So, $^+3 > {}^-4$.

On Thursday, Amy had $^-5$ dollars. Compare $^-5$ and $^-4$.

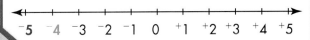

On a number line, values decrease from right to left.

$^-5$ is to the left of $^-4$ on the number line.

So, $^-5 < {}^-4$.

Problem Solving

27. Pedro mixed $\frac{1}{3}$ gallon of pineapple juice with $\frac{2}{3}$ gallon fruit juice to make punch. How much punch does he now have?

28. While at the beach, Lexi collected 23 clamshells, 12 scallop shells, and 4 periwinkle shells. What is the mean number of shells that were collected?

29. Writing to Explain If you used a number line to move 12 spaces to the left from zero, and then moved 5 spaces to the right, on what number would you land?

30. Last month, Sarah's cell phone bill was $80. This month, her bill is $100. Did Sarah owe more money to the phone company this month or last month? Explain.

31. One world record holder for free diving had made a 400-foot dive and a 525-foot dive, each with a single breath. Which dive was deeper? Explain.

32. At 8:00 A.M., the temperature was 14° C. At noon, the temperature had risen 6° C. At 5 P.M., the temperature had dropped 7° C. By 8 P.M., the temperature had dropped another 3° C. What was the temperature at 8 P.M.?

33. Reasoning A number c is 6 units to the right of $^-3$ on a number line. What number is c and is it greater than or less than $^-3$?

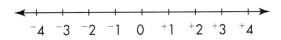

34. Nina deposited $40.00 into her account. Which shows this integer?

A $^-60$ **B** $^-40$ **C** $^+40$ **D** $^+60$

Ordering Integers

How can you write integers in order?

The high temperatures for four cities in Alaska in one day in November are shown at the right.

Write the cities and their temperatures in order from least to greatest.

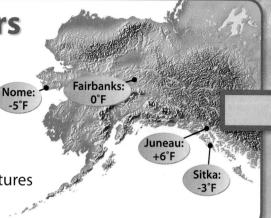

Nome: -5°F

Fairbanks: 0°F

Juneau: +6°F

Sitka: -3°F

NS 1.8 ⚷ Use concepts of negative numbers (e.g., on a number line, in counting, in temperature, in "owing"). Also NS 1.5 Grade 5 ⚷

Guided Practice*

Do you know HOW?

For **1** through **8**, write the integers in order from least to greatest.

1. $^+6, 0, ^-3$

2. $^-9, ^+2, ^-2$

3. $^-5, ^+10, ^-8$

4. $^+4, ^-1, ^+3$

5. $^-13, ^-17, ^+1$

6. $^-19, 0, ^-4$

7. $^-4, ^+16, ^-7$

8. $^+12, ^+18, ^-9$

Do you UNDERSTAND?

9. In the example above, what city had a temperature above 0°F?

10. On the same day, Anchorage had a temperature of $^-1$°F. On the number line above, would it be placed to the right or to the left of Fairbanks?

11. The temperatures throughout the day in a certain city were $^+5$°F, $^-7$°F, $^-3$°F, and $^+10$°F. List the temperatures in order from least to greatest.

Independent Practice

For **12** through **27**, write the numbers in order from least to greatest. You may use a number line to help.

12. $^+2, 0, ^-4$

13. $^-30, ^+12, ^-5$

14. $^-23, ^-25, ^+3$

15. $^-20, ^+6, ^-12$

16. $^+11, ^+18, ^-18$

17. $^-36, ^-9, ^-20$

18. $^+7, ^+2, ^-9$

19. $^-43, ^+21, ^-4$

20. $^-33, ^-78, ^+25$

21. $^-18, ^+13, ^-8$

22. $^+23, ^+45, ^-1$

23. $^-67, ^-87, ^-98$

24. $^+3, ^+4, ^-6$

25. $^-42, ^+10, ^-9$

26. $^-11, ^-44, ^+7$

27. $^+8, ^-8, ^-88$

For another example, see Set C on page 347.

Locate each integer on the number line.

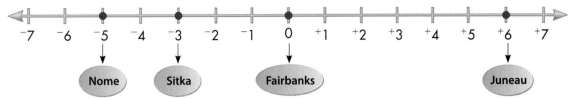

Write the integers from left to right as they appear on the number line.

⁻5, ⁻3, 0, ⁺6

The cities and their temperatures in order from least to greatest are:
Nome (⁻5), Sitka (⁻3), Fairbanks (0), and Juneau (⁺6).

Problem Solving

28. Some of the most extreme temperatures ever recorded on Earth were ⁺136°F in Libya, ⁺134°F in Death Valley, ⁻129°F in Antarctica, and ⁻90°F in Russia. Order these temperatures from least to greatest.

29. Kyle had $14. He gave $5 to a friend and spent $2 on a snack. He then found a $5 bill. Order the numbers ⁺14, ⁻5, ⁻2, and ⁺5 from greatest to least.

30. There are 48 boxes in a warehouse. If there are 22 packages of paper in each box, how many packages of paper are there in the warehouse?

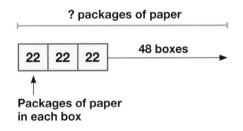

? packages of paper

| 22 | 22 | 22 | 48 boxes |

Packages of paper in each box

31. Edgar plays a game on his computer 6 times. His scores are ⁺4, 0, ⁻2, ⁺8, ⁻9, ⁺6? What are his scores from least to greatest?

A 0, ⁻2, ⁺4, ⁺6, ⁺8, ⁻9

B ⁻2, ⁻9, 0, ⁺4, ⁺6, ⁺8

C ⁺8, ⁺6, ⁺4, 0, ⁻2, ⁻9

D ⁻9, ⁻2, 0, ⁺4, ⁺6, ⁺8

For **32**, use the diagram on the right.

32. The Baltimore Light was built on a foundation that is 82 feet deep. The iron foundation was sunk through a 55-foot layer of mud. Order the heights shown on the diagram from least to greatest.

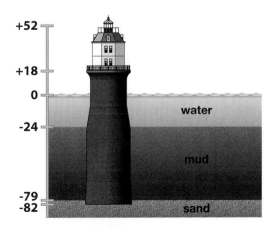

+52
+18
0
water
-24
mud
-79
-82
sand

Lesson

14-4

MR 2.3: Use a variety of
methods, such as words,
numbers, symbols, charts,
graphs, tables, diagrams,
and models, to explain
mathematical reasoning.
Also NS 3.1 ,
MR 2.0, MR 3.2.

Problem Solving

Draw a Picture

Mount Whitney is about 14,491 feet above sea level ($^+$14,491). The Monterey Bay underwater canyon reaches a depth of about 11,800 feet below sea level ($^-$11,800). What is the total distance from the top of Mount Whitney to the bottom of Monterey Bay? Draw a picture to decide.

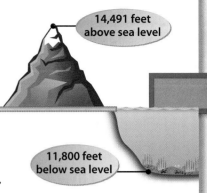

14,491 feet
above sea level

11,800 feet
below sea level

Guided Practice*

Do you know HOW?

Solve the problem.

1. Clarissa had $50 in her checking account. By mistake, she wrote a check for $80. What is the balance in Clarissa's checking account now? Draw a picture to decide.

Do you UNDERSTAND?

2. Why is the distance between the height of Mount Whitney and the depth of Monterey Bay canyon greater than the height of Mount Whitney?

3. Write a Problem Write a problem in which you draw a picture to solve the problem. Then answer your question.

Independent Practice

Solve each problem. Write the answer in a complete sentence.

4. A relay race team has 6 members. Each member runs the same part of a three-mile race. How far does each member run?

5. Thelma, Kay, and Lorraine want to share a foot-long sandwich equally. How much should each of the three friends get?

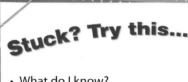

Stuck? Try this....

- What do I know?
- What diagram can I use to help understand the problem?
- Can I use addition, subtraction, multiplication, or division?
- Is all of my work correct?
- Did I answer the right question?
- Is my answer reasonable?

For another example, see Set D on page 347.

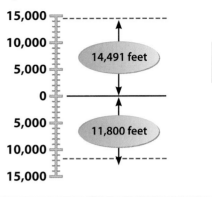

I can draw a picture to solve this problem.

To get the whole distance, I can add the two parts.

14,491 + 11,800 = 26,291

The total distance is 26,291 feet.

For **6** and **7**, use the graph at the right.

6. A school bus picks up 61 students each day. The distance each student lives from school is shown in the graph to the right. How many students live 8 or more miles from school?

7. How many miles from school do most of the students live?

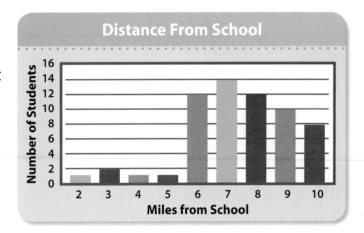

8. The low temperature for one day in May was 64°F. The high temperature for that day was 18°F higher. What was the high temperature?

9. Matea wants to plant flowers along her six foot sidewalk. She will plant one flower at each end and a flower every foot in between. How many flowers will she plant?

Use the drawings at the right for **10** and **11**.

10. Alexis and Shawn each needed to design a banner for field day. They each want their banner to be 5 feet long. Alexis marked 24 inches on her banner. Draw a picture to show how she can use this distance to find 5 feet.

11. Shawn marked 1 yard on his banner. Draw a picture to show how Shawn can use this distance to find 5 feet.

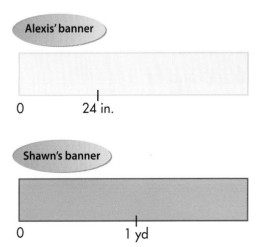

1. Which point on the number line best represents +5? (14-1)

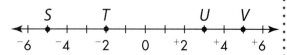

A Point *S*

B Point *T*

C Point *U*

D Point *V*

2. Which statement is true? (14-2)

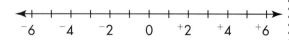

A $+5 < 0$

B $-4 < +2$

C $+6 = -6$

D $-4 > +13$

3. The integers below are listed from least to greatest. Which of the following answer choices could the missing integers be? (14-3)

$-12, \boxed{}, -6, \boxed{}, +3, +8, +10$

A -7, and $+4$

B 0 and $+13$

C -8 and -2

D -13 and -1

4. The deepest point on the Pacific Ocean floor is a little less than 7 miles below sea level. How is 7 miles below sea level written as an integer? (14-1)

A 19

B 17

C 0

D -7

5. Which integer is the least? (14-3)

A $+15$

B -14

C -4

D $+5$

6. Garrison jumped off the side of a boat that was 8 feet above sea level. He went 6 feet below sea level. Draw a picture to help find the total distance he traveled. (14-4)

A 2 feet

B 6 feet

C 8 feet

D 14 feet

7. What is the opposite of 18? (14-1)

A -16

B -18

C $+8$

D $+16$

8. Which statement is true? (14-2)

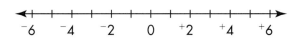

A $+3 < +2$

B $0 < -5$

C $-1 > -6$

D $-4 > -3$

9. Which of the following could represent +$65? (14-1)

A A deposit of $65

B A withdrawal of $65

C Owing $65

D Never having $65

10. Which shows the temperatures in order from least to greatest? (14-3)

A $-6, -4, 0, 12$

B $-6, -4, 12, 0$

C $-4, -6, 0, 12$

D $0, 12, -4, -6$

11. What are the next three numbers in this pattern? (14-1)

+20, +16, +12, +8, ▢ **,** ▢ **,** ▢

A $+4, +2, -4$

B $+4, 0, -2$

C $+4, 0, -4$

D $+4, -4, -8$

12. Which of the following has the greatest value? (14-3)

A A deposit of $4

B Paying $2

C $12 owed

D A withdrawal of $6

13. While vacationing in Alaska, the low temperature for one day was $-6°F$. The high for the same day was only $10°F$ warmer. Draw a picture to help find the high temperature for the day. (14-4)

A $-16°F$

B $+4°F$

C $+10°F$

D $+16°F$

14. Which integer is best represented by point R on the number line? (14-1)

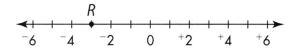

A $+5$

B $+3$

C -3

D -5

15. Which symbol makes the comparison true? (14-2)

$-4 \bigcirc +4$

A $+$

B $>$

C $=$

D $<$

Set A, pages 336–337

Which sentences describe positive integers?
Which sentences describe negative integers?

1. The lake is 500 feet *below* sea level.

2. Liz *gained* 20 feet in the last lap.

3. The store *lost* money today: a total of $85.

4. The hill is 247 feet *high*.

Words like *below* and *lost* describe a negative
integer. Words like *high* and *gain* describe
a positive integer. So, sentences 1 and
3 describe negative integers. Sentences
2 and 4 describe positive integers.

Remember opposites are the same
distance from zero on a number line.

Write an integer for each word
description.

1. 14 degrees below zero

2. A rise of 22 degrees

3. 8 degrees Celsius

4. A drop of 12 degrees Fahrenheit

5. Phil is playing great golf. His score is
2 under par.

6. Stan lost $20 when he left his
wallet on the bus.

7. The trail stopped at 1,424 feet
above sea level.

8. The football team lost fifteen
yards on a penalty.

Set B, pages 338–339

Compare. Use $>$ or $<$ for $\bigcirc$.

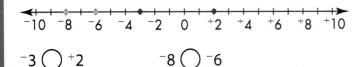

$^-3 \bigcirc ^+2$ $^-8 \bigcirc ^-6$

The integer $^-3$ is to the left of $^+2$ on the
number line. So, $^-3 < ^+2$ or $^+2 > ^-3$.

The integer $^-8$ is to the left of $^-6$ on the
number line. So, $^-8 < ^-6$ or $^-6 > ^-8$.

Remember integers increase as
you move from the left to the right
on a number line.

Compare. Use $>$ or $<$ for the $\bigcirc$.

1. $^+7 \bigcirc ^-3$ 2. $^-9 \bigcirc ^+3$

3. $^-2 \bigcirc ^-9$ 4. $^+8 \bigcirc ^+4$

5. $^-3 \bigcirc ^+4$ 6. $^-6 \bigcirc ^-5$

7. $^-7 \bigcirc ^-4$ 8. $^+5 \bigcirc ^-2$

9. $^-5 \bigcirc ^-7$ 10. $^-1 \bigcirc 0$

11. $^-3 \bigcirc ^-6$ 12. $^-8 \bigcirc 4$

13. $^+5 \bigcirc 0$ 14. $^-10 \bigcirc ^+10$

Set C, pages 340–341

At a town pool, the diving board is 4 feet above the water. The water is at 0 feet, and the shallow end is 3 feet deep. The deep end of the pool is 11 feet deep. The high-dive platform is 12 feet above the water.

What is the order of these numbers from least to greatest?

Start by writing the integers.

$^+4, 0, ^-3, ^-11, ^+12$

Then mark the location of each integer on a number line.

$^-12\ ^-10\ ^-8\ ^-6\ ^-4\ ^-2\ 0\ ^+2\ ^+4\ ^+6\ ^+8\ ^+10\ ^+12$

Finally, write the integers in order from left to right as they appear on the number line.

$^-11, ^-3, 0, ^+4, ^+12$

Remember that when ordering integers, 0 will fall between the negative and positive integers.

Write in order from least to greatest.

1. $^+4, 0, ^-2$ 2. $^-8, ^+3, ^-5$

3. $^-4, ^+12, ^-6$ 4. $^+3, ^-5, ^+7$

5. $^-18, ^-12, ^+2$ 6. $^-16, ^+7, ^-1$

Write in order from greatest to least.

7. $^-1, ^+6, ^+8, ^-6, ^+1$

8. $^-4, ^+7, ^-12, ^-6$

9. $^-4, 0, ^-8, ^+2, ^+3$

10. $^+10, ^-9, ^-5, ^-11, ^+12$

11. $^+2, ^+12, ^-15, ^-10, 0$

12. $^-25, ^-60, ^+26, ^+42, ^-30$

Set D, pages 342–343

A 5-kilometer run had markers at the starting line, the halfway point, and the finish line. Markers were also placed at each kilometer. How many markers were used for the race?

Draw a picture to solve the problem.

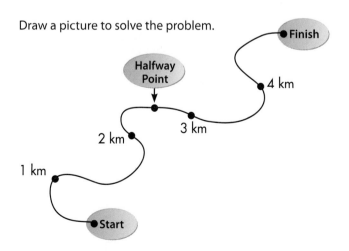

There were 7 markers used for the race.

Remember to draw pictures to represent situations.

Solve each problem.

1. Georgia had $30 in her checking account. By mistake, she wrote a check for $50. What is the balance in Georgia's checking account now? Draw a picture to decide.

2. Jill, Maddie, Kyle, and Paul arranged their desks in a row. Kyle's desk is next to only one other desk. Paul's desk is the third desk. Maddie's desk is next to Jill's. What is the order of their desks?

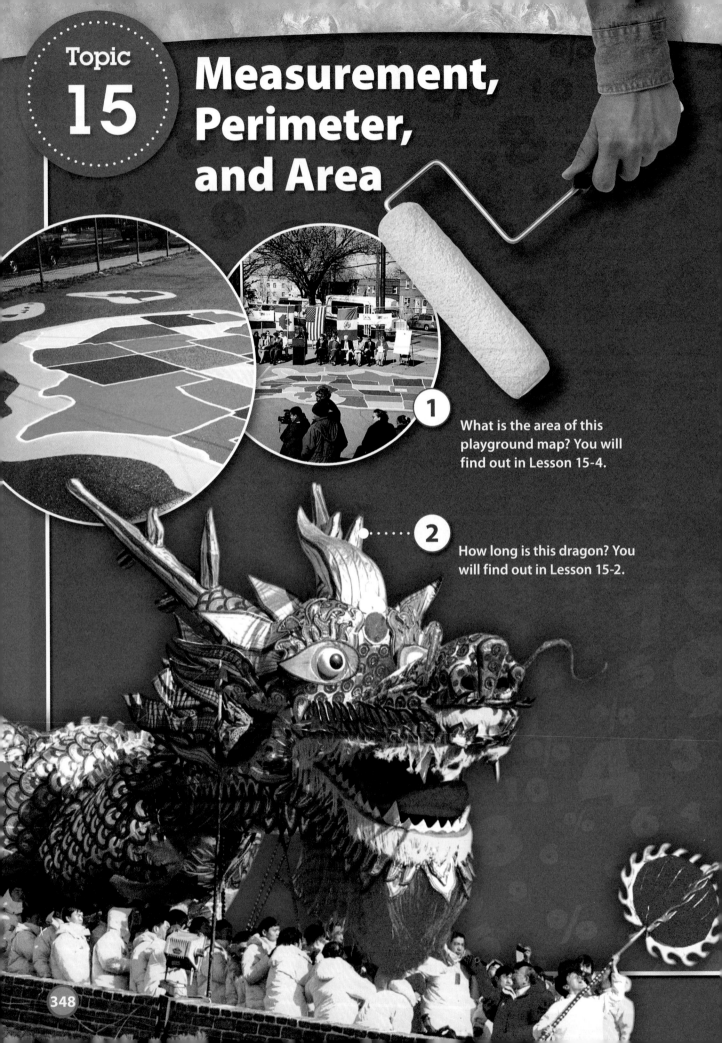

Topic 15

Measurement, Perimeter, and Area

1 What is the area of this playground map? You will find out in Lesson 15-4.

2 How long is this dragon? You will find out in Lesson 15-2.

Review What You Know!

Choose the best term from the box.

> • addition   • multiplication
> • mile   • perimeter

1. The ? is the distance around a figure.

2. A customary unit used to measure long distances is the ? .

3. ? is the operation you use to find the area of a region.

Multiplication Facts

Find each product.

4. 6×5 5. 7×9 6. 8×8

7. 7×4 8. 3×6 9. 5×4

10. 4×9 11. 8×5 12. 9×6

13. 8×4 14. 3×9 15. 8×7

Measurement

Choose the best unit to measure the length of each item. Write inch, foot, yard, or mile.

16. book   17. football field

18. road   19. classroom

20. leaf   21. marathon race

22. **Writing to Explain** Would a yardstick be the best tool to use to measure the length of an ant? Explain.

23. Name two items in your classroom that could best be measured in inches.

3 How tall is the largest model of an ear of corn? You will find out in Lesson 15-1.

4 You can use different shapes to estimate the perimeter of California. You will find out how in Lesson 15-3.

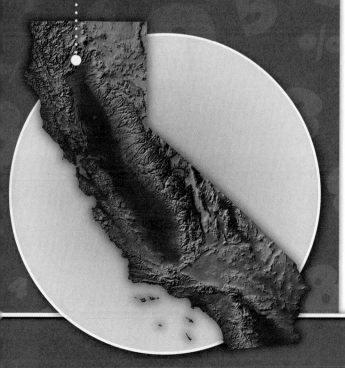

MG 1.4 Grade 3 Carry out simple unit conversions within a system of measurement (e.g., centimeters and meters, hours and minutes).

Customary Measures

What are customary units of measure?

Eva needs to buy a 15-foot cable to hook up her computer. She found one brand of cable in inches and another brand in yards.

How many inches is 15 feet?

How many yards is 15 feet?

15-foot cable

Customary Units of Length	
1 foot	= 12 inches
1 yard	= 36 inches
1 yard	= 3 feet
1 mile	= 5,280 feet
1 mile	= 1,760 yards

Other Examples

Units of Length

Inches (in.), foot (ft), yard (yd), and mile (mi) are customary units of length.

A paperclip is about 1 inch.

A notebook is about 1 foot.

A baseball bat is about 1 yard.

One mile is about four times around the track.

Units of Weight

Ounce (oz.), pound (lb), and ton (T) are customary units of weight.

Customary Units of Weight	
1 lb	= 16 oz
1 T	= 2,000 lb

 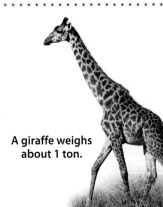

A key weighs about 1 ounce.

A kitten weighs about 1 pound.

A giraffe weighs about 1 ton.

Units of Capacity

Cup (c), pint (pt), quart (qt), and gallon (gal) are customary units of capacity.

Customary Units of Capacity	
1 pt	= 2 c
1 qt	= 2 pt
1 gal	= 4 qt

1 cup (c)

1 pint (pt)

1 quart (qt)

1 gallon (gal)

To change from larger units to smaller units, multiply.

$$15 \textbf{ feet} = \text{ } \textbf{ inches}$$
$$1 \textbf{ foot} = \textbf{12 inches}$$
$$\textbf{15} \times \textbf{12} = \textbf{180}$$

So, 15 feet is equal to 180 inches.

To change from smaller units to larger units, divide.

$$15 \textbf{ feet} = \text{ } \textbf{ yards}$$
$$\textbf{3 feet} = \textbf{1 yard}$$
$$\textbf{15} \div \textbf{3} = \textbf{5}$$

So, 15 feet is equal to 5 yards.

Guided Practice*

Do you know HOW?

In **1** through **4**, find each missing number.

1. 5 T =   lb

2. 8 qt =   gal

3. 21 ft =   yd

4. 9 ft =   in.

Do you UNDERSTAND?

5. What operation do you use if you want to change a larger unit to a smaller unit?

6. Eva's computer weighs 18 pounds. How many ounces does Eva's computer weigh?

Independent Practice

In **7** through **14**, find each missing number.

7. 8 lb =   oz

8. 45 yd =   ft

9. 18 pt =   c

10. 6,000 lb =   T

11. 24 ft =   yd

12. 20 gal =   qt

13. 48 in. =   ft

14. 46 lb 15 oz =   oz

In **15** through **19**, choose the most appropriate unit of length for each. Write *in., ft, yd,* or *mi.*

15. car

16. pencil

17. river

18. a hand

19. airplane

In **20** through **24**, choose the most appropriate unit of weight for each. Write *oz, lb,* or *T.*

20. elephant

21. bird

22 child

23. book

24. truck

DIGITAL

Animated Glossary
www.pearsonsuccessnet.com

Independent Practice

In **25** through **28**, choose the most appropriate unit of capacity for each. Write *c, pt, qt,* or *gal.*

25. watering can

26. carton of milk

27. bathtub

28. drinking glass

In **29** through **36**, compare. Write >, <, or = for each ◯.

29. 1 pt ◯ 2 c

30. 2 gal ◯ 4 qt

31. 50 ft ◯ 16 yd

32. 48 oz ◯ 3 lb

33. 1 lb ◯ 8 oz

34. 100 in. ◯ 9 ft

35. 1 yd ◯ 36 in.

36. 4 pt ◯ 8 qt

Problem Solving

37. Reasoning While grocery shopping, Mrs. Gutierrez bought a small bag of rice and a large bag of noodles. Both packages are different sizes. Can the packages weigh the same? Explain.

38. Number Sense Which number is greater, the number of pounds a box weighs or the number of ounces the same box weighs?

39. Geometry Look at this series of shapes. Which shape comes next in the pattern?

40. A shipping company will not ship items weighing more than 50 lb. Which of the following cannot be shipped with the company?

  A Book   **C** Watermelon

  B Refrigerator   **D** DVD

41. Raymond poured 8 cups of punch. Madison poured 5 pints of punch. Ryan poured 2 quarts of punch. Who poured the most punch?

42. Jeremiah bought 2 pounds of lettuce and 3 pounds of tomatoes for a salad. How many ounces of each did he purchase?

43. In Olivia, Minnesota, there is a giant ear of corn that is about 8 yards tall standing over a roadside gazebo. How many feet is equal to 8 yards?

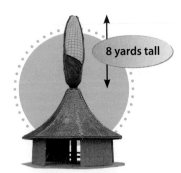

8 yards tall

Algebra Connections

Measurement Tables

How can you use conversion tables to change one customary unit of measure to another customary unit of measure?

There are three types of customary units of measure. They are units for length, capacity, and weight.

Data

Customary Units		
Length	**Capacity**	**Weight**
1 ft = 12 in.	1 pt = 2 c	1 lb = 16 oz
1 yd = 3 ft	1 qt = 2 pt	1 T = 2,000 lb
1 mi = 5,280 ft	1 gal = 4 qt	

Example: How many inches are in 1 mile?

Think *What conversions will I have to use?*

Since the question is asking about miles and inches, customary units of length will be used.

1 mile is 5,280 feet.
1 foot is 12 inches.

Convert miles to inches:
$5,280 \times 12 = 63,360$

There are 63,360 inches in 1 mile.

In **1** through **8**, find each missing number.

1. 2 T = ▢ oz

2. 12 yd = ▢ in.

3. 1 gal = ▢ c

4. 540 in. = ▢ yd

5. 8 qt = ▢ c

6. 2 gal = ▢ c

7. 125 lbs = ▢ oz

8. 100 yd = ▢ in.

In **9** through **16**, compare. Write >, <, or = for each ◯ .

9. 5 T ◯ 16,000 oz

10. 5 gal ◯ 40 c

11. 24 gal ◯ 3 pt

12. 7 qt ◯ 35 c

13. 2 yd ◯ 99 in.

14. 1,000 in. ◯ 9 yd

15. 2 T ◯ 4,000 oz.

16. 80 pt ◯ 11 gal

17. A marathon is about a 25-mile race. If the average person's stride when running is about 3 feet, how many strides will the average person take in a marathon?

18. John says that anything that is measured in customary units can be converted to another customary unit. Is he correct? Explain.

19. The average person drinks 56 pints of water in a week. How many gallons is this?

20. A truck is carrying widgets each weighing 1 oz. The maximum weight of a bridge it needs to go over is 15 T. If the truck weighs 9 T and is carrying 170,000 widgets, can the truck go over the bridge? Explain.

15-2

MG 1.4 Grade 3
Carry out simple unit conversions within a system of measurement (e.g., centimeters and meters, hours and minutes).

Metric Measures

What are metric units of measure?

One of the largest sunflowers ever grown had a height of about 800 centimeters.

How many millimeters is this?
How many meters is this?

800 centimeters

Metric Units of Length

1 cm	= 10 mm
1 dm	= 10 cm
1 m	= 100 cm
1 km	= 1,000 cm

Other Examples

Units of Length

Millimeter (mm), centimeter (cm), decimeter (dm), meter (m), and kilometer (km) are metric units of length.

The thickness of a dime is about 1 millimeter.

A ladybug is about 1 centimeter long.

A snake is about 1 meter long.

4 city blocks is about 1 kilometer.

Units of Mass

Gram (g) and kilogram (kg) are metric units of mass. Mass is the amount of matter in an object.

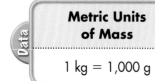

Metric Units of Mass

1 kg = 1,000 g

A dollar bill has a mass of about 1 gram.

A cantaloupe has a mass of about 1 kilogram.

Units of Capacity

Milliliter (mL) and liter (L) are metric units of capacity.

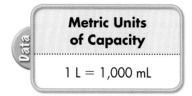

Metric Units of Capacity

1 L = 1,000 mL

An eyedropper can be used to measure 1 milliliter.

Some water bottles hold 1 liter.

To change from larger units to smaller units, multiply.

800 centimeters = ▢ millimeters.

1 cm = 10 mm

800 × 10 = 8,000

So, 800 centimeters is equal to 8,000 millimeters.

The sunflower was 8,000 millimeters tall.

To change from smaller units to larger units, divide.

800 centimeters = ▢ meters.

100 centimeters = 1 meters

800 ÷ 100 = 8

So, 800 centimeters is equal to 8 meters.

The sunflower was 8 meters tall.

Guided Practice*

Do you know HOW?

In **1** through **4**, find each missing number.

1. 42 cm = ▢ mm   **2.** 56 L = ▢ mL

3. 65 kg = ▢ g   **4.** 30 km = ▢ m

In **5** through **8**, choose the most appropriate unit of measure.

5. length of a belt   **6.** drinking glass

7. highway   **8.** bleach in a bottle

Do you UNDERSTAND?

9. Look at the data chart above. Which is the larger unit of measure, a meter or a kilometer?

10. Which is the smaller unit of measure, a gram or a kilogram?

11. What operation do you use if you want to change a smaller unit to a larger unit?

Independent Practice

In **12** through **27**, find each missing number.

12. 230 km = ▢ m   **13.** 64 L = ▢ mL   **14.** 32 kg = ▢ g   **15.** 6 cm = ▢ mm

16. 16 kg = ▢ g   **17.** 57 dm = ▢ cm   **18.** 6,113 m = ▢ dm   **19.** 552 km = ▢ m

20. 86 m = ▢ cm   **21.** 64 L = ▢ mL   **22.** 8,000 g = ▢ kg   **23.** 4,000 mL = ▢ L

24. 9 km = ▢ dm   **25.** 970 mm = ▢ cm   **26.** 6,113 m = ▢ dm   **27.** 9,000 mL = ▢ L

*For another example, see Set B on page 378.   Lesson 15-2   **355**

In **28** through **30**, choose the most appropriate unit of measure.

28. strawberry: g or kg

29. bicycle: g or kg

30. fish tank: mL or L

In **31** through **35**, tell whether the unit measures length, mass, or capacity.

31. liter   **32.** gram   **33.** kilometer   **34.** decimeter   **35.** kilogram

For **36** through **38**, compare. Write >, <, or = for each ◯.

36. 1 kg ◯ 1 g   **37.** 100 mL ◯ 1 L   **38.** 10 cm ◯ 1 dm

Problem Solving

For **39**, use the table to the right.

39. The Sorensens are purchasing a new car. The table compares the gas mileage of their used car to that of the car they are buying. Round each decimal to the nearest tenth.

Miles per Gallon

Type of Car	City Driving	Highway Driving
New Car	27.21	31.50
Used Car	17.86	22.09

40. Estimation The mass of 5 tomatoes is about 1 kilogram. Estimate the mass of 1 tomato in grams.

41. Number Sense Which number would be greater, the number of liters of juice in a pitcher or the number of milliliters of juice in the same pitcher?

42. In the year 2000, the world's largest Chinese dancing dragon was part of a celebration at the Great Wall of China. It took 3,200 people working inside the dragon to move it. Which is the best estimate of the length of the dragon?

   A 3,048 mm   **C** 3,048 dm

   B 3,048 cm   **D** 3,048 m

43. Which measure is **NOT** equal to 6 meters?

   A 60 kilometers

   B 60 decimeters

   C 600 centimeters

   D 6,000 millimeters

eTools, Practice, Review
www.pearsonsuccessnet.com

Mixed Problem Solving

The John Muir Wilderness extends along the crest of the Central Sierra Nevada of California. The 581,143 acres of land includes snow-capped mountains, meadows, trails, lakes, and streams. The John Muir Wilderness is also home to the endangered Sierra Nevada Bighorn Sheep. Since the late 19th century, there has been a decrease in the number of sheep. The chart shows the number of Sierra Nevada Bighorn Sheep in various years.

Year	Number of Sheep
1977	250
1986	310
1995	100
2004	250

1. How many more Sierra Nevada Bighorn Sheep were there in 1986 than in 1977?

2. How many more Sierra Nevada Bighorn Sheep were there in 2004 than in 1995?

3. From which year to which year did the population of sheep increase by the greatest amount?

4. What was the difference in the number of sheep between 1986 and 1995?

5. The California Wilderness Act increased the acreage of the John Muir Wilderness by 81,000 acres. About how many acres was the John Muir Wilderness before the increase?

6. One of the favorite trails in the John Muir Wilderness is the John Muir Trail. The trail is 211 miles long. If a group of hikers wanted to hike about $\frac{1}{2}$ the distance of the trail in 7 days, how far should they hike each day?

7. If the mountain climber climbed $\frac{1}{4}$ of the distance up Arrow Peak one day and then climbed another $\frac{1}{3}$ of the distance to the next day, what fraction of the climb did he complete?

$\frac{1}{4}$ of the way up the hill

MG 1.4 Understand and use formulas to solve problems involving perimeters and areas of rectangles and squares. Use those formulas to find the areas of more complex figures by dividing the figures into basic shapes. Also **MG 1.0, AF 1.4.**

Perimeter

Hands-On
metric ruler

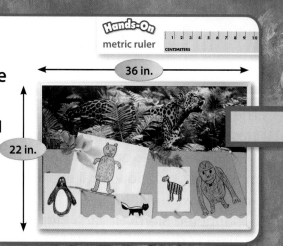

← 36 in. →

22 in.

How do you find the distance around an object?

Fred wants to put a border around the bulletin board in his room. How much border will he need?

Perimeter is <u>the distance around a figure.</u>

Another Example How do you estimate and find the perimeter of different figures?

Estimate and find the perimeter of the hexagon below.

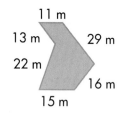

11 m

13 m   29 m

22 m

16 m

15 m

Use rounding to estimate:
$30 + 20 + 20 + 20 + 10 + 10 = 110$

Add the actual numbers:
$29 + 16 + 15 + 22 + 13 + 11 = 106$

The perimeter of the hexagon is 106 m.

Find the perimeter of the square below. All 4 sides of a square are the same length. So, the formula is:

$P = s + s + s + s$
or, $P = 4 \times s$

9

$s = 9$
$P = 4 \times 9$
$P = 36$

The perimeter of the square is 36 cm.

Explain It

1. How can you use addition to find the perimeter of a square? How can you use multiplication?

2. Why couldn't you use a formula to find the perimeter of the hexagon? Could you ever use a formula to find the perimeter of a hexagon? Explain.

One Way

Measure to find the length of each side. Then add to find the perimeter.

36 + 22 + 36 + 22 = 116

The perimeter of the bulletin board is 116 inches.

Another Way

Use a formula.

Perimeter = (2 × length) + (2 × width)

$P = (2 \times \ell) + (2 \times w)$

$P = (2 \times 22) + (2 \times 36)$

$P = 44 + 72 = 116$

The perimeter of the bulletin board is 116 inches.

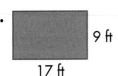

width

length

Guided Practice*

Do you know HOW?

For **1** through **4**, estimate, and then find the perimeter of each figure.

1.
11 in.　16 in.
13 in.

2.
9 ft
17 ft

3.
12 mm
6 mm
15 mm　17 mm
21 mm

4.
13 m

Do you UNDERSTAND?

5. How can you use a formula to find the perimeter of any regular polygon?

6. How can you estimate to see if the value you found for the perimeter of Fred's bulletin board is reasonable?

7. Fred is making a frame for an autographed photo of his favorite soccer player. If the picture is 8 inches by 10 inches, how much wood will Fred need for the frame?

Independent Practice

Leveled Practice For **8** through **10**, measure the sides and find the perimeter of each figure.

8.
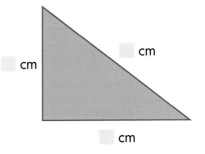
cm
cm
cm

9.
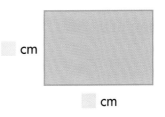
cm
cm

10.
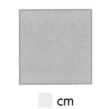
cm

*For another example, see Set C on page 378.

For **11** through **18**, estimate, and then find the perimeter of each figure.

11. 39 in.

12. 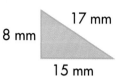 12 ft

16 ft

13. 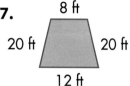 22 yd

14.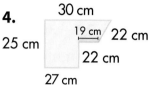
30 cm
25 cm
19 cm 22 cm
22 cm
27 cm

15.
14 m

16.
8 mm   17 mm
15 mm

17.
8 ft
20 ft   20 ft
12 ft

18.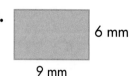
6 mm
9 mm

Problem Solving

19. Tom drew the 2 rectangles at the right. What is the difference between the perimeter of Rectangle A and the perimeter of Rectangle B?

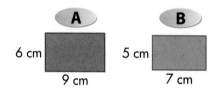

A   B

6 cm   5 cm

9 cm   7 cm

A   3 cm   **B**   6 cm   **C**   12 cm   **D**   54 cm

20. Reasoning Which has a greater perimeter, a 28-inch square or a 21-inch by 31-inch rectangle? Explain.

21. Charles wanted to estimate the perimeter of California, so he drew several polygons and placed them over a map of the state. Estimate the perimeter of California to the nearest hundred.

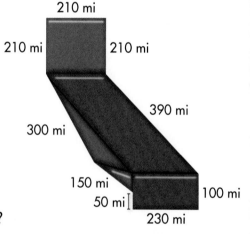

210 mi

210 mi   210 mi

390 mi

300 mi

150 mi

50 mi

100 mi

230 mi

22. Writing to Explain Paula built a play area for her dog in the shape of a regular pentagon. If the perimeter is 35 feet, what is the length of each side of the play area?

23. Myles gets to play on the computer every time he reads 120 pages. If he reads 10 pages a night, how many nights will he have to read before he gets to play on the computer?

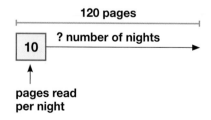

120 pages

? number of nights

10

pages read
per night

24. Think About the Process James wants to draw a rectangle with a perimeter of 42 units and a length of 13 units. How can he determine the width?

A   Subtract 13 from 42, then divide by 2.

B   Multiply 13 by 2.

C   Add 13 to 42. Then divide by 2.

D   Multiply 13 by 2. Subtract the product from 42. Divide the difference by 2.

Algebra Connections

What's the Conversion Rule?

How can you use tables to find out how two units are related?

The rules for converting one unit into another are not always given. Sometimes it is necessary to compare two different units.

A dram is a small customary unit of weight.

How many drams are there in an ounce?

Drams	Ounces
32	2
64	4
	5

Think *How are these units related?*

32 drams ÷ 2 = 16 drams per ounce

Does this check?

64 drams ÷ 4 = 16 drams per ounce

How many drams are there in 5 ounces?

5 × 16 = 80 drams

In **1** through **4**, complete the tables and find the rule of conversion.

1.

Dash	Teaspoon
8	1
16	2
24	
32	

8 dashes per teaspoon

2.

Bushel	Peck
	8
4	16
6	
7	28

4 pecks per bushel

3.

Quart	Peck
16	2
24	3
40	5
56	

8 quarts per peck

4.

Gallon	Hogshead
	1
126	
252	4
315	5

63 gallons per hogshead

5. A "stone" is an old unit of weight used in Ireland and England to measure potatoes. A stone is 14 pounds, and 160 stones make up a "long ton." How many pounds is a long ton?

6. A furlong is a unit of length still used today in racing and agriculture. A race that is 8 furlongs is 1 mile. How many feet are in 1 furlong?

7. A famous novel by Jules Verne is titled *20,000 Leagues Under the Sea*. A league is a nautical measurement equal to 3 miles. The deepest point in the ocean is about 6.84 miles. How many leagues deep can you actually go?

8. Neil is reading a sign of old measures of volume from England. He sees that there are 2 pecks in 1 kenning. There are 2 kennings in 1 bushel. There are 2 bushels in 1 strike. There are 4 strikes in 1 quarter. There are 4 quarters in 1 chaldron. Write a number sentence to show the number of pecks in a chaldron.

Area of Squares and Rectangles

MG 1.1 Measure the area of rectangular shapes by using appropriate units, such as square centimeter (cm²), square meter (m²), square kilometer (km²), square inch (in.²), square yard (yd²) or square mile (m). Also **AF 1.4, MG 1.4, MG 1.0.**

How can you find the area of a figure?

A small can of chalkboard paint covers 40 square feet. Does Mike need more than one small can to paint one wall of his room?

Area is <u>the amount of space needed to cover a figure.</u> Area is measured in square units.

Guided Practice*

Do you know HOW?

For **1** through **4**, find the area of each figure.

1.
7 in
3 in

2.
5 m
4 m

3.
14 ft
8 ft

4.
9 cm

Do you UNDERSTAND?

5. What is the formula for the area of a square? Explain how you know.

6. Mike plans to paint another wall in his room blue. That wall measures 12 feet by 8 feet. How much area does Mike need to paint?

Independent Practice

Leveled Practice In **7** and **8**, measure the sides and find the area of each figure.

7.
cm
cm

8.
cm
cm

In **9** through **16**, find the area of each figure.

9.
4 ft
9 ft

10.
6 mm
6 mm

11.
5 in.
7 in.

12.
4 yd
8 yd

For another example, see Set D on page 378.

One Way

Measure to find the length of each side. You can also count the square units to find area.

8 ft

6 ft

$6 \times 8 = 48$

The area of Mike's wall is 48 square feet.

Another Way

You can use a formula to find area.

Area = length × width

$A = \ell \times w$

$A = 6 \times 8$

$A = 48$

width

length

The area of Mike's wall is 48 square feet. He will need more than one small can of paint.

13.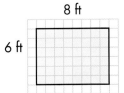
14 m
3m

14.
13 mm
9 mm

15.
11 cm
9 cm

16. 4 yd

Problem Solving

17. Reasoning Jen's garden is 4 feet wide and has an area of 28 square feet. What is the length of the garden?

18. Diane drew a polygon with 4 sides and 1 set of parallel sides. What type of polygon did Diane draw?

19. Writing to Explain Leah says the area of a rectangle is always greater than its perimeter. Jules says the perimeter of a rectangle is always greater. Who is correct?

20. Mr. Chen is putting tile down in his kitchen. The kitchen is 16 feet long and 8 feet wide. The tile costs $5 per square foot. How much will it cost Mr. Chen to tile his kitchen?

21. Helen's sandbox is 6 feet long and 5 feet wide. What is the area of the sandbox?

  A 11 sq ft

  B 22 sq ft

  C 30 sq ft

  D 36 sq ft

22. Number Sense At the first bus stop, 18 people got on. At the next stop, 12 people got off and half as many as this got on. At the third stop, 6 people got off and 2 got on. At the fourth stop, half the people on the bus got off. How many people are left on the bus?

23. The playground map of the United States is a rectangle with a width of 25 feet. Its length is 10 feet longer than its width. Find the area of the map.

DIGITAL

Animated Glossary, eTools
www.pearsonsuccessnet.com

Area of Irregular Shapes

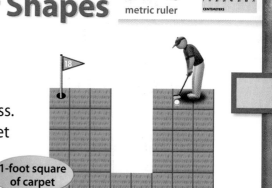

How can you find the area of an irregular figure?

Mr. Fox is covering a miniature golf course hole with artificial grass. How many 1-foot squares of carpet will Mr. Fox need to cover the miniature golf course hole?

1-foot square of carpet

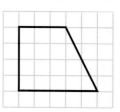

MG 1.4 Understand and use formulas to solve problems involving perimeters and areas of rectangles and squares. Use those formulas to find the areas of more complex figures by dividing the figures into basic shapes. Also **AF 1.4, MG 1.1, MG 1.0.**

Another Example **How can you estimate area?**

Some shapes contain partial square units.

Estimate the area of the trapezoid to the right.

One Way

Count the whole square units. Then estimate the number of units made from combining partial squares.

There are 14 whole square units. The partial square units make about 2 more square units.

14 + 2 = 16

The trapezoid has an area of about 16 square units.

Another Way

Draw a rectangle around the trapezoid and find the rectangle's area.
$A = 4 \times 5 = 20$

Find the area outside the trapezoid but inside the rectangle.

There are about 4 square units not in the trapezoid.

Subtract to find the difference between the two areas.

$20 - 4 = 16$

The trapezoid has an area of about 16 square units.

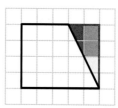

Explain It

1. Why is the answer of 16 square units considered an estimate?

2. Can the trapezoid be divided into rectangles to find the area?

Count the square units to find the area.

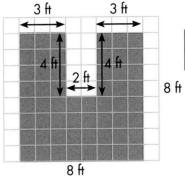

3 ft   3 ft
4 ft   4 ft
2 ft
8 ft
8 ft

The area of the golf course hole is 56 square feet.

Divide the hole into rectangles. Find the area of each rectangle and add.

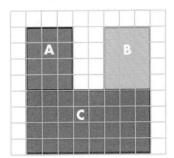

Rectangle A
$A = 4 \times 3 = 12$

Rectangle B
$A = 4 \times 3 = 12$

Rectangle C
$A = 4 \times 8 = 32$

Add the areas: $12 + 12 + 32 = 56$
The area of the golf course hole is 56 square feet.

Guided Practice*

Do you know HOW?

For **1** and **2**, find the area of each figure.

1.

2.

4 cm
3 cm
9 cm
6 cm

For **3** and **4**, estimate the area of each figure.

3.   **4.**
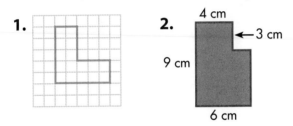

Do you UNDERSTAND?

5. **Writing to Explain** Could the golf course hole be divided into any other set of rectangles?

6. Suppose Mr. Fox bought 75 square feet of artificial grass. How much artificial grass will be left over?

7. Mr. Fox decided the area of the hole was too large. What would the new area of the hole be if he only uses rectangles A and C in the example above?

Independent Practice

For **8** and **9**, measure and find the area of each figure.

8.
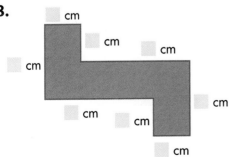
cm
cm
cm
cm
cm
cm
cm
cm

9.
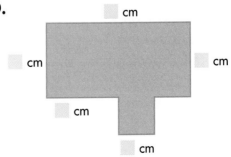
cm
cm
cm
cm
cm

For **10** through **13**, estimate the area of each figure.

10.

11.

12.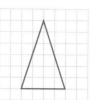

13.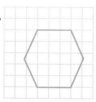

14. (Think) About the Process Jared drew the figure to the right on grid paper. Which is **NOT** a way in which the figure could be divided to find the total area?

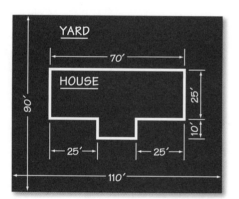

   A $(4 \times 6) + (3 \times 3)$

   B $(3 \times 7) + (4 \times 2) + (4 \times 1)$

   C $(4 \times 6) + (3 \times 7)$

   D $(2 \times 4) + (3 \times 3) + (4 \times 1) + (4 \times 3)$

15. **Writing to Explain** Laurie's family is building a new house. The design for the house is shown to the right. What is the area of the new house? How big will their yard be?

16. **Algebra** Write an algebraic expression to represent the phrase "six times a number is 24." Solve the expression

17. **Writing to Explain** Each student on a field trip got a sandwich, a salad, and a juice. If you know that there were 10 students on the field trip, would you be able to tell how much they paid for lunch in all? Why or why not?

18. Mrs. Washington drew a triangle on grid paper. The base of the triangle is 6 units long. The triangle is 8 units tall. Draw a picture of Mrs. Washington's triangle on grid paper. Estimate the area.

19. Mandy designed a patch to add to her quilt. What fraction is colored blue?

   A $\frac{2}{8}$

   B $\frac{4}{8}$

   C $\frac{8}{8}$

   D $\frac{8}{4}$

Algebra Connections

Repeating Shape Patterns

Look at the shapes below. Can you identify a pattern?

The pattern is 1 triangle, 2 circles, and 1 square.

Example: Name the 10th shape in the pattern at the left.

Think *Where does the pattern repeat itself?*

The pattern of 1 triangle, 2 circles, 1 square repeats after 4 shapes.

First group of shapes   Second group of shapes

$$4 + 4 + 2 = 10.$$

Add two more

The 2nd shape in the pattern is a circle, so the 10th shape is also a circle.

In **1** through **10**, name the shape asked for in each pattern.

1. What is the 15th shape?

2. What is the 9th shape?

3. What is the 12th shape?

4. What is the 28th shape?

5. What is the 11th shape?

6. What is the 45th shape?

7. What is the 31st shape?

8. What is the 21st shape?

9. What is the 50th shape?

10. What is the 19th shape?

For **11** through **12**, find the shape asked for in each pattern.

11. Silvana used 7 red mugs, 6 purple mugs, and 8 green mugs in the display. How many mugs did she use in all?

12. Peter used 20 placemats in the display. The mats were blue, orange, and yellow. Arrange them in a pattern.

Lesson

15-6

MG1.3 Understand that rectangles that have the same perimeter can have different areas.
Also MG1.0 Understand perimeter and area.

Same Perimeter, Different Area

Can rectangles have the same perimeter but different areas?

Beth has 12 feet of fence to build a rectangular pen for her rabbits. She wants the pen to have as much space as possible. Which rectangular pen has the greatest area?

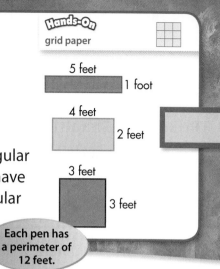

Hands-On
grid paper

5 feet / 1 foot

4 feet / 2 feet

3 feet / 3 feet

Each pen has a perimeter of 12 feet.

Guided Practice*

Do you know HOW?

For **1** through **4**, use grid paper to draw two different rectangles with the given perimeter. Tell the dimensions and area of each rectangle. Circle the one that has the greater area.

1. 16 feet

2. 20 centimeters

3. 24 inches

4. 40 meters

Do you UNDERSTAND?

5. In the example at the top, what do you notice about the area of the rectangles as the shape becomes more like a square?

6. Alex is building a rabbit pen with 25 feet of fence. What rectangle can he build that has the greatest possible area?

Independent Practice

For **7** through **10**, use grid paper to draw two different rectangles with the given perimeter. Tell the dimensions and area of each rectangle. Circle the one that has the greater area.

7. 10 inches

8. 22 centimeters

9. 26 yards

10. 32 feet

For **11** through **14**, describe a different rectangle with the same perimeter as the one shown. Then tell which rectangle has the greater area.

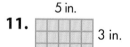

11. 5 in. / 3 in.

12. 4 ft / 3 ft

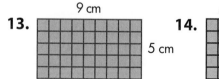

13. 9 cm / 5 cm

14. 4 m / 5 m

DIGITAL
eTools
www.pearsonsuccessnet.com

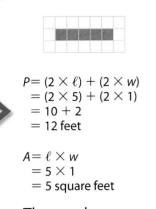

$P = (2 \times \ell) + (2 \times w)$
$= (2 \times 5) + (2 \times 1)$
$= 10 + 2$
$= 12$ feet

$A = \ell \times w$
$= 5 \times 1$
$= 5$ square feet

The pen has an area of 5 square feet.

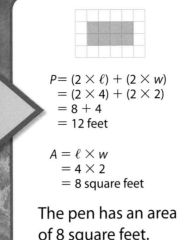

$P = (2 \times \ell) + (2 \times w)$
$= (2 \times 4) + (2 \times 2)$
$= 8 + 4$
$= 12$ feet

$A = \ell \times w$
$= 4 \times 2$
$= 8$ square feet

The pen has an area of 8 square feet.

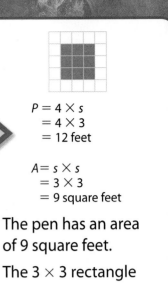

$P = 4 \times s$
$= 4 \times 3$
$= 12$ feet

$A = s \times s$
$= 3 \times 3$
$= 9$ square feet

The pen has an area of 9 square feet.

The 3×3 rectangle has the greatest area.

Problem Solving

15. Reasoning The rectangles at the right have the same perimeter. Without measuring or multiplying, how can you tell which has the greater area, rectangle X or rectangle Y?

16. Writing to Explain Karen drew a rectangle with a perimeter of 20 inches. The smaller side measured 3 inches and the longer side of the rectangle was 7 inches. Is she correct?

17. Suppose you arrange 48 counters into groups. The first group has 3 counters. Each group after that has 2 more counters than the group before. How many groups do you need to make to use all 48 counters?

18. Estimation Three towns are sharing the cost of library repairs for a regional high school. The total cost will be $7,200. If the cost is shared equally, will each town pay more or less than $3,000?

19. Mr. Gardner is building a fence around his garden. He has a total of 42 ft of fencing to make the perimeter. How much fencing should he use along the width and length to create the pen with the largest possible area?

For **20**, use the diagram at the right.

20. Which statement about the rectangles is true?

    A They both have the same width.

    B They both have the same length.

    C They both have the same perimeter.

    D They both have the same area.

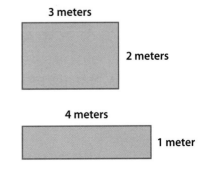

MG 1.2 Recognize that rectangles that have the same area can have different perimeters.
Also **MG 1.0, AF 1.4.**

Same Area, Different Perimeter

Can rectangles have the same area but different perimeters?

In a video puzzle game, you have 16 castle tiles to make a rectangular castle, and 16 water tiles for a moat. How can you completely surround the castle with water?

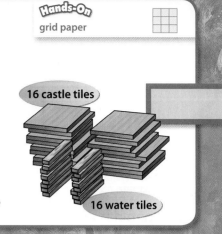

Hands-On
grid paper

16 castle tiles

16 water tiles

Guided Practice*

Do you know HOW?

For **1** through **4**, find two different rectangles that have the given area. Give the dimensions and perimeter of each rectangle, and tell which one has the smaller perimeter.

1. 6 square feet

2. 36 square yards

3. 64 square meters

4. 80 square inches

Do you UNDERSTAND?

5. In the example above, what do you notice about the perimeter of the rectangles as the shape becomes more like a square?

6. In Round 2 of the video puzzle game, you have 24 castle tiles. What is the fewest number of water tiles you will need to surround your castle?

Independent Practice

For **7** through **10**, use grid paper to draw two different rectangles with the given area. Tell the dimensions and perimeter of each rectangle. Circle the one that has the smaller perimeter.

7. 9 square inches   **8.** 18 square feet   **9.** 30 square meters   **10.** 32 square centimeters

For **11** through **14,** describe a different rectangle with the same area as the one shown. Then tell which rectangle has a smaller perimeter.

11.
6 m
4 m

12.
3 yd
4 yd

13.
5 ft
4 ft

14.
8 cm
2 cm
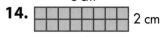

DIGITAL

eTools
www.pearsonsuccessnet.com

Make rectangles that have an area of 16 square units. Find the perimeter of each rectangle.

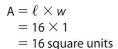

$A = \ell \times w$
$\quad = 16 \times 1$
$\quad = 16$ square units

$P = (2 \times \ell) + (2 \times w)$
$\quad = (2 \times 16) + (2 \times 1)$
$\quad = 32 + 2$
$\quad = 34$ units

$A = \ell \times w$
$\quad = 8 \times 2$
$\quad = 16$ square units

$P = (2 \times \ell) + (2 \times w)$
$\quad = (2 \times 8) + (2 \times 2)$
$\quad = 16 + 4$
$\quad = 20$ units

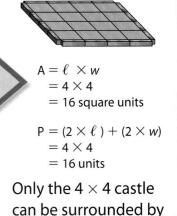

$A = \ell \times w$
$\quad = 4 \times 4$
$\quad = 16$ square units

$P = (2 \times \ell) + (2 \times w)$
$\quad = 4 \times 4$
$\quad = 16$ units

Only the 4 × 4 castle can be surrounded by 16 water tiles.

Problem Solving

15. Writing to Explain Park School and North School cover the same area. In physical education classes, each student runs one lap around the school. At which school do the students have to run farther?

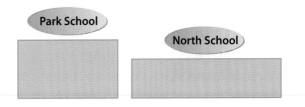

16. Estimation Sue bought 2 sweaters for $18.75 each and mittens for $11.45. About how much money will she get in change if she pays with 3 twenty-dollar bills?

17. Geometry Which of the following shapes cannot be congruent to a rectangle: a square, a rhombus, a quadrilateral, or a circle?

18. Number Sense The perimeter of rectangle P is 12 feet. The perimeter of rectangle Q is 18 feet. Both rectangles have the same area. Find the area and the dimensions of each rectangle.

19. Ms. Fisher is using 64 carpet tiles to make a reading area in her classroom. Each tile is a square that measures 1 foot by 1 foot. What is the length and width of the rectangular area she can make with the smallest possible perimeter?

20. Which statement about the rectangles to the right is true?

A They both have the same width.

B They both have the same length.

C They both have the same perimeter.

D They both have the same area.

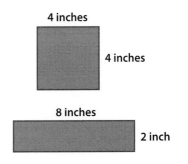

MR 1.2 Determine when and how to break a problem into simpler parts. Also MR 1.0, 2.3, MG 1.0.

Problem Solving

Solve a Simpler Problem and Make a Table

Each side of a triangle cracker below is one inch long. If there are 12 triangle crackers in a row, what is the perimeter of the figure?

1 inch

Guided Practice*

Do you know HOW?

1. Cora is cutting a piece of paper to get equal sized pieces. After the first cut, she stacks the two pieces and makes another cut. After she makes the second cut, she stacks the pieces again. If this pattern continues, how many pieces will she have after the fourth cut?

Do you UNDERSTAND?

2. How was the problem above broken into simpler problems?

3. **Write a Problem** Write a problem that you can solve by making a table.

Independent Practice

Solve.

4. Troy is helping his father build a fence. Each section of the fence has a post at each end. Make a table showing how many posts will be needed if there are 1, 3, 5, 10, 15, or 20 sections of the fence. Look for a pattern.

5. How many posts will be needed if the fence has 47 sections?

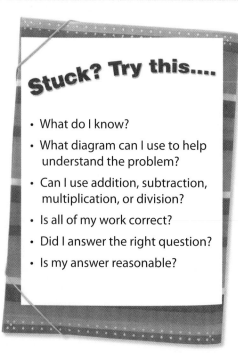

Stuck? Try this....

- What do I know?
- What diagram can I use to help understand the problem?
- Can I use addition, subtraction, multiplication, or division?
- Is all of my work correct?
- Did I answer the right question?
- Is my answer reasonable?

For another example, see Set G on page 379.

Change the problem into problems that are simpler to solve.

Look at 1 triangle, then 2 triangles, then 3 triangles.

perimeter = 3 inches

perimeter = 4 inches

perimeter = 5 inches

The perimeter is 2 more than the number of triangles.

Number of triangles	1	2	4
Perimeter (inches)	3	4	6

So, for 12 triangles the perimeter is 14 inches.

Problem Solving

6. Helen is part of a 32-player one-on-one basketball tournament. As soon as a player loses, she is out of the tournament. The winners will continue to play until there is one champion. How many games are there in all in this tournament?

7. The figure below is a square. If sides A and B are doubled, will this figure still be a square?

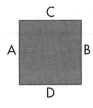

For **8** through **10,** use the table at the right.

8. The missing classes in the schedule to the right are Math, Science, Reading, Spelling, and Social Studies. Math is after morning break. Spelling is at 9:40. Reading and Science are the two afternoon classes. At what time is Math class?

9. What class is at 8:45?

10. Science class is before Reading. What time is Science class?

Class Schedule

Data

Morning	Afternoon
8:30: Opening	12:15:
8:45:	1:00: Break
9:30: Break	1:30:
9:40:	1:55: Recess
10:25: Recess	2:05: Art, Music or P.E.
10:55:	2:40: Pack Up
11:30: Lunch	2:45: School's Out

11. Six friends are playing checkers. If each friend plays against every other friend once, how many games of checkers will they play all together?

12. Mr. McNulty's classroom library has 286 books. If he buys 12 books each month for five months, how many books will he have in all?

13. Jolene, Timmy, Nicholas, Paul, and Kathryn are all planting in a community garden. If each of their plots holds 7 rows and 13 columns, how many plants will they be able to grow all together?

14. Thomas is training for a marathon. He runs for 2 miles and then he walks for a half a mile. If he trains by running 22 miles every day, how many miles would he walk?

15. Every day James spends $\frac{5}{10}$ of an hour on the phone, $\frac{6}{12}$ of an hour reading, and $\frac{3}{6}$ of an hour on the computer. Use the fraction strips to the right to tell which activity James spends the most time doing.

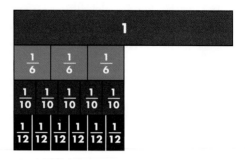

16. Maya is putting 3 ice cubes in each red cup and 4 ice cubes in each blue cup. The cups alternate colors starting with red. How many ice cubes will she use if she has 15 cups?

17. Shaina has a 30-inch necklace she wants to have cut into five 6-inch bracelets for her friends. The jeweler chargers $3 for each cut. How much does Shaina need to pay for the cuts?

18. Danielle can type 15 words per minute. How many minutes will it take her to type 105 words?

Minutes	1	2	3
Words typed	15	30	45

Think About the Process

19. It takes a plumber 4 minutes to cut a pipe. Which expression would you use to find how long it took the plumber to cut a pipe into 7 pieces?

A $4 + 7$

B 4×4

C 7×4

D 7×7

20. On every train car there are two connectors, one at the front and one at the back. These connectors are there so each car can be linked with another car. If a train has 30 cars how would you find out the number of connections made?

A The number of cars minus 1

B The number of connectors on all the cars minus 1

C Same as the number of cars

D The number of cars plus 1

Find the product. Estimate to check
if the answer is reasonable.

1.	523 $\times\ \ 64$	**2.**	502 $\times\ \ 67$	**3.**	45 $\times\ 30$	**4.**	37 $\times\ 45$

5.	64 $\times\ 23$	**6.**	9,431 $\times\ \ \ \ 15$	**7.**	5,050 $\times\ \ \ \ 4$	**8.**	24,028 $\times\ \ \ \ \ \ 4$

Find the quotient. Estimate to check
if the answer is reasonable.

9. $428 \div 7$ **10.** $2\overline{)408}$ **11.** $568 \div 8$ **12.** $70 \div 4$

13. $2\overline{)509}$ **14.** $639 \div 3$ **15.** $5\overline{)555}$ **16.** $307 \div 4$

Error Search Find each answer that is not correct.
Write it correctly and explain the error.

17. $\dfrac{1}{5}$
      $+\ \dfrac{1}{10}$
      $\overline{\ \ \ \dfrac{3}{10}}$

18.   21
      $\times\ 15$
      $\overline{126}$

19. $\dfrac{123\ \text{R4}}{4\overline{)496}}$

20.   3.76
      $-\ 1.94$
      $\overline{2.22}$

21. $15.32
      $\times\ \ \ \ \ \ 5$
      $\overline{\$76.60}$

Number Sense

Estimating and Reasoning Write whether each
statement is true or false. Explain your answer.

22. The sum of $497 + 435$ is 3 less than 935.

23. The difference of $863 - 281$ is greater than 700.

24. The product of 5 and 8,914 is closer to 40,000 than 45,000.

25. The expression $(12 + 8) \div 4$ equals 5.

26. The quotient of $351 \div 9$ is greater than 40.

27. The product of 7 and 52 is 14 more than 350.

1. Maggie's ping-pong table is 9 feet long and 5 feet wide. Which equation could be used to find the area of the rectangular playing surface of the ping pong table? (15-4)

A $A = 9 \times 5$

B $A = 9 + 5$

C $A = (2 \times 9) + (2 \times 5)$

D $A = 2 \times (9 \times 5)$

2. Each cube has 6 faces. If Tandra stacks 2 cubes on top of each other, she can see 10 faces. If Tandra stacks 7 cubes one on top of the other, how many faces of the cubes will she be able to see? (15-8)

Cubes	2	3	4	5	6	7
Faces	10	14	18			

A 42

B 32

C 30

D 28

3. What is the area of a square with each side 9 inches long? (15-4)

A 81 square inches

B 72 square inches

C 36 square inches

D 18 square inches

4. Which statement is true about the garden plots shown below? (15-6)

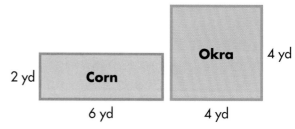

A They both have the same width.

B They both have the same length.

C They both have the same area.

D They both have the same perimeter.

5. Which of the following could be best measured in liters? (15-2)

A How heavy an apple is

B How heavy a feather is

C Water in an eye dropper

D Lemonade in a pitcher

6. A diagram of Izzi's bedroom is shown below. What is the area of her room? (15-5)

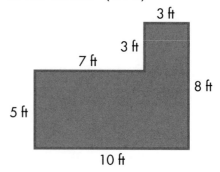

A 44 square feet

B 59 square feet

C 74 square feet

D 80 square feet

7. Howie used 20 feet of edging to design four different gardens. He wants the garden with the greatest area. Which should Howie use? (15-6)

A
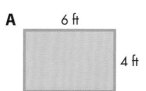
6 ft
4 ft

B
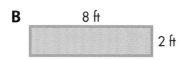
8 ft
2 ft

C
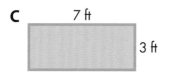
7 ft
3 ft

D
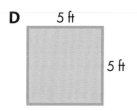
5 ft
5 ft

8. The mouth on the Statue of Liberty is 36 inches wide. How many feet wide is the Statue of Liberty's mouth? (15-1)

A 3 feet

B 4 feet

C 108 feet

D 432 feet

9. Mia's balcony is 4 feet wide and 6 feet long. What is the perimeter? (15-3)

A 10 feet

B 14 feet

C 20 feet

D 24 feet

10. How many grams are in 224 kilograms? (15-2)

A 2,240

B 22,400

C 224,000

D 2,224,000

11. Which unit would best measure the weight of a pair of scissors? (15-1)

A Pounds

B Ounces

C Tons

D Kilograms

12. Mrs. Gee has 24 carpet squares. How should she arrange them so that she has the smallest perimeter? (15-7)

A 12 by 2 rectangle

B 1 by 24 rectangle

C 4 by 6 rectangle

D 8 by 3 rectangle

13. What is the perimeter of the flag? (15-3)

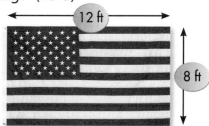
12 ft
8 ft

A 96 feet

B 40 feet

C 28 feet

D 20 feet

Set A, pages 350–352

6 tons = ▢ pounds

To change from a larger unit to a smaller unit, multiply

1 T = 2,000 lb
6 × 2,000 = 12,000

So, 6 tons = 12,000 pounds.

Remember to check if your answers are reasonable using units you already know.

1. 8 T = ▢ lb   **2.** 12 qt = ▢ gal

3. 30 ft = ▢ yd   **4.** 5 ft 8 in. = ▢ in.

Set B, pages 354–356

400 centimeters = ▢ meters

To change from a smaller unit of length to a larger unit, divide.

1 m = 100 cm
400 ÷ 100 = 4

So, 400 centimeters = 4 meters.

Remember when converting metric units, use multiples of ten.

1. 32 kg = ▢ g   **2.** 8 L = ▢ mL

3. 45 cm = ▢ mm   **4.** 20 km = ▢ m

Set C, pages 358–360

Add to find the perimeter of the rectangle.

14 + 14 + 6 + 6 = 40 m

 6 m
14 m

You can use a formula to find the perimeter.

$P = (2 \times \ell) + (2 \times w)$
$P = (2 \times 14) + (2 \times 6)$
$P = 28 + 12 = 40$ m

The perimeter of the rectangle is 40 m.

Remember you can use a formula to find perimeter. Find the perimeter of each figure.

1. 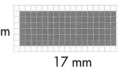 54 mm   **2.** 14 ft

Set D, pages 362–363

You can count square units to find area.

Use a formula to calculate area.

$A = \ell \times w$
$A = 7 \times 6$
$A = 42$

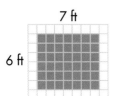
7 ft
6 ft

The area of the rectangle is 42 square feet.

Remember you can draw a diagram to help visualize the problem.

Find the area of each figure.

1.
9 mm
17 mm

2. 16 cm

Set E, pages 364–366

Divide a figure into rectangles to find area.

Rectangle A
$A = 9 \times 6$
$A = 54$

Rectangle B
$A = 4 \times 2$
$A = 8$

$54 + 8 = 62$ square feet

Remember you can count the units to find the area.

Find the area of each figure.

1.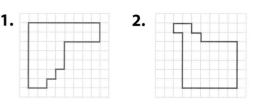

2.

Set F, pages 368–371

Draw a different rectangle with the *same perimeter* as the one shown, and find its area.

8 ft
3 ft

$P = (2 \times \ell) + (2 \times w)$ $A = \ell \times w$
$\quad = (2 \times 8) + (2 \times 3)$ $= 8 \times 3$
$\quad = 16 + 6$ $= 24$ square feet
$\quad = 22$ ft

A 7 ft by 4 ft rectangle has the same perimeter.

7 ft
4 ft

$A = 7 \times 4 = 28$ square feet
$A = 28$ square feet

Remember that two rectangles can have the same area, but different perimeters.

Draw two different rectangles with the perimeter listed. Find the area of each rectangle.

1. $P = 24$ feet

2. $P = 40$ centimeters

Draw two different rectangles with the area listed. Find the perimeter of each rectangle.

3. $A = 64$ square feet

4. $A = 80$ square yards

Set G, pages 372–374

Each side of each triangle is two inches. What is the perimeter of the figure with 5 triangles?

2 in
2 in

The perimeter increases by 2 in.

Number of Triangles	1	2	3	4	5
Perimeter	6 in.	8 in.	10 in.	12 in.	

The perimeter of 5 triangles is 14 inches.

Remember you can break the problem apart and solve.

1. Each side of a square is one inch. If there are 14 squares in a row, what is the perimeter of the figure?

Data and Graphs

1 This long-horned beetle can grow to 7 inches long. How many kinds of beetles are there? You will find out in Lesson 16-2.

2 Emperor penguins cannot fly, but they are great swimmers. How deep can an Emperor penguin dive? You will find out in Lesson 16-4.

3

The Akashi Kaiko Bridge in Japan, shown above, is the longest suspension bridge in the world. How does this bridge compare in length to the Golden Gate Bridge shown below? You will find out in Lesson 16-2.

Review What You Know!

Vocabulary

Choose the best term from the box.

- data
- scale
- survey
- line plot

1. A ? is a series of numbers along the axis of a graph.

2. Collected information is called ?.

3. A ? is a display of data along a number line.

Division

4. 454 ÷ 5

5. 612 ÷ 3

6. 336 ÷ 4

7. 625 ÷ 5

8. 387 ÷ 3

9. 878 ÷ 7

Interpreting Data

Use the bar graph. How much higher is

10. Peak 1 than Peak 3?

11. Peak 3 than Peak 4?

12. **Writing to Explain** Why is this statement incorrect? The heights of Peak 2 and Peak 4 have the greatest difference.

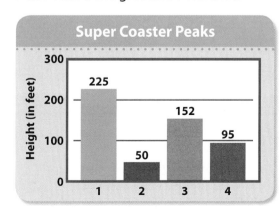

Super Coaster Peaks

Data from Surveys

How do you take a survey and record the results?

Pizza Plus took a survey to decide which high school team they should sponsor.

In a survey, information is collected by asking different people the same question and recording their answers.

SDAP 1.1 Formulate survey questions; systematically collect and represent data on a number line; and coordinate graphs, tables, and charts. Also SDAP 1.0.

Please Take One

Which of these high school sports teams do you think Pizza Plus should sponsor?

❏ Football

❏ Baseball

❏ Basketball

Guided Practice*

Do you know HOW?

For **1** through **3**, use the tally chart below.

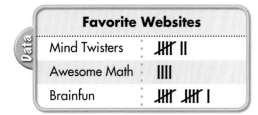

Favorite Websites	
Mind Twisters	ЖЖ II
Awesome Math	IIII
Brainfun	ЖЖ ЖЖ I

1. How many people were surveyed?

2. How many people in the survey liked the Awesome Math website best?

3. Which website was the favorite of more people than any other?

Do you UNDERSTAND?

4. In the survey at the top, do you know whether people thought Pizza Plus should sponsor the soccer team? Why or why not?

5. What question do you think was asked for the survey below?

High School Games Attended Last Year	
Football	12
Basketball	5
Soccer	14
Baseball	8

Independent Practice

For **6** through **8**, use the table at the right.

6. How many people liked using a pencil the best?

7. How many people were surveyed?

8. Which type of project was the favorite of more people than any other?

Favorite Type of Drawing Project	
Pencil	7
Ink	7
Paint	9
Charcoal	4

*For another example, see Set A on page 398.

Step 1

Write a survey question.

"Which of these high school sports teams do you think Pizza Plus should sponsor: football, baseball, or basketball?"

Step 2

Make a tally chart and record the data.

Count the tallies and record the results.

Team to Sponsor

Data		
Football	JHT JHT III	13
Basketball	JHT III	8
Baseball	JHT JHT I	11

Step 3

Explain the results of the survey.

Football was chosen by the most people. So, Pizza Plus should sponsor the football team.

Problem Solving

For **9** through **12**, use the tally chart at the right.

9. How many of the people surveyed have pet fish?

10. Which type of pet was owned by the most people?

11. Reasoning Can you tell how many people were surveyed? Why or why not?

12. Reasoning Can you tell how many of the people surveyed have no pets? Why or why not?

Pets Owned

Data	
Dog	JHT JHT
Cat	JHT IIII
Fish	JHT III
Hamster	III
Snake	III

13. Elisa bought a camera for $29.50 and 2 rolls of film for $3.50 each. How much did Elisa spend in all?

For **14** and **15**, use the table at the right.

14. What was the total count for each type of show?

15. How many people were surveyed?

Favorite Type of TV Show

Data	
Action	4
Animated	3
Comedy	8
Sports	5

16. **Think About the Process** At a barbeque, 8 out of 10 people ate hot dogs and 4 out of 5 people ate hamburgers. Which number sentence shows that the same fraction of people ate hot dogs and hamburgers?

A $10 - 8 = (5 - 4) + 1$

B $10 + 8 = 2 \times (5 + 4)$

C $\frac{10}{8} = \frac{5}{4}$

D $\frac{8}{10} = \frac{4}{5}$

SDAP 1.3 Interpret one-and two-variable data graphs to answer questions about a situation. Also SDAP 1.0.

Interpreting Graphs

How can you read a bar graph?

A bar graph uses bars to show data.

About how many more species of animals are in the Minnesota Zoo than the Phoenix Zoo?

The scale consists of numbers that show the units used on a graph.

The interval is the amount between tick marks on the scale.

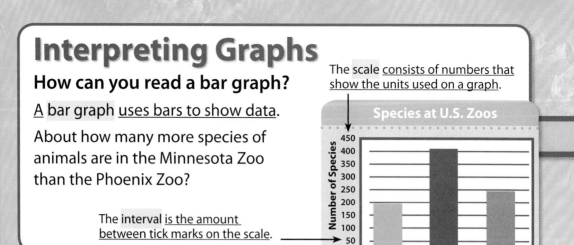

Species at U.S. Zoos

Guided Practice*

Do you know HOW?

For **1** and **2**, use the bar graph below.

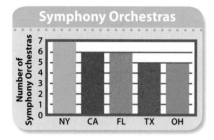

Symphony Orchestras

1. Which state shown on the graph has the most symphony orchestras?

2. Which state has the same number of symphony orchestras as Texas?

Do you UNDERSTAND?

3. What is the interval of the scale for the bar graph above?

4. The Miami Metro Zoo has 300 species of animals. Which zoos have a fewer number of species than the Miami Metro Zoo?

5. **Writing to Explain** Explain how you find the difference between the number of species at the San Francisco Zoo and the Phoenix Zoo.

Independent Practice

For **6** through **8**, use the bar graph at the right.

6. About how much longer does a lion live than a giraffe?

7. Which animals have the same average lifespan?

8. The average lifespan of a gorilla is 20 years. How would you change the graph to add a bar for gorillas?

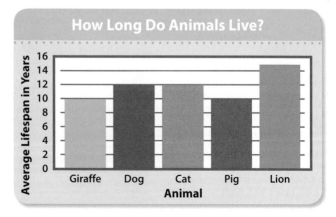

How Long Do Animals Live?

For another example, see Set B on page 398.

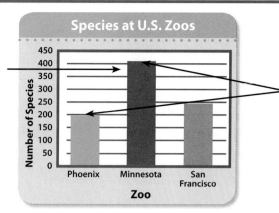

Species at U.S. Zoos

The purple bar is just above the number 400. The Minnesota Zoo has about 400 species of animals.

Skip count by 50s from the top of the green bar (Phoenix Zoo) until you are even with the top of the purple bar (Minnesota Zoo). Count: 50, 100.

The Minnesota Zoo has about 200 more species than the Phoenix Zoo.

Problem Solving

For **9** through **12**, use the graph at the right.

9. Describe the scale of the graph. **The scale goes from 5,000 feet to 15,000 feet.**

10. What impression does the graph give? **See margin.**

11. **Reasoning** Why is the graph misleading? **See margin.**

12. The Akashi-Kaikyo Bridge is almost 4,000 feet longer than the Golden Gate Bridge. Which bridge shown in the graph is about half the length of the Akashi-Kaikyo Bridge? **Brooklyn Bridge**

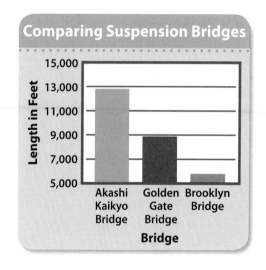

For **13** through **15**, use the graph at the right.

13. There are over 350,000 species of beetles. How does this compare to the number of species shown for moths and butterflies? **See margin.**

14. Which two insects have about the same number of species? **Flies & Wasps and Bees**

15. **Reasoning** How is the graph misleading? **See margin.**

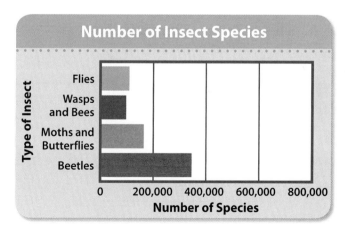

Lesson

16-3

SDAP 1.2 Identify
the mode(s) for sets of
categorical data and the
mode(s), median, and
any apparent outliers
for numerical data sets.
Also **SDAP 1.0**, and
SDAP 1.1.

Line Plots

How can you organize data using a line plot?

A line plot <u>shows data along a number line</u>. Each X represents one number in the data set. An outlier <u>is any number that is very different than the rest of the numbers</u>.

The table below shows the average life spans of certain animals in years. Make a line plot to organize the data.

Average Animal Life Span (years)						
Dog	Cat	Cow	Pig	Lion	Deer	Black Bear
12	12	15	13	13	10	32

Average
Life Span:
32 years

Guided Practice*

Do you know HOW?

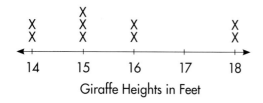

Giraffe Heights in Feet

1. How many giraffes are 14 feet tall?

2. What is the most common height of the giraffes?

3. How tall is the tallest giraffe on the line plot?

4. Is the number 18 an outlier?

Do you UNDERSTAND?

5. Which animals listed above have a life span of 13 years?

6. Writing to Explain How do you know that the life span of the bear is an outlier by looking at the line plot?

7. A kangaroo has an average life span of 7 years. If you included this information on the line plot above how would it affect the line plot?

Independent Practice

For **8** through **13**, draw a line plot for each data set and identify any outliers.

8. 6,9,3,11,26

9. 13, 16, 18, 3, 25

10. 18, 17, 11, 15, 29, 14, 16

11. 15,16, 2, 31,12

12. 17, 17, 16, 18, 21

13. 25, 28, 22, 24, 27, 28, 21

DIGITAL
Animated Glossary
www.pearsonsuccessnet.com

For another example, see Set C on page 398.

Read the line plot.

The most Xs are above 12 and 13, so the most common life spans of the animals in the table are 12 years and 13 years.

The greatest life span shown is 32 years and the shortest lifespan shown is 10 years.

Identify any outliers.

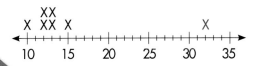

The number 32 is far away from the rest of the numbers on the line plot.

The life span of the black bear, 32 years, is an outlier.

Problem Solving

For **14** through **16**, use the data to the right.

14. Trisha's swimming coach recorded the time it took her to swim a lap last week. Make a line plot of Trisha's lap times.

15. Which day is an outlier in the data?

16. If you made a line plot of Trisha's time using 0 and 5 minutes as the boundaries, would the outlier be more or less obvious than if the boundaries of your line plot were 50 and 75 seconds? Explain.

Data

Day	Time
Monday	55 seconds
Tuesday	57 seconds
Wednesday	51 seconds
Thursday	72 seconds
Friday	51 seconds

17. Algebra A sheet of coupons is set in an array with 6 coupons in 12 rows per sheet. How many coupons are there on 100 sheets?

18. Writing to Explain Bob listed the weights of his friends (in pounds). They were 87, 93, 89, 61, and 93. Bob said there were no outliers. Is Bob correct?

19. Six friends shared some CDs. Each friend received 3 CDs. How many CDs were there in all?

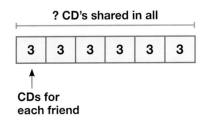

20. Henry and some friends went to play miniature golf. Their scores are shown below. Make a line plot of their scores.

51, 70, 52, 51, 48, 54, 55, 52, 52

Mean

How can you find the mean?

SDAP 1.1 Grade 5
Know the concepts of
mean, median, and mode;
compute and compare
sample examples to show
that they may differ.
Also **SDAP 1.0.**

Finding the mean of a set of data tells what is typical of the numbers in the set. The mean, or average, is found by adding all the numbers in a set and dividing by the number of values.

Kara's quiz scores were 7, 7, and 10. What was her average quiz score?

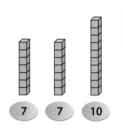

7   7   10

Guided Practice*

Do you know HOW?

In **1** through **6**, find the mean of each group of numbers.

1. 2, 6, 19   **2.** 13, 24, 15, 28, 25

3. 64, 72, 56   **4.** 8, 7, 20, 145

5. 3, 5, 30, 38   **6.** 20, 58, 190, 84

Do you UNDERSTAND?

7. Writing to Explain Why do you need to divide by 4 to find Kara's average test score?

8. Juan's bowling scores were 88, 96, and 113. What is his mean score?

Independent Practice

Leveled Practice For **9** through **27**, find the mean.

9. Add: $3 + 2 + 16 =$ ▨
Divide: ▨ $\div 3 =$ ▨

10. Add: $1 + 5 + 2 + 4 =$ ▨
Divide: ▨ $\div 4 =$ ▨

11. Add: $56 + 32 + 62 =$ ▨
Divide: ▨ $\div 3 =$ ▨

12. 80, 248, 68   **13.** 15, 38, 25, 22   **14.** 35, 45, 75, 85   **15.** 16, 25, 86, 45

16. 2, 2, 16, 16   **17.** 1, 3, 5, 2, 4   **18.** 56, 72, 84, 68   **19.** 80, 248, 68

20. 15, 38, 25, 22   **21.** 35, 45, 75, 85   **22.** 87, 33, 123   **23.** 52, 19, 71, 26

24. 12, 112, 221   **25.** 8, 21, 28   **26.** 1, 1, 106   **27.** 102, 123, 9, 358

DIGITAL
Animated Glossary
www.pearsonsuccessnet.com

For another example, see Set D on page 399.

To find the average, the items are combined and then divided equally.

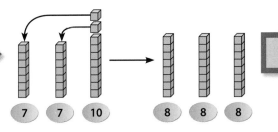

| 7 | 7 | 10 | | 8 | 8 | 8 |

Kara's average quiz score is 8.

Kara's test scores were 82, 76, 94, and 88.

Add the scores.

```
  2
  82
  76
  94
+ 88
 340
```

Divide the sum by the number of addends.

```
    85
 4)340
  -32
    20
  - 20
     0
```

Kara's average test score is 85.

Problem Solving

28. Number Sense The mean of 16, 16, and 16 is 16. The mean of 15, 16, and 17 is also 16. Find 3 other sets of numbers that have the mean of 16.

29. Algebra What number goes in the box to make this number sentence true?
$(8 - 2) \times 4 = 6 \times$ ▢

30. Geometry Use geometric terms to describe one common characteristic of the shapes in each group.

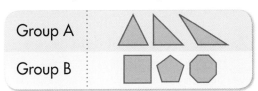

Group A

Group B

31. Reasoning Jacob worked 5 hours on Thursday, 4 hours on Friday, and 6 hours on Saturday. The number of hours he worked on Sunday did not change the mean. How many hours did Jacob work on Sunday?

Use the chart at the right for **32** through **34**.

32. Estimate how deep an Emperor Penguin dives in yards?

Tip *Remember 1 yard = 3 feet.*

33. How many fewer feet does a Peruvian Petrel dive than a Thick-billed Murre?

34. Find the mean of the dives as listed in the table.

Deepest Dives of Birds in Feet	
Emperor Penguin	1,772 ft
Thick-billed Murre	689 ft
Peruvian Petrel	272 ft

Data

35. Which of these is the number six million, sixteen thousand, one hundred six?

A 6,160,106   **B** 6,106,106   **C** 6,016,106   **D** 6,016,160

Median, Mode, and Range

How do you find and use median, mode, and range?

The median is the middle number when the numbers in a data set are listed in order. The mode is the number or numbers that occur most often in the data. The range is the difference between the greatest and the least number in the data set.

What is the median, mode, and range for the heights in inches of a group of fourth graders listed below?

Height (in inches)
57, 55, 50, 52, 51, 56, 55

Data

Guided Practice*

Do you know HOW?

In **1** through **4**, find the median, mode, and range of each set of data.

1. 41, 15, 51, 51, 41

2. 36, 54, 43, 43, 67, 43, 39, 66

3. 11, 67, 34, 14, 42, 12, 34, 62, 33, 57

4. 42, 62, 54, 50, 62, 60, 48

Do you UNDERSTAND?

5. In the example above, how many numbers are less than the median? How many numbers are greater than the median?

6. **Writing to Explain** Can a group of numbers have more than 1 mode?

7. Does every set of data have a mode? Explain.

Independent Practice

In **8** through **16**, find the median, mode, and range of each set of data.

8. 58, 54, 62, 58, 60

9. 8, 9, 8, 10, 13, 3, 15, 15, 8, 13, 14

10. 23, 46, 52, 41, 41, 52, 66

11. 42, 13, 41, 41, 57, 52, 36

12. 6, 4, 12, 12, 5, 7, 8

13. 31, 63, 24, 15, 15, 26, 53

14. 56, 76, 66, 86, 59

15. 43, 64, 24, 14, 32, 47, 63, 63, 79

16. 49, 19, 45, 45, 48, 21, 19

DIGITAL

Animated Glossary
www.pearsonsuccessnet.com

*For another example, see Set E on page 399.

<table>
<tr>
<td>

Find the median.

List the data in order from least to greatest, and find the middle number.

50, 51, 52, 55, 55, 56, 57

The median is 55.

</td>
<td>

Find the mode.

Find the number or numbers that occur most often.

50, 51, 52, 55, 55, 56, 57

The mode is 55.

</td>
<td>

Find the range.

Subtract the greatest value minus the least value.

50, 51, 52, 55, 55, 56, 57

$57 - 50 = 7$
The range is 7.

</td>
</tr>
</table>

Problem Solving

17. Geometry The perimeter of a triangle is $\frac{5}{6}$ inches. Two sides are $\frac{1}{8}$ inch each. What is the length of the third side?

18. Reasoning Liz said that the mode of the set of data below is 6. Is Liz correct? Explain.

2, 4, 6, 4, 4, 6, 6

19. Geometry If side A of a rectangle is 12.87 cm, and side B is 4.89 cm what is the perimeter of the rectangle?

20. Writing to Explain Could 23 be the median of 6, 8, 23, 4, and 5? Explain.

For **21** through **23**, use the chart to the right. Each X represents how much a person bought at the bake sale.

21. How many people bought 2 items?

22. What is the mode of the data.

23. How many people bought 3 or more items?

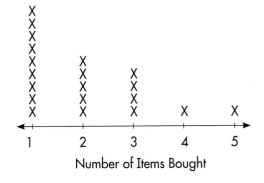

24. What division sentence do the beads to the right model?

   A $24 \div 6 = 4$

   B $24 \div 8 = 3$

   C $29 \div 5 = 5\,R\,4$

   D $28 \div 4 = 4\,R5$

MR 2.3 Use a variety of methods, such as words, numbers, symbols, charts, graphs, tables, diagrams, and models, to explain mathematical reasoning. Also SDAP 1.3.

Problem Solving

Make a Graph

Students in two fourth-grade classes completed a survey about their favorite hobbies. How were the two classes similar? How were they different?

Data

Mr. Foster's Class	
Favorite Hobby	**Tally**
Swimming	卌 卌 卌
Cycling	卌 卌
Art	卌

Data

Mrs. Lopez's Class	
Favorite Hobby	**Tally**
Swimming	卌 卌 I
Cycling	卌 卌 III
Art	卌

Guided Practice*

Do you know HOW?

Solve. Make a graph.

1. Jo recorded the number of snowy days for three months in a tally chart. Make a bar graph using this data. Which month had the most snowy days?

Data

Month	Tally Snowy Days	Number
December	卌	5
January	卌 卌 I	11
February	卌 III	8

Do you UNDERSTAND?

2. How could you make different bar graphs to display the same data from the tally charts above?

3. Suppose you added the numbers from both classes to make one data table. Which hobby was most popular overall?

4. **Write a Problem** Write a problem that uses the data charts above. Then answer your question.

Independent Practice

For **5** and **6**, use the table below.

Data

	Morning	Afternoon	Evening
Cars	142	263	120
Trucks	42	181	64

5. Make two graphs of this data, one for cars and one for trucks.

6. Why is it useful to use the same scale for both graphs?

Stuck? Try this....

- What do I know?
- What diagram can I use to help understand the problem?
- Can I use addition, subtraction, multiplication, or division?
- Is all of my work correct?
- Did I answer the right question?
- Is my answer reasonable?

*For another example, see Set F on page 399.

Make a bar graph for each data chart.

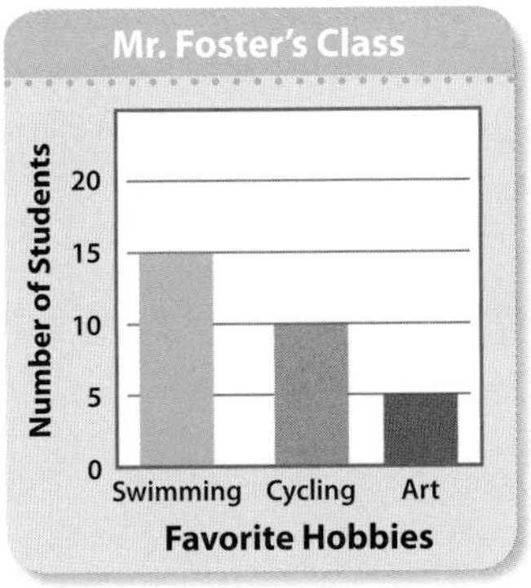

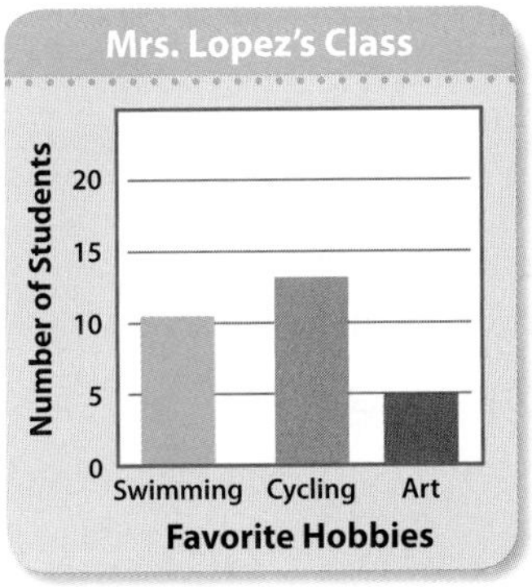

Mr. Foster's Class

Number of Students
20
15
10
5
0

Swimming Cycling Art
Favorite Hobbies

Mrs. Lopez's Class

Number of Students
20
15
10
5
0

Swimming Cycling Art
Favorite Hobbies

Read the graphs.
Make comparisons.

How are they similar:

Art was the least popular hobby in both classes, and the same number of students in each class liked art.

How are they different:

Swimming was the favorite hobby in Mr. Foster's class, and cycling was the favorite hobby in Mrs. Lopez's class.

For **7** through **10**, use the tally chart below.

Data

Activity	2008	2009
Newspaper	卌 卌	卌 卌
Dance Troupe	卌	卌 I
Book Club	卌	卌
Marching Band	IIII	卌 I

7. The fourth grade students chose which of four activities they wanted to join. Make a bar graph for 2008 and another bar graph for 2009.

8. If 3 people in 2009 left the book club to join the dance troupe, which club would have the most students?

9. Identify two clubs in 2009 that together were chosen by more than half of the fourth grade students.

10. How many more students joined a club in 2009 than in 2008?

For **11** through **13**, use the table to the right.

11. Who rode 15 miles less than Sherry in Week 1?

12. Which person biked fewer miles in Week 2 than in Week 1?

Data

Name	Week 1	Week 2
Peter	17 miles	26 miles
Sherry	25 miles	29 miles
Jorgé	22 miles	20 miles
Carla	10 miles	20 miles

13. Reasoning Use the table to compare the total miles ridden in Week 1 to the total miles ridden in Week 2. Which was greater?

For **14** and **15**, use the diagram to the right.

14. Stella picks one marble from Bag 1. How many possible outcomes are there?

15. **Writing to Explain** How many marbles will Stella have to take from Bag 3 to guarantee she will draw a blue marble?

For **16** and **17**, use the table at the right.

16. Marcia recorded the number of sit-ups and push-ups she did last week. Make two graphs using the data in the table.

17. Compare the number of sit-ups each day to the number of push-ups. What pattern do you notice? What can you conclude?

Marcia's Sit-ups and Push-ups		
Day	Sit-ups	Push-ups
Monday	25	12
Tuesday	21	16
Thursday	55	24
Friday	32	12
Sunday	68	28

For **18** and **19**, use the diagram at the right.

18. Ms. Michael planted the flowers in her garden in an array. After she fills in the fifth row, how many flowers will her garden have?

19. If Ms. Michael continues to plant using the same pattern of colors, what will be the colors of the next three flowers that she plants?

Think About the Process

20. There are 14 park benches in the park. Each bench holds 4 people. Which number sentence shows the greatest number of people who can sit on park benches at one time?

A $14 \times 4 =$ ▢

B $14 + 4 =$ ▢

C $14 \times 14 =$ ▢

D $4 \times 4 =$ ▢

21. Hanna walked to and from school on Monday, Wednesday, and Friday. What information is needed to find how far she walked?

A The distance from home to school

B Who she walked with

C The number of streets she crossed

D The time school starts

Find the difference. Estimate to check
if the answer is reasonable.

1. 54.3 − 0.28   **2.** 14.8 − 3.76   **3.** 15.23 − 3.17

4. 25.78 − 9.8   **5.** 18.1 − 3.45   **6.** 12.7 − 3.81

Find the product. Estimate to check if the answer is reasonable.

7.	23,418	**8.**	6,223	**9.**	33,478	**10.**	406	**11.**	4,000
×	5	×	2	×	5	×	36	×	12

Find the sum. Estimate to check if the answer is reasonable.

12.	12,345	**13.**	4,402	**14.**	403	**15.**	5,474	**16.**	13,985
+	87,654	+	3,912	+	737	+	723	+	7,539

Error Search Find each answer that is not correct.
Write it correctly and explain the error.

17. 33.90
   + 25.76
   —————
    58.66

18. 34,890
   ×   8
   —————
  279,120

19. $1.05
   2)$2.10

20. $\frac{5}{6}$
   − $\frac{1}{4}$
   —————
    $\frac{4}{2}$

21. 5,007
   ×   35
   —————
  175,215

Number Sense

Estimating and Reasoning Write whether each statement is true or false.
Explain your answer.

22. The product of 3 and $5.87 is greater than $18.

23. The sum of 59,703 and 24,032 is greater than 70,000,
but less than 90,000.

24. The difference of 466 − 103 is 3 less than 366.

25. The product of 21 and 4,076 is greater than 80,000.

26. The quotient of 534 ÷ 6 is greater than 90.

27. The sum of 11.35 and 5.2 is less than 16.

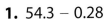

1. Which subject was the favorite of more students than any other? (16-1)

Favorite Books

Social Studies	JHT II
Math	JHT IIII
Language Arts	II
Science	JHT

A Social Studies

B Math

C Language Arts

D Science

2. Each student picked an individual activity during Fun Day.

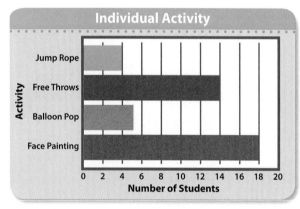

How many more students chose face painting than free throws? (16-2)

A 4

B 6

C 14

D 18

3. What is the median for this set of data? (16-5)

60, 10, 55, 60, 45, 50, 60

A 40

B 50

C 55

D 60

4. Mrs. Chi made a bar graph of the number of books students read over summer break.

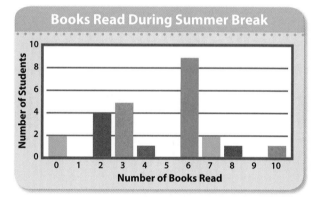

How many students read fewer than 3 books during summer break? (16-2)

A 4

B 5

C 6

D 11

5. What is the range for this set of data? (16-5)

12, 10, 48, 64, 36, 48, 12, 32, 48

A 10

B 36

C 48

D 54

6. As part of a class fundraiser, students received money for each lap they ran around the school's parking lot.

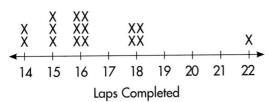

Laps Completed

What is the outlier in this set of data? (16-3)

A 8

B 16

C 22

D There is no outlier in this data set.

7. Mr. Romanoski went on a 9 day business trip. The miles he drove each day are listed below. What is the mode for the miles he drove? (16-5)

45, 53, 19, 45, 47, 52, 53, 45, 51

A 34

B 45

C 53

D 45 and 53

8. Peter and his friends bowled one game. Their scores were 83, 76, 89, 91, and 76. What was the range of their scores? (16-5)

A 15

B 69

C 76

D 89

9. The graphs below show the number of times an answer choice was used on two different tests. Which conclusion can be made? (16-6)

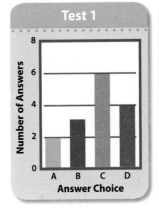
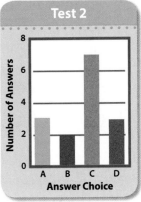

A Answer C was used most often in both tests.

B Answer B was used the least in both tests.

C Answer D was used the same number of times in both tests.

D No conclusions can be made.

10. Jared's scores on his last four math assignments are listed below. What was his mean score? (16-4)

82, 76, 82, and 100

A 24

B 79

C 82

D 85

Set A, pages 382–383

How many people in the survey liked to watch the rings?

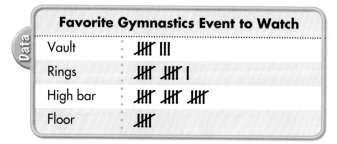

Favorite Gymnastics Event to Watch	
Vault	JHT III
Rings	JHT JHT I
High bar	JHT JHT JHT
Floor	JHT

Eleven people liked to watch the rings best.

Remember that you can answer a question by taking a survey.

1. How many people in the survey liked to watch the vault best?

2. Which event was named by more people than any other event?

3. Can you tell from the survey whether people liked to watch the uneven bars? Explain.

Set B, pages 384–385

Which animal has about 34 teeth?

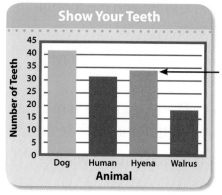

The bar that is just below the line for 35 is the one for hyenas.

Hyenas have about 34 teeth.

Remember that looking at the scale can help you interpret the data.

1. What is the graph about?

2. What is the scale of the graph? What is the interval?

3. Which animal has 32 teeth?

4. About how many more teeth does a dog have than a human?

Set C, pages 386–387

The data set shows the number of goals scored by each team in a soccer tournament:

4, 8, 7, 0, 3, 3, 7, 4, 6, 1, 2, 7, 6, 4, 2, 7, 2, 6, 7, 4

Draw a line plot for the data.

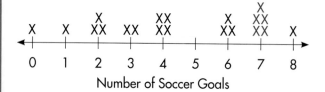

The most common number of goals scored is **7.** There are no outliers.

Remember that an outlier is a number that is very different from the rest of the numbers in a line plot.

1. How many soccer teams scored 3 goals?

2. How many teams scored more than 5 goals?

3. What was the most goals scored by a team?

4. How many teams scored only 2 goals?

Set D, pages 388–389

What is the mean of 77, 95, 78 and 86?

Add the numbers in the set

```
  3
  77
  95
  78
+ 86
 336
```

Divide the sum by the number of addends.

```
    84
4)336
  -32
   16
 - 16
    0
```

The mean of the set is 84.

Remember that the mean is found by adding all the numbers in a set first.

Find the mean of each group of numbers.

1. 5, 8, 17   **2.** 18, 19, 14, 29, 35

3. 68, 73, 51   **4.** 6, 2, 22, 146

5. 10, 10, 30, 34 **6.** 28, 52, 195, 89

Set E, pages 390–391

What is the median, mode, and range of this set of numbers?

12, 4, 8, 3, 26, 8, 17, 6, 12, 7, 5, 23

The median is the middle number when the data is ordered.

3, 4, 5, 6, 7, 8, 8, 12, 12, 17, 23, 26

The median is 8.

The mode is the number or numbers that occur most often. The mode is 8 and 12.

The range is the greatest value minus the least value.

26 – 3 = 23. The range is 23.

Remember there can be more than one mode.

Find the median, mode, and range of each set of data.

1. 1, 3, 10, 8, 7, 3, 11

2. 48, 50, 62, 50, 54

3. 92, 99, 100, 99, 106, 99, 97

4. 80, 85, 87, 80, 89

Set F, pages 392–394

How can you use a bar graph to find which team is in second place in the standings?

Volleyball Wins	
Hawks	10
Lions	14
Falcons	12
Bears	7

Choose a scale. Choose an interval. Make a bar for each team. Label the axes and give the graph a title.

The Falcons are in second place.

Remember to use a scale that starts at 0 and goes beyond the highest number in the data when you draw a bar graph.

1. How can you check whether the bars on the graph are correctly drawn?

2. What is the interval of the graph?

3. Which team came in third place?

Length and Coordinates

1

Where was the world's largest American flag displayed? You will find out in Lesson 17-1.

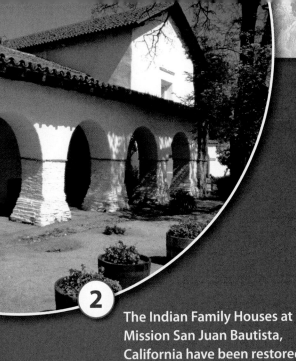

Review What You Know!

2

The Indian Family Houses at Mission San Juan Bautista, California have been restored. How many rooms did these houses have? You will find out in Lesson 17–2.

3

The Empire State Building is a famous landmark in New York City. Where is this landmark located? You will find out in Lesson 17-3.

Vocabulary

Choose the best term from the box.

> • area   • perimeter
> • foot   • meter

1. A __?__ is the customary unit of length equal to 12 inches.

2. The distance around a figure is its __?__.

3. A metric unit of length is the __?__.

4. The number of square units needed to cover a region is the __?__.

Perimeter

Find the perimeter of each polygon.

5. 2 in. 2 in. 2 in.

6. 3 ft 1 ft 1 ft 3 ft

7. 1 m 1 m 2 m 2 m 1 m 3 m

8. 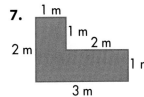 1 cm 1 cm 1 cm 1 cm 1 cm

Addition and Subtraction Facts

Write a subtraction fact for each addition fact.

9. $8 + 8 = 16$

10. $4 + 7 = 11$

11. $6 + 6 = 12$

12. $9 + 5 = 14$

13. **Writing to Explain** Explain how you could subtract $146 - 51$ using mental math.

Lesson
17-1

MG 2.0 ⚷ Use two-
dimensional coordinate
grids to represent points
and graph lines and
simple figures.

Ordered Pairs

How do you name a point located on a coordinate grid?

A coordinate grid <u>is used to show ordered pairs</u>. An ordered pair is <u>a pair of numbers that name a point on a coordinate grid</u>. Where is point *D* located on the grid?

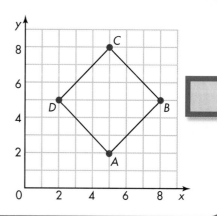

Guided Practice*

Do you know HOW?

For **1** through **6**, write the ordered pair, or name the point.

1. *C*   2. *E*

3. *D*   4. (4, 1)

5. (3, 4) 6. (0, 3)

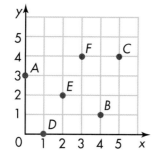

Do you UNDERSTAND?

7. **Writing to Explain** Without plotting the points, how can you tell that a point at (12, 6) is to the right of a point at (10, 6)?

8. In the example above, which point is at (5, 8)?

9. The coordinates for point *M* are (8, 3). Does point *M* lie inside or outside of the diamond above?

Independent Practice

For **10** through **18**, write the ordered pair for each point.

10. *I*   11. *J*   12. *K*

13. *L*   14. *M*   15. *N*

16. *O*   17. *P*   18. *Q*

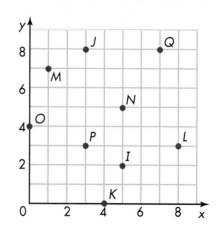

Animated Glossary
www.pearsonsuccessnet.com

For another example, see Set A on page 414.

A location on a coordinate grid is named by an ordered pair (x, y) of numbers.

The x-coordinate, <u>or the first number, tells how many units to move to the right</u>.

The y-coordinate, <u>or second number, tells how many units to move up</u>.

Point D is located at (2, 5).

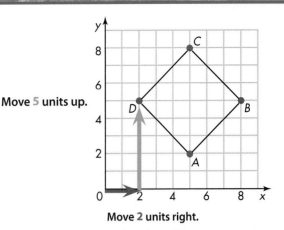

Move **5** units up.

Move **2** units right.

For **19** through **26**, name the point for each ordered pair.

19. (4, 4)　　**20.** (1, 3)　　**21.** (4, 1)　　**22.** (3, 6)

23. (2, 7)　　**24.** (6, 2)　　**25.** (6, 7)　　**26.** (0, 5)

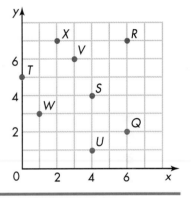

Problem Solving

27. Joanne, Terry, and Shira drank 2 liters of lemonade in all. How many liters did Terry drink if all three drank equal amounts of lemonade?

28. Place these ordered points on a graph: (2, 4), (2, 6), and (2, 8). What do you notice about these points?

29. Bernice ran a 26-mile marathon in 4 hours. In the first two hours, she ran 7 miles each hour. If she also ran equal distances in the third and fourth hours, how many miles did she run in the fourth hour?

30. Geometry A square measures 8 inches by 8 inches. A rectangle measures 4 inches by 16 inches. Both figures have the same area, 64 square inches. Which figure has a greater perimeter?

31. Geometry The largest United States flag ever created was displayed at the Hoover Dam. The flag measures 255 feet by 505 feet. How many feet wider is the flag than it is long?

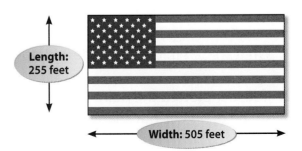

Length: 255 feet

Width: 505 feet

17-2

MG 2.0 ⟶ Use two-dimensional coordinate grids to represent points and graph lines and simple figures.

Shapes on Coordinate Grids

Hands-On grid paper

How can you use a coordinate grid to draw shapes?

Naomi is making a banner for the baseball team. She uses ordered pairs in the table at the right to draw the shape. What is the shape of the banner?

x	y
2	3
2	7
8	3
8	7

Another Example How can you draw shapes on a coordinate grid?

Jasper is making cut-out shapes. He uses the ordered pairs in the table. What shape is he making?

x	y
3	3
9	3
3	7

Step 1

Plot the ordered pairs on the coordinate grid.

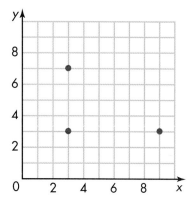

Step 2

Draw a line to connect the ordered pairs.

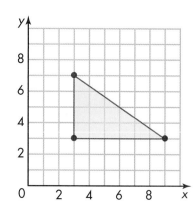

The shape is a triangle.

Explain It

1. What shapes might be made with four ordered pairs?

2. If Jasper plotted the point (5, 3), would that change the shape of his cut-out shape?

Plot each set of ordered pairs on a coordinate grid.

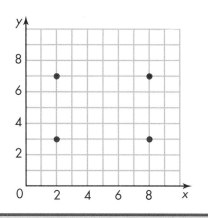

Draw a line to connect the ordered pairs.

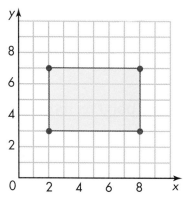

The shape of the banner is a rectangle.

Guided Practice*

Do you know HOW?

For **1** and **2**, plot each set of ordered pairs on a coordinate grid. Name the shape.

1. (2, 3), (6, 3), (6, 8)

2. (8, 5), (8, 0), (3, 0), (3, 5)

Do you UNDERSTAND?

3. **Writing to Explain** If you are given four ordered pairs, is it possible that the shape is a triangle?

4. In the example above, what do you know about the points (2, 3) and (8, 3)?

Independent Practice

For **5** through **10**, plot each ordered pair on a coordinate grid. Use grid paper to help.

5. (3, 6)

6. (7, 2)

7. (0, 4)

8. (5, 3)

9. (1, 8)

10. (9, 12)

For **11** through **13**, use the coordinate grid to the right.

11. If you connect the points, what is the shape of *ABCD*?

12. What shape do you make if you connect the points *MNOP*?

13. How are the points (9, 3), (9, 8), and (9, 14) alike?

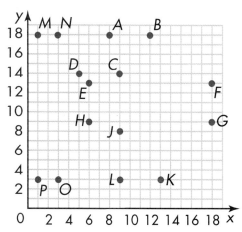

Animated Glossary, eTools
www.pearsonsuccessnet.com

For **14** and **15**, use the coordinate grid at the right.

14. Abe used the coordinate grid to make a diagram for a kite. What is the shape of his kite?

15. Name the point on the kite that is on line *AB* and line *CD*?

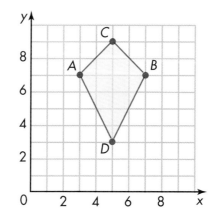

16. Marge is using software to design a tree house. In the program, she inputs these points to draw a window: (2, 3), (6, 3), and (1, 7), and (7, 7).

   a What is the shape of the window?

   b Marge decides to add another point to her design. What shape does she make if she plots the point (4, 9) to her design?

For **17** and **18**, use the diagram at the right.

17. The map shows two family houses at Mission San Juan Bautista. The larger house had 22 rooms, and the smaller house had 11 rooms. How long was the smaller house?

18. How many more rooms are in the larger house than in the smaller house?

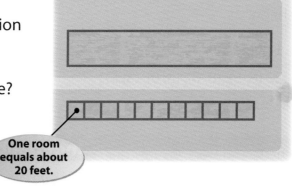

One room equals about 20 feet.

19. Geometry Fred says that an octagon must have a greater perimeter than a pentagon because it has more sides. Do you agree or disagree? Explain.

20. Algebra On a car trip, the Smith family car can go 350 miles on a full tank of gas. How many miles can the car go on *n* tanks of gas?

21. With your pencil, start at (1, 1). Then, move up 4 units. Move three units right. Then, move 4 units down. Finally, move 3 units left. What shape have you made?

   A Triangle   **C** Rectangle

   B Square   **D** Pentagon

22. **Think About the Process** Wally bought 3 greeting cards that were the same price. He spent $18. Which expression shows how to find the cost of each card?

   A 18 ÷ 3   **C** 18 + 3

   B 18 × 3   **D** 18 − 3

Find the quotient. Estimate to check if the answer is reasonable.

1. $2\overline{)947}$ **2.** $6\overline{)478}$ **3.** $303 \div 3$ **4.** $112 \div 5$

5. $4\overline{)506}$ **6.** $612 \div 6$ **7.** $5\overline{)441}$ **8.** $83 \div 9$

9. $56 \div 6$ **10.** $555 \div 8$ **11.** $2\overline{)37}$ **12.** $536 \div 7$

Find the difference. Estimate to check if the answer is reasonable.

13. 5,810
   − 389

14. 4,087
   − 496

15. 381
   − 126

16. 214
   − 65

17. 2,000
   − 1,325

18. 3,847
   − 829

19. 424
   − 397

20. 4,040
   − 2,546

21. 4,830
   − 2,968

22. 4,321
   − 1,234

Error Search Find each answer that is not correct. Write it correctly and explain the error.

23. $\dfrac{1}{3}$
   $+ \dfrac{7}{12}$
   $\overline{\dfrac{11}{12}}$

24. 16,840
   × 6
   101,046

25. $4\overline{)569}$ = 141 R5

26. 45.76
   + 12.78
   58.54

27. 20,000
   × 5
   10,000

Number Sense

Estimating and Reasoning Write whether each statement is true or false. Explain your answer.

28. The difference of 3,289 − 1,199 is less than 1,000.

29. The *r* in the equation $4 + r = 9$ is equal to 13.

30. The expression $(4 + 20) \times 2 \div (4 \times 2)$ is 24.

31. The difference of 34.07 and 9.93 is closer to 24 than 25.

MG 2.2 ⊶
Understand that the length of a horizontal line segment equals the difference of the x–coordinates.

MG 2.3 ⊶
Understand that the length of a vertical line segment equals the difference of the y–coordinates.

Lengths of Horizontal and Vertical Line Segments

Hands-On
grid paper

How can you calculate the length of a horizontal or vertical line segment?

You can use ordered pairs to find length or distance. The x-value tells distance to the right. The y-value tells the distance up.

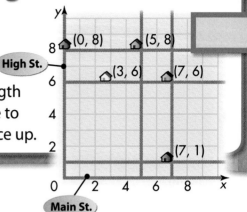

Guided Practice*

Do you know HOW?

Find the distance between the ordered pairs. Use grid paper to help.

1. (1, 3), (1, 8)   **2.** (2, 3), (12, 3)

3. (4, 3), (3, 3)   **4.** (2, 3), (2, 1)

5. (7, 15), (7, 2)   **6.** (7, 3), (1, 3)

7. (4, 4), (8, 4)   **8.** (35, 1), (12, 1)

Do you UNDERSTAND?

9. Writing to Explain If you are given two ordered pairs, how can you tell if they lie on a vertical line or on a horizontal line?

10. Which house did you start at if walking two blocks to the right and two blocks up brings you to another house?

11. What is the distance from the blue house to Main Street? to High Street?

Independent Practice

For **12** through **23**, find the distance between the ordered pairs. Use grid paper to help.

12. (2, 7), (6, 7)   **13.** (6, 7), (6, 4)   **14.** (6, 4), (6, 0)   **15.** (11, 8), (1, 8)

16. (8, 3), (8, 8)   **17.** (4, 9), (9, 9)   **18.** (0, 3), (1, 3)   **19.** (15, 6), (15, 12)

20. (5, 7), (5, 0)   **21.** (1, 9), (9, 9)   **22.** (10, 6), (4, 6)   **23.** (18, 10), (21, 10)

DIGITAL

eTools
www.pearsonsuccessnet.com

How far is the red house from the green house?

Compare the ordered pairs: (7, 1)
                                        (7, 6)

The *x*-values are the same.

Because the points lie on a vertical line, you subtract the y-values to find the distance.

6 − 1 = 5

The distance between the red and green houses is 5 units.

How far is the blue house from the purple house?

Compare the ordered pairs: (0, 8)
                                        (5, 8)

The *y*-values are the same.

Because the points lie on a horizontal line, you subtract the x-values to find the distance.

5 − 0 = 5

The distance between the purple and blue houses is 5 units.

Problem Solving

For **24** through **26**, use the coordinate grid at the right.

24. What two points have a vertical distance of 8 units between them?

25. What is the horizontal distance between point *A* and point *F*?

26 Is the horizontal distance between points *A* and *F* greater than or less than the vertical distance between points *D* and *E*? Explain.

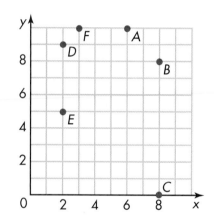

For **27** through **29**, use the map at the right.

27. How many vertical blocks separate the New York Public Library and the Empire State Building?

28. How many horizontal blocks separate the New York Public Library and Grand Central Station?

29. How many total blocks would you walk from the Empire State Building to Grand Central Station?

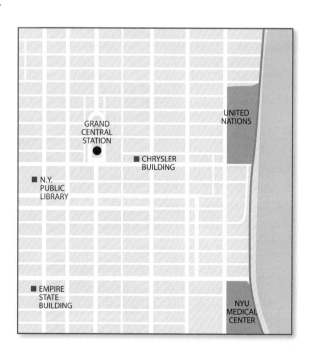

MR 2.2 Apply strategies and results from simpler problems to more complex problems.
Also **MR 2.0**

Problem Solving

Solve a Simpler Problem

If you are riding in a taxi, the shortest distance between two points is usually NOT a straight line.

Find the distance (the number of blocks) from school to the post office and then home. Arrows show one-way streets.

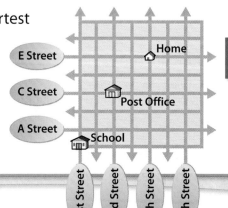

Guided Practice*

Do you know HOW?

Use a simpler problem to solve.

1. Suppose you walk from *A* to *B*. You walk 7 blocks without repeating a block. Find one way to make this walk.

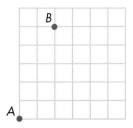

Do you UNDERSTAND?

2. Find another way to travel from school to the post office to home. Is the total distance the same as the total distance in the example above?

3. **Write a Problem** Write a problem in which you use a simpler problem to solve. Then answer the problem you wrote.

Independent Practice

Solve each problem. Write the answer in a complete sentence.

4. Rosa walked three blocks west, two blocks north, one block east, and two blocks south. How many blocks was she from where she started?

5. Lionel lives 13 blocks south of the library. Randy's house is four times as many blocks south as Lionel. How many blocks and in what direction does Randy need to travel to get to the library?

Stuck? Try this....

- What do I know?
- What diagram can I use to help understand the problem?
- Can I use addition, subtraction, multiplication, or division?
- Is all of my work correct?
- Did I answer the right question?
- Is my answer reasonable?

I can solve a simpler problem.

First, I'll find the distance from school to the post office.

I can take 1st Street 3 blocks. Then I can take C Street 2 blocks and get to the post office.

3 + 2 = 5

That is 5 blocks.

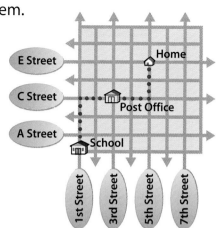

Now I can go from the post office to home.

I can go 2 more blocks on C Street. Then I can go 2 blocks on 5th Street.

2 + 2 = 4.

That is 4 more blocks.

5 + 4 = 9, so it is 9 blocks from school to home.

For **6** and **7**, use the map at the right.

6. How far is it from Walter's house to the park if each unit represents 1 block?

7. Nancy rides her bike from her house to Jerry's house, and then to the park. How many blocks did she ride her bike?

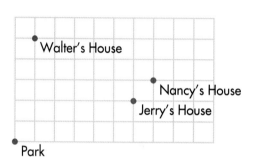

Use the map at the right for **8** through **10**. In the map, each square equals 5 miles.

8. How many miles is it from Smithberg to McAllen?

9. How many miles by highway is it from McAllen to Providence?

10. How many miles by highway is it from Smithberg to Providence?

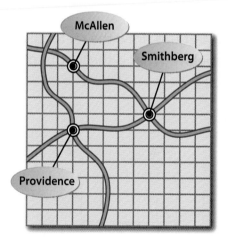

11. Hayley has set a goal to read all 26 books on the library's Best Books list. She plans to read 2 books each week. How long will it take Hayley to read all the books?

26 books in all

2 — weeks

books to be read each week

12. In a Double Dutch tournament, the winning team jumped 447 times in two minutes. The second place team jumped 375 times in 2 minutes. How many more jumps did the winning team make?

A 65 jumps   **C** 75 jumps

B 72 jumps   **D** 82 jumps

1. Which coordinates name point *R*? (17-1)

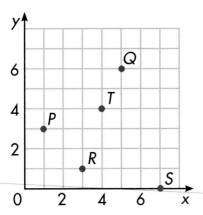

A (1, 3)

B (3, 1)

C (5, 6)

D (7, 0)

2. Marques drew the rectangle shown below. What is the length of $\overline{YZ}$? (17-2)

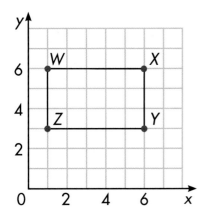

A 3 units

B 5 units

C 8 units

D 16 units

3. How can you find the number of units from point *H* to point *C*? (17-3)

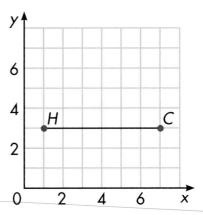

A Subtract 7 – 1

B Subtract 7 – 3

C Subtract 3 – 1

D Subtract 3 – 3

4. Telly is drawing a right triangle on the grid below. Which of the following could be the coordinates of her other point? (17-2)

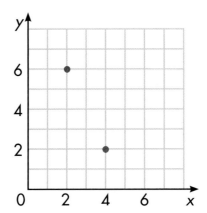

A (0, 2)

B (3, 2)

C (4, 5)

D (4, 6)

5. What is the length of the line segment? (17-3)

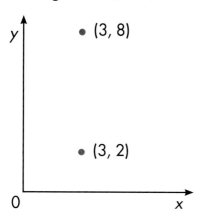

A 1 unit

B 5 units

C 6 units

D 8 units

6. Which point is at (6, 3)? (17-1)

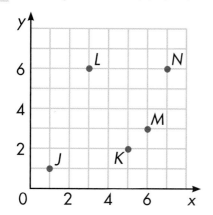

A Point *J*

B Point *K*

C Point *L*

D Point *M*

7. The city bus leaves the bus station, goes to the zoo, then the science museum, then to the amusement park, and then back to the bus station. Find the shortest distance (the number of blocks) the bus travels during one route. (17-4)

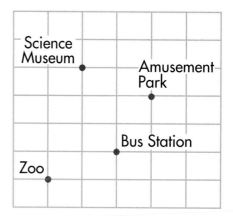

A 14 blocks

B 15 blocks

C 16 blocks

D 20 blocks

8. What is the distance between (6, 9) and (6, 2)? (17-3)

A 3 units

B 4 units

C 7 units

D 11 units

9. How can you find the distance between (4, 2) and (4, 5)? (17-3)

A Subtract 4 – 2

B Subtract 5 – 4

C Subtract 4 – 4

D Subtract 5 – 2

Set A, pages 402–403

Write the ordered pair for point *M*.

Move **4** units to the right.
The *x*-value is 4.

Move **7** units up.
The *y*-value is 7.

The ordered pair
for *M* is (4, 7).

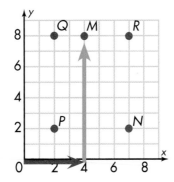

Remember that the first coordinate
is the *x*-value, and the second
coordinate is the *y*-value.

Write the ordered pair or name
the point.

1. *A*   **2.** *C*   **3.** *D*   **4.** *F*

5. (7, 4)   **6.** (6, 2)   **7.** (5, 2)   **8.** (6, 9)

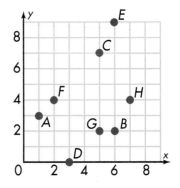

Set B, pages 404–406

Plot the points (3, 6), (3, 2), (8, 2), (8, 6).
What shape do the points make?

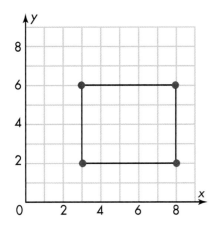

The shape is a rectangle.

Remember to connect each point to
make a closed figure.

Plot each set of ordered pairs.
Name the shape.

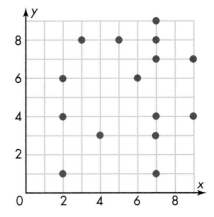

1. (2, 4), (2, 6), and (6, 6)

2. (2, 1), (4, 3), (7, 1), and (7, 3)

3. (3, 8), (5, 8), (7, 8), and (7, 9)

Set C, pages 408–409

What is the length of $\overline{AB}$?

Compare the ordered pairs:
(4, 8)
(4, 6)

The *x*-values are the same. Because the points lie on a vertical line, you can subtract the *y*-values to find the distance.

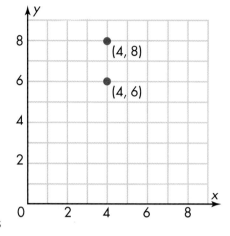

The length of $\overline{AB}$ is $8 - 6 = 2$ units.

Remember that if the *y*-values are the same, the line is horizontal.

Find the distance between the ordered pairs.

1. (5, 8) and (1, 8)

2. (4, 3) and (10, 3)

3. (5, 4) and (4, 4)

4. (2, 5) and (2, 2)

5. (5, 17) and (5, 2)

6. (9, 3) and (2, 3)

Set D, pages 410–411

Find the shortest driving distance (the number of blocks) from school to the park and then home.

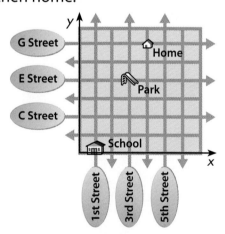

Break the problem into simpler parts.

School to park: I can go 4 blocks up on 1st Street and 2 blocks right on E Street to get to the park. That is 6 blocks.

Park to home: I can go up 2 more blocks on 3rd Street and 1 block right on G Street to get home. That is 3 blocks.

The shortest distance is $6 + 3 = 9$ blocks.

Remember that you can break a problem into simpler parts.

Use a simpler problem to solve. Arrows show one-way streets.

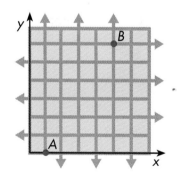

1. Suppose you walk from *A* to *B*. You walk 10 blocks without repeating a block. Find one way to make this walk.

Formulas and Equations

1

California produces between 2,000,000 to 2,500,000 bales of cotton each year. In the fields, cotton is compressed into modules that can weigh more than 6 tons. How many bales are in one module? You will find out in Lesson 18-2.

2

The Thrust SSC was the first land vehicle to go faster than the speed of sound. How fast did this supersonic car go? You will find out in Lesson 18-5.

Review What You Know!

Vocabulary

Choose the best term from the box.

> • capacity   • length
> • yard   • volume

1. A _?_ is a unit of length equal to 3 feet.

2. _?_ represents the amount a container can hold in liquid units.

3. The _?_ of a solid figure is the number of cubic units needed to fill it.

Capacity

Choose the best unit to measure the capacity of each. Write cups or gallons.

4. bathtub   5. fish tank

6. soup bowl   7. mug

8. gasoline tank   9. sugar in a recipe

Weight

Choose the best unit to measure the weight of each. Write ounces or pounds.

10. bicycle   11. slice of bread

12. pencil   13. bag of wood chips

14. bowling ball   15. bunch of bananas

Area and Volume

16. What is the width of a rectangle if its area is 16 square feet and its length is 8 feet?

17. **Writing to Explain** The length of the edge of a cube is 4 feet. Find the volume.

3

In 1969, Apollo 11 became the first space mission to land people on the moon. How long did the trip to the moon take? You will find out in Lesson 18-1.

4

Kudzu is the world's fastest growing plant. How fast can this weed grow? You will find out in Lesson 18-3.

Formulas and Equations

How are formulas used to solve problems?

Erin went cross-country skiing for 2 hours at an average speed of 10 miles per hour. How far did Erin ski in all?

Use the formula distance = rate × time.

AF 1.4 Use and interpret formulas (e.g., area = length × width or A = ℓw) to answer questions about quantities and their relationships. Also AF 1.0, AF 1.5 ⚷ .

10 miles per hour

Other Examples

The formula for finding the area of a rectangle is area = length × width.

What is the area of the rectangle to the right?

A = ℓ × **w**

18 × 4 = 72 square centimeters

4 cm

18 cm

Guided Practice*

Do you know HOW?

For **1** and **2**, use the formula **A** = ℓ × **w** to find the area of each rectangle.

1. ℓ = 4cm, w = 8 cm

2. ℓ = 12 ft, w = 25 ft

Do you UNDERSTAND?

3. If Erin skied for 4 hours, would the distance formula change?

4. Trudy rode her bike for 6 hours at a speed of 5 miles per hour. Use the distance formula to find how far Trudy rode.

Independent Practice

For **5** through **8**, use the formula below to find the perimeter of a rectangle.
Perimeter = (2 × length) + (2 × width)
P = (**2** × ℓ) + (**2** × **w**)

5. ℓ = 5 in., w = 9 in.

6. ℓ = 12 cm, w = 8 cm

7. ℓ = 10 in., w = 24 in.

8. ℓ = 16 m, w = 6 m

*For another example, see Set A on page 434.

To find the distance, use a formula.

distance = rate × time

$d = r × t$

Identify the value of each variable.

Rate in miles per hour

$r = 10$ The rate is the speed.

Time in hours

$t = 2$

Substitute the values into the formula to find d, the distance in miles.

$d = r × t$

$d = 10 × 2$

$d = 20$

Erin skied 20 miles.

For **9** through **12**, use the following formula to find the cost of a tank of gas.

Cost = price per gallon × number of gallons

$C = p × g$

9. $p = \$2.45, g = 8$ **10.** $p = \$2.35, g = 9$ **11.** $p = \$2.50, g = 10$ **12.** $p = \$2.60, g = 8$

Problem Solving

13. *Apollo 11* was the first mission to land people on the moon. Launched in 1969, the flight to the moon took about 75 hours. The average speed of the spacecraft was 5,200 kilometers per hour. Use the formula $d = r × t$ to find the distance from Earth to the moon.

14. Geometry Write and solve an equation to find the perimeter of the figure below where $x = 7$. Use *P* for perimeter.

7 inches

For **15** and **16**, use the table at the right.

15. Which state has the greater part of its area in land, Rhode Island or Hawaii?

16. Which state has the least part of its area in land, Hawaii or Florida?

Data	State	Part of Area that is Land
	Florida	$\frac{41}{50}$
	Hawaii	$\frac{16}{25}$
	Rhode Island	$\frac{2}{3}$

17. Think About the Process The sum of *x* plus *y* equals 32. If $x = 14$, which equation can be used to find the value of *y*?

   A $y - 14 = 32$　**C** $14 + y = 32$

   B $x - y = 32$　**D** $x + 14 = 32$

18. Geometry A square has a side *s*. Which expression will help you find its area?

   A $s + s + s + s$　**C** $s × s$

   B $s + s$　**D** $4 × s$

Addition and Subtraction Patterns and Equations

How can you find a rule and complete a table?

AF 1.5 Understand that an equation such as $y = 3x + 5$ is a prescription for determining a second number when a first number is given. **AF 1.1, Grade 5** Use information taken from a graph or equation to answer questions about a problem situation.

In the table, let x represent the home team score, and let y represent the visiting team score. How are x and y related? What is the rule? What is the missing number?

	x	y
1st Quarter	14	10
2nd Quarter	16	12
3rd Quarter	19	15
4th Quarter	20	

Guided Practice*

Do you know HOW?

For **1** through **4**, copy and complete each table. Find each rule.

1.

x	y
26	14
21	9
16	4
14	

2.

x	y
6	12
7	13
8	14
9	

3.

x	8	13	16	19
y	23	28	31	

4.

x	18	14	11	10
y	9	5	2	

Do you UNDERSTAND?

5. In the table above, are the x- and y-values increasing or decreasing from quarter to quarter?

6. In the example above, explain why the rule is subtract 4 and not add 4.

7. **Writing to Explain** How could you find the missing number in the table at the top without knowing the rule?

8. Tony earns $7 and saves $2. When he earns $10, he saves $5. When he earns $49, he saves $44. If e is the amount he earns, what expression tells the amount he saves?

Independent Practice

For **9** through **14**, copy and complete each table. Find each rule.

9.

x	5	9	13	16
y	14	18	22	

10.

x	6	8	12	15
y	2	4	8	

For another example, see Set B on page 434.

Find the rule.

Each number in the *y* column is 4 less than the number in the *x* column.

$$14 - 4 = 10$$
$$16 - 4 = 12$$
$$19 - 4 = 15$$

In symbols, the rule is $y = x - 4$.

Use the rule $y = x - 4$ to find the missing number when $x = 20$.

$$y = 20 - 4$$
$$y = 16$$

The missing number is 16.

11.

x	y
12	17
9	14
6	11
3	

12.

x	y
7	5
13	11
20	18
29	

13.

x	y
8	16
6	14
4	12
2	

14.

x	y
16	13
24	21
34	31
39	

Problem Solving

Beatrice stitches a pattern for a quilt she is making. For each square (*x*), there is a set number of circles (*y*).

Number of Squares (x)	Number of Circles (y)
2	
5	13
6	14
8	16

15. What is the rule for the table?

16. How many circles are there when there are two squares?

17. The number of boys in the school chorus is 6 less than the number of girls. Let *x* stand for the number of girls, and let *y* stand for the number of boys. Write an equation to show the relationship. If the pattern continues, how many boys are there in the chorus when there are 22 girls?

18. A hardware store owner has 31 washers to put in 6 drawers. If he divides the washers equally, how many washers will be left over?

  A 25 washers   **C** 1 washer

  B 5 washers   **D** 0 washers

19. Reasoning At harvest time, most of the cotton in the fields is compressed into modules. A large module weighs 7 tons. How many bales of cotton are in a large module?

Tons of Cotton	1	3	5	7
Bales of Cotton	4	12	20	

Multiplication and Division Patterns and Equations

A.F 1.5: Understand that an equation such as y = 3x + 5 is a prescription for determining a second number when a first number is given. AF1.1 Grade 5.

How can you describe a rule with words or symbols?

The table shows how many note cards Josie buys in 2, 4, or 7 boxes. Based upon the pattern, how can Josie find the number of cards when x is 8?

Number of Boxes (x)	Number of Note cards (y)
2	30
4	60
7	105
8	

Guided Practice*

Do you know HOW?

For **1** through **3**, use the table below to answer the questions.

Number of Tickets (x)	4	8	12	16	20
Price of Tickets (y)	$12	$24	$36		$60

1. What is the rule in words?

2. What is the rule in symbols?

3. What is the missing number?

Do you UNDERSTAND?

4. Using the table above, how many note cards are there in one box?

5. How many note cards would there be in 14 boxes?

6. Writing to Explain Explain how you could use what the table shows for the number of note cards in 7 boxes to find the number in 14 boxes.

Independent Practice

For **7** through **12**, copy and complete each table. Find each rule.

7.

x	3	5	7	9
y	9	15	21	

8.

x	6	8	12	16
y	3	4	6	

9.

x	y
56	8
35	5
14	2
7	

10.

x	y
6	24
8	32
24	96
28	

11.

x	y
36	4
45	5
54	6
63	

12.

x	y
10	50
15	75
20	100
25	

*For another example, see Set C on page 434.

Find the rule.

To find how many cards are in each box, divide.

$$30 \div 2 = 15$$
$$60 \div 4 = 15$$
$$105 \div 7 = 15$$

In symbols, the rule is $y = x \times 15$.

Use the rule $y = x \times 15$ to find the missing number when $x = 8$.

$$y = 8 \times 15$$
$$y = 120$$

There are 120 notecards in 8 boxes.

Problem Solving

13. Kudzu is the world's fastest growing weed. Copy and complete the table to the right to find out the rule for the growth rate of kudzu. What is the rule in words?

Day	Inches
1	12
2	24
3	
4	
5	
6	72

14. Writing to Explain Cheryl wrote the equation $q \div 25 = d$, where q represents quarters and d represents dollars, to express the number of quarters in 1 dollar. Is Cheryl's equation correct? Explain.

15. Number Sense How do you know that the solution of $100 - k = 70$ is less than 70?

16. Reasoning Don, Wanda, and Stu play on softball, basketball, or football teams. Each person plays only one sport. Wanda doesn't play football. Don doesn't play softball or football. Stu doesn't play basketball or softball. What team does each person play on?

17. Measurement The surface of a rectangular table is 5 feet long and 4 feet wide. What is the area of the top of the table?

A 14 square feet C 18 square feet

B 16 square feet D 20 square feet

18. A waiter earned $3 in tips on Monday, $7.50 in tips on Tuesday, and $12 in tips on Wednesday. If the pattern continues, how much will he make in tips on Friday?

19. Cami bought a book for $12.52 and a bookmark for $1.19. How much change would she get if she paid with a $20 bill?

A $6.19 C $9.29

B $6.29 D $13.71

Lesson

18-4

MG 2.1 ⟶ Draw the points corresponding to linear relationships on graph paper (e.g., draw 10 points on the graph of the equation y = 3x and connect them by using a straight line). Also MG 2.0 ⟶ .

Graphing Equations

Hands-On grid paper

How do you use a table to make a graph?

Dee earns $2 each time she washes the dishes.

The rule for the table is "multiply by 2."

Graph the equation: $y = 2 \times x$

Total earned

Number of times Dee washes dishes

Dishes x	Money y
0	$0
1	$2
2	$4
3	$6

Guided Practice*

Do you know HOW?

Complete the table.

1.

Hours worked x	0	1	2	3
Money earned y	$0	$4	$8	▨

Do you UNDERSTAND?

2. In the graph above, why is there a point at (0,0)?

3. How much would Dee earn if she washed the dishes 5 times?

4. Plot the ordered pairs from the table in Exercise 1.

Independent Practice

For **5** through **14**, use the equation $y = x - 3$.
Find the value of y for each value of x.

5. $x = 3$ **6.** $x = 5$ **7.** $x = 15$ **8.** $x = 11$ **9.** $x = 9$

10. $x = 24$ **11.** $x = 29$ **12.** $x = 31$ **13.** $x = 12$ **14.** $x = 18$

For **15** through **22**, graph each equation on a separate coordinate grid.

15. $y = 4 \times x$ **16.** $y = x + 2$ **17.** $y = x + 1$ **18.** $y = x + 3$

19. $y = 3 \times x$ **20.** $y = x + 5$ **21.** $y = x + 8$ **22.** $y = x - 2$

DIGITAL eTools
www.pearsonsuccessnet.com

For another example, see Set D on page 435.

Make a table based on the rule.

x	Rule y = 2 × x	(x, y)
0	y = 2 × 0	(0, 0)
1	y = 2 × 1	(1, 2)
2	y = 2 × 2	(2, 4)
3	y = 2 × 3	(3, 6)

Plot the ordered pairs.

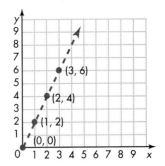

The dashed line shows the graph of the equation $y = 2 \times x$. It is a straight line.

Problem Solving

23. Writing to Explain Kathleen is making fruit smoothies. She needs 12 bananas. She has 5 bananas. Jarrod gave her 2 more bananas. How many more bananas does Kathleen need? Is the diagram drawn correctly?

12 bananas

5 bananas	?

$5 + 7 = 12$, so Kathleen needs 7 more bananas.

Use the table at the right to answer **24** through **26**.

x	y
0	0
1	5
2	10
3	15
6	
7	
8	

24. Complete the table where the x-values are 6, 7, and 8.

25. Graph the ordered pairs in the table you completed.

26. What pattern do you notice between the y-values in the table?

27. Mike made a square using square tiles. Which could be the number of tiles he used?

  A 2 tiles   **C** 9 tiles

  B 5 tiles   **D** 10 tiles

28. Four friends are sharing a bag of 24 pretzels equally. Write an equation to find how many pretzels, p, each friend will get.

29. Find the value of $y = 2x + 2$ when $x = 3$.

  A 6   **C** 10

  B 8   **D** 12

30. A music store sold 28 classical CDs and 57 country music CDs in one day. How many CDs did the store sell that day?

MG 2.1 Draw the points corresponding to linear relationships on graph paper (e.g., draw 10 points on the graph of the equation $y = 3x$ and connect them by using a straight line). Also **MG 2.0** .

More Graphing Equations

How do you use a graph to solve problems?

Jenna is buying lunch and has a coupon for $2 off. Let x = the regular price for lunch. Graph the equation $y = x - 2$.

Use x = 2, 3, 4, 5, and 6.

Other Examples

Find 5 ordered pairs on the graph of $y = 2x + 1$. Make a table. Choose 5 values for x. Then, evaluate $2x + 1$ for each value of x.

x	y = 2x + 1	(x, y)
0	$y = (2 \times 0) + 1$	(0, 1)
1	$y = (2 \times 1) + 1$	(1, 3)
2	$y = (2 \times 2) + 1$	(2, 5)
3	$y = (2 \times 3) + 1$	(3, 7)
4	$y = (2 \times 4) + 1$	(4, 9)

Graph the coordinates shown in the table.

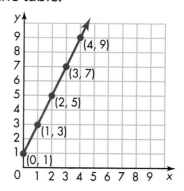

Five ordered pairs on the graph of $y = 2x + 1$ are (0, 1), (1, 3), (2, 5), (3, 7), and (4, 9).

Guided Practice*

Do you know HOW?

Complete the table.

1.

y = 3x + 1	
x	y
4	
6	
8	
10	

2.

y = x + 4	
x	y
2	
4	
6	
8	

Do you UNDERSTAND?

3. How much would Jenna pay for a lunch that costs $8 if she had used her coupon?

4. Graph the coordinates from the table in Exercise 2.

*For another example, see Set D on page 435.

x	y = x − 2	(x, y)
2	y = 2 − 2	(2, 0)
3	y = 3 − 2	(3, 1)
4	y = 4 − 2	(4, 2)
5	y = 5 − 2	(5, 3)
6	y = 6 − 2	(6, 4)

Make a table of values.

Graph the coordinates shown in the table.

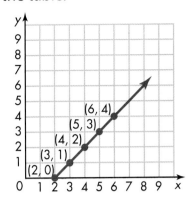

Independent Practice

For **5** through **16**, find five ordered pairs on the graph of each equation. Then graph each equation.

5. y = x + 9

6. y = 2x + 6

7. y = 9x + 3

8. y = 8x

9. y = 3x − 5

10. y = 10x − 4

11. y = 5x + 9

12. y = 6x + 7

13. y = 11x − 1

14. y = 12x − 12

15. y = 4x − 2

16. y = 7x + 4

Problem Solving

17. Geometry The U.S. five-dollar bill and ten-dollar bill are shown below. Are their shapes similar, congruent, or both? Explain.

18. Number Sense When you divide a number by 8, can the remainder be 7? Explain.

19. Algebra What number goes in the box to make the number sentence below true?

(6 − 3) × 4 = 6 × ▢

20. Corrine is packing books into boxes. Each box can hold 12 books. Copy and complete the table to the right.

Number of boxes (x)	Number of books (y)
1	12
2	
3	
4	

Use the line plot at the right to answer **21** through **23**.

The line plot shows the high temperature in degrees Fahrenheit for the first 14 days of October.

21. How many days had shown a high temperature greater than 75°F?

22. What was the most common high temperature in the first 14 days of October?

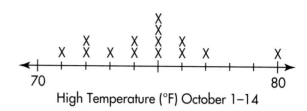

High Temperature (°F) October 1–14

23. How many more days had a high temperature of 75° than 80°?

24. The Thrust SSC jet-car set a land speed record of 766 miles per hour. Starting at 0 miles per hour, the Thrust SSC's speed increased at an average speed of about 40 miles per hour each second. Copy and complete the graph to find the speed at 10 seconds and at 15 seconds.

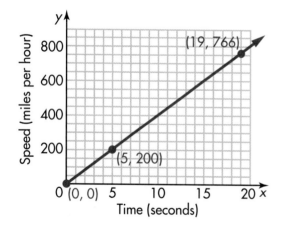

25. **Think About the Process** Look at the graph below. Point T is at $(6, 4)$. Point U is at $(1, 4)$. How can you find the number of units from point T to point U?

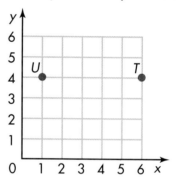

A Add $4 + 6$

B Add $1 + 6$

C Subtract $6 - 4$

D Subtract $6 - 1$

26. **Writing to Explain** Explain why half of Region A is not larger than half of Region B.

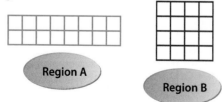

Region A

Region B

27. The numbers in the pattern below increase by the same amount each time. What are the next three numbers in this pattern?

1, 3, 5, 7, ▢ **,** ▢ **,** ▢

A 9, 11, 13   **C** 8, 13, 21

B 6, 7, 9   **D** 7, 8, 9

Mixed Problem Solving

A hurricane is a dangerous storm that can cause a lot of damage. Hurricanes are classified by their wind speed.

1. If a hurricane has wind speeds that reach 190 kilometers per hour, what category of hurricane is it?

Hurricane Ratings	
Category of Hurricane	**Wind Speed (kilometers per hour)**
1	119 to 153
2	154 to 177
3	178 to 209
4	210 to 249
5	Greater than 249

2. In one season, eight hurricanes made landfall on the eastern seaboard of the United States. Three of the storms had wind speeds of 160 kph, four of the storms had recorded wind speeds of 140 kph, and the rest had wind speeds of 249 kph. How many more Category 2 hurricanes were there than Category 5 hurricanes?

3. A hurricane has a recorded wind speed of 122 kph. Two days before making landfall, its wind speed was recorded at 244 kph. How many times greater was the wind speed of the hurricane two days before making landfall? What category of hurricane was it when it made landfall?

4. Storm surge is one measurement used to rate hurricanes. What is the range in storm surge for Category 2 hurricanes?

Storm Surge in Hurricanes	
Category of Hurricane	**Storm Surge (meters)**
1	1.2–1.5
2	1.6–2.4
3	2.5–3.7
4	3.8–5.5
5	> 5.5

5. If a hurricane had a wind speed of 139 kilometers per hour, between which numbers would the measurement of its storm surge fall?

6. Hurricanes are given male and female names that follow one another in sequence and in alphabetical order. In one season, 15 hurricanes were named. The first hurricane in the series was given a female name. How many hurricanes were given male names in that season?

15 named hurricanes

F	?	?	?	?	?	?	?	?	?	?	?	?	?	?

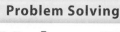
MR 2.3 Use a variety of methods, such as words, numbers, symbols, charts, graphs, tables, diagrams, and models, to explain mathematical reasoning. Also **SDAP 1.0.**

Make a Table

Color tiles are placed around horse tiles. How many color tiles are used for 4 horses? 5 horses?

Number of Horse Tiles	1	2	3	4	5
Number of color tiles	8	10	12		

| 1 horse, 8 color tiles | 2 horses, 10 color tiles | 3 horses, 12 color tiles |

Guided Practice*

Do you know HOW?

Make a table to solve the problem.

1. Troy is making a row of attached fenced-in sections for each type of vegetable in his garden. He sets a post in each corner. How many posts will he need for 4 fenced-in sections ?

Do you UNDERSTAND?

2. Why do the number of color tiles change by 2 in the example above while the number of horses change only by 1?

3. **Write a Problem** Write a problem in which you make a table. Then answer your question.

Independent Practice

4. Marianne visited her aunt for 6 days. On the first day, her aunt gave her $0.10. On the second day, she received $0.20. On the third day, she received $0.30. Make a table to show how much money she received each day of the week.

5. How would you use color tiles to show how much money Marianne received altogether?

6. John went strawberry picking. He picked 12 berries per minute. How many berries did John pick in 5 minutes?

Stuck? Try this....

- What do I know?
- What diagram can I use to help understand the problem?
- Can I use addition, subtraction, multiplication, or division?
- Is all of my work correct?
- Did I answer the right question?
- Is my answer reasonable?

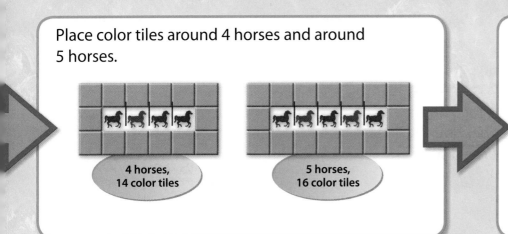

Place color tiles around 4 horses and around 5 horses.

4 horses, 14 color tiles

5 horses, 16 color tiles

Look for a pattern in the table.

The number of horse tiles changes by 1 each time. The number of color tiles changes by 2 each time. My answer seems reasonable.

For **7** and **8**, use the pattern of pennies at the right.

7. The pattern shows how many pennies that Omar and Samantha each have. Make a table to display the data.

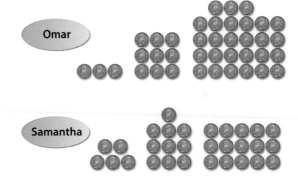

Omar

8. If the pattern continues, how many pennies will Omar have when Samantha has 30 pennies?

Samantha

9. A sale at the grocery store is represented by the table below. Copy and complete the table. How many cans do you need to buy to get 6 free cans?

Cans bought	2	4	6	▨	▨	▨
Free Cans	1	2	3	▨	▨	▨

10. Suppose you have 21 paper clips. How many rows can you make if you continue the pattern below?

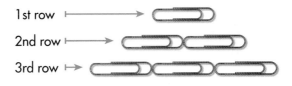

1st row
2nd row
3rd row

11. Dottie's class is working on science projects. Ocean projects make up $\frac{5}{8}$ of the projects, and $\frac{1}{6}$ of the projects are about the planets. The rest of the class is working on an electricity project. What fraction of student projects are about the ocean and planets?

? Ocean and planet projects

$\frac{5}{8}$	$\frac{1}{6}$

1. Mrs. Heathersby drove for 5 hours at a speed of 50 miles per hour. How far did she travel? Use the distance formula below. (18-1)

   $d = r \times t$

   A 10 miles

   B 250 miles

   C 500 miles

   D 2,500 miles

2. What is the rule for the table? (18-2)

x	y
16	29
19	32
22	35
25	38

   A $y = x - 12$

   B $y = x + 12$

   C $y = x - 13$

   D $y = x + 13$

3. What is the missing number in the table? (18-3)

x	y
36	9
24	6
20	5
8	

   A 2

   B 3

   C 4

   D 5

4. What is the missing number in the table? (18-5)

x	y = 2x + 2
1	4
2	6
3	8
4	

   A 4

   B 8

   C 10

   D 12

5. What is the rule for the table? (18-3)

x	4	6	8	9
y	32	48	64	72

   A $y = x \div 8$

   B $y = x \times 8$

   C $y = x - 8$

   D $y = x + 8$

6. What is the missing number in the table? (18-2)

x	y
13	8
27	22
31	26
36	

   A 33

   B 32

   C 31

   D 30

7. Tom drew the graph below. Which equation did he use? (18-4)

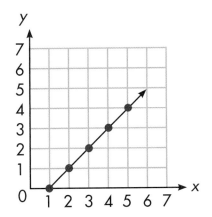

A $y = x - 1$

B $y = x + 1$

C $y = x$

D $y = 1 - x$

8. Anna plotted 3 points of a straight line onto a grid. Which could be the coordinates of another point on the line? (18-5)

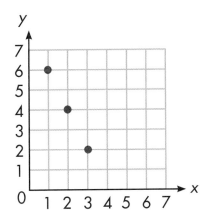

A $(0, 7)$

B $(3, 1)$

C $(4, 1)$

D $(4, 0)$

9. How many batteries would there be in 9 packages? (18-3)

Number of Packages	Number of Batteries
4	24
7	42
10	60
12	72

A 46

B 48

C 52

D 54

10. A walking path through a nature area has concrete pillars connected by wooden paths to form rectangles as shown in the diagram below. How many concrete pillars are needed for 6 rectangles? Use the table to solve the problem. (18-6)

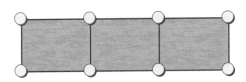

Rectangles	1	2	3	4	5	6
Pillars	4	6	8			

A 16

B 14

C 12

D 10

Set A, pages 418–419

Jeanne rode her bike for 3 hours at a speed of 5 miles per hour. How far did Jeanne ride?

d = r × t

Identify the value of each variable.

Rate in miles per hour: **r = 5**
Time in hours: **t = 3**

Substitute the values into the formula.

d = r × t
d = 5 × 3
d = 15 miles

Remember to use values of known variables to find the value of the unknown variable.

Copy and complete the table using the formula for a rectangle with a length that is 8 inches greater than its width.

1.

Width (inches) w	Length (inches) $\ell = w + 8$
3	
5	
10	

Set B, pages 420–421

Find the rule and the missing number.

Each *y*-value is 6 more than the corresponding *x*-value. In symbols, the rule is:

$y = x + 6$
$15 + 6 = 21$

The missing number is 21.

x	y
12	18
13	19
14	20
15	

Remember that you can use an inverse operation to check your answer.

Find a rule and the missing number.

1.

x	37	34	31	27
y	29	26		19

Set C, pages 422–423

How many notebooks are in 9 boxes? Choose an operation and find a rule.

Words: Multiply the number of boxes by 5.

Symbols: $y = x \times 5$
Use the rule to find the missing value.

$9 \times 5 = 45$

There are 45 notebooks in 9 boxes.

Boxes x	Notebooks y
3	15
5	25
8	40
9	

Remember to choose the operation that helps you find the missing number.

Number of Tickets, x	3	5	10	14
Total Price, y	$18	$30	$60	

Robyn used this table to find the total price of different numbers of tickets to a play.

1. What is the rule in words? in symbols?

2. What is the missing number?

Set D, pages 424–428

Randy earns $20 each time he mows a lawn. How much will he earn for mowing 4 lawns? Use the rule to make a table.

Lawns x	Rule: y = x × 20	Money: y
0	y = 0 × 20	0
1	y = 1 × 20	$20
2	y = 2 × 20	$40
3	y = 3 × 20	$60

Graph the ordered pairs. The graph of the equation $y = x \times 20$ is a line.

Extend the line. Randy earns $80 for mowing 4 lawns.

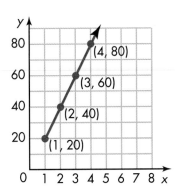

Remember to find at least three coordinates.

1. Copy and complete the table.

x	y = x × 8	(x, y)
3	y = ☐ × 8	(3, 24)
6	y = ☐ × 8	(☐, ☐)
9	y = ☐ × 8	(☐, ☐)
12	y = ☐ × 8	(☐, ☐)

2. Use the coordinates in the table to copy and complete the graph.

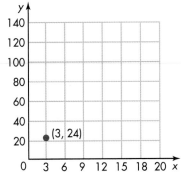

3. Use your graph to find the y-value when $x = 15$.

Set E, pages 430–431

At the fair, Zoe rode 3 rides every half hour, and Pat rode 2 rides every half hour. How many rides did Pat ride while Zoe had 12 rides?

Use counters. Record your results in a table.

3 rides for Zoe
2 rides for Pat

6 rides for Zoe
4 rides for Pat

Rides for Zoe	3	6	9	12
Rides for Pat	2	4	6	8

Pat took 8 rides in the time Zoe took 12 rides.

Remember that making a table can help you solve a problem.

1. Geoff washed 8 cars each hour at a car wash. Bryce washed 6 cars an hour. Use counters to copy and complete the table.

Geoff	8	16	24	32
Bryce	6	☐	☐	☐

2. How many cars did Bryce wash while Geoff washed 16 cars? while Geoff washed 24 cars?

Congruence and Symmetry

1

How many lines of symmetry does the Transamerica Building in San Francisco have? You will find out in Lesson 19-2.

Review What You Know!

Vocabulary

Choose the best term from the box.

- symmetry
- congruent
- rotation
- reflection

1. The _?_ of a figure is the mirror image.

2. Two figures are _?_ if they have the same shape and same size.

3. A figure has _?_ if it can be folded along a line so that both parts match exactly.

4. When a figure changes position by moving about a point, it is a _?_.

2 In this M.C. Escher drawing, what are some of the ways these horses have been moved? You will find out in Lesson 19-1.

3 The Megaray is one of the world's largest kites measuring 66 meters long and 38 meters across. What is the kite's area? You will find out in Lesson 19-1.

Solid Figures

Name the solid figure for each object.

5.   6.   7.

Shapes

Identify each shape.

8.   9.   10.

11.   12.   13.

14.   15.   16.

17. **Writing to Explain** Explain how the figures in Exercise 8–10 are alike and how they are different.

MG 3.3 Identify congruent figures.

Congruent Figures

When are figures congruent?

Figures that are the same size and shape are congruent.

You can use translations, reflections, and rotations to test if two figures are congruent.

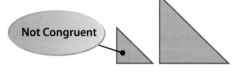
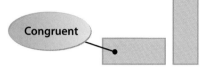

Congruent

Not Congruent

Guided Practice*

Do you know HOW?

For **1** through **4**, tell if the figures in each pair are congruent.

1.    2.

3.    4.

Do you UNDERSTAND?

5. If one of the house shapes above is rotated $\frac{1}{4}$ turn, will the two shapes still be congruent?

6. **Writing to Explain** Can a circle and a square ever be congruent? Why or why not?

Independent Practice

For **7** through **15**, tell if the figures in each pair are congruent.

7.    8.    9.

10.    11.   12.

13.    14. 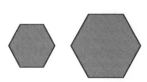   15.

*For another example, see Set A on page 448.

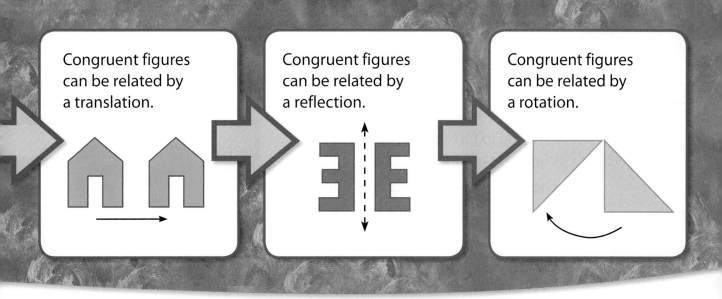

Congruent figures can be related by a translation.

Congruent figures can be related by a reflection.

Congruent figures can be related by a rotation.

Problem Solving

For **16** and **17**, describe everything that is the same and everything that is different about each pair of figures. Then tell if the figures are congruent.

16.

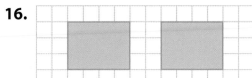

17.

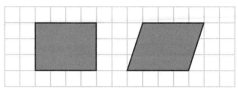

18. In the M.C. Escher drawing at the right, which horse(s) are a translation of the horse labeled X?

   A   Horse A   **C**   Horse A and C

   B   Horse B   **D**   Horse A, B, and C

Symmetry Drawing 78 By M.C. Escher

19. How many days are in 52 weeks?

   A   59 days   **C**   365 days

   B   364 days   **D**   366 days

20. Reasoning Use the diagram below. Frida wrote a message on paper and held it up to a mirror. What does the message say?

21. On a bus ride, Jasmine counted 24 taxis and 12 bicycles. How many wheels did she count in all?

MG 3.4 Identify figures that have bilateral and rotational symmetry.

Line Symmetry

What is a line of symmetry?

A figure is symmetric <u>if it can be folded on a line to form two congruent halves that fit on top of each other.</u>

<u>The fold line is called</u> a line of symmetry. This truck has one line of symmetry.

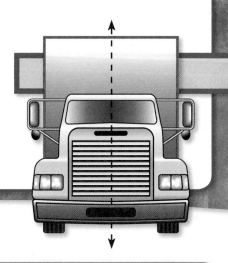

Guided Practice*

Do you know HOW?

For **1** and **2**, tell if each line is a line of symmetry.

1. 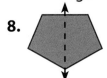   **2.**

For **3** and **4**, tell how many lines of symmetry each figure has.

3.    **4.**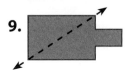

Do you UNDERSTAND?

5. Do some figures have no lines of symmetry?

6. How many lines of symmetry does the figure below have?

7. Writing to Explain How many lines of symmetry does a bicycle tire have?

Independent Practice

For **8** through **11**, tell if each line is a line of symmetry.

8.    **9.**   **10.**    **11.**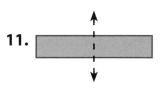

For **12** through **15**, tell how many lines of symmetry each figure has.

12.   **13.**   **14.**   **15.**

*For another example, see Set B on page 448 .

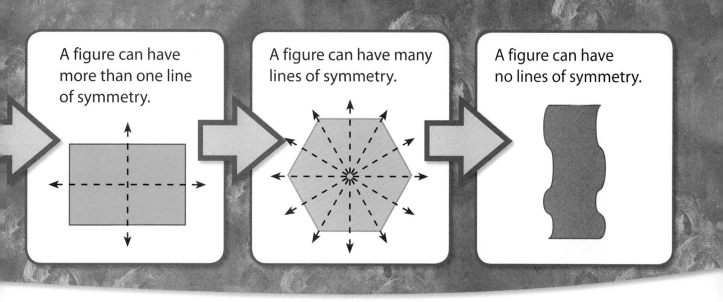

A figure can have more than one line of symmetry.

A figure can have many lines of symmetry.

A figure can have no lines of symmetry.

For **16** through **23**, trace each figure and draw lines of symmetry if you can.

16.

17.

18.

19.

20.

21.

22.

23.

24. How many lines of symmetry does a scalene triangle have?

25. How many lines of symmetry does an isosceles triangle have?

26. Reasoning Vanessa drew a figure and said that it had an infinite number of lines of symmetry. What figure did she draw?

27. Draw a quadrilateral that does not have a line of symmetry.

28. The Transamerica Building in San Francisco has one line of symmetry. Use the picture at the right to describe where the line of symmetry is.

29. Write 5 capital letters that have at least one line of symmetry?

30. How many lines of symmetry does a square have?

    A None   **C** 4 lines

    B 2 lines   **D** 6 lines

DIGITAL   Animated Glossary
www.pearsonsuccessnet.com

MG 3.4 Identify figures that have bilateral and rotational symmetry. Also MG 3.5.

Rotational Symmetry

Hands-On
set of polygons

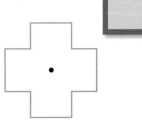

What is rotational symmetry?

When a figure can rotate onto itself in less than a full turn, the figure has rotational symmetry.

If you rotate this figure $\frac{1}{4}$ turn, it has rotated 90°. This figure has rotational symmetry.

Guided Practice*

Do you know HOW?

Does the figure have rotational symmetry? Write yes or no.

1.

2.

3.

4.

Do you UNDERSTAND?

5. A figure that has been rotated a $\frac{1}{4}$ turn has been rotated ▨ degrees.

6. A figure that has been rotated 180° has been rotated ▨ turn.

7. A figure that has been rotated a $\frac{3}{4}$ turn has been rotated ▨ degrees.

Independent Practice

In **8** through **15**, does the figure have rotational symmetry? Write yes or no. Give the least angle measure and turn that will rotate the figure onto itseslf.

8.

9.

10.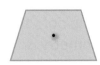

11.

12.

13.

14.

15.

DIGITAL
Animated Glossary, eTools
www.pearsonsuccessnet.com

*For another example, see Set C on page 449.

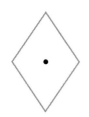

This figure has rotational symmetry. It must be rotated 180°, or a $\frac{1}{2}$ turn, to land on itself.

This figure has rotational symmetry. It can be rotated 90°, 180°, or 270°, or a $\frac{1}{4}$ turn, a $\frac{1}{2}$ turn, or a $\frac{3}{4}$ turn, to land on itself.

This figure does not have rotational symmetry. It must be rotated 360°, or a full turn, to land on itself.

Problem Solving

For **16** and **17**, fill in and use the table to the right.

16. Valerie has 16 yards of fencing material to build a dog run. She wants to put the fence around a rectangular area. Complete the table to the right for the possibilities of the fencing.

17. Which area is the largest? What is another name for this shape?

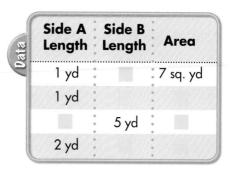

Side A Length	Side B Length	Area
1 yd		7 sq. yd
1 yd		
	5 yd	
2 yd		

18. Measurement A backyard is in the shape of an equilateral triangle. One side measures 17 feet. What is the perimeter of the backyard?

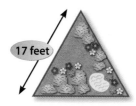

17 feet

19. Which capital letter below has rotational symmetry?

A **N**   C **T**

B **Y**   D **E**

20. Where would the parentheses have to go to make this equation true?

$$18 - 2 + 12 - 8 = 20$$

21. The Megaray Kite has an area of almost 1,500 square meters. Suppose the wind suddenly changes and the kite moves 25 meters East. Has the shape or size of the kite changed? Explain.

Lesson

19-4

MR 2.2 Apply strategies and results from simpler problems to more complex problems. Also **MR 2.0, MG 3.0.**

Problem Solving

Draw a Picture

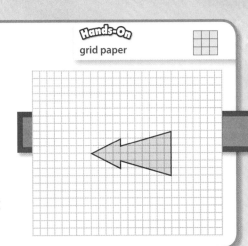

Hands-On
grid paper

Lisa has been asked to draw a large arrow that is exactly the same shape as the one shown on the grid at the right.

Make a large arrow that is exactly the same shape. Explain how you know it is the same shape.

Guided Practice*

Do you know HOW?

For **1** and **2**, make a large figure that is exactly the same shape. Explain how you know it is the same shape.

1.

2.

Do you UNDERSTAND?

3. Suppose that you drew the arrow above so that it was pointing vertically. Would the shape of the arrow change?

4. Draw a picture of a shape. Then triple each side.

Independent Practice

Solve.

5. Draw a large figure. Then draw a smaller figure that is exactly the same shape.

6. If you were to cut out a hexagon to make a stop sign similar to the shape below, how would you draw it to make it twice the size?

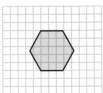

Stuck? Try this....

- What do I know?
- What diagram can I use to help understand the problem?
- Can I use addition, subtraction, multiplication, or division?
- Is all of my work correct?
- Did I answer the right question?
- Is my answer reasonable?

Plan

What do I know? The dimensions of the arrow are 4 units by 4 units by 7 units by 6 units. The arrow is 11 units long from left to right.

What am I asked to find? To make an arrow that is exactly the same shape

Solve

Double the length of each side.

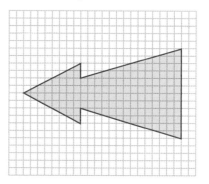

The shapes are the same because the lengths of each side were doubled.

7. Stephen is listening to a book on tape. The book has 17 chapters and each chapter is about 22 minutes long. How many minutes will it take to listen to the complete book?

8. Six people are taking part in a charity walk. Two people walked for 8 miles, three people walked for 6 miles, and one person walked for 10 miles. How many miles did they walk in all?

9. Which can be rotated less than one complete turn and look exactly the same?

A B   C H

B V   D R

10. Which of the following shapes has exactly four lines of symmetry?

A   C

B   D

11. Jackie and Kendall are part of their school's relay race team. Each member of the team has to run for one-half mile of a 3-mile race.

   a Draw a picture to help you find how many members are on the relay team.

   b How many other members are on the relay team besides Jackie and Kendall?

12. Lawrence's father said that he would put 12 dollars into Lawrence's savings account for every 20 dollars Lawrence put into it. If after a year his father had put 96 dollars into Lawrence's account, how much did Lawrence put into his account?

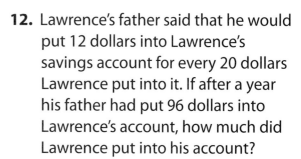

eTools
www.pearsonsuccessnet.com

1. Four of Mrs. Li's students decorated a bulletin board using shapes with lines of symmetry. Whose shape has 4 lines of symmetry? (19-2)

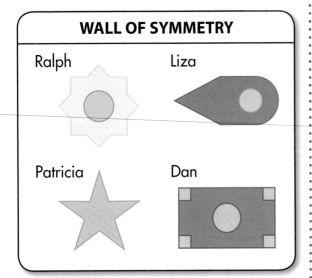

WALL OF SYMMETRY

Ralph   Liza

Patricia   Dan

A Ralph

B Liza

C Patricia

D Dan

2. Milton built two congruent flower beds. Which could be the flower beds he built? (19-1)

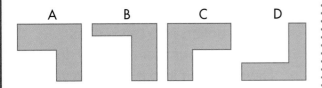

A   B   C   D

A A and B

B A and C

C A and D

D B and C

3. How many lines of symmetry does an equilateral triangle have? (19-2)

A 0

B 1

C 2

D 3

4. Cassidy made this shape for her school's basketball team.

Which shape below is the same shape? (19-4)

A

B

C

D

5. Which figure below has rotational symmetry? (19-3)

A

B

C

D

6. How many lines of symmetry does the logo below have? (19-2)

A 0

B 1

C 2

D 4

7. Which lists all the ways this figure could be rotated and land on itself? (19-3)

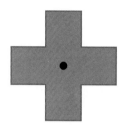

A 90° only

B 90° and 180°

C 90°, 180°, and 270°

D This figure has no rotational symmetry.

8. Which figure is congruent to the figure on the right? (19-1)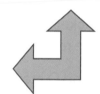

A

B

C

D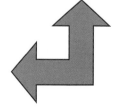

Set A, pages 438–439

Are the figures congruent? If so, tell if they are related by a reflection, translation, or rotation.

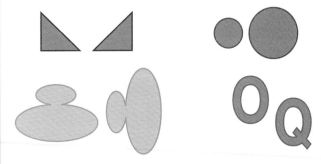

The triangles are the same size and shape, so they are congruent. They are related by a reflection.

The circles are not the same size, so they are not congruent.

The stacked oval shapes are congruent. They are related by a rotation.

The O and Q are different shapes. They are not congruent.

Remember that you can use translations, reflections, and rotations to find if two figures are congruent.

Are the figures in each pair congruent?

1.    2.

3.    4.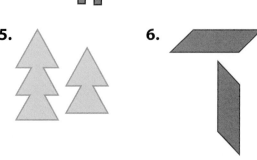

5.   6.

Set B, pages 440–441

How many lines of symmetry do the figures have?

Fold the figure along the dashed line. The two halves are congruent and fit one on top of the other.

It has one line of symmetry.

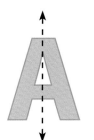

The figure may be folded five ways that result in congruent figures that fit on top of each other.

This figure has five lines of symmetry.

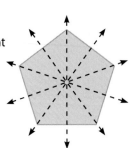

Remember that figures can have many lines of symmetry.

Draw the lines of symmetry for each figure.

1.   2. C

3.   4.

Set C, pages 442-443

What kind of rotation does the figure make?

This figure can be rotated 90°, or a $\frac{1}{4}$ turn, to land on itself.

This figure can be rotated 180°, or a $\frac{1}{2}$ turn, to land on itself.

This figure can be rotated 90°, 180°, or 270°, or a $\frac{1}{4}$ turn, a $\frac{1}{2}$ turn, or a $\frac{3}{4}$ turn, to land on itself.

Remember, a figure has rotational symmetry if it can rotate onto itself in less than a full turn.

1.

2.

3. **E**

4. ◆

Set D, pages 444-445

Make a letter "T" that is exactly the same shape. Explain how you know it is the same shape.

What do I know? The letter is 11 units in vertical height and spans 9 units horizontally.

What am I asked to find? To make a letter T that is exactly the same shape.

Double the dimensions of the figure.

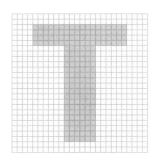

Remember to measure the figure before you draw it.

1. Draw a letter "L" that is exactly the same shape. Explain how you know it is the same shape.

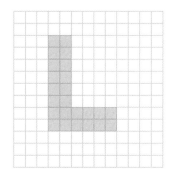

Topic
20

Probability

1 How many passengers can fit in each cabin of the London Eye Ferris Wheel? You will find out in Lesson 20-3.

Vocabulary

Choose the best term from the box.

- likely
- outcome
- probability
- tree diagram

1. A _?_ is a display that shows all possible outcomes.

2. The possible result of a game or experiment is the _?_.

3. A _?_ event is one which will probably happen.

Chance

Give the chance of each outcome for the yellow part of the spinner.

4.

____ out of ____

5.

____ out of ____

6.

____ out of ____

7.

____ out of ____

Fractions

Write a fraction to describe the part of each region or set that is shaded.

8.

9.

10. Writing to Explain Would you eat more if you ate $\frac{1}{4}$ of a small pizza or $\frac{1}{4}$ of a medium pizza?

2

Radar dishes are used to predict where a tornado will touch down. How many times did tornados touch down in California in 2005? You will find out in Lesson 20-4.

3

When people race model boats, each person uses a different radio signal to control their boat. How do the racers make sure they do not use the same radio signal? You will find out in Lesson 20-1.

SDAP 2.1 Represent all possible outcomes for a simple probability situation in an organized way (e.g., tables, grids, tree diagrams).

Finding Combinations

Hands-On
2-color counters and color tiles

How can you find all the possible combinations?

Jay's dentist is giving out dental floss and toothbrushes. Jay will get one toothbrush and one kind of floss. How many different combinations can Jay choose?

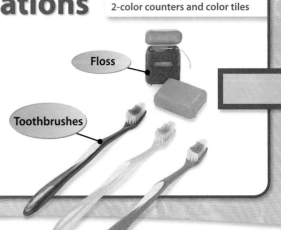

Floss

Toothbrushes

Guided Practice*

Do you know HOW?

For **1** and **2**, find the number of possible combinations. Use objects to help.

1. Choose one of the letters A or B and one of the numbers 1 or 2.

2. Choose one of the letters A, B, C, or D and one of the numbers 1 or 2.

Do you UNDERSTAND?

3. **Writing to Explain** In Exercises 1 and 2, does it matter whether you choose the letter first or the number first? Explain.

4. In the example above, if a third kind of dental floss is offered, how many combinations can Jay choose?

Independent Practice

For **5** and **6**, copy and complete the table to find the number of possible combinations. Use objects to help.

5. Choose one color counter and one color tile.

	Red Counter	Yellow Counter
Blue tile	●	○ ■
Green tile	● ■	■

6. Choose a coin and a bill.

	Quarter	Dime	Nickel	Penny
1-Dollar bill	■	🪙	🪙	🪙
5-Dollar bill	🪙	■	🪙	🪙

DIGITAL
eTools
www.pearsonsuccessnet.com

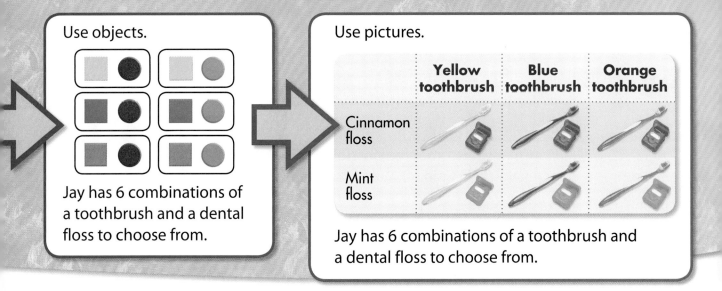

Use objects.

Jay has 6 combinations of a toothbrush and a dental floss to choose from.

Use pictures.

	Yellow toothbrush	Blue toothbrush	Orange toothbrush
Cinnamon floss			
Mint floss			

Jay has 6 combinations of a toothbrush and a dental floss to choose from.

For **7** and **8**, use objects or pictures to find the number of possible combinations.

7. Choose one pet dog, cat, or rabbit and one pet sitter Jill, Marta, or Dave.

8. Choose one of 3 books and one of 8 CDs to bring on a bus trip.

Problem Solving

9. In a model boat race, each person uses a different radio signal. The radio signal is changed using switches on the radio controller. Each switch can be "on" or "off." If there are 4 switches, one combination could be off-on-on-on-off. How many combinations are possible with 4 switches?

 If there are 2 switches, there are 2 × 2, or 4 combinations. If there are 3 switches, there are 2 × 2 × 2 = 8 combinations.

10. Jane made 19 silver dollar pancakes. She took 7 and then gave an equal number to each of her two sisters. How many silver dollar pancakes did each sister get?

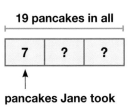

19 pancakes in all

7	?	?

↑
pancakes Jane took

11. Reasoning Mr. Fines needed to buy numbers for an address plaque for his new store. He ordered the numbers 1, 3, and 5. If he could arrange the numbers in any order, what are the possible combinations for his store's address?

12. Tommy had a doctor's appointment at 4:45. He needs 15 minutes to get ready and 20 minutes to drive. At what time does Tommy need to get ready?

SDAP 2.1 Represent all possible outcomes for a simple probability situation in an organized way (e.g., tables, grids, tree diagrams).

Outcomes and Tree Diagrams

What are the possible results?

<u>Each possible result is an</u> outcome. How many outcomes are possible when you spin Spinner 1 and Spinner 2?

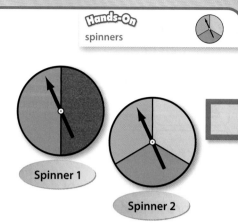

Hands-On
spinners

Spinner 1

Spinner 2

Guided Practice*

Do you know HOW?

For **1** and **2**, use the diagrams below.

Bag 1

Bag 2

1. List all the possible outcomes for picking one card from Bag 2.

2. Make a tree diagram to show all the possible outcomes for picking one card from Bag 1 followed by a card from Bag 2.

Do you UNDERSTAND?

3. What number sentence can you use to find the number of possible outcomes in Exercise 2?

4. **Writing to Explain** In the example at the top, why is Blue Blue an outcome but Red Red is not?

5. A board game uses Spinner 1. On each turn, you must spin Spinner 1 twice. How many outcomes are possible for each turn?

Independent Practice

For **6** through **8**, make a tree diagram to list all the possible outcomes for each situation.

6. Spin Spinner 3 once and toss the number cube once.

7. Pick one card from Bag 3 and toss the number cube once.

8. Pick one card from Bag 3 and spin Spinner 3 once.

 When you make a tree diagram, you can list the outcomes in any order you like.

Bag 3   Number Cube   Spinner 3

DIGITAL

Animated Glossary, eTools
www.pearsonsuccessnet.com

For another example, see Set B on page 464.

Make a tree diagram. A tree diagram is a display that shows all possible outcomes.

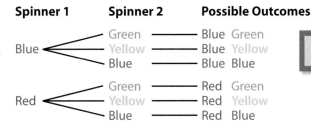

Spinner 1	Spinner 2	Possible Outcomes
Blue	Green	Blue Green
	Yellow	Blue Yellow
	Blue	Blue Blue
Red	Green	Red Green
	Yellow	Red Yellow
	Blue	Red Blue

There are 6 possible outcomes.

Multiply.

There are 2 outcomes for Spinner 1 and 3 outcomes for Spinner 2.

$$3 \times 2 = 6$$

There are 6 possible outcomes.

For **9** and **10**, multiply to find the number of possible outcomes.

9. Flip a coin and toss a number cube that is numbered 1 through 6.

10. Pick one card from each of two piles. One pile has the cards labeled F, I, T, P, N, C, and O. The other has the cards labeled A, R, S, and Q.

Problem Solving

For **11** and **12**, use the diagram at the right.

Some games use shapes other than a cube to allow for more outcomes.

11. How many outcomes are there for one toss of the octahedron and one toss of the dodecahedron?

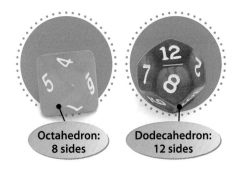

Octahedron: 8 sides Dodecahedron: 12 sides

12. Reasoning You toss the octahedron and dodecahedron and add the two numbers. What is the least possible total? The greatest possible total?

For **13**, use the diagram at the right.

13. Wearing a blindfold, you toss two rings. Both tosses land on a bottle. List all the possible outcomes.

14. In 2002, California had 3 tornadoes touch down. In 2004, 7 more tornadoes touched down. In 2005, there were 3 times as many tornadoes than in 2004. How many tornadoes touched down in Calfornia in 2005?

SDAP 2.2 Express outcomes of experimental probability situations verbally and numerically (e.g., 3 out of 4; $\frac{3}{4}$). **SDAP 2.0** Make predictions for simple probability situations.

Writing Probability as a Fraction

How can you find probability?

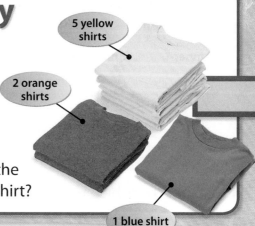

5 yellow shirts

2 orange shirts

1 blue shirt

Katie is organizing T-shirts for 8 members of her team. She has 3 different colored shirts: blue, orange, and yellow. Without looking, what is the probability of Katie picking a yellow shirt?

Another Example **How can you describe probability?**

Remember you have learned to use fractions to describe parts of sets, regions, and distances on number lines. In this lesson, you will learn how fractions can be used to describe probability.

An impossible event has a probability of 0. A certain event has a probability of 1. Any other event has a probability between 0 and 1.

Katie is **certain** to pick a shirt.

Katie is **likely** to pick a shirt that is yellow.

Katie is **unlikely** to pick a shirt that is blue.

It is **impossible** for Katie to pick a green shirt.

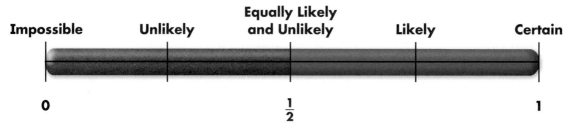

Impossible	Unlikely	Equally Likely and Unlikely	Likely	Certain
0		$\frac{1}{2}$		1

Explain It

1. How likely is it that Katie will pick an orange shirt? Explain.

2. What is the probability of picking a blue shirt?

You can use fractions to describe the probability of an event.

Probability <u>is the likelihood that an event will happen</u>.

$$\text{Probability} = \frac{\text{number of favorable outcomes}}{\text{number of possible outcomes}}$$

$$P = \frac{\text{number of yellow shirts}}{\text{number of shirts in all}}$$

$$P = \frac{5}{8}$$

The probability of picking a yellow shirt is $\frac{5}{8}$.

Guided Practice*

Do you know HOW?

For **1** through **4**, find the probability of selecting a tile, without looking, from those below.

1. Crescent

2. Not a circle

3. Heart or crescent

4. Diamond

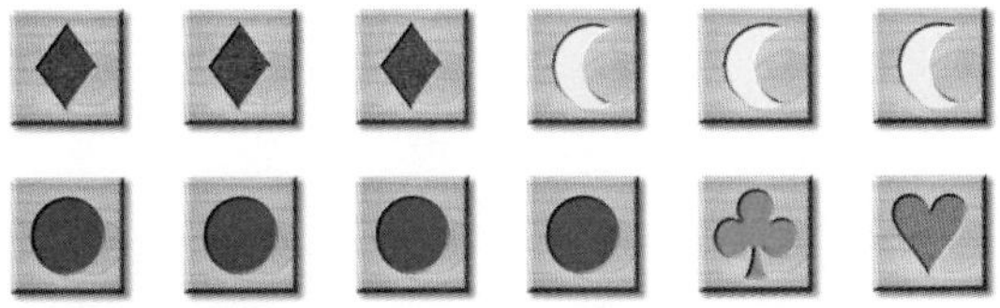

Do you UNDERSTAND?

5. In the example above, what is the probability of picking a blue or an orange shirt?

6. Describe an event that is impossible.

Independent Practice

For **7** through **14**, write the probability of selecting, without looking, the card or letter described.

7. a consonant that is not M

8. the letter D, E, G, O, S, T, or U

9. a blue, orange or green card

10. a letter that is not G

11. a yellow card

12. the letter X

13. the letter Q

14. a vowel

Animated Glossary
www.pearsonsuccessnet.com

*For another example, see Set C on page 465.

For **15** through **18**, write the probability and tell whether it is likely, unlikely, impossible, or certain to land on red when each spinner is spun once.

15.

16.

17.

18.

19. **Geometry** Rectangle A is 4 feet by 6 feet. Rectangle B is 1 yard by 2 yards. Which rectangle has a greater perimeter?

20. How many windows are in a 9-story building if there are 28 windows per story?

21. Look at the problem below.

$$\triangle + 9 = \square$$

If $\triangle = 4$, what is $\square$?

22. **Estimation** Heather has read 393 pages of the latest "Girl Wizard" book. Irene has read 121 fewer pages than Heather. If there are 439 pages in the book, about how many pages does Irene have left to read?

For **23** through **25**, use the bags at the right.

23. Which bag shows a certain outcome if a red tile is picked?

24. What is the likelihood of picking a green tile out of Bag D?

25. What is the probability of picking a green tile out of Bag C?

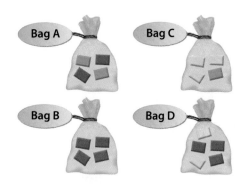

For **26**, use the table at the right.

26. Each cabin of the London Eye Ferris wheel can hold up to 25 passengers. Jared is waiting for Samantha to get off the London Eye. He knows she will get out of Cabin 1, or Cabin 2. What is the probability that she is in Cabin 2? Write the probability as a fraction in simplest terms.

Cabin Number	Number of People
1	15
2	25

Algebra Connections

Changing Patterns

Algebra is a language of patterns, rules, and symbols. Sometimes the patterns stay the same, but sometimes the patterns change. To identify a changing number pattern, first look at the pattern of numbers.

Ask Yourself:

How is each number related to the number to the left and to the right of it?

Example: Look at this pattern of numbers.

8, 10, 14, 20, 28, 38, 50, 64

What is the next number in the pattern?

Think *What is the difference between each number in the pattern and the following number?*

$+2, +4, +6, +8, +10\dots$

$64 + 16 = 80$

80 is the next number in the pattern.

. . . .

For **1** through **6**, find the next two numbers.

1. 2, 2, 4, 4, 8, 8, 16, 16, ▪, ▪

2. 5, 10, 9, 18, 17, 34, 33, 66, ▪, ▪

3. 14, 12, 16, 14, 18, 16, 20, 18, ▪, ▪

4. 6, 9, 8, 11, 10, 13, 12, 15, ▪, ▪

5. 4, 8, 10, 20, 22, 44, 46, ▪, ▪

4. 8, 24, 12, 36, 18, 54, ▪, ▪

For **7** through **15**, find the pattern.

7. 1, 2, 4, 7, 11, 16

8. 2, 7, 9, 15, 17, 24

9. 4, 5, 8, 9, 12, 13

10. 7, 9, 10, 12, 13, 15

11. 2, 4, 12, 48, 240

12. 8, 13, 23, 21, 26, 36, 34

13. 2, 4, 16, 32, 128, 256

14. 5, 10, 11, 22, 23, 46

15. 4, 8, 12, 6, 10, 14, 7

16. It takes 40 minutes to bake a batch of muffins. Two batches of muffins takes 1 hour 20 minutes, 3 batches take 2 hours. How long will it take to make 4 batches of muffins?

17. Linda has three houseplants. She buys two more, then gives one away to her friend, Jayne. If Linda repeats this process five more times, how many house plants will she have?

Lesson

20-4

MR 3.1 Evaluate the reasonableness of the solution in the context of the original situation. Also **MR 2.6**, **SDAP 1.0**.

Problem Solving

Use Reasoning

Mary, Kristen, Deborah, and Amy met on vacation. They are from New York, Georgia, Nevada and Maine. Amy is from New York, and Kristen is not from Georgia. If Deborah is from Nevada, where is Mary from?

Amy is from New York

Deborah is from Nevada

Guided Practice*

Do you know HOW?

Make a chart and use logical reasoning to solve. Write the answer in a complete sentence.

1. Tony has 4 rabbits named Lenny, Emma, Beau, and Blossom. One is orange, one gray, one black, and one spotted. Emma is orange. Beau is not gray. Blossom is spotted. What color is Lenny?

Do you UNDERSTAND?

2. In the example above, when a "Y" is placed in a cell, why does an "N" get placed in the other cells in the same row and column?

3. Write a Problem Write a problem using the reasoning strategy.

Independent Practice

Solve each problem. Write the answer in a complete sentence.

4. There are 5 people in the Robinson family: Harry, Barb, Roger, Laurie, and Carrie. Their ages are 37, 36, 13, 10, and 5. Barb is the oldest and Carrie is the youngest. Laurie is 13. Harry is not 10. He is older than Roger. How old is Roger?

5. Six dancers want to form a triangle so that the same number of dancers is on each side. How should they stand? Draw a picture to solve.

Stuck? Try this....

- What do I know?
- What diagram can I use to help understand the problem?
- Can I use addition, subtraction, multiplication, or division?
- Is all of my work correct?
- Did I answer the right question?
- Is my answer reasonable?

Make and fill in the table with the information you know.

	NY	GA	NV	ME
Mary				
Kristen		N		
Deborah			Y	
Amy	Y			

Each row and each column can have only one Yes because each woman can be from only one of the four states.

Fill in the row with No's (N) where there is one Yes (Y).

Complete the table. Use reasoning to draw conclusions.

	NY	GA	NV	ME
Mary	N	Y	N	N
Kristen	N	N	N	Y
Deborah	N	N	Y	N
Amy	Y	N	N	N

There are 3 No's in each row or column because three of the four choices are incorrect.

Mary is from Georgia.

---

6. What comes next in the pattern to the right?

7. Wendy, Chris, Lauren, and Santiago live on four different streets: Highland, East, Brook, and Elm. Wendy lives on Highland. Lauren lives on Elm. Chris does not live on East. What street does Santiago live on?

	Brook	East	Elm	Highland
Chris		No		
Lauren			Yes	
Santiago				
Wendy				Yes

8. Eric and his friends are playing volleyball. They made a total of 6 groups. If there are 4 players on each team, how many people are playing volleyball?

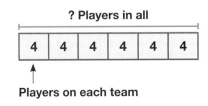

? Players in all

| 4 | 4 | 4 | 4 | 4 | 4 |

Players on each team

9. Vicki has a bag with 6 blue marbles, 4 red marbles, 7 green marbles, and 8 yellow marbles all the same size. If she pulls out one marble without looking, which color is she most likely to choose?

A Blue   **C** Green

B Red   **D** Yellow

10. Weddell, Von Bellingshausen, Cook, Palmer, and Wilkes each explored Antarctica. Two were British, and one was Russian. The other two were from the United States. Palmer and Wilkes were from the same country. Cook was British. Weddell was from the same country as Cook. Which country was Von Bellingshausen from?

1. Newell and Mateo are playing a game. The spinner for the game is shown below.

If Mateo spins the spinner twice, what are all the possible outcomes? (20-2)

A 2 pinks or 2 yellows

B 2 yellows or 1 pink and 1 yellow

C 2 pinks or 1 pink and 1 yellow

D 2 pinks or 2 yellows or 1 pink and 1 yellow

2. Alyssa can buy one of 4 jewelry kits and one of 4 dolls. How many different combinations can she buy? (20-1)

A 16

B 12

C 8

D 4

3. A fish tank has 2 black fish, 4 white fish, 12 orange fish, and 2 red fish. If one fish is pulled out randomly, which color is most likely to be picked? (20-3)

A Black

B White

C Orange

D Red

4. Which tree diagram shows the possible outcomes for spinning each spinner shown? (20-2)

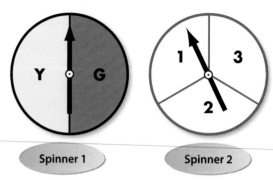

Spinner 1   Spinner 2

A

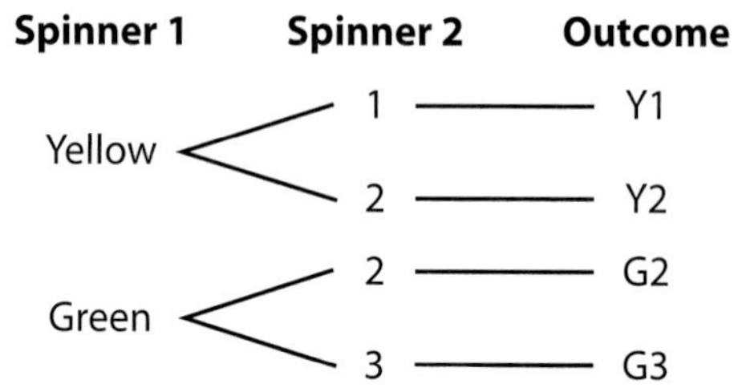

Spinner 1	Spinner 2	Outcome
Yellow	1	Y1
	2	Y2
Green	2	G2
	3	G3

B

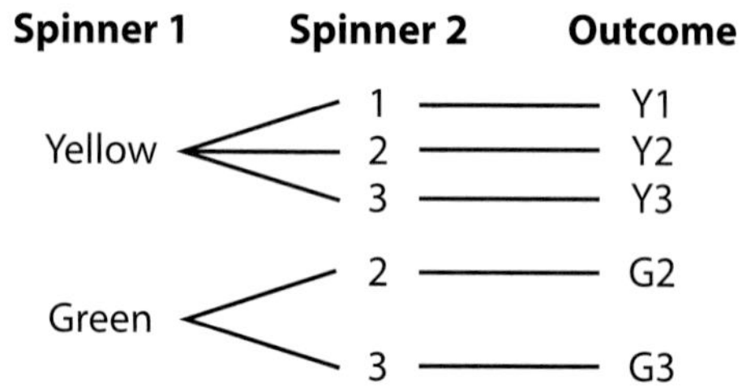

Spinner 1	Spinner 2	Outcome
Yellow	1	Y1
	2	Y2
	3	Y3
Green	2	G2
	3	G3

C

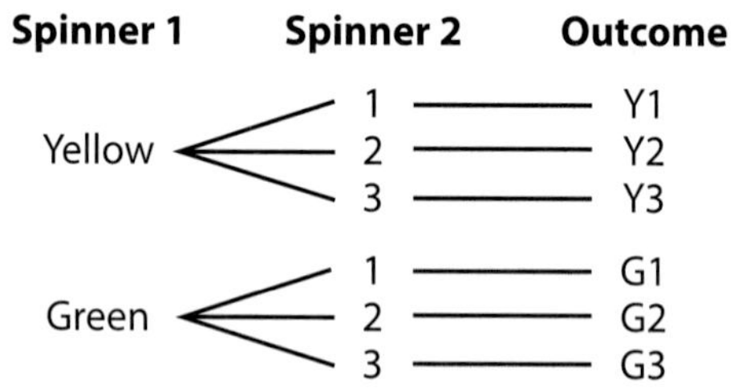

Spinner 1	Spinner 2	Outcome
Yellow	1	Y1
	2	Y2
	3	Y3
Green	1	G1
	2	G2
	3	G3

D

Spinner 1	Spinner 2	Outcome
Yellow	1	Y1
	2	Y2
	3	Y3
Green	1	G1
	2	G2

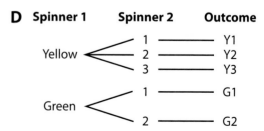

5. The four children in the Wininger family are Ryan, Makena, Jackson, and Whitney. Each child attends Skyline Elementary. There is a child in Kindergarten, 1st grade, 3rd grade, and 5th grade. Makena is in 5th grade. Jackson is not in 1st grade. If Whitney is in 3rd grade, what grade is Ryan in? (20-4)

	K	1	3	5
Ryan				
Makena				
Jackson				
Whitney				

A Kindergarten

B 1st grade

C 3rd grade

D 5th grade

6. If Kinesha selects a balloon, without looking, from the ones below, what is the probability she will select a heart shaped balloon? (20-3)

A $\frac{1}{8}$

B $\frac{3}{8}$

C $\frac{4}{8}$

D $\frac{3}{5}$

7. Ben, Gracie, Josh, and Avery all attend Glenn Oaks School. They each get to school in a different way. They come either by bus, walking, riding a bike, or in a car. Ben walks to school. Gracie does not come in a car. If Josh rides the bus, how does Avery get to school? (20-4)

A Bus

B Walking

C Riding a bike

D Car

8. There are 15 pieces of fruit in the fruit bowl. There are 8 bananas, 2 apples, 4 kiwi, and 1 peach. Which fruit would it be impossible for Regan to pick? (20-3)

A Pear

B Banana

C Peach

D Apple

9. Payton can choose steak, chicken, or pork, and one side of peas, corn, squash, green beans, potatoes, okra, or spinach for his main dish. How many different combinations can he choose? (20-1)

A 10

B 18

C 21

D 28

Set A, pages 452–453

Choose one color and one shape.
Colors: Red or blue or green

Shapes: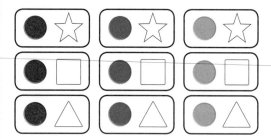

How many combinations are there?

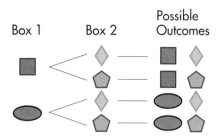

In all, there are 9 combinations.

Remember that the order does not matter when you count combinations.

Find the number of possible combinations.

1. Choose milk or juice plus a side of mashed potatoes, a baked potato, or green beans.

2. Choose a backpack, soft suitcase, or hard suitcase, and then choose one of 5 colors.

Set B, pages 454–455

List the outcomes for picking a square or oval from Box 1, and a diamond or pentagon from Box 2. How many outcomes are possible?

You can make a tree diagram.

Box 1   Box 2   Possible Outcomes

Multiply.

There are **2** outcomes for Box 1 and 2 outcomes for Box 2.

$$2 \times 2 = 4$$

There are 4 possible outcomes.

Remember you can use a tree diagram or multiply to find the number of possible outcomes.

Find the number of possible outcomes for picking a shape from:

1. Bag 1

2. Bag 2

3. Bag 1 and Bag 2

4. Bag 2 and Bag 3

Set C, pages 456–458

Beatrice wrote each letter of her name on a slip of paper and put the slips in a bag. If Beatrice draws one slip from the bag, what is the probability that she will draw a vowel?

The probability of drawing a vowel can be expressed as a fraction.

$$\frac{\text{number of vowels}}{\text{number of letters}} = \frac{4}{8}$$

The probability of drawing a vowel is $\frac{4}{8}$ or $\frac{1}{2}$ in simplest form.

Remember that you can draw a picture to list all of the possible outcomes.

Write the probability of selecting each shape when you select a tile from the tiles below, without looking.

1. Diamond
2. Circle
3. Heart
4. Crescent
5. Clover or diamond
6. Not a diamond

Set D, pages 460–461

Margaret put blue, green, yellow, and orange book covers on her math, science, spelling, and history books. She did not put green on her math book. She put blue on her science book, and yellow on her history book. What color cover did she put on her spelling book? Use logical reasoning to solve.

	Math	Science	Spelling	History
Blue	No	Yes	No	No
Green	No	No	Yes	No
Yellow	No	No	No	Yes
Orange	Yes	No	No	No

Remember you can use information from the problem to draw conclusions.

Use logical reasoning to solve. Copy and complete the table to help you.

	5	6	8	10
Larry			Y	
Evelyn	Y			
Terri				Y
Vivian		Y		

1. Each person gets off an elevator on either the 5th, 6th, 8th, or 10th floor. When Larry gets off, he says bye to Terri. Terri is the last person in the elevator. Evelyn is the first person off the elevator. Vivian gets off after Evelyn. Where does each person get off?

Glossary

A.M. Time between midnight and noon.

acute angle An angle that is less than a right angle.

acute triangle A triangle with three acute angles.

addends The numbers that are added together to find a sum.
Example: 2 + 7 = 9

addend

algebraic expression An expression with variables.

analog clock Shows time by pointing to numbers on a face.

angle A figure formed by two rays that have the same endpoint.

area The amount of space needed to cover a figure. It is measured in square units.

array A way of displaying objects in rows and columns.

Associative Property of Addition Addends can be regrouped and the sum remains the same.

Associative Property of Multiplication Factors can be regrouped and the product remains the same.

average The mean, found by adding all numbers in a set and dividing by the number of values.

bar graph A graph using bars to show data.

benchmark fractions Fractions that are commonly used for estimation: $\frac{1}{4}$, $\frac{1}{3}$, $\frac{1}{2}$, $\frac{2}{3}$, and $\frac{3}{4}$.

breaking apart Mental math method used to rewrite a number as the sum of numbers to form an easier problem.

capacity The amount a container can hold.

center A point within a circle that is the same distance from all points on a circle.

centimeter (cm) A metric unit of length. 100 centimeters = 1 meter

century A unit of time equal to 100 years.

certain (event) An event that is sure to occur.

chord Any line segment that connects any two points on the circle.

circle A closed plane figure in which all the points are the same distance from a point called the center.

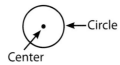

circle graph A graph in the shape of a circle that shows how the whole is broken into parts.

common factor A factor that two or more numbers have in common.

Commutative Property of Addition Numbers can be added in any order and the sum remains the same.

Commutative Property of Multiplication Factors can be multiplied in any order and the product remains the same.

compatible numbers Numbers that are easy to compute mentally.

compensation Adding and subtracting the same number to make the sum or difference easier to find.

composite number A whole number greater than 1 with more than two factors.

cone A solid figure with a base that is a circle and a curved surface that meets at a point.

congruent figures Figures that have the same shape and size.

coordinate grid A grid used to show ordered pairs.

coordinate plane A grid that extends to include both positive and negative numbers.

cube A solid figure with six congruent squares as its faces.

cup (c) A customary unit of capacity.

customary units of measure Units of measure that are used in the United States.

cylinder A solid figure with two congruent circular bases.

data Pieces of collected information.

day A unit of time equal to 24 hours.

decade A unit of time equal to 10 years.

decimal point A dot used to separate dollars from cents or ones from tenths in a number.

decimeter (dm) A metric unit of length equal to 10 centimeters.

degrees Celsius (°C) A metric unit of temperature.

degrees Fahrenheit (°F) A standard unit of temperature.

denominator The number below the fraction bar in a fraction; The total number of equal parts in all.

diameter A line segment that connects two points on a circle and passes through the center.

difference The answer when subtracting two numbers.

digital clock Shows time with numbers. Hours are separated from minutes with a colon.

digits The symbols used to write a number: 0, 1, 2, 3, 4, 5, 6, 7, 8, and 9.

Distributive Property Breaking apart problems into two simpler problems. *Example*: (3 × 21) = (3 × 20) + (3 × 1)

divide An operation to find the number in each group or the number of equal groups.

dividend The number to be divided.

divisibility rules The rules that state when a number is divisible by another number.

divisible Can be divided by another number without leaving a remainder. *Example*: 10 is divisible by 2

divisor The number by which another number is divided. *Example*: 32 ÷ 4 = 8
↑
Divisor

edge A line segment where two faces of a solid figure meet.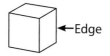

←Edge

elapsed time The amount of time between the beginning of an event and the end of the event.

equally likely (event) Just as likely to happen as not to happen.

equation A number sentence that uses the equal sign (=) to show that two expressions have the same value.

equilateral triangle A triangle in which all sides are the same length.

equivalent Numbers that name the same amount.

equivalent fractions Fractions that name the same region, part of a set, or part of a segment.

expanded form A number written as the sum of the values of its digits. *Example*: 2,000 + 400 + 70 + 6

face A flat surface of a solid that does not roll. 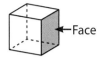←Face

fact family A group of related facts using the same set of numbers.

factors The numbers multiplied together to find a product.
Example: $3 \times 6 = 18$
↖ ↗
Factor

fair game A game in which each player is equally likely to win.

fluid ounce (fl oz) A customary unit of capacity.
1 fluid ounce = 2 tablespoons

foot (ft) A customary unit of length.
1 foot = 12 inches

fraction A symbol, such as $\frac{2}{3}$, $\frac{5}{1}$, or $\frac{8}{5}$, used to name a part of a whole, a part of a set, a location on a number line, or a division of whole numbers.

front-end estimation A way to estimate a sum by adding the first digit of each addend and adjusting the result based on the remaining digits.

gallon (gal) A customary unit of capacity. 1 gallon = 4 quarts

gram (g) A metric unit of mass.

hexagon A polygon with 6 sides.

hour A unit of time equal to 60 minutes.

hundredth One part of 100 equal parts of a whole.

Identity Property of Addition The sum of any number and zero is that number.

Identity Property of Multiplication The product of any number and one is that number.

impossible (event) An event that cannot occur.

improper fractions A fraction in which the numerator is greater than or equal to the denominator.

inch (in.) A customary unit of length.

inequality A number sentence that uses the greater than sign (>) or the less than sign (<) to show that two expressions do not have the same value.

integers Consists of whole numbers and their opposites.

intersecting lines Lines that cross at one point.

interval A number which is the difference between two consecutive numbers on the scale of a graph.

inverse operations Two operations that undo each other. Addition and subtraction are inverse operations. Multiplication and division are inverse operations.
Example: 7 + 10 = 17; 17 − 10 = 7
        6 × 5 = 30; 30 ÷ 5 = 6

isosceles triangle A triangle that has at least two equal sides.

key Part of a pictograph that tells what each symbol stands for.

kilogram (kg) A metric unit of mass. 1 kilogram = 1,000 grams

kilometer (km) A metric unit of length. 1 kilometer = 1,000 meters

leap year A unit of time equal to 366 days.

likely (event) An event that probably will happen.

line A straight path of points that goes on and on in two directions.

line graph A graph that connects points to show how data changes over time.

line of symmetry A line on which a figure can be folded so that both halves are congruent.

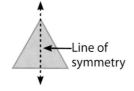

Line of symmetry

line plot A display of data along a number line.

line segment A part of a line that has two endpoints.

liter (L) A metric unit of capacity.

mass The amount of matter that something contains.

mean An average, found by adding all numbers in a set and dividing by the number of values.

median The middle number in an ordered data set.

meter (m) A metric unit of length.

mile (mi) A customary unit of length. 1 mile = 5,280 feet

millennium A unit for measuring time equal to 1,000 years.

milliliter (mL) A metric unit of capacity.

millimeter (mm) A metric unit of length.

minute A unit of time equal to 60 seconds.

mixed number A number that has a whole number and a fraction.

mode The number or numbers that occur most often in a data set.

month One of the 12 parts into which a year is divided.

multiple The product of any two whole numbers.

net A pattern used to make a solid.

Example: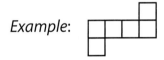

number expression An expression that contains numbers and at least one operation. A number expression is also called a numerical expression.

numerator The number above the fraction bar in a fraction.

obtuse angle An angle that is greater than a right angle.

obtuse triangle A triangle in which there is one obtuse angle.

octagon A polygon with 8 sides.

ordered pair A pair of numbers that names a point on a coordinate grid.

ordinal numbers Numbers used to tell order.

ounce (oz) A customary unit of weight.

outcome A possible result of a game or experiment.

outlier A number in a data set that is very different from the rest of the numbers.

overestimate An estimate that is greater than the exact answer.

P.M. Time between noon and midnight.

parallel lines In a plane, lines that never intersect.
Example:

parallelogram
A quadrilateral in which opposite sides are parallel.

parentheses ( ) Grouping symbols. They can show which operation can be done first.

partial products Products found by breaking one factor in a multiplication problem into ones, tens, hundreds, and so on and then multiplying each of these by the other factor.

pentagon A plane figure with 5 sides.

perimeter The distance around a figure.

period In a number, a group of three digits, separated by commas, starting from the right.

perpendicular lines Two intersecting lines that form right angles. *Example*:

pictograph A graph using pictures or symbols to show data.

pint (pt) A customary unit of capacity. 1 pint = 2 cups

plane figure A figure with only two dimensions.

plot To locate and mark a point named by an ordered pair on a grid.

point An exact location in space.

polygon A closed plane figure made up of line segments.

pound (lb) A customary unit of weight. 1 pound = 16 ounces

prediction An informed guess about what will happen.

prime number Any whole number greater than 1 that has exactly two factors, the number itself and 1.

probability A number telling the likelihood an event will happen.

product The answer to a multiplication problem.

pyramid A solid figure whose base is a polygon and whose faces are triangles with a common vertex.

Q

quadrilateral A polygon with 4 sides.

quart (qt) A customary unit of capacity. 1 quart = 2 pints

quotient The answer to a division problem.

R

radius Any line segment that connects the center to a point on the circle.

range The difference between the greatest value and the least value in a data set.

ray A part of a line that has one endpoint and continues endlessly in one direction.

rectangle A quadrilateral with 4 right angles.

rectangular prism A solid figure whose faces are all rectangles.

rectangular pyramid A solid figure with a rectangle for its base and triangles for all other faces.

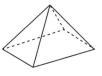

reflection
To turn a plane
figure over.

remainder The number that remains
after the division is complete.

rhombus A quadrilateral
in which opposite sides
are parallel and all sides
are the same length.

right angle An angle
that forms a square corner.

right triangle A triangle in which
there is one right angle.

rotation Moves
a figure about a point.

rotational symmetry A figure that
rotates onto itself in less than a full turn
has rotational symmetry.

rounding Replacing a number with
a number that tells about how many
or how much.

scale Numbers that show the units
used on a graph.

scalene triangle A triangle in which
no sides are the same length.

second A unit of time.
60 seconds = 1 minute

side Each of the line segments
of a polygon.

similar figures Figures that have the
same shape and may or may not have
the same size.

simplest form A fraction in which the
numerator and denominator have no
common factors other than 1.

solid figure A figure that has length,
width, and height.

solution The value of the variable that
makes an equation true.

solve Find a solution to an equation.

sphere A solid figure which
include all points the same
distance from a point.

square A quadrilateral
with 4 right angles and all
sides the same length.

square pyramid A solid
figure with a square base
and four faces that are
triangles.

standard form A way to write a
number showing only its digits.
Example: 2,613

straight angle An angle that forms
a straight line.

sum The result of adding
numbers together.

survey Collecting information by
asking a number of people the same
question and recording their answers.

symmetric A figure is symmetric if it can be folded into two congruent halves that fit on top of each other.

tablespoon (tbsp) A customary unit of capacity.
1 tablespoon = 3 teaspoons

teaspoon (tsp) A customary unit of capacity.
3 teaspoons = 1 tablespoon

tenth One of ten equal parts of a whole.

ton (T) A customary unit of weight.
1 ton = 2,000 pounds

translation
A change in the position of a figure that moves it up, down, or sideways.

trapezoid A quadrilateral with only one pair of parallel sides.

tree diagram A display to show all possible outcomes.

trend A pattern in the data on a line graph, shown by an increase or decrease.

triangle A polygon with 3 sides.

triangular prism A solid figure with two bases that are triangles and the other three faces are rectangles.

underestimate An estimate that is less than the exact answer.

unfair game A game in which each player doesn't have the same chance of winning.

unlikely (event) An event that probably will not happen.

variable A symbol or letter that stands for a number.

vertex (plural, vertices) The point where two rays meet. The point where the sides of a polygon meet. The point where three or more edges of a solid figure meet.

volume The number of cubic units needed to fill a solid figure.

week A unit of time equal to 7 days.

weight A measure of how light or heavy something is.

word form A number written in words. *Example*: Four thousand, six hundred, thirty-two

x-value The first number in an ordered pair.

yard (yd) A customary unit of length.
1 yard = 3 feet

year A unit of time equal to 365 days or 52 weeks or 12 months.

y-value The second number in an ordered pair.

Zero Property of Multiplication The product of any number and zero is zero.

Index

A

Act it out and use reasoning, 126–128

Acute angle, 197, 442–443

Acute triangle, 201

Addition and subtraction,
28–43, 296–299
decimals, 296–308
draw a picture and write an equation, 44–47, 260–262, 342–343
equations, solving, 320–321, 420–421
estimating, 32–33, 297–297
extra information, 34–35
fractions, 252–259
inverse operations, 298
mental math, 32–33, 296–297
missing information, 34–35
modeling addition and subtraction of decimals, 298–301
number sentences, 44–47
pictures, 44–47, 342–343
whole numbers, 32–33, 36–41
zeros, subtracting across, 42–43

Algebra connections
addition and subtraction, 31
changing patterns, 367
missing numbers and operations, 361
multiplication number sense, 103
number patterns, 275
properties and equations, 73
repeating shapes and patterns, 281
solving equations, 171

Algorithms, expanded, 96–99, 140–143

Angles, 196–197, 442–443
acute, 197, 442–443
obtuse, 197, 442–443
right, 197, 442–443
straight, 197

Area, 362–366, 368–371
irregular shapes, 364–365
regular shapes, 362–363

Arrays, 60
multiplication with 2-digit numbers, 140–143

Associative property of addition, 29

Average, 388–389

B

Bar graph, 384

C

Calculator, finding area with, 367

Capacity cup (c), 350–352
customary units, 350–352
gallon (gal), 350–352
liter (L), 354–356
metric units, 354–356
milliliter (mL), 354–356
pint (pt), 350–352
quart (qt), 350–352

Centimeter (cm), 354–356

Changing patterns
length, perimeter, area, 367

Chord, 204–205

Circle, 204–205

Combinations
probability and statistics, 452–453

Commutative property
of addition, 29
of multiplication, 62

Compatible numbers, 138

Compensation, 28

Composite numbers, 180–181

Cone, 208

Congruence. *See* Transformations, symmetry, and congruence

Connections to earlier lessons, 56, 70, 302, 324, 456

Coordinate planes, 402–409
Connections to earlier lessons, 56, 70, 302, 324, 456

Counting on, 28

Cube, 206

Cup (c), 350–352

Customary units of measurement,
350–352. *See* also Metric units of measurement; individual units

Cylinder, 208

Units of measurement,
350–352
area, 358–359
length, 358–359
metric units, 358
perimeter, 358–359

Use objects and make a table,
284–285

Use reasoning, 460–461

Variables, 118–121, 320–326,
426–428

Vertices, 207

Weight ounce (oz), 350–352
pound (lb), 350–352
ton (T), 350–352

Whole numbers adding, 36–39
addition and subtraction, 32–33,
36–41
comparing and ordering, 10–13
estimating sums and differences
of, 32–33
number lines, 278–281
rounding, 24–27
subtracting, 40–41

Word form, 4

Work backward, 328–329

Writing to explain, 242–244

Yard, 350–352

**Zero property of
multiplication,** 63

Zeros division with 1-digit
divisors, zeros in the quotient,
176–177
place value and, 14–15
subtracting across, 42–43